Mental Floss

A
Daily Routine for
Intellectual and Spiritual Hygiene

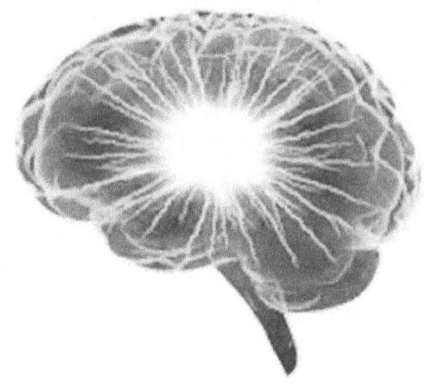

Volume Five

Philip M. Hudson

Copyright 2017 by Philip M. Hudson.
The book author retains sole copyright to his contributions to this book.

Published 2017.
Printed in the United States of America.

All rights reserved.

No portion of this book may be reproduced, stored in a retrieval system, or transmitted in any form or by any means – electronic, mechanical, photocopy, recording, scanning, or other – except for brief quotations in critical reviews or articles, without the prior written permission of the author.

ISBN 978-1-943650-35-4

Library of Congress Control Number 2016953037

Google images.

This book was published by BookCrafters
Parker, Colorado.
bookcrafterscolorado@gmail.com

This book may be ordered from
www.bookcrafters.net
and other online bookstores.

Table of Contents

Acknowledgements..1

Preface..3

Introduction...5

List of Essays..9

Essays..13

Author's Note..417

Appendix One (Alphabetical List of Essays: Volumes 1 - 6).......................419

Appendix Two (Topical List of Essays: Volumes 1 - 6)...............................433

About the Author...451

Also by the Author..453

Acknowledgements

In these essays, I have attributed quotations to original authors whenever possible, as well as when I have editorialized their ideas. In many cases, however, my language will naturally reflect the teachings of leaders and members of The Church of Jesus Christ of Latter-day Saints.

The list of those who have contributed to the construction of these essays is endless. As I have collected my own thoughts, I have realized how heavily I have borrowed from the towering examples of those who, over the years, have been my mystical mentors, my sensible chaperones, my spiritual guides, my surrogate saviors, my compassionate critics, and everything in between.

They are my avatars, manifestations of deity in bodily forms, my na'vi, the visionaries, who communicate with God on a level to which I can only aspire, and my tsaddik, whom I esteem as intuitive interpreters of biblical law and scripture. They are my divine teachers incarnate. They have shown me the way, stretched my mind, reinforced my faith, strengthened my testimony, lifted my spirits, helped me to discover my wings, provided of their means, given immaterial support, emboldened me with words of encouragement, cheered me on with wise counsel, taught me humility, been there to steady me, soothed my troubled soul, stepped in to nurture me, led me to fountains of living water, wet my parched lips with inspired counsel, bound up my wounds, offered listening ears, and extended open arms.

Every family member, teacher, student, classmate, business associate, mentor, friend, priesthood brother, relief society sister, ordinance worker, and temple patron with whom I have come in contact has influenced me. Every author, poet, journalist, essayist, thespian, satirist, and lyricist, has moved me in some positive way. They have taught me to find the silk purse in every sow's ear and the silver lining in every cloud. When I have been given a lemon, they have shown me how to find the recipe for lemonade.

From their positive influence, I have learned that there is so much good in the worst of us, and so much bad in the best of us, that it hardly behooves any of us to talk about the rest of us. I have done my best to keep tempests in teapots where they belong, and to put them in perspective. I have tried to retain the joyful anticipation of the optimistic little boy, who, when faced with the daunting task of shoveling up an enormous pile of manure in a horse stall near his home, enthusiastically set about his task with the exclamation: "There's got to be a pony in there, somewhere!"

Well did the poet long ago teach: "No man is an island, entire of itself. Every man is a piece of the continent, a part of the main. If a clod be washed away by the sea, Europe is the less, as well as if a promontory were, as well as if a manor of thy friends or of thine own were. Any man's death diminishes me, because I am involved in mankind, and therefore never send to know for whom the bell tolls. It tolls for thee." (John Donne).

When I think of the influence of a multitude of angels thinly disguised as my family, friends, and peers, I remember the words of Sir Isaac Newton, who, when pressed to reveal the great secret behind his accomplishments, simply replied: "I stood on the shoulders of giants." Of course, at the end of the day, I alone am responsible for the contents of this volume. But I hope my interpretations of principles and doctrine will cultivate your interest to dig deeper into the themes woven into the tapestry of these essays, by turning to the scriptures and seeking inspiration from the Spirit. My only goal is to help you to expand your insights into the telestial mile markers, the terrestrial truths, and the celestial guidelines that I have attempted to embed within these essays.

Preface

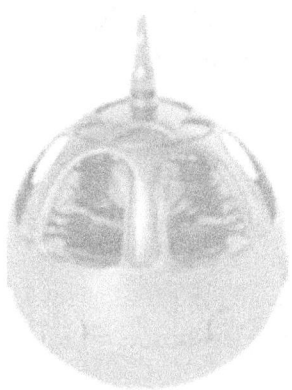

I have learned to love the scriptures, and I often think of St. Hilary, who wrote in the third century: "Scripture consists not in what we read, but in what we understand." In these essays, I have consistently tried to find a scriptural foundation and a spiritual confirmation as my thoughts have ranged over a wide variety of subjects. For me, it has been exciting to find that the ideas swirling around inside my head can generally be anchored to, and find relevance in, the scriptures, because holy writ give me a sense of coherence and stability. Every time an idea explodes in my brain, it causes me to stop and think: "Somewhere in this, there is a new essay hiding!" On a much smaller scale, I feel as Albert Einstein must have, when the mathematical equivalents to scripture study crystallized, and he said of the experience: "A storm broke loose in my mind."

I believe the Spirit has the generative power to energize, vitalize, and quicken our axons and dendrites and craft a neural environment that stimulates creative thought. Those who have experienced the illumination of the Spirit know what Einstein meant when he said: "A splendid light dawned on me." So, the challenge for each of us is to enlist the aid of the Holy Ghost to assist in understanding, whenever and however we process the world around us.

Every time I proofed an essay (and I did this many times) I found myself scribbling additional notes in the margins, and thinking to myself, "Why didn't I see that before." That is precisely what I hope will be the experience of those who read these essays, and that in the process they will be instructed by the Spirit to be led in directions that will later prove to be of value.

I would expect that each of you who consider these essays will be uniquely impacted and that they will touch you differently when you re-visit them. When I am long-gone, perhaps the considerable thought that went into their production will generate a palpable bond between us that will span the years separating us, and the gulf that then divides us will be bridged by our shared energies to establish the foundation for an eventual joyous reunion.

One of the reasons why I am somewhat obsessed with writing is that I enjoy the rush when I find wisdom and great treasures of knowledge, and even hidden treasures. I have found doctrinal themes that are pearls that cannot be discerned after only a cursory glance. I hope that within these pages you will find the seeds that generate within you a quest for greater understanding. I have enjoyed this process of discovery, and heartily recommend it to you.

I had the opportunity to visit the Holy Land many years ago. We stopped, too briefly, at the ruins of Qumran. There, the Dead Sea Covenanters had lived, and in their scriptorium, I was able to pause and reflect upon their Eleventh Hymn that had been preserved in caves high above their community. It reads: "Behold, for mine own part I have reached the intervision, and through the spirit thou has placed within me, come to know Thee, my God." In a similar fashion, Moses wrote: "But now mine own eyes have beheld God; but not my natural, but my spiritual eyes, for my natural eyes could not have beheld; for I should have withered and died in his presence; but his glory was upon me; and I beheld his face." (Moses 1:11).

I am continually reminded of Nephi's counsel to press forward with complete dedication and steadfastness, or confidence with a firm determination in Christ, having a perfect brightness of hope, or perfect faith, and charity, or a love of God and of all men. If we do this, feasting upon the word of Christ, or receiving strength and nourishment from the scriptures, and endure to the end in righteousness, we shall have eternal life, which is the greatest of God's gifts. (2 Nephi 31:20). It is with love, then, that I extend to you the invitation to enjoy these essays. Take them at face value, and use them as a springboard to your own personal levels of discovery, as you are taught by the Spirit to move in the direction of your dreams.

Introduction

If they are fortunate, novice quilters quickly learn a bit of wisdom from the Amish, who make some of the finest quilts in the world. On purpose, the Amish build mistakes into their projects, because they believe that any attempt on their part to design and produce a flawless creation would be a mockery of God, Who alone is perfect. The humility of the Amish makes me think of my own weak attempts to put my thoughts to paper. In His infinite wisdom, God knows very well that I do not need to consciously plan on lacing my efforts with errors. That will come quite naturally, without the need for me to intentionally contribute to my short-comings.

Perhaps these essays will do little more than help to define quirks in my personality. Each of us is different, and many things, including our family and friends, the circumstances in which we find ourselves, the quality of our education, and our own personalities, inspire and mold our oral and written expressions. I would like to think that all of these influences have been encouraging, affirmative, and constructive.

Most of these essays weave and wobble their way to a conclusion, although finality has not been my goal. As a thinker, writer and teacher who values careful scholarship, I would rather leave the door ajar for the reader, to allow the shafts of the light of understanding to creep in as the dawning of recognition awakens interest in particular subject areas. I would hope that within the pages of these essays there is enough latitude to allow for divergent opinions and independent ideas, not to mention constructive criticism. I hope these essays pose more questions than they answer. If, as I laid down my thoughts utilizing around one hundred fifty thousand words, I misstated myself a few times, or flat-out got it wrong, I ask the patient indulgence and gentle correction of the reader.

I find that no matter how often I have re-read an essay, I continue to come up with different ways of expressing myself. The ink on the page may barely have dried before I am busy at work on a significant revision. There is no way to complete the process, and I have given up trying to do so. So this printed volume is a work in progress. I think of it as a living and breathing entity because, even in its imperfection, it is my hope that it has the generative power to stimulate intellectual, philosophical, imaginative, and spiritual thought processes. If this volume has any real value, it would be to provoke inquiry in the minds of all who ponder its theses.

The essays are arranged alphabetically and not topically. Both appendices at the end of the volume contain a comprehensive list of the essays in all six volumes. In Appendix One, these are referenced by volume, to make it easier to find a subject. In Appendix Two, they are referenced topically in 155 distinct categories.

The essays are random in their subject matter and sequentially follow no particular pattern. Most are religious in nature, while some are more philosophical; several are theoretical, a few are serendipitous, and one or two are whimsical. If any seem indecipherable, I invite you to recall Albert Einstein's observation: "That which is impenetrable to us really exists. Behind the secrets remains something subtle, intangible, and inexplicable. Veneration for this force beyond anything that we can comprehend is my religion." My own faith is less esoteric, and promises an understanding of some of the very things that one of the greatest minds of the Twentieth Century found "subtle, intangible, and inexplicable." Quite simply, because of my faith-based heritage, these essays do more than scratch the surface of inquiry; they reach beyond the mathematical equations and plumb the depth and measure the breadth of my understanding of our place in the cosmos. I hope they do the same for you, dear reader.

The various topics were conceived in the white-hot crucible of thought that is common to all of us, charged by 10 to 20 billion cerebral cortical neurons, each with 60 to 100 dendrites and axons making 60 to 240 trillion interconnections. Recent estimates suggest that our brains can store around one petabyte of information (four quadrillion bytes – more than the entire Internet).

One of the titles for an essay still under construction is: "Before I Lose My Mind" and another is "If My Mind Were Stolen." Since eighty-five thousand irreplaceable neurons in our brains die every day, (31 million per year) I'd better get busy. I'll try to remember that the best way to arouse creative expression is to "read ourselves full, think ourselves straight, pray ourselves hot, and let ourselves go!" When we do this, we nurture nature so that it can caper.

Numerous essays were generated by "What if...?" questions, and many germinated in conversations with family and friends and during church meetings, when creative juices were flowing. Current events stimulated some, the observation of both disciplined and egregious behavior prompted others, and cultural norms and excesses provoked more than a few. Just as a chef might throw a number of ingredients into a "slow cooker" and let them simmer for hours on the stove, some of these essays only found shape and substance over time as they were nurtured in the subconscious recesses of my mind. The reduction sauce that instilled flavor in other essays was the product of the distillation of weeks, months, and even years of contemplation, and yet, now and then, one would quickly sizzle into existence as if the idea had been thrown into a cauldron of boiling oil.

Whereas Einstein said: "A storm broke loose in my mind" when he recalled the thought processes leading to equations that have helped to define the universe, my own experiences were generally more like the whispers of a gentle breeze, and I do not pretend to have provided much in the way of meaning to even my little corner of the cosmos.

When, in just 24 days, Handel created the 259 pages of musical score that comprise "The Messiah," the notes came to him so quickly that he could barely keep up, as he furiously scratched out the oratorio on whatever paper was handy. After he had written the "Hallelujah Chorus" in a fervor of divine inspiration, he exclaimed that he had "seen all heaven before him." At the end of the manuscript, in acknowledgement of his own puny efforts, he wrote the letters "SDG" that stood for "Soli Deo Gloria" or "To God alone the glory." On a much smaller scale, we have all had similar experiences with light and knowledge, and I have been permitted on more than a few occasions to catch a glimpse of the flurry of activity that takes place just beyond the parted veil. Revelatory experiences that have been both nurturing and stimulating have sometimes found their way into the grammar of my essays.

Too often, though, my thoughts and expressions can be "carefully disguised with hypocrisy and glittering words," as Einstein put it. Although I do fancy myself a wordsmith, I have tried to avoid pedestrian expressions, idle language, and lazy scholarship. (See, for example, my essay in Volume One entitled "Brevity"). I do not pretend to be an authority on any of the subjects of these treatises, but if their factual tone is sometimes disengaging, the truth is that I typically experienced a deep personal involvement in the expression of the principles that illuminate their themes. There are those among us who can write out pi (π) to tens of thousands of digits. In

2005, in China, Chao Lu memorized π to 67,890 digits, which was a world record. I cannot come close to that, 3.14 being the extent of my knowledge of this irrational number, but I have been blessed with an imperfect ability to grasp concepts and expand them to proportions that seem to me to be at once both timely and timeless. There is an endless list of things I'd like to write about to which I hope to someday turn my attention. I want to explore the themes of Misplaced Keys, the Genesis Project, The Possibility of Intelligent Life on Earth, Doctrinal Dogma, Glowing in The Dark, Prophetic Priorities, Laziness as a Learned Response, Great and Spacious Buildings, Images and Likenesses, Illegal Aliens in Heaven, Where is Away When You Pass Away, and The Middle of Nowhere, to name a few. In the meantime, I hope you like these essays as much as I have enjoyed creating them.

List of Essays

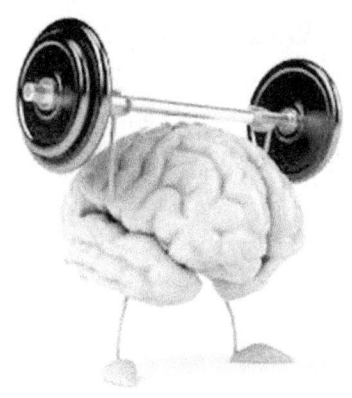

Agency And Youth	13
Attributes Of God	15
Bah! Humbug!	23
Baptism And Accountability	27
Blood, Covenant, And Land Israel	35
Born Again Christians	43
A Change Of Heart	49
Choose The Harder Right	55
Choose Ye This Day	67
Christ's Church Is Restored	73
Citizenship In The Church And Kingdom	77
A Coat Of Many Colors	83
Commitment	89
Connections	97
Construction Zone: Proceed With Caution	107
Covenants	117
Dancing With The Stars	123
Diversity	143
Doctrinal Switch Points	149
Enduring To The End	153
Establishing The Word	157
Faith Is Like A Screw	165
Fate	169
Father, Forgive Them	171
Finding Balance In Our Lives	183

Friendship	193
General Conference: The Super Bowl Of Spiritual Symposia	197
God Is NowHere	205
God's Tactical Flashlight	211
Heaven Can Wait	223
How Then Can I Do This Great Wickedness?	231
I Am A Child Of God	237
In Defense Of The Family	243
In Defense Of The Prophet Joseph Smith	249
Joseph Smith's History	255
Joseph Smith's World	257
Jumping Out Of Our Skin	263
Keep Smiling	277
Lest We Forget	289
Light And Truth	293
Living Water	299
Lost Books Of The Bible	307
Marriage And Family Are Ordained Of God	315
May The 4th Be With You	321
Our Father In Heaven Knows Us	327
Our Neighbors	341
Pennies From Heaven	345
Plan Of Salvation	349
Premortal Life	363
Preparation	371
Pride	377
Priesthood Keys	385
Primer On Addressing Deity	391
Primer On Personal Revelation	395
Proper Prior Planning Prevents Poor Priesthood Performance	405
Recognizing The Church Of Jesus Christ	409

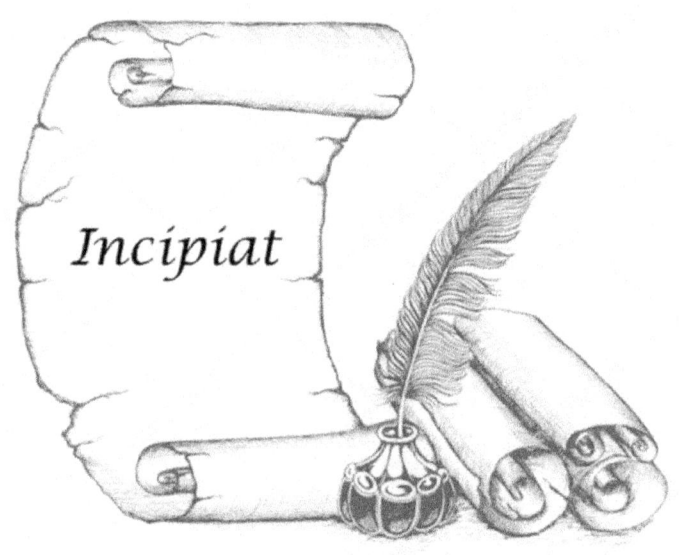

"You are, and always
will be, independent in that stage of
development to which your voluntary decisions
and divine powers have led. There are limits all along the
way to what you can be and do. But you are not a billiard ball.
No power in the universe can coerce your complete assent
or dissent. This thesis on capacity translates Bergson's
metaphor into breathtaking fact: 'The universe is
a machine for the making of gods.'"
(Truman Madsen).

Agency
And Youth

Latter-day prophets have consistently taught that our youth were among the most valiant spirits in the pre-earth existence. During the War in Heaven, those who stood with the Savior sought to preserve agency as a foundation principle of the Plan of Salvation, while those who rebelled and fought with Lucifer sought to control the minds of their brothers and sisters through the devious manipulation of ideology. (See Abraham 3:27 & Revelation 12:7). Those who were zealous in the defense of their freedom of expression kept their first estate, and were added upon. They were blessed to be able to come to earth, to fill the measure of their creation.

During the pre-mortal conflict that pitted contrasting ideologies against each other, the principle of free will, together with the natural consequences related to its expression, prevailed, and when the victorious spirits were given their opportunity to experience mortality, they grasped it with a passion for the freedom to choose their own destiny, that had become ingrained within their nature. Consequently, when those spirits who have come to earth to dwell in mortal clay sense that they are being controlled by compulsion, "in any degree of unrighteousness" whatsoever, their innate tendency is to resist with the same tenacity they exhibited in their pre-mortal life.

Therefore, we need to be very careful how we relate with our youth in every situation involving the exercise of agency. It is helpful to appreciate and to put into context where they have come from, because that helps us to understand why they act as they do.

If God
had wanted
to be permissive, He
would have given us Ten
Suggestions, rather than
Ten Commandments.

Attributes Of God
Related To The Ten Commandments

#1. Because He is "the Father of heaven and earth, the Creator of all things from the beginning," (Mosiah 3:8), He has commanded: "Thou shalt have no other gods before me." (Exodus 20:3). Disciples of Christ emulate His example and are temperate in their behavior. They have learned the principles of self-regulation, and to control sensual and devilish desires. Disciples would never attempt to displace God with golden calves. They have been liberated from enslavement to drunkenness, and selfish indulgence. "Wo unto them that rise up early in the morning, that they may follow strong drink, that continue until night, and wine inflame them!" cautioned Isaiah. (2 Nephi 15:11). Such miscreants are blinded to the work of the Lord that is before their very eyes. "They regard not the work of the Lord, neither consider the operation of his hands." (2 Nephi 15:12). They are held captive because they have no knowledge of God. "Their honorable men are famished, and their multitude dried up with thirst." (2 Nephi 15:13).

The condition of those who have not learned to control their passions is characterized by a hell that "hath enlarged herself, and opened her mouth without measure; and their glory, and their multitude, and their pomp, and he that rejoiceth, shall descend into it. And the mean (or common) man shall be brought down, and the mighty man shall be humbled, and the eyes of the lofty shall be humbled." (2 Nephi 15:14-15). "But the Lord of Hosts will be exalted in judgment, and God that is holy shall be sanctified in righteousness." (2 Nephi 15:16).

#2. Because He knows how susceptible we are to the siren song that escapes the lips of "gods of silver, and gold, of brass, iron, wood, and stone, which see not, nor hear, nor know, (Daniel 5:23), He has commanded: "Thou shalt not make unto thee any graven image." (Exodus 20:4). Satan uses telestial toys that are the corruptible treasures of the earth as weak counterfeits of God. These stand in opposition to celestial sureties and the incorruptible riches of eternity. Jeremiah asked: "Shall a man make gods unto himself, and they are no gods?" (Jeremiah 16:20). In His Preface to the Doctrine and Covenants, the Lord declared of those who lived at the time of Joseph Smith: "They seek not the Lord to establish his righteousness, but every man walketh in his own way, and after the image of his own god, whose image is in the likeness of the world, and whose substance is like that of an idol, which waxeth old and shall perish in Babylon, even Babylon the great, which shall fall." (D&C 1:16).

"Wo unto those that worship idols (in the Last Days), for the devil of all devils delighteth in them." (2 Nephi 9:37). In the final analysis, the seducer can only rule in the earth by manipulating those whose misplaced worship focuses on idols, who have traded their celestial birthright for a mess of pottage, who have traded their agency for the rush that accompanies carnality and sensuality. Standing in grand opposition to that bogus sensory stimulation is priesthood power, which is the "rule of God and is the only legitimate power that has a right to rule upon the earth. When the will of God is done on the earth, as it is done in heaven, no other power will bear rule." (John Taylor, J.D., 5:187).

One of the most unfortunate consequences of falling down before false Gods is that many who do so then harden their hearts against the Lord, and "become like unto a flint." (2 Nephi 5:21). When the inevitable sparks fly, their combustible hatred bursts into flames that are fanned by the winds of intolerance toward their fellow men, and that are fueled by fear, prejudice, ignorance, and narrow-mindedness. The resulting fragility of the pathways through which inspiration flows effectively cripples the capacity to respond to promptings of the Spirit. It is a frightening thing when barriers to revealed communication from the heavens are thrown up, and the word of God is esteemed as a thing of naught. Faithlessness and conscious non-conformity to gospel principles propel the headstrong and stubborn on an accelerating downward death-spiral that leads straight into the gaping mouth of hell.

#3. Because He knows how fruitless it is to swear by heaven, or earth, or by any other oath (see James 5:12), He has commanded: "Thou shalt not take the name of the Lord thy God in vain." (Exodus 20:7). Our Father in Heaven has intimate experience with children who have become blasphemers, and who seek in vain to usurp His very authority. Lucifer was a son of the morning, a light-bearer, but he "became Satan, yea, even the devil, the father of all lies, to deceive and to blind men, and to lead them captive at his will, even as many as would not hearken unto (the) voice" of our Savior. (Moses 4:4). Primarily because his actions demonstrated his contempt for the God in Whose name he spoke in vain, Lucifer became Perdition, or "utter ruin." His progression was halted, because his rebellion against the order of heaven was characterized by the most inappropriate behavior. It was to no effect, after all, that he rebelled against the light, while basking in its warmth. He blasphemed the name of his Father while yet in His presence.

#4. Because He knows how important it is to allow us time to recharge our spiritual batteries, and to rest from our labors, and to pay our devotions to Him, (see D&C 59:10), He has commanded us: "Remember the sabbath day, to keep it holy." (Exodus 20:8). First it was called the Holy Sabbath, then the Sabbath, then Sunday. Now, it is called the Weekend. The time that was prepared especially for us, to ponder and pray, has been replaced with a desire to wander and play. Nevertheless, holy days must never be confused with holidays. "Wherefore, the Sabbath was given unto man for a day of rest; and also that man should glorify God." (J.S.T. Mark 2:26-27). The Lord has given us the Sabbath to help us to have the Spirit more fully in our lives.

Today, we no longer stone to death those who violate the Law of the Sabbath, yet we die spiritually when we deliberately alienate ourselves from God's influence, because our actions throw up an effective roadblock to our eternal progression. "Broad is the gate, and wide the way that leadeth to the deaths; and many there are that go in thereat, because they receive me not, neither do they abide in my law." (D&C 132:25). God has prepared the Sabbath as a "work release program" for us, to see how we will behave when we are left on our own, after having received instruction regarding what we ought to do.

#5. Because we have "one God and Father of all, who is above all," (Ephesians 4:6), He has commanded: "Honor thy father and thy mother." (Exodus 20:12). The title "Elohim" is the plural form of the Northwest Semitic noun El, ("God"), and is accepted as the majestic title of deity. Genesis 1:27 reads: "So God created man in his own image, in the image of God created he him, male and female created he them." This scripture, as well as the teachings of the temple endowment, suggest that Heavenly Parents, male and female, participated jointly in the creative process. In ways that others cannot appreciate, Latter-day Saints recognize the responsibility of mortal parents to provide nurturing environments for the spirit children of our Heavenly Father that have been entrusted to their care. Fathers and mothers have sacred roles and responsibilities, are partners with Deity, and stand with divine role models before the human family to see that the measure of our creation is fulfilled.

#6. Because he has "life in himself," (John 5:26), and because His Son is "the way, the truth, and the life," (John 14:6), He considers it abhorrent to take life, and has commanded: "Thou shalt not kill." (Exodus 20:13). Joseph Smith gave a name to the Three Act Play in which we are all willing participants, calling it "the Plan of Salvation." He characterized it as "one of heaven's best gifts to mankind." ("Teachings," p. 207). Alma variously called it The Merciful Plan of the Father, The Plan of Mercy, The Plan of Redemption, The Plan of Happiness, and the ever-popular Great Plan of Happiness. (Alma 42:8). Whereas the most successful play on Broadway closes its run after a few years at most, the Plan of Salvation has been around since before our first parents attended opening night of the Second Act, Scene One, in the Garden in Eden. Its run will extend beyond mortality into the eternities, where the Third Act will engage the attention of its participants forever. With this perspective, we can easily see why taking the life of another is a heinous act. Doing so dictates an unauthorized re-write of essential elements of the Play/Plan, and erodes the very foundations upon which the promise of the Plan rests.

"Wo unto the murderer who deliberately killeth, for he shall die." (2 Nephi 9:35). The sin of intentionally killing another robs that individual of agency and self-determination with abrupt, total, and irreversible finality. Such a brutal act of selfishness positions the transgressor beyond the power of the Atonement, and so the doctrine of Blood Atonement, wherein the transgressor must atone with his own blood for his sins, was taught among the Nephites.

#7. Because "marriage is ordained of God unto man," and is the order of heaven, (D&C 49:15), He has commanded: "Thou shalt not commit adultery." (Exodus 20:14). Possibly the most significant difference that accounts for the superiority of the Plan of Salvation over any other lifestyle is the process whereby the gospel of Jesus Christ is internalized by His disciples. This phenomenon is called sanctification by the Spirit. A major purpose of the gospel is to provide those principles, covenants, and ordinances that enable us to become sanctified so that we may be worthy to bask in a state of holiness in the presence of our Heavenly Father. Through sanctification, we are cleansed from the effects of sin by a spiritual renewal that prepares us to pass by the angels who stand as sentinels as we approach the veil, ready to enter the presence of the Lord. All we must do in preparation is submit to His will, yield our hearts to Him, be obedient to the teachings of His church, enter into a covenant relationship with Him, and endure to the end in righteousness. "If (we) do these things blessed are (we), for (we) shall be lifted up at the last day." (3 Nephi 27:22).

The scriptures are quite clear about those who violate the covenant of chastity. "Wo unto them who commit whoredoms, for they shall be thrust down to hell." (2 Nephi 9:36). A whore can also be a corrupt or idolatrous individual, organization, or community. Thus, the worship of idols of any kind is a whoredom, and is adulterous in a figurative sense. We worship idols when we turn our backs on the sacred covenants of the priesthood, in acts of defiance akin to infidelity. Idol worship is in diametrical opposition to those who come to the marriage supper of the Lamb with their lamps of oil filled to overflowing.

When the gospel drives the law into our inward parts, so that it is written upon our hearts, a mighty change takes place as we experience the process of sanctification. (See Jeremiah 31:33). When we are born again, the desired result of all gospel-oriented teaching has been achieved. When we are sanctified, we have no more disposition to do evil. Our "minds become single to God, and the days will come that (we) shall see him; for he will unveil his face unto (us)." (D&C 88:68).

When we forsake our sins, come unto Christ, call on His name, obey His voice, and keep His commandments including the Law of Chastity, we shall see His face and know that He is. (See D&C 93:1).

#8. God knows how it feels to be violated by those who unceremoniously take what is not theirs. He asked those who had withheld of their increase: "Will a man rob God? Yet ye have robbed me." (Malachi 3:8). Therefore, He has commanded: "Thou shalt not steal." (Exodus 20:15). However, this injunction is not what motivates the disciples of Christ to exercise moral discipline. Instead, they do not steal because they have consistently listened to the whisperings of the Spirit. They have exercised their agency to build up their spiritual muscles, by repetitively choosing that which is right, simply because it is right. They have established neural and physiological pathways that have crystallized into habit patterns that make it easier to do the right thing.

Simply having good values is not enough. Modern society has failed miserably to instill high standards in the rising generation. We live in a culture that believes that truth is relative, and that it is up to individuals to decide what is right or wrong. As a result, the stage is set for disaster. When "every man walketh in his own way, and after the image of his own god," the erosion of moral discipline is inevitable. (D&C 1:16). When that happens, stop-gap measures of external control are often implemented to manipulate behavior. But an increased reliance on laws that attempt to instill integrity in the absence of a moral compass says something about our culture. The world seeks change by exerting external influence, and fails miserably. The gospel implements lasting change by transforming the inner vessel, and succeeds brilliantly. The Spirit does this by reinvigorating and calibrating that moral compass so that it is oriented toward discipline.

#9. The scriptures bear record of the awful scene that unfolded during the betrayal of Christ. Matthew recorded: "Now the chief priests, and elders, and all the council, sought false witness against Jesus, to put him to death." (Matthew 26:59). In anticipation of the risk of irreparable damage to character, God has commanded: "Thou shalt not bear false witness against thy neighbor." (Exodus 20:16). Those who have His image engraven upon their countenances will recognize their solemn responsibility to be His witness, at all times, and in all places. "Who shall ascend into the hill of the Lord," asked the Psalmist, "or who shall stand in his holy place" to partake of the Divine Nature? "He that hath clean hands and a pure heart; who hath not lifted up his soul unto vanity, nor sworn deceitfully." (Psalms 24:4-5).

Those who bear false witness qualify only for telestial glory. If we view the forces operating in the vortex of life as naturally occurring opposites, false witness is a particularly damaging sin, since it poisons the atmosphere in which choices must be made. It leaves all within its sphere of influence gasping for air. Its fiction may compellingly distort the facts in ways that makes the righteous application of agency very difficult.

#10. The Savior knows from firsthand experience that Satan will use our desire for the world's goods to destroy us. For in the wilderness, He too was tempted of the devil. Even when the deceiver "sheweth him all the kingdoms of the world, and the glory of them; And saith unto him, All these things will I give thee, if thou wilt fall down and worship me," Jesus was, nevertheless, able to declare "Get thee hence, Satan." (Matthew 4:1-11). Thus, are we commanded: "Thou shalt not covet." (Exodus 20:17). Those who desire profane telestial baubles will never find meaning in their lives if they continue to ignore the Plan of Happiness and treat its integral elements superficially and carelessly, only because they are not tangible telestial toys. They think that only if they have more, will they be satisfied. But because they reject the principles upon which happiness is founded, ultimately, they will be frustrated. Those who use their agency inappropriately and make poor investment choices with their time and talents will be left with only a wad of counterfeit currency with which to make late payments with interest tacked on for bad behavior. In their efforts to gain, they will seldom obtain, and more rarely retain feelings of true happiness. Never learning the hard lessons of life, they will continually covet the things with which the gods of wood and stone tempt them, but that ironically are those things that are powerless to redeem them from their misery.

"Cogito, ergo sum."
I think, therefore I am. If we think, then we have proof that we exist. Likewise, if we feel the Spirit or have spiritual promptings, then we have self-evident proof that spirit exists.

Bah! Humbug!

"Marley was dead, to begin with. There is no doubt whatever about that. The register of his burial was signed by the clergyman, the clerk, the undertaker, and the chief mourner. Scrooge signed it. Old Marley was as dead as a doornail." (Charles Dickens, "A Christmas Carol," p. 1).

In the seven years since Marley's death, Ebenezer Scrooge had become even more cold-hearted; a miser who despised Christmas and everything for which it stood. He was the embodiment of winter, bringing to mind images of darkness, despair, sadness, and death. As Dickens put it: "The cold within him froze his old features, nipped his pointed nose, made his eyes red, his thin lips blue, and spoke out shrewdly in his grating voice." He was "a squeezing, wrenching, grasping, scraping, clutching, covetous old sinner!" He had been transformed by the inexorable erosion from endless waves beating upon his cold, pinched heart.

One fateful Christmas Eve, Scrooge was visited by Marley and the ghosts of Christmas Past, Present, and Future. In a memorable exchange, he told Marley's ghost: "But you were always a good man of business, Jacob!" "Business," cried the ghost, wringing its hands again. "Mankind was my business. The common welfare was my business; charity, mercy, forbearance, and benevolence were all my business. The dealings of my trade were but a drop of water in the comprehensive ocean of my business."

And then, there was remorse in his voice, for opportunities missed, and potential denied: "At this time of the rolling year," the spectre said, "I suffer most. Why did I walk through crowds of fellow beings with my eyes turned down, and never raise them to that blessed Star which led the Wise Men to a poor abode? Were there no homes to which its light would have conducted me?"

Over the course of the night, like the Prodigal Son, Ebenezer Scrooge first hit rock-bottom, and only then was able to change his nature. We are encouraged to realize that there were no boundaries or restrictions put upon him as he dragged himself back out of his misery to face the better angels of his nature. In the process, he regained the opportunity to restore the nurturing atmosphere of hearth and home to the benefit of others, particularly the Cratchett family, including Tiny Tim.

The ghosts that appeared to him on Christmas Eve gave him a chance to be "born again," to recommit himself to obey the higher standard from which he had strayed. In a larger sense, the spiritual transformation of Ebenezer Scrooge teaches us that our Heavenly Father's Plan is designed to save even the worst of His children, but only after they have changed their nature. With renewed confidence, we feel a glimmer of hope, inasmuch as we sometimes feel equally undeserving of His unconditional love and grace.

My own conversion was less dramatic than that of Ebenezer Scrooge, and yet my feelings relating to my journey cannot be easily expressed in words. I do know that by the grace of our Heavenly Father, my eyes have been opened. The Savior helps me to forget my bad days and to focus on becoming better; to love my family, to be more responsible towards others, and to help them, to sacrifice myself through His love, to be a willing participant in the creation of a little bit of heaven on earth, to make a small contribution to the spirit of Christmas throughout the year, and to assist others on their journey to Christ.

Dickens wrote of Scrooge after his transformation: "It was always said of him, that he knew how to keep Christmas well." May that be said of each of us, as well! As Tiny Tim observed: "God Bless Us, Every One!"

"Little
children are redeemed
from the foundation of the world
through mine Only Begotten. Wherefore,
they cannot sin, for power is not given
unto Satan to tempt little children,
until they begin to become
accountable before me."
(D&C 29:46-47).

Baptism
And Accountability

In The Church of Jesus Christ of Latter-day Saints, children are not baptized until they have reached what is characterized as "the age of accountability." Members cite the teachings of early church leaders, as well as the scriptures, to justify the practice. For example, Joseph Smith's Translation of the Bible, in Genesis 17:11, clearly states: "Children are not accountable before me until they are eight years old." The Doctrine & Covenants adds further clarification to this doctrine: "Little children are redeemed from the foundation of the world through mine Only Begotten. Wherefore, they cannot sin, for power is not given unto Satan to tempt little children, until they begin to become accountable before me." (D&C 29:46-47).

I have researched the Catholic doctrines relating to original sin, purgatory, hell, and limbo, and I must say that it has left me just as confused as the Catholic apologists themselves seem to be. Suffice to say, that the teachings of The Church of Jesus Christ of Latter-day Saints categorically denounce the concept that unbaptized children, or aborted fetuses for that matter, must necessarily go to hell, limbo, or purgatory, because of the consequences associated with original sin. The breath of fresh air of latter-day revelation is unequivocal: "Children who die before they arrive at the years of accountability are saved in the Celestial Kingdom of heaven." (D&C 137:10).

Sixteen hundred years ago, on the American Continent, the doctrine of baptism was equally clear. At a time when the task of writing upon metal plates was not only laborious but also dangerous, Moroni nevertheless made it his mission to record an extensive treatise relating to the baptism of children, knowing that his words would provide invaluable clarification following the confusion of concepts that was the consequence of the Great Apostasy. He wrote: "Behold I say unto you that this thing shall ye teach - repentance and baptism unto those who are accountable and capable of committing sin; yea, teach parents that they must repent and be baptized, and humble themselves as their little children, and they shall all be saved with their little children. And their little children need no repentance, neither baptism.

Behold, baptism is unto repentance to the fulfilling the commandments unto the remission of sins. But little children are alive in Christ, even from the foundation of the world; if not so, God is a partial God, and also a changeable God, and a respecter to persons; for how many little children have died without baptism! Wherefore, if little children could not be saved without baptism, these must have gone to an endless hell.

Behold I say unto you, that he that supposeth that little children need baptism is in the gall of bitterness and in the bonds of iniquity; for he hath neither faith, hope, nor charity; wherefore, should he be cut off while in the thought, he must go down to hell. For awful is the wickedness to suppose that God saveth one child because of baptism, and the other must perish because he hath no baptism. Wo be unto them that shall pervert the ways of the Lord after this manner, for they shall perish except they repent.

Behold, I speak with boldness, having authority from God; and I fear not what man can do; for perfect love casteth out all fear. And I am filled with charity, which is everlasting love; wherefore, all children are alike unto me; wherefore, I love little children with a perfect love; and they are all alike and partakers of salvation. For I know that God is not a partial God, neither a changeable being; but he is unchangeable from all eternity to all eternity. Little children cannot repent; wherefore, it is awful wickedness to deny the pure mercies of God unto them, for they are all alive in him because of his mercy.

And he that saith that little children need baptism denieth the mercies of Christ, and setteth at naught the atonement of him and the power of his redemption. Wo unto such, for they are in danger of death, hell, and an endless torment. I speak it boldly; God hath commanded me. Listen unto them and give heed, or they stand against you at the judgment-seat of Christ.

For behold that all little children are alive in Christ, and also all they that are without the law. For the power of redemption cometh on all them that have no law; wherefore, he that is not condemned, or he that is under no condemnation, cannot repent; and unto such baptism availeth nothing— But it is mockery before God, denying the mercies of Christ, and the power of his Holy Spirit, and putting trust in dead works." (Moroni 10:10-23).

David O. McKay taught that the time between a child's birth and the age of accountability is ideally suited to teach the principles of the gospel. In fact, in Primary class settings, not to mention in nurturing home environments, children are like little sponges, soaking up the basic doctrines of the kingdom. He further taught that the time between a child's eighth birthday and their sixteenth year is ideal for them to be trained in the application of the principles of the gospel.

Then, President McKay taught, when a child has reached the age of sixteen and is emerging into young adulthood, it is time to trust them in the correct application of the principles they have learned and that have been incorporated through practice into their lives.

The scriptures affirm: "And again, inasmuch as parents have children in Zion, or in any of her stakes which are organized, that teach them not to understand the doctrine of repentance, faith in Christ the Son of the living God, and of baptism and the gift of the Holy Ghost by the laying on of the hands, when eight years old, the sin be upon the heads of the parents. For this shall be a law unto the inhabitants of Zion, or in any of her stakes which are organized. *And their children shall be baptized for the remission of their sins when eight years old*, and receive the laying on of the hands. And they shall also teach their children to pray, and to walk uprightly before the Lord." (D&C 68:25-28 italics mine).

It may be that the underlined portion of the scripture cited above is simply a clarification of the doctrine of accountability; that children cannot be received into the church unless they have "arrived unto the years of accountability before God, and (are) capable of repentance." (D&C 20:71). Elsewhere in the Doctrine & Covenants, the teaching is clear that only children who have reached the age of accountability, and from that time forward are capable of sin, need to be baptized. "For all men must repent and be baptized, and not only men, but women, and children who have arrived at the years of accountability." (D&C 18:42).

All who are baptized follow the example of the Savior. "If it so be that ye believe in Christ, and are baptized, first with water, then with fire and with the Holy Ghost, following the example of our Savior, according to that which he hath commanded us, it shall be well with you in the day of judgment." (Mormon 7:10). They are baptized to fulfill all righteousness. "And Jesus, answering, said unto (John), Suffer me to be baptized of thee, for thus it becometh us to fulfill all righteousness. (J.S.T. Matthew 3:43). They are baptized in order to keep the commandments. "Baptism cometh by faith unto the fulfilling the commandments." (Moroni 8:25). By so doing, they "enter in at the strait gate. "Enter ye in at the strait gate: for wide is the gate, and broad is the way, that leadeth to destruction." (Matthew 7:13). As they are immersed in the healing waters, they are born again. "Nicodemus saith unto him, How can a man be born when he is old? can he enter the second time into his mother's womb, and be born? Jesus answered, Verily, verily, I say unto thee, Except a man be born of water and of the Spirit, he cannot enter into the kingdom of God." (John 3:4-4).

But children who have reached the age of accountability are not baptized for the remission of sins. "Every spirit of man was innocent in the beginning; and God having redeemed man from the fall, men became again, in their infant state, innocent before God." (D&C 93:38). As the poet observed: "Heaven lies about us in our infancy. Shades of the prison house begin to close upon the growing boy. But he beholds the light and whence it flows; he sees it in his joy. The youth, who daily farther from the east must travel, still is nature's priest. And by the vision splendid, is on his way attended. At length, the man perceives it die away, and fade into the light of common day." (William Wordsworth).

That fading light is the consequence of the corrosive nature of sin, the opposition in all things that is necessary part of our mortal experience. In the absence of baptism, which is the lynchpin of the Plan of Salvation, all must be lost. Fortunately, the Lord reveals truth to those who are spiritually ready to understand it, and from the beginning provided a pathway that all might humble themselves as little children.

During the Creation, "God made two great lights; the greater light to rule the day, and the lesser light to rule the night. (Genesis 1:16, see also Moses 2:16, and Abraham 3:5-6, and 4:16). It is illuminating to think of the greater light as the gift of the Holy Ghost, and the lesser light as the Light of Christ. The purpose of the Light of Christ would be to provide enough light that all of Heavenly Father's children might be led to His doorstep, where the greater light of the Holy Ghost would be waiting to welcome them, through the portal of baptism, into celestial glory.

The experience of baptism is akin to having been born again, which implies a re-writing of the record of our lives. We cannot go back and start a new beginning, but we can begin now to make a new ending. Every man's and every woman's life is a fairytale waiting to be written. (Attr. to Hans Christian Anderson). With confidence, we can await the further light and knowledge the Lord has promised to send to us. "For God, who commanded the light to shine out of darkness, hath shined in our hearts, to give the light of the knowledge of the glory of God in the face of Jesus Christ." (2 Corinthians 4:6).

Because "unto whomsoever much is given, of him shall much be required," newly baptized members of the church receive the gift of the Holy Ghost, beside the waters of purification. (J.S.T. Luke 1:57). The intensity of this ordinance allows us to discover for ourselves the very personal levels of the experiences of the Savior. When He speaks of "knowing Him," The Savior must be referring to a special sense of the word. It is not enough that we know about Him, by reading the Gospels, or by listening to others speak of Him. We must know Him through the bonds of common experience and common feeling. Our baptism serves this purpose as an immersion in the tangible element of Spirit.

But then, how can we be expected to keep the Spirit with us after our baptism, and after our confirmation, and the bestowal of the gift of the Holy Ghost? It is in the ordinance of the Sacrament that we renew our covenant of baptism. As Alma said unto his brethren beside the waters of Mormon: "As ye are desirous to come into the fold of God, and to be called his people, and are willing to bear one another's burdens, that they may be light; Yea, and are willing to mourn with those that mourn; yea, and comfort those that stand in need of comfort, and to stand as witnesses of God at all times and in all things, and in all places that ye may be in, even until death, that ye may be redeemed of God, and be numbered with those of the first resurrection, that ye may have eternal life. Now I say unto you, if this be the desire of your hearts, what have you against being baptized in the name of the Lord, as a witness before him that ye have entered into a covenant with him, that ye will serve him and keep his commandments, that he may pour out his Spirit more abundantly upon you?" (Mosiah 18:8-10).

This clearly articulated covenant of baptism applies to all who wish to have their sins forgiven, who are "for all the laws of God; whose flesh is cleansed, shining bright in the waters of purification, even in the waters of baptism. They shall be given a new name in due time to walk perfect in all the ways of God." (From "The Serek Scroll," discovered in 1947, in caves high above Qumran). But the covenant also applies to eight year olds, who have just celebrated a milestone by reaching the age of accountability.

The suggestion that little children need to be baptized for the remission of sins denies the power of the Atonement of Jesus Christ. For they "cannot repent; wherefore, it is awful wickedness to deny the pure mercies of God unto them, for they are all alive in him because of his mercy. And he that saith that little children need baptism denieth the mercies of Christ, and setteth at naught the atonement of him and the power of his redemption. Wo unto such, for they are in danger of death, hell, and an endless torment. I speak it boldly; God hath commanded me. Listen unto them and give heed, or they stand against you at the judgment-seat of Christ. For behold that all little children are alive in Christ." (Moroni 8:19-22).

The ordinances of baptism and the bestowal of the gift of the Holy Ghost, received by eight year old children, are the physical expressions of our desire to teach the doctrine of Christ. As Nephi explained: "I suppose that ye ponder somewhat in your hearts concerning that which ye should do after ye have entered in by the way. If ye will enter in by the way, and receive the Holy Ghost, it will show unto you all things what ye should do. Behold, this is the doctrine of Christ." (2 Nephi 32:1, & 5-6). By following this doctrine, we "begin to be accountable." (D&C 29:47). We learn how to repent, by beginning the process as we have been taught. (See D&C 90:34, Alma 14:1, & Mormon 2:10).

The baptism of eight year old children is the culmination of a process begun much earlier, as their caregivers preach, teach, and expound the principles of the gospel, exhorting them to be baptized, and thereafter to worthily partake of the Sacrament. Little ones are introduced to the concepts and truths pertaining to the principles of the Plan of Salvation. Afterward, the principles are brought into focus and illustrated in meaningful ways. Then, their charges are introduced to instruction that expounds, or enlarges upon the principles, with an expansion of understanding. Finally, little children are exhorted to incorporate the principles into their own lives. Ownership is encouraged through personal witness or testimony, as the worth of the principles is validated. When commitment level reaches critical mass, priests stand ready with the authority to baptize. The administration of the ordinance becomes the outward evidence of personal dedication to obedience. It is the public manifestation of a covenant relationship made with God. It is the ultimate expression of self-reliance, because it is a voluntary surrender of agency to a higher power. It is an expression of "Thy will, and not my will, be done." It becomes a promise and a covenant that young and impressionable children can grasp.

The waters of baptism are a ready invitation to little children, the very ones who are humble, meek, poor in spirit, and pure in heart. When Elisha directed Naaman to wash in the River Jordan seven times in order to be cured of his leprosy, this proud captain of the host of the King of Syria at first refused. But "his servant came near, and spake unto him, and said, My father, if the prophet had bid thee do some great thing, wouldest thou not have done it? How much rather then, when he saith to thee, Wash, and be clean?" Then, with the faith of a little child, "he went down, and dipped himself seven times in Jordan, according to the saying of the man of God: and his flesh came again like unto the flesh of a little child, and he was clean." (2 Kings 5:13-14).

"Strait is the gate, and narrow is the way, which leadeth unto life, and few there be that find it." (Matthew 7:14). Baptism at the age of eight captures the heart of a little child before it has been exposed to the cankering influence and corrosive elements of the world, before their hearts are set upon temporal things, and their spirituality has been so weakened that the things of God are no longer part of their daily experience. Better than the rest of us, little children have a capacity to "lay aside the things of this world, and seek for the things of a better." (D&C 25:10).

The story is told of a kindergarten teacher who walked up and down the rows of desks in her classroom of children, observing their work. She stopped beside one little girl and asked what her drawing was. She replied, "I'm drawing a picture of God." The teacher paused, and then said, "But no one knows what God looks like."

Without missing a beat or looking up from her paper, the little girl replied, "They will in a minute." Though tender in years, this child had what adults might call "focus."

Newly baptized children very quickly realize that, in the Sacrament, Heavenly Father has provided a way for them to experience the mystical or spiritual transformation to a self-centered life to a Christ-centered life. It becomes an ordinance that allows them to regularly recommit themselves to internalize every truth, and every principle relating to eternal progression, and to then endure to the end, not in wickedness, but in righteousness. Others may consider that to be a heavy burden for one so young to bear, but countless witnesses have testified how it has become, for them, the perfect law of liberty.

As they begin to be accountable, their repentance might not be perfect, but as long as they are learning, their spiritual awakening is surely acceptable to the Lord. We may take solace in the scriptures, where, although we are admonished 154 times to be perfect, we are also encouraged 129 times to "learn" and 995 times to "begin." Thus, we read in the scriptures how "the people began to repent of their iniquity; and inasmuch as they did the Lord did have mercy on them." (Ether 11:8). As our "brethren in Zion begin to repent...the angels rejoice over them." (D&C 90:34). We have all witnessed how, when the Lord's anointed servants have "made an end of speaking unto the people, many of them did believe on his words, and began to repent, and to search the scriptures." (Alma 14:1). Even the best among us have seen "that they must perish, (except) they began to repent of their iniquities and cry unto the Lord." (Ether 9:34). With an awakening understanding, Nephi's rebellious brethren "began to see that the judgments of God were upon them, and that they must perish save that they should repent of their iniquities." (1 Nephi 28:15).

In much the same way, the Holy Ghost works on the conscience of children, gently guiding them past the first principles and ordinances of the gospel, onward to covenants relating to the priesthood and the temple. "For behold, thus saith the Lord God: I will give unto the children of men line upon line, precept upon precept, here a little and there a little; and blessed are those who hearken unto my precepts, and lend an ear unto my counsel, for they shall learn wisdom; for unto him that receiveth I will give more," (2 Nephi 28:30), "till we all come in the unity of the faith, and of the knowledge of the Son of God, unto a perfect man, unto the measure of the stature of the fulness of Christ." (Ephesians 4:13).

"For this is the covenant that
I will make with the house of Israel
after those days, saith the Lord; I will put my
laws into their mind, and write them in their hearts:
and I will be to them a God, and they shall be to
me a people: And they shall not teach every
man his neighbour, and every man his
brother, saying, Know the Lord:
for all shall know me, from
the least to the greatest."
(Hebrews 8:10-11).

Blood, Covenant, And Land Israel

In order to better understand Israel and her role in the events that are unfolding in the Last Days, she must be viewed from different perspectives. These allow us to appreciate the influence that her physical and spiritual qualities have had upon her neighbors. There is also the added element of adoption to be considered, that increases many-fold her capacity to change the world in preparation for the Second Coming. In one sense, Israel may simply be viewed as those in whom the blood of Israel flows. Another perspective explores the expanding influence of those within Gentile nations who have made a covenant with God to forsake the world and to join His people. As Paul taught the elect of God who had thereby become Israelites by adoption: "Ye are all the children of God by faith in Christ Jesus. For as many of you as have been baptized into Christ have put on Christ. There is neither Jew nor Greek, there is neither bond nor free, there is neither male nor female: for ye are all one in Christ Jesus. And if ye be Christ's, then are ye Abraham's seed, and heirs according to the promise." (Galatians 3:26-29).

A third point of view considers those whose ancestors have occupied the Holy Land since biblical times. Many of these are descendants of Abraham and have deeply rooted ties that will surely figure prominently in the events surrounding the fulfillment of prophecy in the Last Days, such as the gathering of Israel and preaching of the gospel. For a greater appreciation of the complex issues relating to Arab-Israeli relations in the Promised Land, see "Of The House of Israel," by Daniel Ludlow, in the "Ensign," 1/1991, "How Should Latter-day Saints View the Conflict in Israel?" by Kelly Ogden, in "Meridian Magazine," 9/6/2013, and "Peace in the Holy Land," by Kelly Ogden and David B. Galbraith, published in the "Liahona," 12/1997.

Some voices remain silent, while others are vocal, but all the world has witnessed how Israel has been "gathered home to the lands of (her) inheritance, (to be) established in all (her) lands of promise." (2 Nephi 9:2). That process has been going on long enough for us to acknowledge that there are many lands of inheritance, and many lands of promise, all of which reflect the broad strokes with which Heavenly Father paints His portrait of the children of the covenant.

In the first Area Conference of the church held in Mexico City, in August, 1972. Bruce R. McConkie stated: "Of this glorious day of restoration and gathering, a

Nephite prophet said: 'The Lord... has covenanted with all the house of Israel,' that 'the time comes that they shall be restored to the true church and fold of God'; and that 'they shall be gathered home to the lands of their inheritance, and shall be established in all their lands of promise.' (2 Nephi 9:1-2).

Now I call your attention to the facts, set forth in these scriptures, that the gathering of Israel consists of joining the true church; of coming to a knowledge of the true God and of his saving truths; and of worshiping him in the congregations of the Saints in all nations and among all peoples. Please note that these revealed words speak of the folds of the Lord; of Israel being gathered to the lands of their inheritance; of Israel being established in all their lands of promise; and of there being congregations of the covenant people of the Lord in every nation, speaking every tongue, and among every people when the Lord comes again.

The place of gathering for the Mexican Saints is in Mexico; the place of gathering for the Guatemalan Saints is in Guatemala; the place of gathering for the Brazilian Saints is in Brazil; and so it goes throughout the length and breadth of the whole earth. Japan is for the Japanese; Korea is for the Koreans; Australia is for the Australians; every nation is the gathering place for its own people." (See also: Bruce Satterfield, "The Scattering and Gathering of Israel," B.Y.U. Idaho).Therefore, as we participate in the Gathering, it would help if we were clear about the following:

Blood Israel

The term "blood Israel" could be applied to those who are Israelites by lineage. Today, it is largely the Jews who are "blood Israel." They are of the lineage of Abraham, Isaac, Jacob, and primarily his son Judah. They are the modern-day personification of the ancient covenant people of the Lord.

An angel had asked Nephi, who considered himself a Jew: "Rememberest thou the covenants of the Father unto the House of Israel?" (1 Nephi 14:8). He was speaking of the Abrahamic Covenant that was familiar to Nephi. This covenant has been only imperfectly preserved in the Book of Genesis: "Behold, my covenant is with thee, and thou shalt be a father of many nations. Neither shall thy name any more be called Abram, but thy name shall be Abraham; for a father of many nations have I made thee. And I will make thee exceeding fruitful, and I will make nations of thee, and kings shall come out of thee. And I will establish my covenant between me and thee and thy seed after thee in their generations for an everlasting covenant, to be a God unto thee, and to thy seed after thee." (Genesis 17:4-7).

The full force of the covenant promised to Abraham was that he would have numberless descendants who would be entitled to receive the gospel, the priesthood, and the ordinances of exaltation. God would establish the same covenant with all the generations of Abraham's children. They would ultimately carry the gospel to the nations of the earth and, through them, extend the blessings of God to all mankind. It is the intent of the Abrahamic Covenant to give all of Heavenly Father's children an equal opportunity to participate in and receive the blessings of the Plan of Salvation.

Covenant Israel

There are also those who, by accepting Christ and His covenants, become adopted members of the House of Israel, and who thus have equal claim upon the blessings of Abraham. These individuals could be termed "covenant Israel."

Today, "covenant Israel" is in a position to recognize and understand its relationship with God because of the clarification of principles and doctrines that have accompanied the restoration of the gospel. We learn that the Savior had originally explained to his servant Abraham: "My name is Jehovah, and I know the end from the beginning; therefore my hand shall be over thee. And I will make of thee a great nation, and I will bless thee above measure, and make thy name great among all nations, and thou shalt be a blessing unto thy seed after thee, that in their hands they shall bear this ministry and priesthood unto all nations. ...And I will bless them that bless thee, and curse them that curse thee; and in thee (that is, in thy priesthood) and in thy seed (that is, thy Priesthood), for I give unto thee a promise that this right shall continue in thee, and in thy seed after thee (that is to say, the literal seed, or the seed of the body) shall all the families of the earth be blessed, even with the blessings of the gospel, which are the blessings of salvation, even of life eternal." (Abraham 2:8-11).

Adoption is a process whereby Heavenly Father accepts with a sacred covenant (the Abrahamic Covenant) the parenting rights and responsibilities relating to His children. Because of His determination to honor all of the provision of the covenant, His offspring are empowered to enjoy the status that had formerly defined the relationship between them and their biological parents. Adoption enlarges the scope of their potential so that it may exponentially expand to eternal proportions. It has the power to bring us, the spirit children of our Heavenly Father, back into the fold so that we may, once again, dwell in the light of truth.

When we are converted to the gospel, we do not need to be the literal descendants of Abraham in order to qualify to receive from God the blessings of the Abrahamic Covenant. Literal descendants of Abraham are not the only people whom He calls His covenant people. Speaking to Abraham, God said, "As many as receive this gospel shall be called after thy name, and shall be accounted thy seed and shall rise up and bless thee, as their father." (Abraham 2:10). Thus, the two groups of people cited above who are included in the covenant made with Abraham are: (1) Abraham's righteous literal descendants and (2) those who have been adopted into his lineage by accepting and living the gospel of Jesus Christ. (See 2 Nephi 30:2).

In the Last Days, "as many of the Gentiles as will repent (shall become) the covenant people of the Lord; and as many of the Jews as will not repent shall be cast off; for the Lord covenanteth with none save it be with them that repent and believe in his Son, who is the Holy One of Israel." (2 Nephi 30:2). These are God's covenant people.

As a result of my exposure to the church beginning with a short film ("Man's Search for Happiness") at Flushing Meadows during the 1964 World's Fair, I learned about the covenants God wishes to make with me. For example, I learned about God's morality and the Covenant of Chastity. I learned about His charity and His commandment to love Him and each other. I learned about the principle of consecration as I studied the example of His Son. I learned about His compassion and the Law of the Fast. When I humbled myself, and learned about His perfection, I better understood the importance of the Word of Wisdom. As I sought to become more like Him, His commandment to seek knowledge made more sense to me. As I pondered the gift of His Son, I began to understand the Law of Sacrifice. As I tried to honor the Law of the Sabbath, my thoughts turned to His creation of the world, and how He had rested from His labors on the seventh day.

As I considered my covenant relationship with God, I thought about specific blessings, including my right to guidance from the Holy Ghost. I thought about the priesthood, and women's privileges, blessings, rights, and responsibilities relating to femininity. I thought about eternal family life in the Celestial Kingdom.

I learned that the covenants we make with God have the ability to place us beyond the reach of the adversary, and that obedience gives us the priesthood and spiritual power necessary to overcome evil and obtain exaltation. The teachings of the Prophet Joseph Smith snapped into sharp focus, that "salvation consists of a man's being placed beyond the power of his enemies, meaning the enemies of his progression, such as dishonesty, greediness, lying, immorality, and other vices." (Nauvoo, 5/21/1843, see also "Teachings," p. 297-298).

As I continued to make covenants, I learned more and more about my responsibilities relating to my relationship with God. I was promised that the gates of hell would not prevail against me, and that the Lord God would disperse the powers of darkness from before me, and cause the heavens to shake for my good and His name's glory. (See D&C 21:6). I learned about my duty to keep His commandments. When I realized the Lord had promised Abraham that through his descendants the gospel would be taken to all the earth, I learned something about my sacred duty to share my new-found faith with others.

The beauty of my adoption into the House of Israel has been to claim the privileges associated with His rights and responsibilities, and to be continually learning about The New and Everlasting Covenant, including the covenants made at my baptism, with my ordination to the Melchizedek Priesthood, during the sacrament, and in the temple. I know that these covenants are everlasting and have been ordained by His authority. I know that although His covenants may have been new to me, they will never be changed, for He has given them to His children each time He has dispensed the gospel. (See Ezekiel 37:26). I know by personal example that He is no respecter of persons. (See Acts 10:34).

I am the lucky recipient of the new covenant made with the House of Israel and with the House of Judah, and I will put His law in my inward parts, and write it in my heart. He will be my God, and I will be counted among His people. (See Jeremiah 31:31-34). Because of His love for me, I have learned how to personalize the "contract provisions" of the New and Everlasting Covenant. I have agreed to repent, be baptized, receive the Holy Ghost, the Oath and Covenant of the Priesthood, the endowment, the covenant of marriage in the temple, and to follow and obey Christ to the end of my life. Heavenly Father has promised, in turn, that I will receive exaltation in the Celestial Kingdom. (See D&C 132:20-24). The potential of that promise is hard for me to understand. I only know that the commandments were designed with me in mind, that they are for my benefit, and that if I am faithful, I may have a part in sharing the beauties and the blessings of both heaven and earth. One day, my family and I may live once again in His presence, to partake of His love, compassion, power, greatness, knowledge, wisdom, glory, and dominions.

I am overjoyed that my Father in Heaven established His Covenant to release me from my bondage to sin, and to set me free to take advantage of every feature of the Plan of Salvation. Without His Covenant in my behalf, I realize that the Plan would have been frustrated. I am thrilled to know that covenants have set me free from the bands of death. I believe the words of King Benjamin, who said: "There is no other name given whereby salvation cometh, therefore, I would that ye should take upon you the name of Christ, all you that have entered into the covenant with God." (Mosiah 5:8).

My covenants have set me free to reach my potential. I have learned to know the truth of Benjamin's words, that those who enter into the Covenant "are born of him." (Mosiah 5:7). I understand what it means to be a "Born Again Christian," to be in a covenant relationship with the Lord.

As the Lord revealed to Joseph Smith, so have I learned that the "greater priesthood administereth the gospel and holdeth the key of the mysteries of the kingdom, even the key of the knowledge of God. Therefore, in the ordinances thereof, the power of godliness is manifest. And without the ordinances thereof, and the authority of the priesthood, the power of godliness is not manifest unto men in the flesh." (D&C 84:19-21).

Land Israel

As great as are the blessings of "Blood Israel" and "Covenant Israel," there are those who have inhabited and worked the land since ancient times, and who have been included by the Lord to be counted among those who will receive the blessings of Abraham. These are those whom we might identify as "Land Israel."

Moses taught: "And if a stranger sojourn with thee in your land, ye shall not vex him. But the stranger that dwelleth with you shall be unto you as one born among you, and thou shalt love him as thyself; for ye were strangers in the land of Egypt." (Leviticus 19:33-34).

Isaiah dualistically prophesied: "For the Lord will have mercy on Jacob, and will yet choose Israel, and set them in their own land: and the strangers shall be joined with them, and they shall cleave to the house of Jacob." (Isaiah 14:1).

Heaven's admission policy welcomes Land Israel, along with Blood Israel and Covenant Israel. Persons of any race, creed, color, or national origin are accepted for admission to heaven provided they maintain ideals and standards in harmony with those of The Church of Jesus Christ of Latter-day Saints, and meet heaven's requirements. These are baptism, and the ordinances of the Melchizedek Priesthood.

It may come as a surprise to some, to realize that Israel comes in many different colors. It speaks Arabic, Dutch, Fijian, Mandarin, Russian, and dozens of other languages. It lives in well over 3,000 stakes, in practically every country in the world, from Algeria to Zimbabwe. It has over 15 million members who are red, yellow, brown, black, and white. Israel wears a sarong, a grass skirt, a blue collar, a lava lava, a tupeno, a business suit, and a kilt. It lives in igloos, huts, and high-rise condominiums. Most important of all, it shares a common destiny, and a testimony that Jesus is the Christ, and that His love, indeed, makes the world go round. Today, it is more important than ever to remember the words of President Harold B. Lee, who reminded us that "there is no United States of America in heaven." The great equalizer in the sight of God is obedience by His children to His will.

The key to Israel's liberation from bondage, to her freedom to become, is an adjustment in her attitudes reflected in her desire to be born again. To paraphrase Helen Keller, the real tragedy is not the Israelite who is born without sight, but those of blood, covenant, and land Israel who do not have vision.

"The role of Israel as the depository of true religion is almost self evident," declared Abba Eban, "the freeing of mankind from the idolatry which obstructs its salvation. For as Isaiah understood, there can be no redemption for man unless he conquers self-deification. He must abandon the worship of his own creations, and liberate himself from his lust for power, avarice, domination, and the cult of the state. There can be no redemption until man recognizes his moral obligations as transcendent and divine.

No form of government, no level of material well-being," he continued, "will save man. He will be redeemed only when 'towers fall, and Jerusalem triumphs over Babylon.' What is at stake, finally, is not only intelligence, but feeling. Man has to change his heart. Salvation, the prophets tell us, is preconditioned by repentance. The redeeming act of God waits upon Israel's initiative." ("My People: The Story of The Jews," p. 59-60).

There is a
divine spark in each of us
that never goes out. It may
be dimmed by the ashes
of transgression, but it
is never completely
snuffed out.

Born Again Christians

"Now I say unto you that ye must repent and be born again; for the Spirit saith if ye are not born again ye cannot inherit the kingdom of heaven; therefore, come and be baptized unto repentance, that ye may be washed from your sins, that ye may have faith on the Lamb of God, who taketh away the sins of the world, who is mighty to save and to cleanse from all unrighteousness." (Alma 7:14).

To receive eternal life, we must be "born again" as we are transformed to become "new creatures in Christ," with a renewal of our determination to follow Him, wherever that journey make take us. (2 Corinthians 5:17). But without His sustained divine nourishment, it is inevitable that we will, sooner or later, die spiritually. Perhaps this is why the figurative counterpart to water is so dramatic, for except we "be born of water and of the spirit," there is no way we "can enter into the kingdom of God." (John 3:5). Of this flowing, spiritual spring, Truman Madsen wrote: "If we do not drink, if we die of thirst while only inches from the fountain, the fault comes down to us. For the free, full, flowing, living water is there." ("Christ and The Inner Life," p. 31).

Being physically immersed in water symbolizes the burial of our past sins, and it is only as we emerge from the font that our new life begins. In fact, after King Benjamin's discourse exhorting his people to a renewed commitment to their covenants, they "all cried with one voice, saying: Yea, we believe all the words which thou hast spoken unto us; and also, we know of their surety and truth, because of the Spirit of the Lord Omnipotent, which has wrought a mighty change in us, or in our hearts, that we have no more disposition to do evil but to do good continually. And we, ourselves, also, through the infinite goodness of God, and the manifestations of his Spirit, have great views of that which is to come; and were it expedient, we could prophesy of all things. And it is the faith which we have had on the things which our king has spoken unto us that has brought us to this great knowledge, whereby we do rejoice with such exceedingly great joy. And we are willing to enter into a covenant with our God to do his will, and to be obedient to his commandments in all things that he shall command us, all the remainder of our days, that we may not bring upon ourselves a never-ending torment, as has been spoken by the angel, that we may not drink out of the cup of the wrath of God." (Mosiah 5:1-5).

This declaration of commitment set the stage for Benjamin to get to the very heart of his doctrinal message. "Therefore, he said unto them: Ye have spoken the words that I desired; and the covenant which ye have made is a righteous covenant. And now, because of the covenant which ye have made, ye shall be called the children of Christ, his sons, and his daughters; for behold, this day he hath spiritually begotten you; for ye say that your hearts are changed through faith on his name; therefore, ye are born of him, and have become his sons and his daughters." (Mosiah 5:6-7).

The Lord told Alma what it means to be born again: "Marvel not," He said, "that all mankind, yea, men and women, all nations, kindreds, tongues, and people, must be born again; yea, born of God, changed from their carnal and fallen state to a state of righteousness, being redeemed of God, becoming his sons and daughters; And thus they become new creatures; and unless they do this, they can in nowise inherit the kingdom of God." (Mosiah 27:25-26).

So important did Alma consider the necessity of spiritual rebirth, that he was moved to declare: "I am called…to preach unto my beloved brethren, yea, and every one that dwelleth in the land; yea, to preach unto all, both old and young, both bond and free; yea, I say unto you the aged, and also the middle aged, and the rising generation; yea, to cry unto them that they must repent and be born again." (Alma 5:49).

When Aaron had taught Lamoni's father, the king asked: "What shall I do that I may have this eternal life of which thou hast spoken? Yea, what shall I do that I may be born of God, having this wicked spirit rooted out of my breast, and receive his Spirit?" Then Aaron explained: "If thou desirest this thing, if thou wilt bow down before God, yea, if thou wilt repent of all thy sins, and will bow down before God, and call on his name in faith, believing that ye shall receive, then shalt thou receive the hope which thou desirest." (Alma 22:15-18).

Alma had asked the brethren of the church the same thing: "And now behold, I ask of you, have ye spiritually been born of God? Have ye received his image in your countenances? Have ye experienced this mighty change in your hearts?" (Alma 5:14). Then, he asked the $64,000.00 follow-up question: "If ye have felt to sing the song of redeeming love, I would ask, can ye feel so now?" (Alma 5:26). If not, all would not be lost as a result of their failure to maintain their forward momentum. A recommitment to their covenant of baptism would allow them to re-enter the fold, for being born again can be a process, as well as a point.

"And now," Nephi asked, "after ye have gotten into this strait and narrow path, I would ask if all is done? Behold, I say unto you, Nay; for ye have not come thus far save it were by the word of Christ with unshaken faith in him, relying wholly upon the merits of him who is mighty to save." After our baptism and receipt of the gift of the Holy Ghost, we must "press forward" with complete dedication and "steadfastness," or confidence and a firm determination in Christ, "having a perfect brightness of hope," or perfect faith, and charity, or "a love of God and of all men." If we do this, "feasting upon the word of Christ," or receiving strength and nourishment from the scriptures, and endure to the end in righteousness, we "shall have eternal life," that is the greatest gift that God can bestow. (2 Nephi 31:19-20).

Nephi's formula is, pure and simple, a statement of cold logic that has been made more savory by exposure to the warming tray of plain doctrine. "This is the way," he said, "and there is none other way nor name given under heaven whereby man can be saved in the kingdom of God. And now, behold, this is the doctrine of Christ, and the only and true doctrine of the Father, and of the Son, and of the Holy Ghost." (2 Nephi 31:21). Alma the Younger came to know this in the most intensely personal way possible. "I have seen my Redeemer," he testified, "and he shall come forth and shall redeem all mankind who believe on his name." (Alma 19:13). During a glorious manifestation, the Lord had told him: "Marvel not that all mankind, yea, men and women, all nations, kindreds, tongues, and people, must be born again, yea, born of God, changed from their carnal and fallen state, to a state of righteousness, being redeemed of God, becoming his sons and daughters." (Alma 27:25). He related how, after having been born again, his limbs had received strength, allowing him to stand upon his feet to manifest unto the people that he "had been born of God." (Alma 36:23).

The scriptures do not record whether Nicodemus received the same infusion of the holy element when Jesus "said unto him, Verily, verily, I say unto thee, Except a man be born again, he cannot see the kingdom of God.... Marvel not that I said unto thee, Ye must be born again." (John 3:3 & 7). But we do know that Peter later taught the principle of "being born again, not of corruptible seed, but of incorruptible, by the word of God." (1 Peter 1:23). His fellow apostle John confirmed: "Whatsoever is born of God overcometh the world: and this is the victory that overcometh the world." (1 John 5:4). These are they who are insulated from the carnality, sensuality, and devilish nature of men, insomuch that "whosoever is born of God sinneth not." (1 John 5:18). These are they to whom Jesus Christ gave "power to become the sons of God, even to them that believe on his name: Which were born, not of blood, nor of the will of the flesh, nor of the will of man, but of God." (John 1:12-13).

The unconditional promise is that "every one that doeth righteousness is born of him." (1 John 2:29). "Every one that loveth is born of God, and knoweth God." (1 John 4:7). Immediately after his conversion, Alma sensed the transformation that had occurred, and declared: "Behold I am born of the Spirit." (Mosiah 27:24). He elaborated: "After wading through much tribulation, repenting nigh unto death, the Lord in mercy hath seen fit to snatch me out of an everlasting burning, and I am born of God." (Mosiah 27:28). Although he had been "saved," there was subsequently much work to do, as he patiently endured to the end in righteousness.

Alma later told his son Helaman: "I would not that ye should think that I know these things of myself, but it is the Spirit of God which is in me which maketh these things known unto me; for if I had not been born of God I should not have known these things." (Alma 36:8). He related to Helaman that following his spiritual rebirth, he had "labored without ceasing, that (he) might bring souls unto repentance; that (he) might bring them to taste of the exceeding joy of which (he) did taste; that they might also be born of God, and be filled with the Holy Ghost." (Alma 36:24). As a result of his ministry, he reported: "Many have been born of God, and have tasted as I have tasted, and have seen eye to eye as I have seen." (Alma 36:26). Similarly, Parley P. Pratt said of his own pentecostal experience: "I have received the holy anointing, and I can never rest until the last enemy (that is, unresolved sin) is conquered, (spiritual) death destroyed, and truth reigns triumphant." (J.D., 1:15).

All who have thus been born again are set free by the perfect Law of Liberty to reach their potential. As Paul taught the Romans: "We are buried with him by baptism into death: that like as Christ was raised up from the dead by the glory of the Father, even so we also should walk in newness of life." (Romans 6:3). When we are born again we are as the acorns of a potential oak, for we have been vitalized by a nurturing influence to reach the full stature of our spirits.

"Behold, he changed their hearts; yea, he awakened them out of a deep sleep, and they awoke unto God. Behold, they were in the midst of darkness; nevertheless, their souls were illuminated by the light of the everlasting word."
(Alma 5:7).

A
Change Of Heart

For whatever reason, it is the heart, and not the head, that is the repository of feeling. We have all felt the pain and anguish of heartache, something that is qualitatively and quantitatively different from a headache. At special moments in our lives, our hearts leap for joy, but curiously, we never seem to describe the experience as if our heads were exploding with happiness. Our hearts race with excitement, even as our heads spin with dizziness. A particularly handsome young man may be described as a heartthrob, but rarely as a head case. Kindred spirits are closer to our hearts than to our heads. Instinct draws a baby close to a mother's nurturing breast, and little ones are comforted by the steady beat of her heart. The weak and timid, who are faint of heart, respond to the sweet influence of the Spirit better than to the analytical power of the rational mind. When we are broken-hearted, we are receptive to the teachable things of the kingdom, which is a far cry from the terrifying confusion of a broken mind that is out of synch with reality, or that lacks clarity because of a dim wit. A racing heart may be calmed by a strong will, but when a storm breaks loose in the head there may be no easy remedy for the ensuing nervous exhaustion or breakdown.

Those who listen to their hearts are sensitive, compassionate, empathetic, intuitive, caring, and considerate. When it is only our heads that influence us, we are too often callous, unfeeling, pitiless, harsh, cold-hearted, (brr!) or even (gasp!) heartless. When we begin to lose our minds, others may first charitably describe us as eccentric, and only later harshly label us as demented. But when our hearts have been worn out in service, there is no such stigma.

In fact, when we think of Mother Teresa, we recall the capacity of her heart, and not the numerical value of her intellect. It was from her heart that she echoed the words of St. Francis of Assisi, who said: "Preach the gospel at all times, and when necessary use words." Mother Teresa taught: "Give Jesus not only your hands to serve, but your heart to love. Pray with absolute trust in God's loving care for you. Let Him use you without consulting you. Let Jesus fill you with joy, that you may preach without preaching." ("Love: A Fruit Always in Season, Daily Meditations").

A pounding or racing heart may be the first sign of unbridled excitement. But unregulated stimulation of the brain is more commonly manifested as a grand mal seizure accompanied by foaming at the mouth. Endurance athletes may have enlarged hearts due to repetitive workouts involving aerobic exercise, while over-stressed business executives may only have dangerously enlarged heads due to misguided feelings of self-aggrandizement.

It is far better to have a troubled heart that leads us to repentance and reformed behavior, than it is to have a disturbed mind that can only be managed with antipsychotic medication. Those with wounded or broken hearts may heal slowly, but their prognosis is far better than those with irreversible brain injury. A heart may burst with the pride of accomplishment, but well-deserved achievement is easier to deal with than is the big head of one who is all wrapped up in himself. Those of us who have had our hearts stolen may be lucky enough to find our way back to happiness, but those who have lost their minds through trauma, disease, or the manipulation of others, are left with the irreversibility of a hollow core of existence from which there is no easy avenue of escape.

When we are light hearted, we don't have a care in the world; but when we are light headed, we feel only dizziness and disorientation. With heart-felt sorrow, we experience empathy and compassion that cannot be described with words, and that cannot be explained by the rational mind. Some emotions touch our hearts in ways that could never penetrate our thick skulls. If our hearts are like flint, it is because they have become calcified through neglectful inattention or disuse. Sometimes, people are heartless because they are brainless.

We may have a gentle heart, but if we are soft in the head, it is because our brains have turned to mush and our hippocampus is no longer lighting up its neurons. A pounding heart may presage the excitement of new opportunities, but a throbbing head is often the symptom of poorly managed stress. A warm heart implies nurture, but a heart that is as cold as a lump of coal supposes neglect. A warm embrace draws people together into close proximity where hearts can be knits together as one. A sorrowful heart can also be a strong heart, but only when it is sustained by the Spirit.

The average heart contracts 80 times per minute, 4,800 times per hour, and 115,200 times per day. Over the course of a year, the heart beats over 42 million times. In 70 years, that's almost 3 billion beats. An adult heart pumps up to 2,000 gallons of blood daily, about 730,000 gallons per year, or up to 51,000,000 gallons in 70 years, through around 100,000 miles of vessels in a circulatory system that brings nourishment to the 37.2 trillion cells that make up the human body.

The ancients, who knew little about the anatomy or physiology of the circulatory system, mentioned the heart almost 1,500 times in the scriptures. Many, if not all, of the prophets have used the heart as a metaphor for the seat of our deepest emotions. For example, Joseph Smith described his revelatory experience when reading in the Book of James, in the New Testament: "Never did any passage of scripture come with more power to the heart of man than this did at this time to mine. It seemed to enter with great force into every feeling of my heart." (Joseph Smith History 1:12).

The book of Proverbs is a rich source of references to the heart, as in Proverbs 15:13: "A merry heart maketh a cheerful countenance: but by sorrow of the heart the spirit is broken." Or Proverbs 14:30: "A sound heart is the life of the flesh." Or Proverbs 16:23: "The heart of the wise teacheth his mouth, and addeth learning to his lips." Or Proverbs 2:2: "Apply thine heart to understanding." Or Proverbs 8:5: "Be ye of an understanding heart." Or Proverbs 15:14: "The heart of him that hath understanding seeketh knowledge." Or Proverbs 15:30: "The light of the eyes rejoiceth the heart." Or Proverbs 17:22: "A merry heart doeth good like a medicine." Or Proverbs 23:12: "Apply thine heart unto instruction, and thine ears to the words of knowledge." Or Proverbs 3:1: "Forget not my law; but let thine heart keep my commandments." Or Proverbs 3:5: "Trust in the Lord with all thine heart; and lean not unto thine own understanding." Or Proverbs 7:3: "Write (the law) upon the table of thine heart."

The Saints of all ages understand the feelings of the people of Zarahemla, who exclaimed to their prophet Benjamin: "We believe all the words which thou hast spoken unto us; and also, we know of their surety and truth, because of the Spirit of the Lord Omnipotent, which has wrought a mighty change in us, or in our hearts, that we have no more disposition to do evil, but to do good continually." (Mosiah 5:2).

Alma asked the brethren of the church: "Have ye spiritually been born of God? Have ye received his image in your countenances? Have ye experienced this mighty change in your hearts?" (Alma 5:14). Then, by extension, he asked each of us: "And now behold, I say unto you, my brethren, if ye have experienced a change of heart, and if ye have felt to sing the song of redeeming love, I would ask, can ye feel so now?" (Alma 5:26).

Sometimes, in the physical world, our hearts begin to falter. They may skip a beat or two, or we may suffer from arrhythmia (an abnormal heart rhythm), tachycardia (an abnormally rapid heart rate), or bradycardia (an abnormally slow heart rate). We may experience angina, or chest pain that is related to insufficient oxygenated blood reaching the heart muscle. When we experience the symptoms of heart disease, we are quick to initiate protocols designed to restore function. We make dietary changes, join a gym, habitually take the stairs instead of the elevator, and modify other patterns of behavior. We read everything we can about the subject, and follow the counsel of experts in the fields of medicine, physical therapy, and biofeedback. We seek inspiration from lifestyle coaches and self-help gurus. We learn to monitor our cardiovascular health, and we establish benchmarks to more easily gauge our progress toward the achievement of our goals. When we reach a sustainable level of fitness, we eschew lifestyle choices that would compromise our gains.

Although we have been told to "lift up (our) hearts and be glad," (D&C 29:5), scripture teaches us that in the Last Days, it is the heart that will bear the brunt of the consequences of wickedness. Amid signs in the sun, and in the moon, and in the stars, and upon the earth, men's hearts will fail them for fear. (See Luke 21:24-26). In fact, "all things shall be in commotion, and surely, men's hearts shall fail them." (D&C 88:91).

These scriptures, and others, suggest that there will be both physical and spiritual assaults on the integrity of the hearts of the children of men. On the one hand, significant cardiovascular disease may require medicine such as digitalis to treat a weakened heart. A pacemaker may be necessary to restore proper rhythm. In extreme cases, cardiomyopathy may necessitate a heart transplant to sustain life.

But it is a spiritual heart transplant that is of interest to those who have forsaken the world and embraced the lifestyle of the Saints. Those who have had a physical heart transplant find it necessary to take a cocktail of immunosuppressant medication, according to a strict regimen, for the rest of their lives. The same prescriptions must be taken, in specific doses, at the same time every day. The routine must be followed without variation, in order to avoid the risk of failure of the surgical procedure. All doctor's appointments must be kept, every recommended laboratory test must be performed, medication side effects must be monitored, and drug interactions and the signs and symptoms of organ rejection must be addressed.

The same anti-rejection protocols must be followed after we have spiritually been given new hearts and have been born again. For, as the prophet Ezekiel declared: "A new heart also will I give you, and a new spirit will I put within you: and I will take away the stony heart out of your flesh." (Ezekiel 36:26). If we are not vigilant, our new hearts will surely fail us. We need to take a cocktail of immunosuppressant medication in the form of prayer, service, and temple attendance. We need to follow a strict regimen, in the form of regular spiritually aerobic church activity. We need to be diligent with medication that takes form and has substance in the ordinances of the gospel, including the bread and water that is offered on a weekly basis during ward Sacrament services.

We must be diligent to maintain a schedule of regular accountability interviews with our spiritual physicians, and, in particular, to participate in the house calls that take the form of visits from our priesthood leaders. We must take our home and visiting teaching responsibilities seriously. We must be alert to our need for regularly recurring repentance and learn to self-monitor the spiritual promptings that assure us we have received forgiveness of our sins. If we sense that our organ transplant has begun to fail, or if we feel that it is being rejected because of the effects of carnality, sensuality, or devilishness, we must know to whom we can turn for triage, for guidance and direction, so that the destructive elements might be decisively addressed, in order to restore spiritual heart-health, and once again sing the song of redeeming love without starved for celestial air, or experiencing shortness of breath.

We must strengthen our heart transplants by putting our shoulders to the wheel and pushing along. Cycling through the standard works in Sunday School class every four years may seem repetitive, but it is one of God's favorite spin classes. It is no more pedestrian than is a spectacular sunset, no more dreary than a rainbow after a storm, and no more uninteresting than a flight of migratory geese passing overhead on a cold autumn evening. Setting our sights on the scriptures in Seminary class every morning for four years may be daunting, but it establishes a habit pattern that can propel us over the summit of even the most daunting passes, those seeming obstacles to our progression.

Critics might see only frivolous repetition in our efforts to maintain spiritually aerobic health, mistaking reiteration for detachment from an active lifestyle that focuses only on instant gratification. In fact, sooner or later, there is for everyone who has had a spiritual heart transplant a moment in the sun, when the light of understanding illuminates the mind and confirms the divine potential of the new organs that rhythmically beat in our chests. As the morning breaks over the eastern sky, and the sunrise heralds another day, once again the self-evident truth is confirmed: We have been born again. The challenge before us has been met: We have received our new heart with gratitude, and have given ourselves completely to Him. With our new hearts, we enjoy a spiritual element that sustains our forward momentum as we push on into unexplored regions of eternity. Our new hearts not only expose us to an improved lifestyle, but also sustain our very lives. With all diligence, we keep them vital and healthy, knowing that it is from their steady beat that the fundamental issues of life flow, as in a revelatory stream. (See Proverbs 4:23).

Edmund
Dantès observed,
in the concluding lines
of Alexandre Dumas' "The Count
of Monte Cristo," that "only a man who
has felt ultimate despair is capable of feeling
ultimate bliss. It is necessary to have wished for
death, in order to know how good it is to live. Live,
then, and be happy, and never forget that, until
the day God deigns to reveal the future,
the sum of human wisdom will be
contained in these words:
wait and hope."

Choose
The Harder Right

Is it easier to choose wrong, and harder to choose the right? Is it easier to be wicked, and harder to be righteous? Is it easier to be sad, and harder to be happy? Is it easier to just put your life on cruise control, and harder to take the high road that requires greater concentration? Is it easier to go with the flow, and harder to swim upstream, against the current? Is it easier to walk with turkeys, and harder to soar with eagles? Is it easier to just throw in the towel and give up, and harder to continue the good fight? Is it easier to be mediocre or average, and harder to be exceptional? Is it easier to adopt the ways of the world, and harder to measure up to the autobiographical thread within each of us that leads back to Deity? Is it easier to yield to temptation, and harder to resist sin? Is rebellion an easier alternative, and obedience a harder choice? Is it easier to live in a confusing fog of conflicting values, and harder to be grounded and principled?

Is it easier to be immoral, and harder to be virtuous? Is it easier to be slothful and indolent, and harder to be upright? Is it easier to be swayed by secular humanism, and harder to be faithful and submissive to the whisperings of the Spirit that requires an acknowledgement of profound religious truth? Is it easier to be carnal and worldly, and harder to be holy? Is it easier to live in wanton defiance of God's laws, and harder to pattern our lives after obedience? Is it easier to yield to debauchery, and harder to celebrate morality? Is the pursuit of nobility akin to a quest to find the Holy Grail, or are those who attempt to follow the teachings of the Savior only tilting with windmills?

When Joan of Arc was carried to the stake, she was given the opportunity to obtain her freedom by denying her beliefs. Instead, she made this statement: "I know this now. Every man gives his life for what he believes. Every woman gives her life for what she believes. Sometimes people believe in little or nothing, and so they give their lives for little or nothing. One life is all we have, and we live it as we believe in living it, and then it is gone. But to surrender what you are and to live without belief is more terrible than dying, even more terrible than dying young." Resolutely, then, she faced death, still true to her faith and her beliefs. Her final acts on earth were consistent with her convictions.

In France during the Middle Ages, the successor to the throne was known as the Dauphin. During the reign of his father, unscrupulous and crafty counselors tried every means at their disposal to corrupt the Dauphin, to thereby render him ineligible to inherit the throne. In all of their attempts, however, they were unsuccessful. Finally, in resignation, they asked him: "How is it that with all our enticements we have not been able to corrupt your high standards?" His reply was simple: "I am a King's son."

Both Joan of Arc and the Dauphin had established patterns of behavior that were consistent with their beliefs, and that allowed them to act in perfect harmony with their convictions. Many of us assume that all you need is 21 days to make or break a habit, be it good or bad, and that after that, unconscious mechanisms kick into gear, and we find ourselves on autopilot. This number comes from a popular book published in 1960 called "Psycho-Cybernetics" by Maxwell Maltz, a plastic surgeon who noticed his patients seemed to take about three weeks to get used to their new faces. However, the time it takes to make or break a habit may not be that clear-cut. More recent studies show that the average time it takes for a new habit to coalesce is about 10 weeks, but individual times varied from 18 days to almost 9 months. The bottom line is that if you want to internalize a new behavior, you shouldn't despair if three weeks doesn't do the trick. For most people, that's simply not enough time. Stick with virtuous behavior for a bit longer, and you'll end up with a habit you can keep without even thinking about it.

Along the way, as good habits are forged, there will be hurdles to surmount. We know that there needs to be opposition in order for the positive lifestyle promoted by the Plan of Salvation to succeed, and so, any habit formation, even the internalization of gospel principles, must grapple with this tricky phenomenon. Think, for example, of the predicament facing Adam and Eve in the Garden, before the Fall.

Not knowing the mind of God, that opposition is necessary for the enjoyment of eternal happiness, Satan sought what he thought would be the misery of all mankind, and with his congenital short-sightedness and his typical stratagem of promoting half-truths, he offered the forbidden fruit to Eve. "Ye shall be as God," he unwittingly promised, "knowing good and evil." (2 Nephi 2:18).

By innocently addressing this unfamiliar concept of opposition Adam and Eve made the difficult choice, with a little help from Satan, to transgress God's law, having reached the conclusion that there was no other way for them to heed their Father's encouragement to embark upon the path of progress. They chose the harder right, rather than languishing in the amoral stagnation of the easier wrong. Then, their Father visited them and gave them further instruction, including sacred covenants, in order to provide the nurturing matrix within which their newfound habit patterns could take root.

The Savior Himself explained: "It must needs be that the devil should tempt the children of men, or they could not be agents unto themselves; for if they never should have bitter they could not know the sweet. Wherefore, it came to pass that the devil tempted Adam, and he partook of the forbidden fruit and transgressed the commandment, wherein he became subject to the will of the devil, because he yielded unto temptation." (D&C 29:39-40). But Adam was not deceived. His was an intelligent, conscious decision, the result of a clear understanding of the requirements of the gospel Plan. Adam fell that his family might come to know true happiness and develop the moral fiber to consistently choose the harder right. Without understanding all the ramifications of his decision to partake of the fruit of the Tree of Knowledge of Good and Evil, he nevertheless believed that the change to a mortal condition would be necessary because it had been foreordained of God, even though it might come like a flash of lightning and a clap of thunder. In the end, though, he knew the storm would pass and that flowers would bloom. (See "I Ching," The Chinese Book of Change).

The decision made by Adam and Eve in the Garden to choose the harder right rather than the easier wrong obviated the paradox that lay before them, wherein they would have remained forever in "a state of innocence, having no joy, for they knew no misery; doing no good, for they knew no sin." (2 Nephi 2:23). To put it plainly, the Fall paved the way for the introduction of the very priesthood ordinances that had been individually crafted by God to develop good habit patterns within the crucible of opposition in the lone and dreary world.

Spencer W. Kimball continued: We often try to expel from our lives choices that are typified by the harder right, and that might result in "physical pain and mental anguish," and instead "assure ourselves of continual ease and comfort, but if we were to close the doors upon such sorrow and distress, we might be excluding our greatest friends and benefactors." ("Faith Precedes The Miracle," p. 102-103). Suffering can make saints of sinners as they learn patience and self-mastery. These are the very emotions that Adam and Eve must have experienced, and that may actually have sustained them, as they forged a new life together in the telestial world outside the overly protective influences of the Garden, that might have ultimately proved to be suffocating to their spirits.

President Kimball continued, "If we looked at mortality as the whole of existence, then pain, sorrow, failure, and short life would be calamity. But if we look upon life as an eternal thing stretching far into the pre-mortal past and on into the eternal post-death future, then all that happens may be put in proper perspective." ("Faith Precedes The Miracle," p. 102-103). This longitudinal view must have been adopted by our first parents, for it explains why they eagerly anticipated the opportunity to become mortal. "Blessed be the name of God," Adam had declared, "for because of my transgression my eyes are opened, and in this life I shall have joy, and again in the flesh I shall see God. And Eve, his wife, heard all these things and was glad, saying: Were it not for our transgression we never should have had seed, and never should have known good and evil, and the joy of our redemption, and the eternal life which God giveth unto all the obedient." (Moses 5:10-11).

The Plan was carefully crafted to create the conditions for us to come unto Christ within the crucible of the exercise of our free will, as we are prompted and inspired to choose the harder right. Perhaps there is sense, after all, in the seeming chaos of existence, and there is a common thread underlying all experience, whether it be perceived as positive or negative. "For my thoughts are not your thoughts, neither are your ways my ways, saith the Lord. For as the heavens are higher than the earth, so are my ways higher than your ways, and my thoughts than your thoughts." (Isaiah 55:8-9).

We know that we cannot find "happiness in doing iniquity, which thing is contrary to the nature of that righteousness which is in our great and Eternal Head." (Helaman 13:38). We know by experience that if there be no righteousness, there be no happiness." (2 Nephi 2:13). Then, why do we sin, if "wickedness never was happiness?" (Alma 41:10). Why do we allow ourselves to form bad habits that reinforce negative behaviors and outcomes, and that can only lead to suffering, and spiritual death? Why does misery love company? Why can we not get it through our thick heads that it shall surely come to pass, that it is only "the spirits of those who are righteous (who) are received into a state of happiness, which is called paradise, a state of rest, (and) a state of peace?" (Alma 40:12).

Alma the Younger is a good example of one who had seen life from both sides of the fence, and who, after his conversion, would never again look back upon his former life. Nevertheless, his abrupt change of habits was accompanied by indescribable suffering. His rehab was accompanied by a detoxification from sin that we would not wish upon our worst enemies. His description to his son Helaman of his withdrawal symptoms is difficult even to read: "For three days and for three nights," he recounted, "was I racked, even with the pains of a damned soul." (Alma 36126).

But the silver lining in the cloud that overshadowed him was that he was able to measure his happiness against the discomfort of his former sinful life. "And oh, what joy," he wrote, "and what marvelous light I did behold; yea, my soul was filled with joy as exceeding as (had been) my pain!" (Alma 36:20). When he had been born again, his new life was illuminated by a personal witness that "the elements are eternal, and spirit and element, inseparably connected, receive a fulness of joy." (D&C 93:33). Having once made the harder decision to choose the right, it would now become easier for him to sustain a lifestyle that was oriented to happiness. He had learned the hard way, as we all must to some degree, that specific blessings follow obedience to their related laws. For "there is a law, irrevocably decreed in heaven before the foundations of this world, upon which all blessings are predicated. And when we obtain any blessing from God, it is by obedience to that law upon which it is predicated." (D&C 130:20-21). Alma could now bear a personal testimony of Benjamin's counsel that the Lord "doth require that (we) should do as he hath commanded (us); for which if (we) do, he doth immediately bless (us)." (Mosiah 2:24).

Earlier, Benjamin had asked the people of Zarahemla to consider "the blessed and happy state of those that keep the commandments of God." (Mosiah 2:41). Nephi would later observe how "the Lord in his great infinite goodness doth bless and prosper those who put their trust in him." (Helaman 12:1). Satan is always slithering about in the shadows, offering an easier wrong that brings misfortune because it is only a clever caricature and illegitimate illusion of happiness. It is the norm that it is only after much tribulation that the promises of the Lord are fulfilled. (See D&C 58:4). Only our incessant labors in the kingdom, epitomized by the harder right, are worthy of His mighty blessings. (See D&C 21:9).

For example, it may be more convenient to skip our prayers, but it is only when we pray always that the Lord promises to pour out upon us His Spirit, and to bestow upon us His great blessings. (See D&C 19:38). Whether it takes three weeks or nine months, we will be like "the builder who first bridged Niagara's gorge. Before he swung his cable shore to shore, he sent out across the gulf his venturing kite bearing a slender cord for unseen hands to grasp upon the further cliff and draw a greater cord, and then a greater yet, 'til at last across the chasm swung The Cable – then the mighty bridge in air. So may we send our little timid thoughts across the void, out to God's reaching hands, send our love and faith to thread the deep, thought after thought until the little cord has greatened to a chain no chance can break, and we are anchored to the infinite!" (Edwin Markham).

If we want to develop the habit of choosing the harder right, instead of the easier wrong, we must not only say our prayers, but we must also be long suffering. Alma said of those who were firm in the faith that they "were steadfast and immovable in keeping the commandments of God, and they bore with patience the persecution which was heaped upon them." (Alma 1:25).

If we want to develop the habit of choosing the harder right, instead of the easier wrong, we must "be humble, and be submissive and gentle," and be easily "entreated." (Alma 7:23). We must "call on his holy name, and watch and pray continually, that (we) may not be tempted above that which (we) can bear, and thus be led by the Holy Spirit, becoming humble, meek, submissive, patient," and "full of love." (Alma 13:28). If we are patient in all our sufferings (see Alma 20:29), and bear our afflictions with equanimity, the Lord will help us to succeed in our efforts. (See Alma 26:27).

If we want to develop the habit of choosing the harder right, instead of the easier wrong, we must guard ourselves against languishing in the comfort zones and aid stations that are scattered throughout Zion. (See 2 Nephi 28:24). As Benjamin warned the People of Zarahemla: "But this much I can tell you, that if ye do not watch yourselves, and your thoughts, and your words, and your deeds, and observe the commandments of God, and continue in the faith of what ye have heard concerning the coming of our Lord, even unto the end of your lives, ye must perish." (Mosiah 4:30).

If we want to develop the habit of choosing the harder right, instead of the easier wrong, we must endure to the end in righteousness. Only then will we be able to enjoy "eternal life, which gift is the greatest of all the gifts of God." (D&C 14:7). The Lord warned: "All those who will not endure chastening, but deny me, cannot be sanctified." (D&C 101:5). At the same time, Joseph Smith encouraged the Saints: "If thou endure it well, God shall exalt thee on high," and "thou shalt triumph over all thy foes." (D&C 121:8).

If we want to develop the habit of choosing the harder right, instead of the easier wrong, we will view our afflictions in a new light, and experience an epiphany that they really do work together for our good. (See D&C 98:3). During the process of the maturation of our good habit, the Lord will soften our hearts, inasmuch as he will use adversity to bring us down into the depths of humility. (See Alma 62:41).

It just may be that what doesn't make us stronger, kills us, in the sense that it destroys our drive and determination to improve our condition. It was the Dominican priest Henri Didón who, in the opening ceremony of a school sporting event in 1881, first expressed the words that would later become the Olympic Motto: Citius, Altius, Fortius! (Faster, Higher, Stronger!) In this sense, it is the Lord Who is our physical, mental, emotional, and spiritual fitness coach Who "shall consecrate (our) afflictions for (our) gain." (2 Nephi 2:2). In other words, from His perspective, in the workout program He has designed for each of us, if there is no pain, there can be no improvement.

It may take three weeks or three months, but after that, why should our hearts weep and our souls linger in the valley of sorrow, and our flesh waste away, and our strength slacken, because of our afflictions? (See 2 Nephi 4:26). During that initial period, when we are burning fat and building muscle, we need to be as Alma had been, to "be patient in (the) long-suffering and affliction" that often accompanies the creation of spiritual strength. (Alma 17:11).

We remember the dialogue between Edmund Dantès and the priest Abbé Faria that occurred deep within the walls of the prison of the Chateau d'If, in the Alexandre Dumas novel "The Count of Monte Cristo." "What are you thinking?" asked the Abbé smilingly, imputing the deep abstraction in which his visitor was plunged to the excess of his awe and wonder. "I was reflecting, in the first place," replied Dantès, "upon the enormous degree of intelligence and ability you must have employed to reach the high perfection to which you have attained. What would you not have accomplished if you had been free?" "Possibly nothing at all," replied the priest. "The overflow of my brain would probably, in a state of freedom, have evaporated in a thousand follies; misfortune is needed to bring to light the treasures of the human intellect. Compression is needed to explode gunpowder. Captivity has brought my mental faculties to a focus; and you are well aware that from the collision of clouds electricity is produced - from electricity, lightning, and from lightning, illumination."

Finally, at the end of the tale, Dantès observes: "Only a man who has felt ultimate despair is capable of feeling ultimate bliss. It is necessary to have wished for death, in order to know how good it is to live. Live, then, and be happy, and never forget that, until the day God deigns to reveal the future to man, the sum of human wisdom will be contained in these words: wait and hope."

In His infinite wisdom, He has designed all things to give us experience, that it might be for our good. (See D&C 122:7). But He allows the anticipated change to hinge upon our own desire and resourcefulness. Until we are committed and our agency kicks into high gear, "there is hesitancy, the chance to draw back, always ineffectiveness. Concerning all acts of initiative, there is one elementary truth, the ignorance of which kills countless ideas and splendid plans: That the moment we commit ourselves, then Providence moves too. All sorts of things occur to help us that would never have otherwise occurred. A whole stream of events issues from the decision, raining in our favor all manner of unforeseen incidents and material assistance, which no-one could have dreamed would have come our way." (Thomas Hornbein, "Everest: The West Ridge," p. 100).

The process by which good habits are developed is that of testing the mettle of our convictions. We have no proof until we act on the basis of trust. Then comes the confirmation of the reality, as feelings of self-confidence grow and purposeful actions replace tentative overtures. This is why the creation of good habits is so intimately tied to righteousness. The way of the Lord is strait. Our tests during mortality are eminently fair. The rules are simple and the rewards are unmistakably plain. Heavenly Father will not cause us to misplace our trust in a program of spiritual fitness that cannot deliver on its promises.

Still, if we want to develop the habit of choosing the harder right, instead of the easier wrong, we will frequently be confronted by forks in the road, and we would do well to take the road less traveled. As Robert Frost wrote: "I shall be telling this with a sigh somewhere ages and ages hence: Two roads diverged in a wood, and I, I took the one less traveled by, and that has made all the difference." ("The Road Not Taken").

If we want to develop the habit of choosing the harder right, instead of the easier wrong, we must maintain unbridled optimism. Adversity will never end, even if we have a bright and cheerful outlook on life, but the journey will be much more pleasant if we have learned to channel hardship into constructive expressions that lead to positive outcomes.

If we want to develop the habit of choosing the harder right, instead of the easier wrong, we must take a few steps into the darkness before faith, the spiritual strong searchlight, illuminates the way before us. Then, as Helen Keller declared: "Although sinister doubts" may continue to "lurk in the shadow, (we will) walk unafraid towards the Enchanted Wood where the foliage is always green, where joy abides, where nightingales nest and sing, and where life and death are one in the presence of the Lord." ("Midstream").

If we want to develop the habit of choosing the harder right, instead of the easier wrong, we must not allow ourselves to be O.C.D. about it. In other words, we must not be Overly Concerned with Discipleship. At times, we need to just go with the flow of the Spirit, in the sense that we must "not run faster or labor more than (we) have strength." (D&C 10:4). Sometimes, we need to be content to enjoy the glittering facets of the life of the Spirit, wherein we are receptive to flashes of insight as we are cast off into a stream of revelation and carried along in the quickening currents of direct experience with God.

So why, then, does it seem to be more difficult to choose the harder right than the easier wrong? Of all God's creations, Satan is most miserable, and our adoption of his tactics and counterproposal of democratization of the principles of the Plan without priesthood guidance and direction at the Council would make us equally unhappy by denying agency, requiring obedience, relying on compulsion, and preventing progression. Although the plan he proposed in heaven was counterfeit, a fraud, inoperable, and ultimately rejected by the Council, basic elements have been transferred to the mortal battlefield, where a last ditch effort for their acceptance is currently underway in the sweaty arena of agency. And that may explain a lot. A third part of the host of heaven, basking in celestial light, was drawn to Satan's ideology. Here on earth, with an impenetrable veil drawn across our minds, even with the Light of Christ, and even with the gift of the Holy Ghost, and even though the curtains of the Lord's holy habitation have been extended, many of us are still swayed by Satan's siren song.

Elements of the Adversary's flawed ideology can be seen in social, political, cultural, and economic programs, and even in elements of religious ideology that pander to our innate insecurity, lack of initiative, and desire for undeserved entitlements. Those who voluntarily or involuntarily give up their agency in exchange for whatever transient pleasures poor choices may provide, have been snared by Satan and bound by his strong chains. They are enslaved by bad habits. When they feel the heavy cords of oppression around their necks, they realize too late that their poor choices have limited their options, restricted their actions, and fettered the expression of their righteous desires. Habitual sin creates a monotonous and mind-numbing conformity that is the antithesis of the artistic individuality proffered by the Plan. If we allow bad habits to limit our choices, often all that is left in the end is a cold compromise that can leave a hollow core of emptiness in our gut.

Sometimes all too quickly, and sometimes agonizingly slowly, those who have sold their birthright for a mess of pottage are dragged down to a hell on earth that is of their own making. It is very hard to break the bad habits that are the result of repetitive poor choices precisely because agency must be surrendered in order to acquire them, and ironically, "we can never get enough of what we don't need, because what we don't need won't satisfy us." (Dallin Oaks, C.R., 10/1991). We exchange our noble birthright for that mess of pottage.

Heavenly Father does not operate this way. He always honors the eternal principle of agency. As He counseled Adam in the beginning, "thou mayest choose for thyself, for it is given unto thee." (Moses 3:17). This is a riskier course of action, but it is the only way that eternal progression is possible. Choices and opposites are necessary as we stretch our spiritual muscles by reaching out to grasp the brass rings of immortality and eternal life. In the process, rather than enslaving us in good habits, God repeatedly gives us the opportunity to voluntarily recommit ourselves to covenants of obedience to true and eternal principles. Thus, church membership and readily participating in principled activities are vital to our spiritual well being, as is the renewal of the covenants we have made through the ordinances. God has unbridled confidence in our ability to choose the harder right, instead of the easier wrong, and as we do so, a miraculous transformation in our attitude takes place. The Prime Directive to which He adheres demands that we be free to choose, but the deck is fortuitously stacked in our favor because of the Light of Christ and the Gift of the Holy Ghost. And so we are blessed with the physical and spiritual capacity to forge success strategies as we internalize the qualities of high achievers.

The Light of Christ exerts a nurturing influence. Although we must daily travel further from the East, we are nevertheless oriented toward its radiant glow emanating from that distant horizon. It provides us with the regularly recurring reassurance of a religious recalibration that autocorrects our orientation on the eternities with celestial precision. It envelops us in an intuitive appreciation of where we came from, why we are here, and where we are going. As in a heavenly language that is rhythmical, melodious, soothing to our ears, and calming to our souls, when we hear the Spirit quietly whisper: "You're a stranger here," we are struck by the realization that we have "wandered from a more exalted sphere." (Eliza R. Snow, "O My Father"). The Light of Christ personalizes what it means to be anxiously engaged, inspires us to plumb the depths of our commitment to the Savior, sensitizes us to the nobility of His work, and makes us more acutely aware of His glory, by bringing the visions of immortality and eternal life within our purview.

When we resolve to choose the harder right, instead of the easier wrong, we commit ourselves to the arduous process of a spiritual rebirth. When we feel the urge to push His agenda instead of our own, the Light of Christ can be our labor coach, providing us with just the right amount of encouragement to successfully deliver our witness of the Savior without being overbearing.

One exciting element of our resolve to choose the harder right, instead of the easier wrong, is the constant stream of inspiration and revelation that subsequently cascades down from above. This insures that we may walk along illuminated pathways, and allows us to use our faculties of mind, intellect, and spirit to our best advantage, that we might discern between truth and error, and thereby more easily choose the right. It permits us to listen with sensitivity and to be receptive to the cries of the downtrodden and oppressed, to see with a clarity that allows us to be proactively responsive to our environment, and to be benevolently blind to the shortcomings of others who have not yet discovered that the gospel is the perfect law of liberty.

When we resolve to choose the harder right, instead of the easier wrong, as fire in the sky, the air in the theater of life will be charged with an electricity that represents the inevitable merger of the universal encouragement of the Light of Christ, with the pointed and providential guidance provided by the Holy Ghost. When these influences streak in tandem across the heavens, their trajectories will coalesce to trace a flaming trail whose incandescence sparkles over a vast cosmic ocean of thought. Over the ebb and flow of its tide, the Spirit will create an effectual bridge of understanding that is buttressed by the cohesive influence of the mighty foundation of faith. Then, the difficulty of making hard choices will melt away as the morning dew evaporates in the noonday sun.

Those who have chosen what they mistakenly believe to be the easier wrong, those who have voluntarily given up their agency to choose what they have perceived to be the harder right, will find themselves in the grip of bad habits, and will be snared by Satan and bound by his strong chains. The heavy cords he places around their necks will drag them down to hell. Once entrenched, their bad habits will become very hard to consciously and purposefully break, precisely because agency itself has been surrendered in order to acquire them. Those who suffer from the resulting compulsions have reached this condition because of repeated actions, until a point is reached where unlimited freedom leads to unlimited tyranny.

Our habits, for better or for worse, are our constant companions. Completely at our command, they are our greatest helpers or our heaviest burdens. They push us onward and upward, or drag us down to mediocrity. Habits may be easily managed, but we must be firm with them as they coalesce into behavior patterns.

Habit is the servant of all, working with the precision of a machine, to be run for profit or ruin, for she is coldly logical. Those who are firm with her will find that the world will come knocking at their door. But if she is treated carelessly or inattentively, she can easily become death, the destroyer of worlds. (See "Bhagavad Gita").

Perhaps this is what President Monson had in mind, when he cautioned the Saints to choose the harder right, instead of the easier wrong. (See C.R., 4/2016).

Our goal should be to establish spiritual
symmetry and balance in our lives
as we engage the requirements
of the Lord's fitness program.

Choose
Ye This Day

During the 40-year sojourn of Israel in the wilderness of Sinai, Moses had served as its guide, given it God's law, and acted as His spokesman. He was the only leader an entire generation of Israelites had ever known. But the Lord took him home at the end of their journey, just when they were about to face their greatest tests. The Lord had a contingency plan, however, to call Joshua to succeed Moses and to encourage him to fill the shoes of the great lawgiver by being strong, having courage, studying the scriptures, and being obedient. (See Joshua 1:6). Joshua rose to the occasion as he and allowed God to shape his nature. Similarly, as we allow God to mold our character, we can develop divine attributes and accomplish whatever He wants us to do.

Joshua faced daunting challenges when the Lord called him to lead the Israelites. He was not only taking the place of a great trailblazer, but he was also being asked to lead Israel in the conquest and colonization of Canaan. He may have felt as President Spencer W. Kimball did when he said: "This is my feeling for the work at this moment. There are great challenges ahead of us, and giant opportunities to be met. I welcome that exciting prospect and feel to say to the Lord: Give me this mountain! Give me these challenges!" (C.R., 10/1979).

Our own opportunities for growth require strength, moral courage, and the ability to prioritize our time so that we can cut to the quick and focus on matters of substance. Each of us has 168 hours each week, much of it discretionary time to do with as we please. As few as three of these hours are spent in church. We need to ask ourselves: How many hours are wasted "hanging out?" How many hours are squandered watching television, playing video games, or on our computers or our mobile devices? How many hours do we devote to social media?

Perhaps we should budget our time as carefully as we budget our money. Concentrating on the things that really matter endows us with a special capacity to manage the gift of time. We learn to take time with discipline, make time with diligence, find time with care, spend time with thoughtfulness, invest time with wisdom, and share time with pleasure. Turning our attention to the weightier matters of the law gives us a sense of independence, as we learn something new every day. Learning how to control our time can open our hearts and our minds to a breathtaking expansion of understanding. As we practice a learning style that embraces the Spirit, we discover a pattern that becomes our norm.

Heber J. Grant declared: "That which we persist in doing becomes easier for us. Not that the nature of the thing has changed, but our power to do is increased." Spencer W. Kimball understood the capacity of effective time management: "What I am asking for," he said, "is not a flashy, temporary change in performance, but a quiet resolve to lengthen our stride." ("Ensign," 12/1985).

As Josiah Gilbert Holland wrote: "God, give us men! A time like this demands strong minds, great hearts, true faith, and ready hands. Men whom the lust of office does not kill. Men whom the spoils of office cannot buy. Men who possess opinions and a will. Men who have honor; men who will not lie. Men who can stand before a demagogue and damn his treacherous flatteries without winking. Tall men, sun-crowned, who live above the fog in public duty and in private thinking. For while the rabble, with their thumbworn creeds, their large professions and their little deeds, mingle in selfish strife, Lo! Freedom weeps, Wrong rules the land, and Justice sleeps."

"It is not the critic who counts," declared Teddy Roosevelt, "and not he who points out where the strong man stumbled or where the doer of deeds could have done them better. The credit belongs to the man who is actually in the arena, whose face is marred by dust and sweat and blood, who tries and comes up short again and again, who knows the great enthusiasms, the great devotions and spends himself in a worthy cause; who, at best, if he fails, at least fails while daring greatly, so that his place shall never be with those cold and timid souls who know neither victory nor defeat." ("Citizenship In A Republic," 4/23/1910).

John F. Kennedy wrote, in a speech prepared for delivery on the afternoon of November 22, 1963: "We in this country, in this generation, are - by destiny rather than by choice - the watchmen on the walls of world freedom. We ask, therefore, that we may be worthy of our power and responsibility; that we may exercise our strength with wisdom and restraint, and that we may achieve in our time and for all time the ancient vision of peace on earth, and good will toward men. That must always be our goal, and the righteousness of our cause must always underlie our strength. For as was written long ago: 'Except the Lord keep the city, the watchman waketh in vain.'" (Psalms 127:1).

The Sons of Helaman "were all young men, and they were exceedingly valiant for courage, and also for strength and activity. But, behold, this was not all - they were men who were true at all times in whatsoever thing they were entrusted.

Yea, they were men of truth and soberness, for they had been taught to keep the commandments of God and to walk uprightly before him." (Alma 53:20-21).

In order to be successful, the Lord commanded Joshua to study "the book of the law." (Joshua 1:8). Today, familiarity with the scriptures is important for us to succeed in our callings; indeed, in our lives. We cannot "wing it" in matters of substance, leave our fate to chance, or play it by ear in a world that has amazingly little to say. We must have proven protocols in place, study them, and apply them to our circumstances, in order to reach successful conclusions.

When Israel prepared to cross over Jordan, the flow of the river was halted, but not before the priests who carried the ark stepped into the current. (See Joshua 3:13-17). The Lord sometimes asks of us similar tests of faith. Boyd K. Packer said: "Shortly after I was called as a General Authority, I went to Harold B. Lee for counsel. He listened very carefully to my problem and suggested that I see David O. McKay. President McKay counseled me as to the direction I should go. I was very willing to be obedient, but saw no way possible for me to do as he counseled me to do. I returned to Elder Lee and told him that I saw no way to move in the direction I had been counseled to go. He said: The trouble with you is you want to see the end from the beginning. I replied that I would like to see at least a step or two ahead. Then came the lesson of a lifetime. You must learn to walk to the edge of the light, he said, and then a few steps into the darkness; then the light will appear and show the way before you." ("B.Y.U. Today," 3/1991, p. 22-23).

After crossing over Jordan, Israel set up a memorial of 12 stones as a testimony to future generations of the Lord's power, and to remind them that He would continue to bless them as He had their fathers. Today, we celebrate God's power through the ordinance of the Sacrament, by the example of the temple, by the testimony of the Twelve Apostles, and with the benchmarks of our own spiritual experiences. We remember the circumstances associated with our baptism, and our ordination to the priesthood is memorialized every time we exercise its power. The temple worthiness interview is commemorated with a personal recommend signed by our priesthood leaders and by ourselves. All of these experiences are as stones that provide a foundation for opportunities to commemorate God's influence in our lives.

In his final counsel to Israel, Joshua exhorted her to "cleave unto the Lord," or to join together with Him, rather than to "cleave unto the remnant of (the Canaanite) nations." (Joshua 23:8 & 12) Today, we sometimes "cleave unto" the world simply by tolerating its sins. "Vice," can be "a monster of such frightful mien, as to be hated needs but be seen. Yet seen too oft', familiar with its face, we first pity, then endure, and then embrace." (Alexander Pope).

We adopt the lifestyle of the world when we party and play in Idumea, rather than ponder and pray in Zion. We adopt coarse and profane speech. "Dude, we really do. I mean, it's, like, normal." We adopt its manner of dress. Too frequently, the messages on our T-shirts, or festooned with ink on our skin, reflect what we are thinking. But, "this much I can tell you," Mosiah cautioned his people. "If you do not watch yourselves, and your thoughts, and your words, and your deeds...you must perish." (Mosiah 4:30).

We sometimes adopt the values of the world, confusing them with the principles of the gospel. A neighbor of Marion D. Hanks came home with a new boat, and proudly showed it to Elder Hanks, asking for suggestions for a name. Elder Hanks said: "Why don't you call it 'Sabbath Breaker?" This might have been a little harsh, but it illustrates the fact that we all need to be vigilant as we unconsciously establish our priorities.

Near the end of his life, Joshua gave important counsel to Israel. "Choose ye this day whom ye will serve," he declared. "But for me and my house, we will serve the Lord." (Joshua 24:15). We can't serve the true and living God and our worldly gods of wood and stone at the same time. The example of Joshua reminds us of the importance of commitment. "Not tomorrow, not when we get ready, not when it is convenient," taught Marvin J. Ashton, "but 'this day,' straightway, choose whom you will serve. He who invites us to follow will always be out in front of us with His Spirit and influence setting the pace. He has charted and marked the course, opened the gates, and shown the way. He has invited us to come unto Him, and the best time to enjoy His companionship is straightway." (C.R., 4/1983). We can best get on course and stay on it by making a total commitment, as Joshua did, to do the will of our Father.

Joshua's final instructions included the same charge to be strong and to have courage that the Lord had given when He had called him to be a prophet. (See Joshua 23:1-6). Ezra Taft Benson echoed this injunction when he said that two principles are essential for security and peace: "First, trust in God; and second, determine to keep the commandments, to serve the Lord, and to do that which is right. The Lord has made it very clear in the revelations that even though times become perilous, even though we be surrounded by temptation and sin, even though there be a feeling of insecurity, even though men's hearts may fail them and anxiety fill their souls, if we only trust in God and keep his commandments, we need have no fear." (C.R., 10/1950).

"How can religions survive when it is strapped to a wooden restatement of traditions whose meaning as well as application fades unless there is further light from on high?"
(B.H. Roberts).

Christ's Church
Is Restored

Jesus established His church so that His gospel could be taught, the priesthood could be organized, ordinances could be performed, and we could make covenants with our Heavenly Father. He did this so that the Plan of Salvation could be taught, which would allow us to reach our potential as sons and daughters of God.

During the years after His mortal ministry, there was gradual but accelerating apostasy from the truth, culminating in a doctrinal free-fall that shattered any resemblance to the church that had been established by Jesus. The resulting withdrawal of the Spirit has been characterized as the Dark Ages, a time when the formulation of new ideas became almost impossible. "Whenever people choose to disregard, disobey, or distort any gospel principle or ordinance, whenever they reject the Lord's prophets, or whenever they fail to endure in faith, they distance themselves from God and begin to live in spiritual darkness. Eventually, this leads to a condition called apostasy. When widespread apostasy occurs, God withdraws His priesthood authority to teach and administer the ordinances of the gospel." ("Preach My Gospel" manual, p. 33). Without the settling influence of the Spirit, even secular inquiry and discovery is stymied.

Long before, Amos had prophesied that there would be an apostasy. "Behold, the days come, saith the Lord God, that I will send famine in the land, not a famine of bread or a thirst of water, but of hearing the words of the Lord. And they shall wander from sea to sea, and from north even to the east, they shall run to and fro to seek the word of the Lord, and shall not find it." (Amos 8:11-12).

The Lord knew that, after His mortal ministry and that of His chosen Apostles, there would be a long night of darkness, followed by a renewal of faith. Speaking of the Last Days, His prophet Isaiah had written of such a restoration: "Behold I will proceed to do a marvelous work among this people, even a marvelous work and a wonder." (Isaiah 29:14). Joseph Smith became involved in that process simply because he had sought wisdom from God to know what he personally needed to do to find favor with Him. "If any of you lack wisdom," the scriptures had instructed him, "let him ask of God, that giveth to all men liberally, and upbraideth not; and it shall be given him. But let him ask in faith, nothing wavering." (James 1:5-6). Many of us have done the same thing, as we have sought to know God's will.

Joseph's petition was answered in a spectacular fashion. He related: "I saw a pillar of light exactly over my head, above the brightness of the sun, which descended gradually until it fell upon me." (J.S.H. 1:16). Then, he said: "I saw two Personages, whose brightness and glory defy all description, standing above me in the air. One of them spake unto me, calling me by name, and said, pointing to the other – This is My Beloved Son, Hear Him!" (J.S.H. 1:17).

Joseph was told things about the churches that were then on the earth that must have really startled him, for his inquiry had been only to find out which among them was right. "I was answered that I must join none of them," he related, for they were all wrong, and the Personage who addressed me said that all their creeds were an abomination in his sight; that those professors were all corrupt; that they draw near to me with their lips, but their hearts are far from me, they teach for doctrines the commandments of men, having a form of godliness, but they deny the power thereof." (J.S.H. 1:19).

Today, in my community (in Spokane, Washington) there are a lot of churches. Among them are the following fifty: Jehovah's Witness, The Church of The Resurrection, The Cornerstone Pentecostal Church, Jesus is The Answer, The Living Truth Tabernacle, Amazing Grace Fellowship, The Assembly of God, The Crosswind Church, The Glad Tidings Church, The Trinity Lighthouse, The Baptist Church, The Living Water Community Church, The Shiloh Hills Fellowship, Christ Our Hope Bible Church, The Church of The Nazarene, The Catholic Church, The Christian Life Church, The Calvary Chapel, The Presbyterian Church, The Methodist Church, The Holy Temple Church of God in Christ, The Slavic Christian Church, The Refreshing Soaring Church of God in Christ, The Unity Church of Truth, The Life River Fellowship, The Cornerstone Pentecostal Church, The Northview Bible Church, The Lutheran Church, The New Beginnings Church, The Pentecostal Evangelical Church, The River of Life Open Bible Church, The Spokane Dream Center Women's Discipleship, The Unity Church of Truth, The New Hope Christian Reformed Church, The First Church of Christ Scientist, The Church of Christ, The Jesus Lord Church of the Living God International, The Church of Jesus Christ of Latter-day Saints, The Heritage Congregational Church, The First Covenant Church, The All Nations Christian Center, The Christ our Hope Bible Church, The Christ the Savior Orthodox Church, The First Church of The Open Bible, The Shalom Church, The Fellowship of The Messiah, A Fresh Start Ministries, and The Unitarian Universalist Church.

The simple existence of so many churches clearly illustrates that direction from God is needed in order to identify His one true church. This restoration of authority occurred in May and June 1829, when Joseph Smith and Oliver Cowdery were first given the Aaronic Priesthood, and then the Melchizedek Priesthood. John the Baptist, a legal administrator sent from the presence of God, bestowed the Aaronic Priesthood. Peter, James, and John, also legal administrators, bestowed the Melchizedek Priesthood. Later more keys of the priesthood were restored by other messengers who were likewise on God's errand. (See D&C 110:11-16).

This restoration of priesthood authority granted men the power to organize the church. This occurred on April 6, 1830. (D&C 20:1). On that day, Joseph Smith was called by God to be a prophet and the first elder of His church, and Oliver Cowdery was called as the second elder of the church. (D&C 20:2-4). Only the basic framework of the church was set up at that time. It took several years for the church to be organized, in a process that has continued to this day.

The organization of offices within the church followed, in a pattern that had been established in former times (see the 6th Article of Faith), with apostles, prophets, pastors, teachers, and evangelists. The First Principles and Ordinances were restored, which are faith in the Lord Jesus Christ, repentance, baptism by immersion for the remission of sins, and the laying on of hands for the gift of the Holy Ghost. (See the 4th Article of Faith). Upon that humble foundation has been built the great latter-day work that we have today.

"To
every man
there comes in his
life a time when he is
figuratively tapped on the
shoulder and offered a chance
to do a very special thing, unique
to him and fitted to his talents. What
a tragedy if that moment finds him
unprepared or unqualified for
that which would have been
his finest hour."
(Winston Churchill).

Citizenship In The Church And Kingdom

December 7, 2013, the Women's World Cup Downhill ski race was held at Lake Louise, Alberta, Canada, with the temperature dipping to 14 degrees F. below zero, and with a wind chill factor dropping that to 31 degrees F. below zero. The course was two miles long, and the racers completed the run in just under two minutes, which means they averaged over 60 miles per hour. My questions were: "How in the world could they prepare for such a demanding event, held in such pitiless conditions? How could they even "warm up" beforehand, so their muscles could withstand the brutal punishment and their exposed skin the chilling cold?" The only answer I could come up with was that, having been subjected to similar trials before, they must have relied upon a strict and comprehensive protocol that had, aforetime, been rigorously tested, and was now meticulously followed.

We all have conscious and unconscious protocols in place that we need to follow in order to meet challenges and achieve desired results. I have a protocol that works for me each morning when I wake up. I take a hot shower to limber up my muscles and work out the kinks before I begin my day. I know that if I don't slowly work up to my envisioned physical activity level, if I try to take shortcuts, I will pay in spades later on and it will take quite a while for me to even get back to my original starting point.

We also have spiritual protocols or proven formulas to follow, in order to achieve envisioned results. If we want to perform at a level that compliments the full stature of our spirits, but don't follow the protocols required to do so, our best efforts could be stymied, causing us to entirely miss our mark.

In 1952, while serving in the Quorum of the Twelve Apostles, Ezra Taft Benson was asked by Dwight D. Eisenhower, then President of the United States, to serve as the nation's Secretary of Agriculture. With the encouragement of church President David O. McKay, Elder Benson accepted the assignment and served well. In his first General Conference address after becoming Secretary of Agriculture, he said: "I have been happy in the privilege to serve, in a small way at least, this great country and the government under which we live. I am grateful to the First Presidency and my brethren that they have been willing, not only to give consent, but also to give me their blessing as I responded to the call of the Chief Executive." (C.R., 4/1953).

As of 2014, there were 7 senators serving in the Congress of the United States of America, 5 Republicans and 2 Democrats. Harry Reid, the Senate Majority Leader from Nevada, was the highest-ranking elected L.D.S. official in U.S. History. There were 10 Congressmen serving in the House of Representatives, 8 Republicans and 2 Democrats, from American Samoa, Arizona, California, Idaho, and Utah. It was almost 180 years ago (1835) that the church unanimously approved a declaration of beliefs about government. This declaration is recorded in D&C Section 134. It was a protocol, or a formula, given by God, about how to be good citizens. This protocol was articulated just 48 years after the ratification of the U.S. Constitution, in September 1787.

48 years is not a long time. Some of us remember 1965. It was the year that a postage stamp cost a nickel, and "The Sound of Music," with Julie Andrews singing in high alpine meadows, hit the theaters. The Big Bang Theory was experimentally confirmed by Penzias and Wilson. Winston Churchill died, and the Beatles were at the height of their popularity. The BatMobile was created, and the Gateway Arch in St. Louis was completed. Sandy Koufax pitched a perfect game for the Los Angeles Dodgers. Likewise, in context, the Declaration of Beliefs about Government came shortly on the heels of the U.S. Constitution. The Founding Fathers were still fresh in the minds of many citizens in 1835.

That Declaration of Beliefs had a lot to say about the purposes, or role, of civil government in the lives of private citizens. It declared that government was instituted "for the good and safety of society." (D&C 134:1). It promoted the postulate that government was created "for the protection of the innocent and the punishment of the guilty." (D&C 134:6). It endorsed the belief that government existed "for the protection of all citizens in the free exercise of their religious belief" and "for redress of all wrongs and grievances." (D&C 134:7 & 11).

To support and sustain the Declaration of Beliefs, we each need our own personally prepared protocol to help fulfill the purposes of government. L. Tom Perry said that we need to be "actively engaged in supporting and defending the principles of truth, right, and freedom" (C.R., 10/1987). To do so, we should turn to the scriptures for guidance, as we seek to uphold leaders who "administer the law in equity and justice." (D&C 134:3). "Honest men and wise men should be sought for diligently, and good men and wise men ye should observe to uphold; otherwise whatsoever is less than these cometh of evil." (D&C 98:10).

When we do not observe this protocol, "the wicked rule, (and) the people mourn."

(D&C 98:9). Having said that, the church itself "is politically neutral. It does not endorse political parties, platforms, or candidates. Candidates should not imply that they are endorsed by the church or its leaders. Church leaders and members should avoid any statements or conduct that might be interpreted as church endorsement of political parties or candidates." ("Church Handbook of Instructions").

This is interesting, in light of our understanding of the political atmosphere in heaven surrounding the events that transpired at the Council and shortly thereafter. It seems that even though the political spectrum is not black and white, politics can be. Our challenge is to work within the Lord's protocol to achieve a spiritual resolution to the issue of how we can meaningfully participate in the process of government in a republic.

To that end, we must ask ourselves: "What is our responsibility regarding the laws of the land?" The scriptures teach: "Let no man break the laws of the land, for he that keepeth the laws of God hath no need to break the laws of the land. Wherefore, be subject to the powers that be, until he reigns whose right it is to reign, and subdues all enemies under his feet." (D&C 58:21-22). In addition: "That law of the land which is constitutional, supporting that principle of freedom in maintaining rights and privileges, belongs to all mankind, and is justifiable before me. Therefore, I, the Lord, justify you, and your brethren of my church, in befriending that law which is the constitutional law of the land." (D&C 98:5-6). "We believe in being subject to kings, presidents, rulers, and magistrates, in obeying, honoring, and sustaining the law." (12th Article of Faith).

About 20 years after the Declaration of Beliefs about Government was written, Abraham Lincoln declared: "To sin by silence, when words should be spoken, makes cowards of men." So, even as we practice our religion, we must nurture within ourselves an active, participating relationship with our civil government. The Declaration of Beliefs clearly states: "We believe that religion is instituted of God; and that men are amenable to him, and to him only, for the exercise of it, unless their religious opinions prompt them to infringe upon the rights and liberties of others; but we do not believe that human law has a right to interfere in prescribing rules of worship to bind the consciences of men, nor dictate forms for public or private devotion; that the civil magistrate should restrain crime, but never control conscience; should punish guilt, but never suppress the freedom of the soul." (D&C 134:4). It goes on to say: "We do not believe it just to mingle religious influence with civil government, whereby one religious society is fostered and another proscribed in its spiritual privileges, and the individual rights of its members, as citizens, denied." (D&C 134:9).

Joshua drew a line in the sand, when he declared: "Choose you this day whom ye will serve; whether the gods which your fathers served that were on the other side of the flood, or the gods of the Amorites, in whose land ye dwell: but as for me and my house, we will serve the Lord." (Joshua 24:15). Today, members of the church "should do their civic duty by supporting measures that strengthen society morally, economically, and culturally." Latter-day Saints "are urged to be actively engaged in worthy causes to improve their communities and make them wholesome places in which to live and rear families" ("Handbook of Instructions"). "The Family: A Proclamation to The World" (1995), that has been adopted and internalized by members of the church, attests to their commitment to these worthy causes.

We can begin to strengthen our communities by ministering to the needs of others, by serving in elected or appointed public service positions, and by supporting worthy activities. We should always "be anxiously engaged in a good cause, and do many things of (our) own free will, and bring to pass much righteousness. For the power is in (us), wherein (we) are agents unto (ourselves). And inasmuch as (we) do good (we) shall in nowise lose (our) reward." (D&C 58:27-28).

To be anxiously engaged, we need to influence more than we are influenced by others, lead and not follow, and light candles rather than curse the darkness. When it rains, we need to open up our umbrellas, rather than stand around complaining about the foul weather. We need to stem the tide rather than allow ourselves to be passively swept up in it, solve problems rather than ignore them, and pay it forward more than we watch our own backs. We need to have protocols in place that will allow us to fulfill the measure of our creation. We need to recognize that the ultimate power to change rests within ourselves, but then to have the faith to let go and let God.

Victor Frankel declared: "Everything can be taken from us but one thing: the last of the human freedoms - to choose our attitude in any given set of circumstances, to choose our own way. The one thing you can't take away from me is the way I choose to respond to what you do to me. The last of one's freedoms is to choose one's attitude in any given circumstance. Between stimulus and response, there is a space. In that space is our power to choose our response. In our response, lies our growth and our freedom. Forces beyond your control can take away everything you possess except one thing, your freedom to choose how you will respond to the situation."

He continued: "We who lived in concentration camps can remember the men who walked through the huts comforting others, giving away their last piece of bread. They may have been few in number, but they offer sufficient proof that everything can be taken from a man but one thing: the last of the human freedoms — to choose one's attitude in any given set of circumstances, to choose one's own way." ("Man's Search for Meaning").

In June 1965, President David O. McKay spoke to a group from the Physical Facilities Department of the church." He said: "Let me assure you, brethren, that some day you will have a personal Priesthood interview with the Savior, Himself. If you are interested, I will tell you the order in which He will ask you to account for your earthly responsibilities. First, He will request an accountability report about your relationship with your wife… Second, He will…request information about your relationship to each and every child. Third, he will want to know what you have personally done with the talents you were given in the pre (earth) existence. "Fourth, He will want a summary of your activity in your church assignments… Fifth,… if you were honest in all your dealings. Sixth, He will ask for an accountability on what you have done to contribute in a positive manner to your community, state, country and the world." (Reported by Cloyd Hofheins in an address to the Seventies Quorum of the Provo Utah Oak Hills Stake, 5/16/1982). Let us make sure that each of us has protocols in place, so that we can prepare for that joyful occasion when we can sit down one-on-one with the Savior and confidently recount the story of our life.

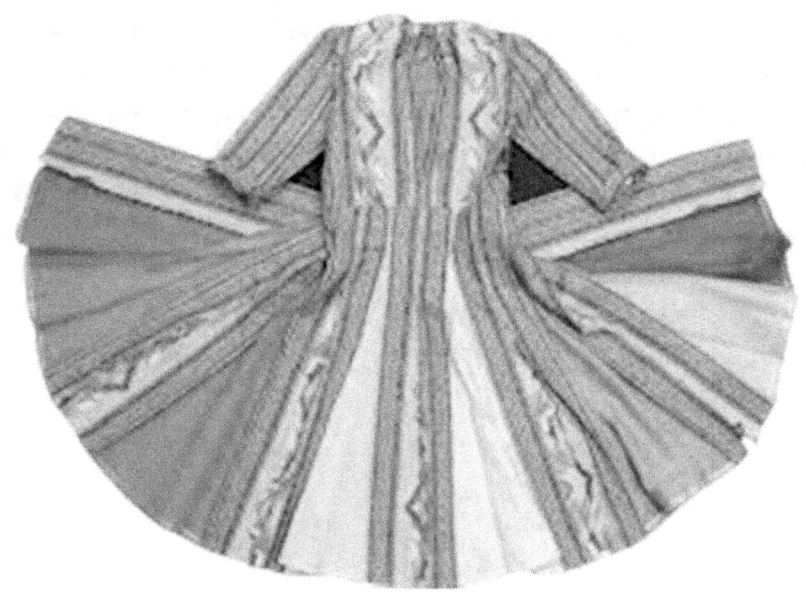

"Israel loved
Joseph more than all
His children, because he
was the son of his old age:
and he made him a coat
of many colours."
(Genesis 37:3).

A Coat
Of Many Colors

It is interesting to think of Joseph's coat of many colors as an allegory for the fabric of our own lives, sewn by our Heavenly Father Himself, with each thread individually tailored to suit our circumstances, and representing, not the drab monotone of the world, but a true Technicolor Dream Coat signifying the glories and riches of eternity. To do so helps us to put the day-to-day elements of the Plan of Salvation in perspective, and to more clearly discern the grey-toned obstacles to our progression so that they may stand out in sharp contrast to the polychromatic backdrop of the design that God has envisioned for each of us.

Joseph's coat was a wonderful expression of his father's love for him, and to wear it must have given him a great deal of pleasure, but it did get him into serious trouble. Had this impressionable youngest son of Jacob kept his counsel to himself after he had received visions of his brethren paying him obeisance, he might have mitigated their growing envy and avoided their subsequent conspiracy against him. "For although a man may have many revelations, and have power to do many mighty works, yet if he boasts in his own strength, and sets at naught the counsels of God, and follows after the dictates of his own will and carnal desires, he must fall and incur the vengeance of a just God upon him." (D&C 3:4).

We all know what happened next: "And the Midianites sold him into Egypt unto Potiphar, an officer of Pharaoh's, and captain of the guard." (Genesis 37:36). Joseph's physical garment was gone, and he would find himself falsely accused and in bondage in Egypt, left in rags in a dark and hopeless dungeon. It would be up to him to seek guidance in reconstructing the coat, if only in his mind's eye, that he might learn to appreciate the significance of each thread that had been so thoughtfully and carefully provided by his Father in Heaven.

I think of Joseph when I read the dialogue between Edmund Dantès and the priest Abbé Faria that occurred deep within the walls of the prison of the Chateau d'If, in the Alexandre Dumas novel "The Count of Monte Cristo." "What are you thinking?" asked the Abbé smilingly, imputing the deep abstraction in which his visitor was plunged to the excess of his awe and wonder. "I was reflecting, in the first place," replied Dantès, "upon the enormous degree of intelligence and ability you must have employed to reach the high perfection to which you have attained. What would you not have accomplished if you had been free?" "Possibly nothing at all," replied the priest. "The overflow of my brain would probably, in a state of freedom, have evaporated in a thousand follies; misfortune is needed to bring to light the treasures of the human intellect. Compression is needed to explode gunpowder. Captivity has brought my mental faculties to a focus; and you are well aware that from the collision of clouds electricity is produced - from electricity, lightning, and from lightning, illumination."

Finally, at the end of the tale, Dantès observes: "Only a man who has felt ultimate despair is capable of feeling ultimate bliss. It is necessary to have wished for death, in order to know how good it is to live. Live, then, and be happy, and never forget that, until the day God deigns to reveal the future to man, the sum of human wisdom will be contained in these words: wait and hope."

As the poet sagaciously observed: "My life is but a weaving between my God and me. I cannot choose the colors. He weaveth steadily. Oft' times He weaveth sorrow, and I in foolish pride, forget He sees the upper, and I, the underside. Not 'til the loom is silent and the shuttles cease to fly, will God unroll the canvas and reveal the reason why. The dark threads are as needful in the weaver's skillful hand, as the threads of gold and silver in the pattern He has planned." (Benjamin Malachi Franklin).

Joseph's coat of many colors teaches us that every cloud has a silver lining. As Helen Keller wrote: "I believe that no good shall be lost, and that all man has willed or hoped or dreamed of good shall exist forever. I believe in the immortality of the soul because I have within me immortal longings. I believe that the state we enter after death is wrought of our own motives, thoughts, and deeds. I believe that my home there will be beautiful with color, music, and speech of flowers and faces I love. Without this faith, there would be little meaning in my life. I should be a mere pillar of darkness in the dark. Observers in the full enjoyment of their bodily senses pity me, but it is because they do not see the golden chamber in my life where I dwell delighted; for dark as my path may seem to them, I carry a magic light in my heart. Faith, the spiritual strong searchlight, illuminates the way, and although sinister doubts lurk in the shadow, I walk unafraid towards the Enchanted Wood where the foliage is always green, where joy abides, where nightingales nest and sing, and where life and death are one in the presence of the Lord." ("Midstream").

Joseph received his coat as a gift from his father, just as we receive ours from our Heavenly Father. We can be sure that the bolts of cloth have been carefully selected and cut to address every exigency in our lives. As Mark E. Petersen observed: "Shall we not be willing to sacrifice our ordinary desires when necessary, and cut our cloth to fit the pattern of revised circumstances" that unfolds before us, with the intention of maximizing our life experiences? ("Ensign," 4/1981). Those evolving circumstances provide for us coats of many colors with enough room stitched into the pattern to allow us to grow into the full stature of our spirits. They are not tailored to be contemporary or fashionable or form fitting. They have not been designed to emphasize our physical form, or to impress the world. Rather, they are of enduring quality, and their fitting has been carefully customized to be comfortably motivating, subtly inspiring, quietly elegant, gently refining, spiritually uplifting, and unobtrusively sophisticated, with an easy grace that belies the power that is intrinsic to the cloth. The purpose of our Father's careful selection of material, meticulous tailoring, and almost obsessive attention to detail, protects us from both the winds of adversity and the wiles of the adversary.

Just as Joseph's siblings were jealous of Jacob's gift, and were likely envious of their younger brother's rapidly evolving spiritual maturity, so too are our contemporaries sometimes resentful of the accomplishments that are facilitated by our own coats of many colors. No matter what other outfits may be in our closets, however, and especially if their design is after the likeness of the world, we must have the courage to push them aside and instead choose modestly uplifting and complementary ensembles. If we then wear our coats with dignity, they will make statements equivalent to that of the cape worn by Superman. Their fabric will have come, not from Krypton, but from Kolob, and the powers thereby derived will be otherworldly and supernatural. If we see in their vibrant colors the Lord and his strength, (and) seek his face continually," (1 Chronicles 16:11), our coats will transform us. They will allow us to be faster than speeding bullets, more powerful than locomotives, and empower us to leap tall buildings in a single bound. Our coats will endow us with the power of God, to give strength to the poor and to the needy in his distress, and to be "a refuge from the storm, (and) a shadow from the heat," even when the blast from the unrighteous and unworthy is as a storm against the fortress of our spiritual security. (Isaiah 25:4).

If we desire the attention and adoration of the world, and are tempted to leave our coats of many colors hanging unused and unattended in the back of our closets, hidden behind our more contemporary outfits, we would do well to attune our ear to our Father, Who quietly reassures us: "Be still, and know that I am God"(D&C 101:16). From the Book of Exodus, Aaron's example teaches that each of us may enjoy the protection afforded by the special clothing that complements, as an ensemble, our coat of many colors. "And thou shalt bring Aaron and his sons unto the door of the tabernacle of the congregation, and wash them with water. And thou shalt put upon Aaron the holy garments, and anoint him, and sanctify him." (Exodus 42:12-13). From time immemorial, the coats of many colors that have been provided by God for His children to wear have shielded them against the power of the destroyer, and have been designed to protect them from his evil influence until they have finished their work on the earth.

As we care for and maintain our coats by repenting and by humbling ourselves sincerely, through faith, God will minister unto us through His holy angels, whose own garments will be pure and white above all other whiteness, whose countenances will be as lightning, and whose personages will be glorious beyond description. (See D&C 20:6 & J.S.H. 1:32).

Like spiritual swaddling clothes, our coats will resonate with intrinsic light that does not trace its origin to pigment and dye. Their power will be evident to even the most hardened skeptics, such as Belshazzar, who summoned Daniel to his court, and said: "I have even heard of thee, that the spirit of the gods is in thee, and that light and understanding and excellent wisdom is found in thee." (Daniel 5:14). The king did not realize it, but the vitality that he sensed in Daniel came from the prophet's own coat of many colors.

The light of the Spirit will give each thread in our own coats a vibrancy and vivacity that is unique to holy vestments. Their colors are fast, and can only fade if we neglect to properly care for and maintain them. Inasmuch as we do not defile them, however, but are true and faithful to the care instructions that are clearly printed on their labels, they will be shields of protection to us. But if we inadvertently or carelessly wash our coats with other garments that have been soiled with the stain of sin, their powers of enchantment will be neutralized.

Each of our individual coats has many colors that make it unique. Psychophysicists tell us that the human eye can distinguish around 10 million different colors, which is really quite remarkable, since there are only three primary colors in the visible light spectrum (red, green, and blue). Isaac Newton, who was the first to use a prism to separate white light (at wavelengths between 390 – 700 nm) into its individual colors, divided the spectrum into seven named colors (red, orange, yellow, green, blue, indigo, and violet). So the arrangement of colors in our individual coats has plenty of latitude to be unique, to fit our individual circumstances.

In general, though, the color red calls us to action, and reminds us that the Savior trod the winepress alone. Orange is a warning to take care that we conform our lives to the Lord's design. Yellow encourages us to seek the light that is gathering in the east. Green brings to mind the power of envy, and our requirement to observe and keep the 10th commandment, and to be content with the cards in the hand that God has dealt us. Blue reminds us to mourn with those that mourn, and to comfort those that stand in need of comfort. Indigo is a color whose depth and brightness represent the profundity of the gospel, and its ability to illuminate truth wherever it may be found. Violet is the color of amethyst, lavender and beautyberries, and reminds us of the garlands festooning the latticework of the celestial city of God. (See Revelation 21:20).

Grey (black and white) is associated with neutrality, conformity, uncertainty, and indifference. It prompts us to choose whom we will serve, and encourages us to stand on the Lord's side. Purple (red and blue) urges us to remember the royal robes of Christ our King. Black (blue, red, and yellow) underscores the necessity of opposition that paves the way to our progression. White (red, orange, yellow, green, blue, indigo and violet) solemnly suggests the comprehensive nature of the ordinances of the priesthood, our temple covenants, and the purity of the Spirit, all of which are necessary if we are to regain the glory of our former home.

From ultraviolet to infrared, our coats of many colors will incorporate into their pattern and design every color of visible light, but they will also resonate with radiation from a spectrum that can only be seen with eyes that have been touched by the hand of God. If we were able to break down that energy with a spiritual prism, we would look beyond the limited horizon of our sight, and see the visions of eternity. "By the power of the Spirit our eyes (would be) opened and our understandings (would be) enlightened, so as to see and understand the things of God." (D&C 76:12).

"Commitment is the courage to begin
without any guarantee of success."
(Goethe).

Commitment

In the church, our hands-on training teaches us that if we plan our work, and then work our plan, we will enjoy success in our endeavors. We know that proper prior planning prevents poor priesthood performance. We dream big, and by establishing deadlines, we facilitate our progress toward the realization of realistic goals. We know by our own experience that work without vision is drudgery, and vision without work is dreamery, but that work with vision is destiny. It is because of our commitment to the cause that we know these things.

We also know that there is a God in heaven, because we have witnessed the universality of commitment. We believe it is a characteristic with which God has blessed both men and beasts. High energy levels of commitment are found within those who are members of The Church of Jesus Christ of Latter-day Saints, but they do not have a lock on this noble character trait. Commitment is not even found solely within the human family; it is also common among those with whom we share rungs on the evolutionary ladder. I have gotten between an agitated cow moose and her calf. I have seen momma bears aggressively protecting their cubs. I have witnessed bald eagles relentlessly riding updrafts looking for food for their chicks back in the nest. Commitment runs deeply; it is not only in our blood, but it also drives the behavior of countless other species. This cannot be happenstance. It must be that, during the creation, the apple did not far fall from the tree.

Commitment is not something that we consciously cultivate. We do not say: Today, I think I'll work on commitment. Instead, it seems to come naturally, but it is actively nurtured by the settled conviction in our minds that we are the acorns of mighty oaks; the offspring of deity. John K. Edmunds, who also served as the President of the Salt Lake Temple, enjoyed a long and distinguished legal career in Chicago. One day, a widow came to him for advice, and when they were finished, she apprehensively asked: "How much do I owe you?" Gently, he responded, "Why don't you pay me what you think it's worth. Greatly relieved, she got out her coin purse, fished around for a quarter, and pressed it into his hand. He looked at the quarter, looked at her, and then got out his own coin purse, and gave her ten cents change. Howard W. Hunter must have been referring to this Christ-like level of commitment, when he counseled: "We need to walk more resolutely and more charitably the path that Jesus has shown. We need to pause to help and lift another, and surely we will find strength beyond our own. If we would do more to learn the healer's art, there would be untold chances to use it, to touch the wounded and the weary, and to show to all a gentle heart."

Commitment begins with a strong sense of intention or focus, but that is only half of the equation. The second half defines a statement of purpose or a plan of action. The difficulty is that we make promises about behaviors and outcomes with the sense of intention or focus, but we then ignore the process necessary to achieve the goal. Envisioned outcomes are simply the byproducts of that dynamic flow of process. If we learn to commit fully to the process, then the outcomes will be what they should be. But, if we commit merely to the outcomes and ignore the process, we have sabotaged both. Wobble and instability will be created by the unequal demands of intention on the one hand, and our lack of purpose or a plan of action on the other. Indecisiveness will condemn any hope of success.

The principle of commitment is ingrained within us from earliest childhood, by processes that come into play even before we are capable of understanding. Think of the promises that were articulated when we received our first blessing as babies, for example. By the authority of the priesthood, blessings were pronounced that contained promises linked to anticipated high levels of future commitment. Later, we had baptismal interviews before we turned eight years of age, preparatory to making a series of commitments related to our membership in the church and kingdom. We reinforce the commitments we have thus made when we participate in the ordinance of the Sacrament, and we make additional covenants when we receive the Melchizedek Priesthood, and later in the temple, that are directly related to a divinely inspired statement of purpose and a plan of action, all of which are buttressed by the powerful spiritual intervention of our Father in Heaven, Who stands ever ready to minister to our needs. Every time we receive a calling in the church, it is accompanied by a priesthood blessing that sets us apart with a statement of purpose and plan of action that vitalizes the utilization of resources related to the successful execution of our responsibility.

Day in and day out, our success is largely determined by our capacity to make and keep commitments. Each time we take the road less traveled, we keep a date with destiny, as we reach greater heights of achievement. As Robert Frost wrote: "I shall be telling this with a sigh somewhere ages and ages hence: Two roads diverged in a wood, and I, I took the one less traveled by, and that has made all the difference." ("The Road Less Traveled").

It is easy to take for granted the blessing that activity in the church teaches us about commitment. As we study the scriptures, we learn to be more patient in our insistent desire for the instant gratification that can neutralize dedicated discipleship.

But it is only after we "have done the will of God, (that we) receive the promise." (Hebrews 10:36). As we learn to recognize the Lord's timetable, our commitment level is protected and shielded from the erosive influence of impatience. We quietly go about out business, "and do the things which the Lord hath commanded, for (we) know that the Lord giveth no commandments unto the children of men, save he shall prepare a way for them that they may accomplish the thing which he commandeth them." (1 Nephi 3:7). We learn to "trust in the Lord with all (our) heart; and lean not unto (our) own understanding." (Proverbs 3:5). "Then shall (our commitment) wax strong in the presence of God." (D&C 121:45).

When we learn how to focus our commitment, and to engage "the Lord (as our) helper, (we) will not fear what man shall do unto (us)." (Hebrews 13:6). We learn about the follow-through element of commitment; that "it is God which worketh in (us) both to will and to do of his good pleasure." (Philippians 2:13). We have proven Him in times past, and can testify: "If any man will do his will, he shall know of the doctrine." (John 7:17). We establish a habit pattern of obedience, and follow the admonition of Paul, to "perform the doing of it; that as there was a readiness to will, so there may be a performance also out of that which (we) have." (2 Corinthians 8:11).

We persevere in a plan of action born of our moral discipline, in part because we know that "reason and experience both forbid us to expect that morality can prevail in exclusion of religious principle." (George Washington). We are concerned because of society's problem keeping its commitments. In a cover story entitled "The Me, Me, Me Generation," in "Time" magazine, (5/20/2013), Joel Stein wrote: "Millennials are lazy, entitled, narcissists, who still live with their parents."

He continued: "Here's the cold, hard data: The incidence of narcissistic personality disorder is nearly three times as high for people in their 20s as for the generation that's now 65 or older, according to the National Institutes of Health. 58% more college students scored higher on a narcissism scale in 2009 than in 1982. Millennials got so many participation trophies growing up, that a recent study showed that 40% believe they should be promoted every two years, regardless of performance. They are also fame-obsessed: Three times as many middle school girls want to grow up to be a personal assistant to a famous person as want to be a Senator, according to a 2007 survey. They're so convinced of their own greatness that the National Study of Youth and Religion found the guiding morality of 60% of Millennials in any situation is that they'll just be able to feel what's right. Their development is stunted: More people ages 18 to 29 live with their parents than with a spouse, according to a recent study. And they are lazy. In 1992, the nonprofit Families and Work Institute reported that 80% of people under 23 wanted to one day have a job with greater responsibility. 10 years later, only 60% did."

Many young adults who fall within the parameters of the Me Generation are active, faithful Latter-day Saints. But it is only because they have been schooled in obedience to the principles of the gospel, that they have not joined their peers as flotsam and jetsam on the sea of life, "tossed to and fro, and carried about with every wind of doctrine, by the sleight of men, and cunning craftiness." (Ephesians 4:14). Instead, the gospel has taught them how to stem the tide; they no longer just go with the flow. Their standard of behavior towers above the lowest common denominator that is the cultural norm. They are "fellowcitizens with the Saints, and with the household of God. (Ephesians 2:19).)

Latter-day Saints are assisted in their ability to internalize commitment to true principles when they receive their temple endowment, and when they return to the temple to review and renew their covenants as they perform vicarious work for the dead. The garment they consciously wear reinforces their commitment with the promise that it will be a shield and a protection to them, as long as they do not defile it.

They receive divine assistance when they are called to positions of responsibility within the church. When they are uniquely set apart to do a particular work in the church, the position becomes theirs. Under priesthood direction, it is clearly stated that the position doesn't belong to anyone else, and no-one else has a right to it. They know that if they do not do the job, it will not be done. Therefore, they accept callings with the intention to carry out the associated responsibilities as though their lives depended on it. Their commitment level becomes unassailable.

Those who have committed their lives and fortunes to the Lord are amazed by what can happen when they set their mind to a task. They have learned that the secret of their success is their acceptance of positions of responsibility without reservation and the performance of their labors with a strong heart. They have found that when the spirit of the gospel flows in their bloodstream, they are quickened by a spiritual power that defies description; and it is then that things really begin to happen. A burning zeal to serve God lifts them to greatness. It gives them authority over their weaknesses, and over the defeats that are a part of life.

Latter-day Saints have learned how to recognize the process that it is necessary to follow in order to achieve envisioned outcomes. They know that "a successful life requires commitment - whole-souled, deeply held, eternally cherished commitment to the principles they know to be true." (Howard W. Hunter).

Disciples have learned to make the distinction between total commitment and a vapid contribution to the cause. They remember the story of the chicken and a pig who were invited to a breakfast, and how the chicken said that he would bring some eggs. He asked the pig if he would provide bacon, to which the pig replied: Yours is a contribution, but mine is a sacrifice. Latter-day Saints know that, ultimately, "what our Father in Heaven will require of us is more than a contribution; it is a total commitment, a complete devotion; all that we are and all that we can be." (Howard W. Hunter, C.R., 10/1959). Hence, the Law of Sacrifice, which is a celestial law.

When Joan of Arc was carried to the stake, she was given the opportunity to save her life and to obtain her freedom by simply denying her beliefs. Instead, she made this statement: "I know this now. Every man gives his life for what he believes. Every woman gives her life for what she believes. Sometimes people believe in little or nothing, and so they give their lives for little or nothing. One life is all we have, and we live it as we believe in living it, and then it is gone. But to surrender what you are and live without belief is more terrible than dying, even more terrible than dying young." Resolutely, then, she faced death, still true to her faith and her beliefs. Her final acts on earth were consistent with her convictions and her commitment.

In France at around the same time that Joan of Arc became a martyr to the cause, the successor to the throne was known as the Dauphin. During the reign of his father, unscrupulous and crafty counselors tried every means at their disposal to corrupt the Dauphin, to thereby render him ineligible to inherit the throne. In all of their attempts, however, they were unsuccessful. Finally, in resignation, they asked him, "How is it that with all our enticements we were not able to corrupt your high standards?" His reply was simple: "I am a King's son." The implications of that statement are eternal in scope.

Both Joan of Arc and the Dauphin had established patterns of behavior that were consistent with their beliefs, and that allowed them to act in perfect harmony with their convictions. Many of us assume that all you need is 21 days to make or break a habit, be it good or bad, and that after that, unconscious mechanisms kick into gear, and we find ourselves cruising along on autopilot. This number comes from a popular book published in 1960 called "Psycho-Cybernetics" by Maxwell Maltz, a plastic surgeon who noticed his patients seemed to take about three weeks to get used to their new faces. However, the time it takes to make or break a habit may not be that clear-cut. More recent studies show that the average time it takes for a new habit to coalesce is about 10 weeks, but individual times varied from 18 to 254 days. The bottom line is that if you want to internalize a new behavior, you shouldn't despair if three weeks doesn't do the trick. For most people, that's simply not enough time. Stick with it for a bit longer, commit to one standard of behavior, and you'll end up with a habit you can keep without even thinking about it. You will have successfully internalized your commitment, with the need for only periodic preventive maintenance.

Choose you this day whom ye will serve," declared Joshua, "but as for me and my house, we will serve the Lord." (Joshua 24:15). President Hunter once remarked during a General Conference address: "There is good reason to make our decision now to serve the Lord. On this Sunday morning, when the complications and temptations of life are somewhat removed, and when we have the time and more of an inclination to take an eternal perspective, we can more clearly evaluate what will bring us the greatest happiness in life. We should decide now, in the light of the morning, how we will act when the darkness of night and when the storms of temptation arrive."

In that valley of decision, belief alone will not be sufficient; we will also need to do Heavenly Father's will with a ready heart. Belief is nothing more than the mental assent to a proposition, but without the critical element of moral responsibility that we call faith. As such, belief alone may very well lack the power to generate positive outcomes. Commitment may very likely be absent, because it simply does not spontaneously follow belief. But, if belief is nurtured by faith, commitment can transform knowledge into the fragrant blossom of testimony. Finally, obedience to the Celestial Law of Consecration just might be the noblest expression of commitment. As Joseph Smith said: "A religion that does not require the sacrifice of all things never has power sufficient to produce the faith necessary (to lead) unto life and salvation." ("Lectures on Faith," p. 58.)

Disciples are committed to live according to active religious principles that immerse them in the gospel every day of the week. As a Church Welfare Program pamphlet stated long ago: "The church cannot hope to save a man on Sunday if during the week it is a complacent witness to the crucifixion of his soul." ("Helping Others to Help Themselves: The Story of the Mormon Church Welfare Program," p. 4). The gospel nurtures commitment with an energetic program that gives vitality to every waking moment.

The Lord revealed something very special about His children, in His preface to the Doctrine and Covenants. He stated that The Church of Jesus Christ of Latter-day Saints is the "only true and living church upon the face of the whole earth." (D&C 1:30). This begs the question: Are we "living members" of the church? If the Lord put His finger to our pulse, would He be able to detect the quickening influence of the Spirit? If He measured our core testimony temperature, would it reflect a burning zeal to embrace the principles of the gospel? Would our actions betray our commitment to do everything we could do to come unto Christ? Would we love God and our neighbors as ourselves? Would our actions reflect who we are and what we believe? If we were on trial, would there be enough evidence to convict us of being Christians?

Are we pressing forward with complete dedication and steadfastness, with confidence and a firm determination in Christ, having a perfect brightness of hope and perfect faith; with charity, or a love of God and of all men. If we do this, if our commitment level is such that we are feasting upon the word of Christ, receiving strength and nourishment from the scriptures, and if we endure to the end in righteousness, we shall have eternal life, which is the greatest gift that God can bestow. (See 2 Nephi 31:20).

Do we listen to the Spirit and constantly seek its direction? Do we pray for the strength to meet our challenges? Do we set our hearts upon the riches of eternity, rather than the things of the world? Do we recognize that spiritual renewal will always trump physical gratification? Have we made a choice regarding whom we will serve? Do we actually strengthen our brethren? Are we anxious to share our joy? Do we put into action our beliefs? Are we anxiously engaged in bringing to pass many good things of our own free will? Do we love one another? Do we keep ourselves unspotted from the world? Do we stand firm, and are we true and living members of the church? Does our level of commitment belie the reality that we have received the promise to be among those "who are come unto Mount Zion, and unto the city of the living God, the heavenly place, the holiest of all?" (D&C 76:66).

"Invisible threads
are the strongest ties."
(Friedrich Nietzsche).

Connections

No one would argue that we are bound to each other by more than genetics. With few exceptions, for example, in the case of monastic ascetics and agoraphobics, we are social creatures. Many years ago, it became apparent to social scientists that our connections can be viewed as a hierarchy. In 1943, Abraham Maslow described a pyramid of need, in a paper entitled "A Theory of Human Motivation." In an ascending order of significance, Maslow described the pattern of our connections as if they were on a path leading to self-transcendence beginning with physiological configurations, and then safety, belongingness, love, esteem, and finally self-actualization. The order of this hierarchy remains a popular framework in sociological research and management training.

I believe that it is even more useful if our connections are viewed in the context of the gospel of Jesus Christ. I believe there are levels of interconnectivity that transcend the behavioral sciences to reveal the core of our existence and to bind us to Him Who "hath also sealed us, and given the earnest of the Spirit in our hearts." (2 Corinthinans 1:22). These are concepts that are foreign to behaviorists who attempt to explain interpersonal conduct by utilizing only tangible terms while skirting metaphysical abstractions that are no less real.

The first category I would suggest is what I call Type 0 or human genome connections. Within this class are the associations that exist only because our species shares the same D.N.A. sequences. Consequently, Type 0 connections relegate us to be as ships passing in the night. We may appear to be similar in construction and in purpose, but at the end of the day there is more of a disconnect between us than anything else that would tie us to each other. Type 0 human genome connections do not require eye to eye contact, and rarely establish bonds because others are really nothing more than nameless faces in the crowd. There is little or no evidence of the emotion that is really the glue that binds us together.

The second category is what I call Type 1 connections. These are real, and allow us to relate to each other through common interests like sports, schools, jobs, cars, and hobbies. But, at the same time, they are casual connections. For example, how many times has each of us said to ourselves: "I know that face; I just can't put a name to it." Type 1 connections are neural in origin, and owe their existence to the molecular basis of memory, but they too often develop along the pathways of short-term, and not long-term, memory. They may be powerful initially, but their intensity often fades with time, as does the afterglow of fireworks exploding in the night sky.

The third category is what I call Type 2 connections, those that are forged through the commanding chemistry of shared experiences, especially those that elicit intense emotion. These visceral connections can last for years, because they trace their foundations to the crisis of uncommonly positive or negative experience that can catalyze our nervous systems with electrifying consequences. We have close associates, life-long friends, and even blood-brothers with whom we have established Type 2 connections that seem unassailable.

But Type 2 connections, like Type 1 connections, can and often do fade with time. Think of the unity that gripped America in the aftermath of 9/11. We can all still visualize members of the U.S. Congress standing on the steps of the Capitol, with arms linked together, singing God Bless America. But how quickly are our Type 2 connections smothered in the marsh gas emitted by our scramble for scarce resources and telestial trash!

Somewhere beyond Type 2 connections, there may come an A-ha! moment when we "see the light." We may have an instant of sudden realization, inspiration, insight, recognition, or comprehension. We might even feel that we have been "born again!" Nicodemus asked: "How can a man be born when he is old? Can he enter the second time into his mother's womb, and be born? Jesus answered, verily, verily, I say unto thee, except a man be born of water and of the Spirit, he cannot enter into the kingdom of God. That which is born of the flesh is flesh; and that which is born of the Spirit is spirit." (John 3:4-6). The Savior used this occasion to teach Nicodemus about Type 3 connections that can only be truly appreciated in the context of deeply moving spiritual experiences.

The Sons of Mosiah had such a moment, when they felt compelled to "impart much consolation to the church, confirming their faith, and exhorting them with long-suffering and much travail to keep the commandments of God." (Mosiah 27:33). Thereafter, their developing connection with the Lamanites motivated them to embark upon a mission in the Land of Lehi that lasted fourteen long years. (See Mosiah 28:9). Ironically, the Lamanites among whom they ministered did not initially understand the power of Type 3 connectivity. But in each of these instances cited, their Type 2 connections evolved into Type 3 connections with the missionaries, with each other, and with the Lord.

There follows in The Book of Mormon a description of what we might do, in order to have and sustain Type 3 connections. Mormon reported that at the conclusion of their mission, the Sons of Mosiah were still the brethren of Alma "in the Lord; yea, and they had waxed strong in the knowledge of the truth; for they were men of a sound understanding and they had searched the scriptures diligently, that they might know the word of God. But this is not all; they had given themselves to much prayer, and fasting; therefore, they had the spirit of prophecy, and the spirit of revelation, and when they taught, they taught with power and authority of God." (Alma 17:2-3). Their mission had given them the perspective whereby they could experience Type 3 connectivity.

Type 3 connectivity can last forever; examples include the bond that can exist between a mother and child, or between "soul-mates" whose match was made in heaven. Both birth and death experiences can generate the intensity to sustain Type 3 connections. Veil experiences in the temple can compellingly and convincingly communicate connections between the living and the dead. In our everyday interpersonal relationships, with Type 3 connections, the expressions "Brother" and "Sister" flow from our lips, even though no actual familial bonds exist.

Type 3 connections are enduring because with them we touch the face of God. Think of the genius of the advertising executives who coined the phrase: "Reach out and touch someone." Perhaps without realizing it, they tapped into our universal need to establish connections with eternity. Paul clearly recognized our desire to establish connectivity with each other and with our Heavenly Father because he wrote to the Ephesians that, by obedience to gospel principles, they would be "no more strangers, but fellowcitizens with the Saints, and with the household of God." (Ephesians 2:19).

From the beginning of time, the traditional family has provided a milieu in which Type 3 connections are generated. Alarmingly, today many families do not recognize the need or possess the tools to consciously cultivate these connections. Rather, they subsist on a meager diet of Type 1 or Type 2 connections, mistakenly thinking that they are experiencing the pinnacle of achievement in human interrelationships while actually settling for mediocrity. Or, perhaps they just do not care, either way. Sometimes, they simply have no interest in expanding their horizons, and they are content to just go with the flow. For whatever reason, they are either unwilling or unable to generate the intrinsic power necessary to create what Latter-day Saints would call "forever families."

With this in mind, we can better appreciate the purpose behind the dissemination since 1995 of The Church of Jesus Christ of Latter-day Saints' statement of belief entitled: "The Family: A Proclamation to The World." We also better understand the meaning of Joseph Smith's teaching that, at every age in the world, the main object of gathering the people of God "was to build unto the Lord a house whereby He could reveal unto His people the ordinances of His house and the glories of His kingdom, and teach the people the way of salvation," which has primarily been to develop Type 3 leading to Type 4 connections. (See below). (H.C., 5:423). We are enjoined: "Thou shalt lay aside the things of this world, and seek for the things of a better." (D&C 25:10).

In essence, both Joseph Smith and the Lord taught that we could not completely nurture our spiritual connections "until the temple (was) completed, where places (could) be provided for the administration of the ordinances of the priesthood." (H.C., 4:603.) When we neglect our religious opportunities, we jeopardize our eternal souls. Sometimes, individuals are baptized after Type 2 connections have propelled them along on their journey toward Type 3 experiences. At other times, those investigating the merits of the church and of Christ may have already had fleeting Type 3 connection experiences, have strongly felt the Spirit, and have then determined to be baptized in order to capture those wonderful feelings with the confident anticipation of enjoying them on a regular basis. These are the pathways along which testimony is nurtured and strengthened.

But, in order to maintain their momentum and make it enduring, new members as well as established members of the church need to have sustaining spiritual experiences that foster Type 3 connectivity. As Gordon B. Hinckley said: "Every convert needs a friend, a responsibility, and nurturing with the good word of God." ("Liahona," 2/1999). If they do not find the resources that are necessary to sustain Type 3 connections, they risk sliding back into Type 2 interconnectivity. They cannot endure for long if they rely only upon the light emitted by Type 1 and 2 connections. They need an external power source in order to become members of the second mile club of Type 3 Interconnectivity, a select group to which they will be invited to join soon after their baptisms. (See Matthew 5:41).

Paul knew what it meant to go the second mile. He ministered among the Corinthian Saints, whom he was pleased to discover had a working relationship with the laws of the gospel, whose expression he characterized as being written upon "tables of stone." He explained the connectivity the Saints had with each other in terms of their second mile commitment: "Ye are manifestly declared to be the epistle of Christ ministered by us, written not with ink, but with the Spirit of the living God; not in tables of stone, but in fleshy tables of the heart." (2 Corinthians 3:3).

Sooner or later, every member of the church is a second miler, who is encouraged to become perfect in Type 3 commitment, and to so live to be worthy of Type 4 commitment. During His mortal ministry, the Savior said "he that shall endure unto the end, the same shall be saved." (Matthew 24:13). Going a step further, He explained to Joseph Smith: "If you keep my commandments (the first mile / Type 3 commitment) and endure to the end (the second mile / Type 4 commitment) you shall have eternal life, which gift is the greatest of all the gifts of God. (D&C 14:7).

Our Type 3 connections are solidified with service, particularly directed at those who cannot provide of their own means to generate equivalent connections. Service in the temple comes to mind. In the ordinances performed by patrons in behalf of the dead, the expression "for and in behalf of" is uttered in baptisms, confirmations, ordination to the priesthood, washing, anointing, in clothing ordinances, in the endowment, and in the sealing together of spouses and children. Temple ordinances give substance to the expression that "no man is an island." The Designer of the Plan created opportunities for us to perform vicarious work, that we might comfortably surround ourselves with Type 3 connections to both the living and the dead, as we establish bonds between all those who have been strengthened by covenants made with God. These can seal us to our forbearers all the way back to Father Adam and Mother Eve, as well as forward to our posterity, forging an unbreakable chain leading all the way to the Celestial Kingdom. We can use Type 3 connections to redeem the dead as well as to pay it forward.

But that is not all we can do. Our Type 3 connections have the power to establish a platform upon which we can build an even more ambitious milieu of connectivity. After the Flood, the ancients built ziggurats that were towers specifically designed to reach all the way to heaven. The Tower of Babel is a good example of these exaggerated church steeples. (See Genesis 11:4). But their architects and builders missed the point. Instead of creating physical structures, they would have more profitably spent their time if they had built relationships or connections with each other. Starting with Type 1 connections, they could have rapidly advanced through Type 2, and on to Type 3. Then, they would have figuratively reached the stars with what I will call the Type 4 level of connection that is described in the scriptures as having one's "Calling and Election" made sure. This is not a relationship that is well understood by either theologians or scriptorians. It requires a profound spiritual comprehension that can only be built upon the foundation of Type 1, 2, and 3 connections.

By design, this essay has purposely saved the best for last. When we achieve Type 4 connectivity, we shift our focus, and our mystical relationship with God becomes a permanent part of our spiritual identity. That is how members of The Church of Jesus Christ of Latter-day Saints have the presumption to declare that it is our destiny to one day rule as kings and queens, and priests and priestesses, in the house of Israel forever, to reign with authority over kingdoms, thrones, principalities, powers, dominions, and exaltations.

But we can't get there if we begin at Type 0, but expect to skip the intermediate steps. That's where the experiences of mortality in the learning laboratory of life come into play. No man is an island unto himself, and when we hear the bell, we need not wonder for whom it tolls, for it tolls for us.

When designing the Plan, God knew that, with only nine months of preparation, we would transition from the eternal world where we had enjoyed the warmth of hearth and home in heaven, to the bleak atmosphere of the lone and dreary world here on earth, and that when we did so, there would be an immediate disconnect that would be brutal and unrelenting in its intensity. The Plan requires that we take this labor of love and somehow postpone our Type 4 pre-mortal proclivities, as we emerge on the world stage surrounded by Type 0 mortal experiences.

In order to counteract that unforgiving reality check, God made it instinctively possible for us to enjoy Type 1 and Type 2 connections that would gently lead us toward Type 3 connections, so that we could eventually have Type 4 connections. He provided a blueprint for survival, and inserted within its many pages of instruction enough information to organize ourselves and prepare every needful thing, so that we might establish a house of prayer, fasting, faith, learning, glory, and order; even the happiest place on hearth and a house of God where dreams come true; where connectivity would not only be magical, but also entirely possible. (See D&C 88:119).

That is why Adam and Eve, who were living in innocence in a Garden setting, were truthfully told that it had been patterned after the order of heaven where they had aforetime lived. When Adam fell that men might be, their physical surroundings in the lone and dreary world were designed to provide a hint of familiarity. If they would be sensitive to the Spirit, they would be able to re-establish their celestial connectivity and have joy. (See 2 Nephi 2:25). They would enjoy communication with the heavens. Adam fell so that God could teach him and his mortal posterity how to re-establish Type 4 eternal connections.

Truly, "the universe is but one great city, full of beloved ones, divine and human, by nature endeared to each other." (Epictetus). Heavenly Father is the Grand Architect of the design that establishes the brotherhood of man even as it confirms His fatherhood, so that in Him "we could live, and move, and have our being; as certain also of (our) own poets have said. For we are also his offspring." (Acts 17:28).

When Cain asked his father Adam if he was his brother's keeper (see Genesis 4:9), he did so not really knowing the answer to the question. But it did expose his failure to comprehend his Type 3 connection with his brother Abel. When the Savior posed the question to the lawyer: "Which now of these three, thinkest thou, was neighbour unto him that fell among the thieves?" He was asking the young man to take a leap of faith, to recognize the spiritual handwriting on the wall, and acknowledge the Type 3 connections he should have had with someone so despised as a Samaritan. (Luke 10:36). Moroni's challenge to come unto Christ is an invitation for us to establish with Him a Type 3 connection, and to stretch our minds and our spirits, that the way might be paved for us to expose ourselves to Type 4 connections that would allow Him to perfect us. (See Moroni 10:32).

Joseph Smith asked the Saints if they could somehow establish a Type 3 connection with each other that was founded on charity. (See D&C 121:45-47). Similarly, Moses instructed all of Israel to regard its neighbors not with Type 0 connectivity, but as Type 3 brothers and sisters. He taught: "And if a stranger sojourn with thee in your land, ye shall not vex him. But the stranger that dwelleth with you shall be unto you as one born among you, and thou shalt love him as thyself." (Leviticus 19:33-34). In short, we establish covenant relationships with God so that we can establish Type 3 connections, leading to Type 4 eternal joy in the Kingdom of Heaven.

Ruth felt this connectivity, when she implored her mother in law Naomi: "Entreat me not to leave thee, or to return from following after thee, for whither thou goest, I will go, and where thou lodgest, I will lodge. Thy people shall be my people, and thy God my God. Where thou diest, will I die, and there will I be buried. The Lord do so to me, and more also, if ought but death part thee and me." (Ruth 1:16-17). Ruth established a profound connection that endured for over eleven hundred years, allowing the Savior to come to earth through her lineage.

The mission statement of our Father in Heaven is to establish Type 4 connections with His children. (See Moses 1:39). Peter taught: "Brethren, give diligence to make your calling and election sure; for if ye do these things, ye shall never fall." (2 Peter 1:10). The Savior likewise taught His disciples: "Then shall the King say unto them on his right hand, Come, ye blessed of my Father, inherit the kingdom prepared for you from the foundation of the world. For I was an hungered, and ye gave me meat. I was thirsty, and ye gave me drink. I was a stranger, and ye took me in; naked, and ye clothed me. I was sick, and ye visited me. I was in prison, and ye came unto me. Then shall the righteous answer him, saying, Lord, when saw we thee an hungered, and fed thee; or thirsty, and gave thee drink? When saw we thee a stranger, and took thee in; or naked, and clothed thee? Or when saw we thee sick, or in prison, and came unto thee? And the King shall answer and say unto them, Verily I say unto you, Inasmuch as ye have done it unto one of the least of these my brethren, ye have done it unto me." (Matthew 25:34-40).

With disappointment, He said to others who never went to the effort to establish

Type 3 or 4 connectivity: "I never knew you: depart from me, ye that work iniquity." (Matthew 7:23). Or, as the Joseph Smith Translation puts it: "Ye never knew me." (J.S.T. Matthew 7:33). Similarly, the J.S.T. changed the wording: "Verily I say unto you, I know you not," (Matthew 25:12), to "Ye know me not." (J.S.T. Matthew 25:11). In both instances, the ball is clearly in our court, to pattern our relationships after the order of the Type 4 connectivity that is characteristic of heaven.

Modern-day revelation speaks of those who, during their mortal probation, establish an unshakable bond with our Father in Heaven and with the Lord Jesus Christ, through unfettered access to the Holy Ghost. "Then shall they be gods, because they have no end; therefore shall they be from everlasting to everlasting, because they continue; then shall they be above all, because all things are subject unto them. Then shall they be gods, because they have all power, and the angels are subject unto them." (D&C 132:20).

Sooner or later, every member of the church will encounter a line drawn in the sand. Those who "endure unto the end, the same shall be saved." (Matthew 24:13). Or, as the Lord explained to Joseph Smith: "If you keep my commandments" by fostering Type 3 connections, "and endure to the end, establishing Type 4 connectivity "you shall have eternal life, which gift is the greatest of all the gifts of God. (D&C 14:7).

"The
stretching of your
faith is immediate pain that
results in ultimate gain. It is in the
waiting, that we become who
we are meant to be."
(Mandy Hale).

Construction Zone:
Proceed With Caution

A better understanding of the principles of the gospel and of the doctrines of the kingdom can help us to better negotiate the minefields of mortality, the conceptual cul de sacs, doctrinal dead-ends, religious roundabouts, and one-way roads that lead to hell, the spiritual stop signs and yield to temptation signs, and the dangerous curves, blind intersections, cross traffic, and speeders on the excess express. Properly identifying these ten pitfalls can help us to internalize the principles of the gospel and the doctrines of the Kingdom of God, that each of us "may act in doctrine and principle pertaining to futurity, according to the moral agency" that the Lord has given to each of us, that we may be accountable for our own sins in the day of judgment. (D&C 101:78).

Principles are laws that definitively explain how things work and why things happen as they do. They form the foundation of doctrine. They have a basis in truth, and so they give definition and vibrancy to doctrine. Principles provide substance and establish the ideal as the standard to which we all should strive. Our testimonies focus on principles rather than on values, and so our witness of truth easily bridges the cultural, economic, political, and social boundaries that would otherwise segregate the Saints. Principles speak to our spirits because everyone is entitled to guidance from the Light of Christ. Our understanding of principles provides immunity from the corrosive contamination of conventional wisdom, and resistance to the twisted influence of private interpretation.

Principles become the homing beacon of the torch of truth. They help us to avoid being caught in the bind of building the church while killing the articles of its faith, or permitting form to triumph over spirit. Principles have vitality because they are alive with interactive communication with God. They are the substance of the currents that are part of the flowing fountain of the church. Principles quicken us to recognize the source of the life-giving water that is ultimately expressed in doctrine.

Doctrine relates to specifics, but it also encompasses the collective foundation of principles. It describes an interrelated system of teachings that provide context for particular subjects. In this milieu, justice and mercy are the principles that relate to the doctrine of Atonement. Repentance is the principle that relates to the doctrine of Forgiveness. Faith and repentance are the principles that relate to the doctrine of baptism for the remission of sins. Vicarious work is a principle that relates to the various doctrines that form the basis of temple work. Moral behavior is a principle that relates to the doctrines that underpin the Law of Chastity. Free will is a principle that relates to the doctrine of self-determination. Service in the kingdom is a principle that is related to the doctrine of foreordination. Guidance by the Spirit is a principle that is related to the doctrine of revelation. Making correct choices is a principle that is related to the doctrine of eternal progression.

Henry B. Eyring said: "We must be cautious and careful not to go beyond teaching true doctrine." This requires that we be sensitive to the whisperings of the Holy Ghost. "His confirmation is invited as we avoid speculation or personal interpretation. One of the surest ways to avoid even getting near false doctrine is to choose to be simple in our teaching. Safety is gained by that simplicity, and little is lost." (C.R., 4/2009).

Jeffrey Holland addressed a similar theme in another General Conference. "The scriptures are not the ultimate source of knowledge for Latter-day Saints," he said. The living God is the ultimate source, and His teaching comes as vibrant revelation. This doctrine is central to the message of the Restoration. "God is engaged in our lives," said Elder Holland, and "continues to speak His word and reveal His truth." (C.R., 4/2008). This basic belief demands that we maintain an open canon of scripture, including continuing revelation.

As we learn about both principles and doctrine, we receive the mysteries of the kingdom of heaven, and have the heavens opened unto us. We "commune with the general assembly and church of the Firstborn, and enjoy the communion and presence of God the Father, and Jesus the mediator of the new covenant." (D&C 107:18-19). We learn how to teach correct principles that relate to doctrine when we are asked, as Antionah asked of Alma: "What does the scripture mean...?" (Alma 12:21).

1). We learn how to avoid conceptual cul-de-sacs. We carefully and cautiously follow the example of Alma, who told Corianton: "Now, my son...I give it as my opinion..." (Alma 40:11). As the High Priest and leader of the church, we can cut him some slack, as he taught his own son.

Written in an era of limited resources, the first issue of the Times and Seasons contained a lead editorial to the elders of the church: "Be careful that you teach not for the word of God, the commandments of men, nor the doctrines of men. Study the word of God and preach it and not your own opinions, for no man's opinion is worth a straw." We have been repeatedly counseled to trust in the

Lord with all our heart and lean not unto our own understanding. (Proverbs 3:5). This is why B.H. Roberts "said after a coherent and vigorous presentation that he loved books; indeed, that in some degree books had made him. But then, in a most vehement way, he said 'But I am not dependent on books. I am dependent for what I really know and really trust, on the direct experience of God.'" (Truman Madsen, "Defender of The Faith," p. 374).

It is our teaching, with all of its wonderful resources, that brings those within the sphere of our influence into the realm of direct experience with God. In fact, "we save ourselves by our teaching, and we save those who will get in tune with the same spirit that we have, when we teach those truths." (Bruce R. McConkie, "The Foolishness of Teaching"). We remember the wise counsel of Paul to Timothy: "And the things that thou hast heard of me among many witnesses, the same commit thou to faithful men, who shall be able to teach others also." (2 Timothy 2:2).

2). We learn to identify the paths leading to doctrinal dead ends. We remember the observation of B.H. Roberts, who believed that the religions of his day were often simply multiplying mirrors and studying angles without actually increasing the light. The Restoration of the gospel, he felt, had done just the opposite.

It may be true that the Lutheran slogan "every man his own priest" has become one of the hinge-pins upon which Protestantism rests. But the resulting anarchy within its denominations is clear evidence that "multiplying mirrors" leads to doctrinal dead ends. The Church of Jesus Christ of Latter-day Saints celebrates authority vested in those who have been called and set apart to administer the ordinances of the priesthood. It categorically refutes the protestant interpretation of scripture that suggests that no person can have any Christian rule over another, in any way.

Latter-day Saints look to inspiration from the Holy Ghost, and to their inspired priesthood leaders, for guidance. They know that learned or authoritative commentaries can help with scriptural interpretation, but as Dallin Oaks taught, "they must be used with caution. Commentaries are not a substitute for the scriptures any more than a good cookbook is a substitute for food. Commentaries refer to everything that interprets scripture, from the comprehensive book-length commentary to the brief interpretation embodied in a lesson or an article, such as this one."

"One trouble with commentaries," he continued, "is that their authors sometimes focus on only one meaning, to the exclusion of others. As a result, commentaries, if not used with great care, may illuminate the author's chosen and correct meaning but close our eyes and restrict our horizons to other possible meanings. Sometimes those other less obvious meanings can be the ones most valuable and useful to us as we seek to understand our own dispensation and to obtain answers to our own questions. This is why the teaching of the Holy Ghost is a better guide to scriptural interpretation than even the best commentary." ("Ensign," 1/1995).

3). We learn how to get off religious roundabouts. We follow the simple and straightforward counsel offered by Moroni, to "come unto Christ, and be perfected in him, and deny (ourselves) of all ungodliness; and if (we) shall deny (our)selves of all ungodliness, and love God with all (our) might, mind and strength, then is his grace sufficient for (us), that by his grace (we) may be perfect in Christ; and if by the grace of God (we) are perfect in Christ, (we) can in nowise deny the power of God." (Moroni 10:32).

If we suddenly and without warning find our heads spinning at 78 rpm on telestial turntables, we don't fret, because experience has thrown us a curve more than once. We know how to get back on the strait and narrow. We also know that worry is interest on a debt that never comes due, so we are optimists who see opportunity in every difficulty, rather than pessimists who see difficulty in every opportunity.

4). We learn that it is a one-way road that leads to hell. Our ears often ring with the lyrics of popular music that may be pleasing to the ear, but promote half-truths. "Living easy, living free; season ticket on a one way ride. Asking nothing; leave me be. Taking everything in my stride. Don't need reason; don't need rhyme. Ain't nothing that I'd rather do. Going down; party time. My friends are gonna be there too. I'm on the highway to hell. No stop signs, speed limit. Nobody's gonna slow me down. Like a wheel, gonna spin it. Nobody's gonna mess me around. Hey, Satan, paying my dues, playing in a rock band. Hey, mamma, look at me. I'm on the way to the promised land. I'm on the highway to hell, and I'm going down all the way. I'm on the highway to hell." (AC/DC, "The Highway to Hell").

The Lord nurtures His children differently. Gordon B. Hinckley said: "I think the best way I could describe the (interactive communication) process is to liken it to the experience of Elijah as set forth in the book of First Kings. Elijah spoke to the Lord, and there was a wind, a great wind, and the Lord was not in the wind. And there was an earthquake, and the Lord was not in the earthquake. And there was a fire, and the Lord was not in the fire. And after the fire a still, small voice, which I describe as the whisperings of the Spirit." (C.R., 10/1996).

Ezra Taft Benson wondered if we take time to listen to the promptings of the Spirit. "Answers to prayer," he said, "come most often by a still voice and are discerned by our deepest, innermost feelings. I tell you that you can know the will of God concerning yourselves if you will take the time to pray and to listen." (C.R., 10/1977). We will be comforted and guided if we put God first, and heed the whisperings of the Holy Ghost.

5). We learn not to yield to the signs of temptation. When dealing in the currency of faith, particularly in large denominations, we always make sure that we have enough cash in our wallets to meet our needs. We make regularly recurring deposits into our spiritual bank accounts, so that in times of emergency or adversity, there will always be enough in reserve to make adequate withdrawals.

We seek divine direction, and have learned how to focus the powers of heaven in our behalf. Because we are on the errand of the Lord, we take advantage of the opportunities He sends our way to be cast off into a stream of revelation as we are carried along in the quickening currents of direct experience with God. We find examples from our daily experiences that will support our thesis on life. We recognize and act upon moments when the Spirit leads us along the path of principle and the direction of doctrine, remembering that President Kimball said: "Seeking the spectacular, we often miss the constant flow of revealed communication that comes." (Munich Area Conference, 1973).

6). We learn that there may be dangerous curves ahead of us on the path of progression. When our faith is tested, and we feel inadequate to meet the demands of those who would challenge our beliefs, we take courage in the example of Alma, who on at least one occasion deferred to the greater wisdom of higher powers. In response to a difficult question from his son Corianton, he simply said: "Now these mysteries are not yet fully made known unto me; therefore I shall forbear." (Alma 37:11).

The Psalmist wrote of those who, trying to make sense of life, "reel to and fro, and stagger like a drunken man, and are at their wits' end." (Psalms 107:27). Daniel described the crisis of confidence of Belshazzar, whose "thoughts troubled him, so that the joints of his loins were loosed, and his knees smote one against another." (Daniel 5:6). When we are not well-grounded in principle and doctrine, the very fibers of our being are disjointed, as well, and fail to hold us together. We lose our physical, emotional, and spiritual coherence. If synaptic activity within our central nervous systems fires sporadically, we can only respond inappropriately and ineffectively in a palsy of principle and a dilemma of doctrine, without hope of spiritual synchronization or expectation of religious recalibration.

Sometimes, those who are not well-grounded need to be jolted out of their complacency in the same way that defibrillator paddles are used to restore normal cardiac rhythm in a heart attack patient. We remember the relevance of the Lord's instruction to Nephi: "Stretch forth thine hand again unto thy brethren, and...I will shock them, saith the Lord, and this will I do, that they may know that I am the Lord their God." (1 Nephi 17:53).

7). Sometimes, when we are approaching blind intersections, we take a deep breath, hold tightly to our faith, and keep quiet. For example, when someone points out that Justice and Mercy have picked a gender, we offer no opinion, but secretly hope for personal enlightenment: "For behold, justice exerciseth all his demands, and also mercy claimeth all which is her own." (Alma 42:24).

We are clear about our purpose, and "make no small plans, for they have no magic to stir men's souls." (Daniel H. Burnham). Whatever we do, we do it well, remembering the words of Abraham Lincoln, who declared: "I will prepare myself, and someday my chance will come." We emphasize the positive aspects of gospel principles and doctrines. We don't shirk our responsibilities or leave our understanding to the whims of fate. We all know about those four people named Everybody, Somebody, Anybody, and Nobody. An invitation to explain doctrine had been extended, and Everybody was sure that Somebody would prepare well ahead of time. Anybody could have done it, but Nobody did. Somebody got angry about it because, although it was Everybody's responsibility, he thought that Anybody could do it, but Nobody realized that not Everybody would take it seriously. It ended up that Everybody blamed Somebody when Nobody did what Anybody could have done. (Anonymous).

8). If we encounter cross traffic during our journey, we learn to be especially vigilant. We are alert to those who would try to trip us up, particularly by wresting the scriptures. (See Alma 41:1). We sympathize with those who kick against the pricks, because they often have only a weak foundation of doctrinal understanding of the gospel, and risk falling into transgression in consequence of their shallow comprehension of principles. As they pick apart the scriptures or the words of the Lord's servants, doctrine is distorted into meaningless fragments without any coherent connection. The sobering warning of Alma to the inhabitants of Ammonihah is ever on our minds: "Behold, the scriptures are before you; if ye will wrest them it shall be to your own destruction." (Alma 13:20).

The Lord told Joseph Smith: I "shall bring to light the true points of my doctrine… that I may establish my gospel, that there may not be so much contention; yea, Satan doth stir up the hearts of the people to contention concerning the points of my doctrine; and in these things they do err, for they do wrest the scriptures and do not understand them." (D&C 10:62-63).

9). We learn to avoid the excessive toll paid by speeders who frequent the Excess Express. The world simply does not recognize the value of balanced nutrition from the good word of God. Instead, it embraces the fleeting rush of artificial sweeteners, the empty calories of convenience, and the hypoglycemia of hypocrisy. The world jostles to and fro on a platform of platitudes before boarding the Excess Express in a vain attempt to take a shortcut to perfection. But the day will come when the worldly-wise will look in the mirror and see themselves as they really are; "that their spiritual bodies have become one sorry sight; no more than skeletons, covered with skin. They will get up to heaven, but never get in. 'Another soul's mine!' they will hear Satan scream. 'Give man something nice, and he'll take the extreme!' OK, I'll admit it; I'll outright confess. For the fast way to hell, take the Excess Express." (Anonymous).

During our own pre-mortal training, we must have recognized that strenuous spiritual exercise would give us vigorous vitality and leave us stronger, and so we surely learned to use our recovery time wisely. We must have developed the capacity to carefully monitor our bodies' vital signs; to feel the spiritual equivalents of oxygen-debt and lactic acid buildup; to monitor the efforts of our minds to keep pace with our spiritual development. We surely experienced brief bursts of energy resulting in spectacular achievement, but more importantly, we discovered that sustained effort over long periods would be more effective in carrying us further along the road leading to eternal life. Our Personal Trainer must have taught us the value of developing endurance, so that when the time would come to turn the other cheek, instead of embracing the carefree lifestyle of the rich and famous, it would be easier to go the second mile simply because of the force of habit.

10). We learn to recognize and to heed the spiritual stop signs that the Holy Ghost strategically places along the crooked path where we are tempted to get our ticket punched. In a very real sense, each of us is confined to a world of our own making, and most of us are trapped within the narrowly defined perceptual prisons we have created for ourselves. The walls of that fortress are reinforced with the razor-wire of limiting beliefs, those stories we tell ourselves that cause us to sabotage our own best efforts. They can damage and even cripple our lives, diminish our abilities, compromise our progress, and prevent us from attaining our goals. Although all of us have limiting beliefs, everyone has the power to change them. Most people, however, don't realize it's possible, and for that matter, aren't even aware that they have made conscious decisions about what they choose to believe and not to believe.

If we learn to let go and let God, and allow His principles and doctrines to regulate our lives, surely He will bless our efforts, and we will feel better about ourselves and about our contributions to the kingdom, no matter how large or small they may be. We will learn that the only way we can increase our strength is to give away that which we have received. We will learn that when we serve our hearts out, we will feel rejuvenated.

We will hear the voice of the Lord, asking: "Hast thou not known? Hast thou not heard, that the everlasting God, the Lord, the Creator of the ends of the earth, fainteth not, neither is weary? There is no searching of His understanding. He giveth power to the faint; and to them that have no might, He increaseth strength… They that wait upon the Lord shall renew their strength; they shall mount up with wings as eagles; they shall run, and not be weary; and they shall walk, and not faint." (Isaiah 40:28 & 30-31).

"Until one is committed,
there is hesitancy, the chance to draw
back, always ineffectiveness. Concerning all
acts of initiative, there is one elementary truth, the
ignorance of which kills countless ideas and splendid
plans: That the moment one definitely commits oneself,
then Providence moves too. All sorts of things occur to
help one that would never have otherwise occurred."
(Tom Hornbein, "Everest: The West Ridge").

Covenants

Technically, members of the church do not have a lock on covenants, per se. You say tomāto, I say tomăto. You say potāto, I say potăto. Broadly speaking, a covenant is a historical term for a treaty or other agreement. It is a legal term, particularly restricting the use of property; for example, Conditions, Covenants, and Restrictions or CC&Rs. Loan covenants define the conditions relating to financial instruments. The United Nations uses the term, as in its International Covenant Council on Civil and Political Rights. The Palestine Liberation Organization uses the term, as in The Palestinian National Covenant of 1964, which outlined the aims of the P.L.O.. So does the I.R.A., as in The Ulster Covenant of 1912, which protested against British home-rule. Covenants also define a series of solemn agreements believed by many to exist between God and Israel. The foundation of the Torah is the belief that God chose the Children of Israel, and made His covenant with them.

The Latter-day Saint concept of religious "covenants" goes back at least to Abraham, but the temple endowment traces its origin all the way to Adam and Eve in the Garden of Eden, and concerns the agreements they made with God. The scriptures teach that Abraham was righteous and refused to worship his father's idols. In recognition of this, the Lord made a covenant with him and his descendants.

That covenant is defined in Abraham 2:11 & in Genesis 17:4-8. In these verses, God promised Abraham that he would have numberless descendants who would be entitled to receive the gospel, the priesthood, and the ordinances of exaltation. God would establish the same covenant with all the generations of Abraham's children. They would ultimately carry the gospel to the nations of the earth and through them, would extend the blessings of God to all mankind. The Abrahamic Covenant is of such power and force that its conditions endow all of Heavenly Father's children with the opportunity to participate in and receive the blessings of the Plan of Salvation.

We do not need to be the literal descendants of Abraham to qualify to participate in this covenant. Literal descendants of Abraham are not the only people whom God calls His covenant people. Speaking to Abraham, God said, "As many as receive this gospel shall be called after thy name, and shall be accounted thy seed and shall rise up and bless thee, as their father." (Abraham 2:10). Thus, two groups of people are included in the covenant made with Abraham: (1) Abraham's righteous literal descendants and (2) those adopted into his lineage by accepting and living the gospel of Jesus Christ. (See 2 Nephi 30:2). It is precisely because of its relationship to the Abrahamic Covenant, that a person's lineage is declared during the administration of a patriarchal blessing.

Today, members of His church make a number of covenants with the Lord. There are baptismal covenants, sacramental covenants, The Oath and Covenant of The Priesthood, and several temple covenants. If God did not make these covenants with His children, if there were no law given, if men could sin with impunity, if they had a free pass, as it were, "what could justice do, or mercy either, for they would have no claim upon the creature? …The works of justice would be destroyed, and God would cease to be God." (Alma 42:21-22).

Latter-day Saints view religious covenants in a way that is uniquely personal and peculiar to their beliefs. They believe that covenants are received only by revelation from God, and are binding contracts, and since He is a party to every gospel covenant, they must necessarily come through revelation. No person can, therefore, enter into such covenants without direct revelation from God. In their minds, it follows that the only ones who can make covenants with God are members of the Church of Jesus Christ who believe in latter-day revelation. (See the 7th Article of Faith).

Latter-day Saints go to a great deal of effort to make covenants with God, because they believe they are integral to the Plan of Salvation that has been designed to bring to pass our immortality, exaltation, and eternal life. They feel that covenants are particularly powerful because they reveal something about the attributes of God Himself. Latter-day Saints believe that covenants accurately describe a heavenly parenting style. God is our Father, and He is perfect in every way. He could give us everything He has, but what He is, we must earn for ourselves, as we struggle to overcome adversity and gain self-mastery. Covenants bridge the gulf between mortality and eternity, by helping us, more than any other thing, to focus our efforts to become as He is.

If it were not possible to become as God is, Latter-day Saints believe that religious covenants would be unnecessary. This provides insight into the world's ignorance relating to the importance that Latter-day Saints attach to the covenants they make with God, particularly in the temple, and it suggests the direction that teaching should follow. As Joseph Smith observed: "Reading the experience of others, or the revelation given to them, can never give us a comprehensive view of our condition and true relation to God. Knowledge of these things can only be obtained by experience through the ordinances of God set forth for this purpose." (H.C., 6:50).

As a result of my exposure to the teachings of the church, beginning with a short film ("Man's Search for Happiness") at Flushing Meadows, New York, during the 1964 World's Fair, I learned that the covenants we make with God reflect His attributes. For example, God is moral, so He gives us the Covenant of Chastity. He has charity, so He commands us to love Him and each other. God is disciplined, so He gives us the Law of Obedience. Because He is a righteous steward, He gives us the Law of Consecration. Because He loves His less fortunate children, He gives us the Law of the Fast. Because His is a perfected, resurrected body, He gives us the Word of Wisdom. Because He is omniscient, He gives us the commandment to seek knowledge. In consequence of the Gift of His Son, He gives us the Law of Sacrifice. Because He rested from His labors on the seventh day, He gives us the Law of the Sabbath.

I learned that our covenant relationship with God releases the power within us to receive specific blessings, for example, the right to enjoy continual guidance from the Holy Ghost. Worthy men receive the right to hold and exercise the priesthood. Women receive the rights, privileges, blessings, and responsibilities relating to femininity. They also receive the right to exercise authority, at sundry times and under special circumstances in the temple. Families receive the blessings of the priesthood relating to eternal life in the Celestial Kingdom.

I learned that the covenants we make with God have the power to put us beyond the long reach of the adversary. Obedience gives us the priesthood and spiritual power necessary to overcome evil and obtain exaltation. The Prophet Joseph Smith explained: "Salvation consists of a man's being placed beyond the power of his enemies, meaning the enemies of his progression, such as dishonesty, greediness, lying, immorality, and other vices." (Sermon delivered at Nauvoo temple site on May 21, 1843. Source: "Joseph Smith Diary").

Those who make covenants have been promised: "The gates of hell shall not prevail against you; yea, and the Lord God will disperse the powers of darkness from before you, and cause the heavens to shake for thy good, and His name's glory." (D&C 21:6). The gates of hell mark the entrance to what has been called 'the Spirit Prison of the Unjust,' where unenlightened souls are allowed to go, to work out their own salvation, and to await the day of their deliverance from the iron grip of Satan. (See Alma 40:11-14).

After joining the church, I quickly learned about my responsibilities relating to the covenant relationship I had established with God. I learned about my duty to keep His commandments. I learned about my responsibility to be a missionary and how my life would fit in with the promise that had been given to Abraham, that through his descendants the gospel would be taken to all the earth.

I am continually learning more about the fulness of the gospel, which is The New and Everlasting Covenant, including the covenants I made at my baptism, at my ordination to the Melchizedek Priesthood, and that I renew during the administration of the Sacrament and before altars in the temple. The Lord calls the covenant everlasting because it has been ordained and ratified by His everlasting authority. He assures us that the foundations of the covenant, meaning the blessings associated with obedience, will never be changed, for He is the same yesterday, today, and forever. He has given this same covenant to Adam, Enoch, Noah, Abraham, and other prophets, during each dispensation of the gospel. The words may change slightly, but the intent and purpose, and the blessings related to obedience, do not. The Lord calls the covenant "new" because each time the gospel is restored after being taken from the earth due to apostasy, it is new to the people who receive it. (See Jeremiah 31:31-34 & Ezekiel 37:26).

As I have matured in the church, I have learned about the "contract provisions" of the New and Everlasting Covenant. Initially, I agreed to repent, be baptized, to receive the Holy Ghost, and then I was taught about the endowment and the covenant of marriage in the temple. With spiritual and priesthood power, I have determined to follow and obey Christ to the end of my life. Heavenly Father has promised me, in turn, that I will receive the blessing of exaltation in His Celestial Kingdom. (See D&C 132:20-24). The scope of that promise is hard for me to understand. I do know that the commandments are for my benefit, and that through faith I may share in the blessings and enjoy the beauties of heaven and earth. I may look forward, once again, to living in His presence, to partake of His love, compassion, power, greatness, knowledge, wisdom, glory, and dominions.

I have learned that my Father in Heaven established His Covenant to release me from my bondage to sin, and to set me free to completely take advantage of all the features of the Plan of Salvation, and particularly of its keystone, the Atonement of Christ. Without His Covenant in my behalf, although I am a very small cog in a very large wheel, I realize that the Plan would be frustrated. I am thrilled to know that covenants have set me free from the iron bands of death. I believe the words of King Benjamin, who said: "There is no other name given whereby salvation cometh, therefore, I would that ye should take upon you the name of Christ, all you that have entered into the covenant with God." (Mosiah 5:8).

The covenants I have made with God have set me free to reach my potential, and I rejoice that I have been born again. Truly, did Benjamin declare that those who enter into the Covenant "are born of him." (Mosiah 5:7). I understand that I am a "Born Again Christian," who has joined the ranks of others who are known to

God, and are in a covenant relationship with Him. (See Mosiah 27:25, Alma 5:14, & 7:14, Mosiah 15:10-11, & Alma 22:15, & 36:24).

As the Lord revealed to Joseph Smith, so have I learned that the "greater priesthood administereth the gospel and holdeth the key of the mysteries of the kingdom, even the key of the knowledge of God. Therefore, in the ordinances thereof, the power of godliness is manifest. And without the ordinances thereof, and the authority of the priesthood, the power of godliness is not manifest unto men in the flesh." (D&C 84:19-21).

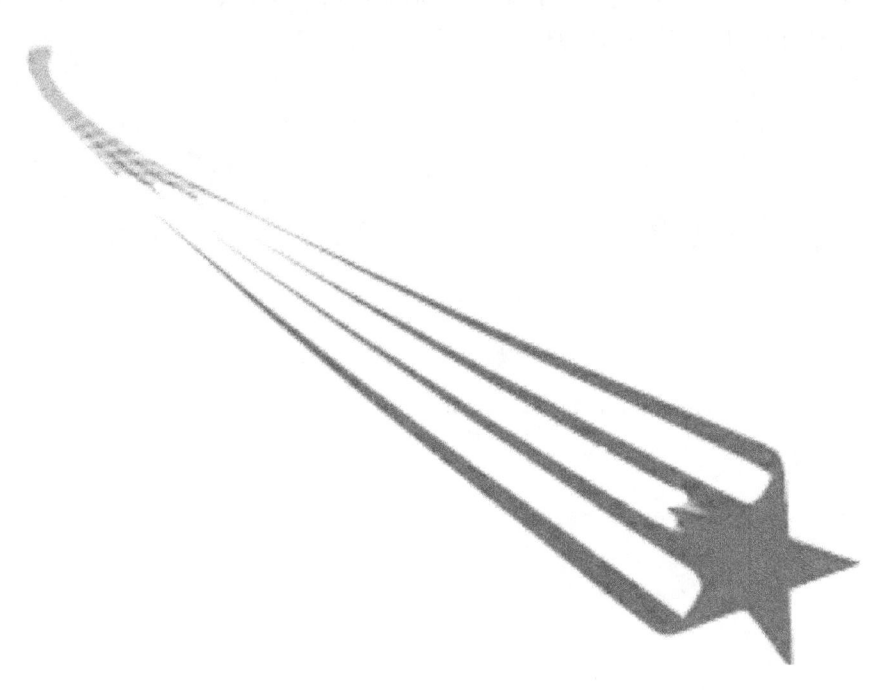

While at the Institute
for Advanced Studies at
Princeton, Albert Einstein was
asked if he might show a visitor his
laboratory. Einstein smiled, picked up
a fountain pen, and pointed it at his head.

Dancing With The Stars

"The Great Silence" is the contradiction between the astronomically high estimates of the probability of extraterrestrial life and its corresponding lack of evidence. After all, we ask ourselves: Hasn't humanity reached the point where it should be "Dancing With The Stars?" Shouldn't we be holding up the Mirror Ball Trophy with our extra-terrestrial quickstep partners? The universe is around 13.7 billion years old and contains something on the order of 70 sextillion (7 x 1022) stars, many of which undoubtedly have planets, so somewhere, at some point in the past, life should have evolved into societies of technologically advanced species who have either intentionally or inadvertently broadcast news of their existence across the far reaches of space. Yet, back in 1950, the physicist Enrico Fermi wondered aloud why no such evidence has been detected. His question ("Where is everybody?") has come to be known as "The Fermi Paradox." It is also known as "Silentium Universi." Basically, the paradox is a conflict between scale and probability on the one hand, and the aforementioned lack of confirming evidence on the other.

The "scale" involved is mind-boggling. There are an estimated 200 to 400 billion stars in the Milky Way Galaxy alone. Somewhere out there should be intelligent life capable of having made its presence known. Think of the electromagnetic signals from earth – for example, all those broadcasts of "Sesame Street" - that have been traveling at the speed of light outward through space since the early years of the 20th century.

The second foundation of the Fermi Paradox, which is probability, is the assumption that extraterrestrials would have developed the ability to overcome scarcity and colonize new habitat, and ultimately to possess the technology to explore neighboring star systems. But after having had so much time (13.7 billion years) in which to do so, no terrestrial evidence of alien life seems to now exist, thereby creating a conflict begging for resolution.

It may be that life is precious and is found relatively infrequently in the cosmos. Perhaps we are unique, after all. Hamlet may have been right when he exclaimed: "What a piece of work is a man, how noble in reason, how infinite in faculties, in form and moving how express and admirable, in action how like an angel, in apprehension how like a god! The beauty of the world, the paragon of animals." (Shakespeare, "Hamlet," Act 2, Scene 3).

It may be that our best efforts to reach out and touch someone, anyone, might be corrupted by an "Observer Effect" that significantly alters the state of the elusive objects of our investigation and makes their detection and measurement more difficult. Perhaps the very devices we have constructed to search for the evidence of alien life have tainted the data that would have otherwise confirmed its existence.

It may be that our neighbors in the infinite reaches of space and time are defined by bounds and conditions that make their detection with our five physical senses impossible. William W. Phelps mused: If only we "could hie to Kolob in the twinkling of an eye, and then continue onward with that same speed to fly, do you think that (we) could ever, through all eternity, find out the generation where Gods began to be, or see the grand beginning, where space did not extend, or view the last creation, where Gods and matter end? Methinks the Spirit whispers, 'No man has found pure space, nor seen the outside curtains where nothing has a place.' The works of God continue, and worlds and lives abound. Improvement and progression have one eternal round. There is no end to matter; there is no end to space; there is no end to spirit; there is no end to race." ("If You Could Hie to Kolob").

Our arguable "nobility" notwithstanding, after 4 billion years of evolutionary development, it is still up in the air whether intelligent life exists on earth, and if it does, will it ever make it past a Type 0 civilization. (See the definition below of Types 0, 1, 2, and 3 civilizations). Perhaps, other cultures have embraced, as we have, an insane policy of Mutually Assured Destruction, (MAD), that has inexorably led to their ultimate annihilation. Perhaps, exponentially expanding technology ultimately proves to be impossible to control by those moving too quickly along its path of hopeful progress toward Type 1 planetary stability. Perhaps alien civilizations too often seal their fate by inadvertently opening a Pandora's Box of unmanageable knowledge, thereby sowing the seeds of their own ruin.

Perhaps technology harbors a fatal flaw and nurtures a hidden Achilles Heel. As Type 0 societies evolve, though they may envision a technological shield of protection, they may instead inadvertently pursue the creation of a dispassionate and amoral "Sky Net." Our own terrestrial storytellers have already described how such a coldly logical machine could one day take on a deadly "life" of its own to bite the hand that had created it. (See the movie: "Terminator 3: Rise of The Machines").

Perhaps intelligent life in the universe has a very difficult time moving beyond our own "Type 0" civilization described by Michio Kaku, with all the petty jealousies, regional conflicts, social and economic inequalities, and sectarian violence that have plagued us for millennia. Kaku has conceptualized "Type 1" planetary civilizations, right out of "Buck Rogers" and "Type 2" interstellar civilizations, like "Star Trek - The Next Generation." He also envisions "Type 3" galactic civilizations on the order of the Empire, in the movie "Star Wars."

Dr. Kaku believes that "in about 100 years our Type 0 civilization will become planetary (a Type 1 civilization). We'll be able to harness all the energy output of earth. We'll play with the weather. The danger period is now (Type 0), because we still have the savagery. We still have the passions. We have sectarian, fundamentalist ideas swirling about, and we also have nuclear, chemical and biological weapons capable of wiping out life on earth."

He sees two mutually exclusive trends developing, the one toward a multi-cultural, scientific, tolerant, nurturing, interactive, and interdependent society, with easy access to educational opportunity, meaningful employment and the satisfaction of temporal needs. The Internet, Facebook, and other social media, rock and roll, fashion, sports, the European Union, NAFTA, and even English as a planetary language are evidence that we are inching in that direction. We are witnessing the genesis of a Type 1 economy and a Type 1 culture. However, we also see its opposite in economic inequality and poverty, organized crime and secret societies, political corruption and terrorism, violence against minorities, cultural myopia, drug and alcohol abuse, sectarian conflicts, and religious fundamentalism, that are all self-destructive reactions against a Type 1 civilization. Whether we make it beyond Type 0 or not is therefore still undecided.

Dr. Kaku continues: "Now, in outer space, we look for signs of intelligent life. So far, we find none. Civilizations like Type 1 should be commonplace in the galaxy. Some people assume, therefore, that Type 0 civilizations are rather common, but only a few of them make it to Type 1 because that society for the first time in its history has the ability to commit planetary suicide. Maybe that is the reason why we don't see evidence of alien life. Maybe they never made it. Maybe one day when we have starships and visit their worlds we'll see atmospheres that are irradiated because they had nuclear war, or atmospheres too hot to sustain life because they had a runaway greenhouse effect. Maybe when we explore the galaxy we'll see the corpses of Type 0 civilizations that never quite made it to Type 1."

At the cosmic speed limit, (the speed at which light travels, or about 6 trillion miles per year), it would take only 120,000 years, (the blink of an eye on a cosmological scale), for a probe or vessel from a Type 2 or 3 civilization to traverse the Milky Way. Our own solar system is a relative newcomer on our 13.2 billion year-old galactic stage, yet we have no indication that life forms have stopped by earth at any time during its own 4.6 billion year history, to leave their calling cards. Perhaps they have, and we are asking the wrong questions, or are looking in the wrong places for the unique signatures that have indelibly marked their passing.

However, unless alien physicists have worked out the details to permit travel at warp speed, where space itself is distorted to shorten the distance between points A and B, the physical evidence of life elsewhere in the galaxy, let alone in the universe, may not exist. Still, there are promising launch platforms, right in our own vicinity, for space-faring visitors. For example, the Alpha Centauri System, (our nearest stellar neighbor), is only 4.2 light years away, almost within shouting distance, about 25.62 trillion miles from earth. A potentially habitable planet, named Proxima Centauri, has been discovered orbiting Alpha Centauri.

In 1977, the United States of America created the cosmic equivalent of the slogan "Kilroy was here" when it sent Voyager 1 out into space like a bottle bobbing on a deep and boundless intergalactic ocean. After forty years, (as of 2017) it had traveled 12.8 billion miles at a constant velocity of 36,387 miles per hour, 0.00005434% of the speed of light, or just over 10 miles per second. At this rate, it will take Voyager 1 about 14,000 years to travel one light year. (Go to Voyager.jpl.nasa.gov/where to see how far Voyager is from the earth, in real time). Light, traveling at 186,200 miles per second, takes over 16 hours to reach the probe that has now passed the Termination Shock of the solar wind (the heliosphere) and has entered interstellar space. In about 40,000 years, Voyager 1 will be as close as it's going to get (about 1.6 light years) to another star: (AC+79 3888 in the Ophiuchus Constellation). Its Golden Record and pictograms describe life on earth. Electroplated upon the exterior of the probe is an ingenious "atomic clock," a sample of the isotope uranium-238 with a half-life of 4.468 billion years. If Voyager 1 has enough specific orbital energy to leave the Milky Way, in 1,288,000,000 years it will enter intergalactic space. It is possible that, one day in the distant future, within the boundaries of a galaxy far, far away, a civilization may stumble upon Voyager 1 and determine its age by calculating the decay of the isotope, and also vector its location of origin. "Twentieth-century" humans would be to them as a voice crying from the dust, for our sun would have long since become a red giant after running out of its hydrogen fuel. Although the earth and its life forms will be destroyed in that process about 5 billion years from now, Voyager would nevertheless remain our enduring legacy, representing a small token of our fleeting influence on the intergalactic stage.

If Voyager were headed in the direction of Proxima Centauri, which happens to be the closest of 51 stars within 16 light years of earth, it would only take 80,376 years to reach it. The earth is about 28,000 light years from the center of the Milky Way Galaxy, which itself is around 120,000 light years in diameter. Its closest major neighbor is the spiral galaxy Andromeda, composed of over a trillion stars 2.6 million light years from earth. These large numbers suggest that intergalactic two-way communication, let alone travel, might just take too much time to complete, even if "ridiculous" or "ludicrous" speed were possible. (See the movie: "Space Balls").

So where is everybody? Let's forget our intergalactic second cousins, (we always considered them a strange bunch, anyway) and just concentrate on our more immediate next of kin who might be living in the neighborhood. In our own Milky Way, astronomers have found evidence of 160 billion of one particularly promising type of red dwarf star, 40% of which (64 billion) are thought to have planets, supposed "M Class" (earth similarity) planets. If conditions on only one in a thousand of those 64 billion has actually germinated life, there could be 64 million planets with thriving life forms. If only one in a thousand of those 64 million has life similar to our own, there could be 64,000 "sister" planets out there in the night sky, embedded within the fuzzy wash of the Milky Way's light. On many of these, alien cosmologists might even now be gazing up in the chill of the evening, wondering if they too are alone in the universe, and their wives might be wondering if they are going to be late for dinner again.

Myths from around the world give the Milky Way its name and explain its origin. The Greeks believed it was created when suckling Heracles dribbled the breast milk of Hera, wife of Zeus, across the night sky. It was also described as the trail to Mount Olympus, the home of the Gods, and as the path of ruin made by the chariot of the Sun God Helios. In Sanskrit, the Milky Way was called Akash Ganga (Ganges of the Heavens), and was considered sacred. Hindu cosmology explains the galaxy as an ocean of milk churned by the gods for a thousand years in order to release Amrita, the nectar of immortal life.

Using our aforementioned calculations relating to the probability of life in the Milky Way Galaxy as a baseline, we may extrapolate that within the 200 to 400 billion galaxies in the known universe there could be as many as 25,600,000 trillion (2.56×10^{19}) "earths" with life just like our own. That mind-boggling number pales in comparison to the endless possibilities within a multiverse, or parallel universes that together might comprise everything that exists and can exist; the entirety of knowable and unknowable space, time, matter, and energy. But that is the subject of another ambitious essay.

Perhaps we have found no proof of extraterrestrial life because we have an over-developed anthropocentric viewpoint. Perhaps we look too closely for evidence of the kinds of activities we would perform, without realizing that extraterrestrial life might behave in entirely different ways that make perfect sense to them, but are completely "alien" to our nature, inclination, experience, or means of detection.

Then there is the distinct possibility that the evolution of life on alien worlds has taken a very different path than it has on earth. To use an example with which we are all familiar, if a comet had not struck earth 70 million years ago, thus effectively ending the cretaceous period with its exponential proliferation of dinosaurs, we might even now look and think like our velociraptor distant cousins. Perhaps alien life is so unlike Homo Sapiens that the gulf separating our species is just too great to bridge with comprehensible communication.

Early in 2012, NASA's planet-hunting Kepler spacecraft confirmed the discovery of the first alien world that lies within the habitable zone of its host star, where temperatures would allow liquid H_2O to exist. New finds bring the space telescope's total haul during its first 16 months of operation to 2,326 planets. The exciting thing about this particular planet, though, is that it is a potentially habitable alien world orbiting a star very much like our own sun.

"As of January 2015, Kepler and its follow-up observations had found exoplanets (planets outside our solar system) in about 440 star systems. In November 2013, astronomers estimated, based on Kepler mission data, that there could be as many as 40 billion rocky, earth-size exoplanets orbiting in the habitable zones of Sun-like stars and red dwarfs within the Milky Way. The nearest such planet may be 3.7 parsecs away, according to the scientists." ("Wikipedia"). (A parsec is a unit of distance used in astronomy, equal to about 3.26 light years).

Using the High Accuracy Radial Velocity Planet Searcher (HARPS) spectrograph at the European Southern Observatory in Chile, astronomers have found within the Milky Way nine more similar exoplanets only slightly larger than earth. The investigators estimate that about 100 such planets lie in the immediate neighborhood of the sun. The "new observations with HARPS suggest that about 40 percent of all red dwarf stars have an 'earth' orbiting in the habitable zone." ("Space: MSNBC.com, 3/28/2012).

It seems plausible that over billions of years, intelligent life should have flourished on at least some of these "M Class" planets that likely permeate our galaxy. The technological accomplishments of humans over the past 50 years, or 5 years, or even the last 5 minutes, beg the question: "Where is everybody?" If intelligent life is out there, why have we detected no evidence of its existence? At the very least, why hasn't its presence revealed itself through the distribution of electromagnetic signals that should be the unmistakable signature of a technologically advanced civilization?

Perhaps we are looking through a very small keyhole into the locking mechanism of what may be the wrong microscopic portion of the night sky. When we gaze up into its vast expanse, the stars that are visible from earth (about 9,096 of them) are nearly all in the Milky Way. Aside from the Large and Small Magellanic Clouds, Andromeda and Triangulum are among fewer than half a dozen discernable galaxies. Centaurus A is the furthest, at a distance from earth of 13.7 million light years. Maybe the evidence of alien life is not only hidden from our optic nerves and occipital lobes, but is also beyond the reach of our most sophisticated instruments.

Perhaps First Contact has not yet been made because members of the United Federation of Planets unerringly adhere to The Prime Directive, Starfleet's General Order #1, the most prominent guiding principle in the fictional universe of "Star Trek: The Next Generation." Interestingly, the Prime Directive, which dictates that there can be no interference with the internal development of pre-warp civilizations, is consistent with the historical real-world concept of Westphalian sovereignty.

The rationale behind the Prime Directive, which is that civilizations with advanced technologies should not alter, modify, revise, amend, adjust, improve, develop, expand, or change in any way the natural development of emerging societies, wherever they may be found, even if the aid is well-intentioned or kept secret, is that to do so might radically influence its natural evolution. This could be detrimental to its society or to its celestial neighbors within the sphere of its expanding powers, or it could be beneficial, but the effect would most certainly not be neutral. In any case, the culture's natural progression, and that of others with whom it might come in contact, would be artificially influenced in ways that would be difficult to anticipate and impossible to control. Regardless of the outcome, there would be no turning back.

So, perhaps aliens have been observing our behavior for some time, but have exercised God-like prudence and restraint when they have been tempted to reveal their presence. Perhaps they are keenly aware of our sense of urgency, but maintain the disciplined reserve that allows us to take the necessary baby steps that might one day lead us to interplanetary familiarity and even camaraderie. Perhaps they ascribe to the philosophy of "milk before meat," and before they make their presence known they have determined to see how our transition from a "Type 0" to a "Type 1" civilization is progressing. Perhaps their patience reflects a more accurate time-line for growth and development than our hasty and imprudent demands for play-dates with extra-terrestrials would dictate.

On the other hand, perhaps alien ambassadors are among us even now in the disguise of the greatest minds of the 20th and 21st centuries, conducting tutorials in disciplines that range from astrophysics to zoology, and everything in between. After First Contact had been made in the motion picture "Close Encounters of The Third Kind," a terrestrial scientist at Devil's Tower was heard to exclaim: "Einstein was right!" To which a colleague replied: "Hell, Einstein was probably one of them!" "Truth is stranger than fiction, but it is because fiction is obliged to stick to possibilities, while truth isn't." (Mark Twain).

Perhaps aliens are among us now, but utilize "cloaking devices" that allow their observation posts to remain hidden from our view until we have independently developed not only the Type 2 technology, but also the maturity, to move with responsibility among the stars in the as yet untresspassed sanctity of space. Cloaking technologies with which we are already familiar include radar absorbing materials, optical camouflage, and minimization of electromagnetic emissions (in the infrared portion of the spectrum) through cooling. Cloaking technologies with which we are only beginning to familiarize ourselves include the utilization of "Metamaterials," artificial substances engineered to have properties that may not be found in nature. These have been theorized to allow EM radiation to pass right through cloaked objects.

Perhaps the natural inquisitiveness of extraterrestrials has been tempered by their appreciation of simple math and sobering terrestrial statistics. In the United States, for example, over a span of 40 years, the annual budget for The National Aeronautical and Space Administration (NASA) has been just under $10 billion (1958–2011), while the budget for the Department of Defense (called "The War Department" until 1947) in just one of those years was $680 billion (2010), or 54% of all federal spending, and the budget for the Department of Homeland Security was $43 billion. (2011). Perhaps extraterrestrials have noted with alarm that the "World Nuclear Club" spends $1 trillion each year to maintain its arsenals, in contrast to the annual U.S. Budget for the International Space Station, which is a paltry $2.1 billion.

Perhaps we have a flawed anthropomorphic assumption about the attitudes of other intelligent species. Perhaps, quite simply, a self-imposed "radio silence" is in effect because they just want to be left alone. Perhaps masters of the universe (Type 3 civilizations) have overcome the ego-centric desire to affirm their prominence in the profane, self-destructive, self-important, and self-aggrandizing ways with which we are all-too familiar. Perhaps as they have become increasingly self-actualized and have honed their capacity to reach their potential, they have effectively extinguished the self-defeating need to draw attention to themselves, especially at the expense of others. Perhaps their unconscious shyness is a highly evolved defense mechanism.

Perhaps their reticence has been carefully cultivated through genetic selection as a self-deprecating personality trait. Perhaps they have achieved a "star power" that transcends the craving for media attention, admiration, adulation, and adoration.

Perhaps their silence is a galactic, self-effacing understatement. Perhaps their P.I.N. is such a jealously guarded secret that they view extra-terrestrial knowledge of their existence as the ultimate form of identity theft. Perhaps they have finally learned how to control the invasive harassment by the paparazzi and the exploitation upon which our supermarket tabloids, not to mention the talking heads on network news, voraciously feed. Perhaps they relish their anonymity and cherish their privacy. Perhaps to hide from prying eyes, they have developed the technological equivalent of the dark glasses worn by our own cultural icons to disguise their identities.

Perhaps alien geneticists have manipulated the genome of their species in order to temper the fires attendant to their transition from Type 0 to Type 1, 2, or 3 cultures. But, in the process, perhaps their zeal to "go where no-one has gone before" has been selectively bred out of their chromosomes, as well. Perhaps they are more comfortable just staying home "for the evening," hunkered down in overstuffed easy chairs with good books to enjoy. Perhaps they have discovered that greener pastures lie on their own side of the fence, and they have finally found the elusive inner peace that had been right in front of their noses all along. Perhaps their tranquility has come at the expense of the primal sense of wanderlust with which we are familiar. Perhaps the excitement that gets our juices flowing and pushes the boundaries of our experience has been suppressed or even extinguished in alien species. Perhaps when they "MapQuest" or "Google" their travel itineraries, they delete without interest earthly attractions that garner our own attention, like the world's largest ball of twine (measuring 41.5 feet in diameter) in Branson, Missouri.

That scenario notwithstanding, there is always the possibility that aliens don't need to pack their bags, gas up the family mini-van, and experience the thrill of the wind in their faces on the open interstellar or intergalactic road. Perhaps they travel at the speed of thought, rather than at the speed of light. (See the movies: "Total Recall" and "K-Pax"). Perhaps they dismiss the temporal and spatial limitations with which we are familiar with a cursory wave of the hand that initiates energy bursts deep within the cerebral cortical grey matter of their highly developed brains. As omniscient Q told Captain Picard: "The universe has been my backyard." ("Star-Trek: The Next Generation." "Deja Q"). In another episode, he exulted: "We are going to have fun! I'll take you to places no human could ever hope to see." ("Opid").

Perhaps, with the evolution of intelligent life, electromagnetic waves are no longer generated because alien communication technologies have become more sophisticated than our crude instruments that emit radiation (at a range between 3 kilohertz and 300 gigahertz, and corresponding wavelengths from 1 millimeter to 100 kilometers). Perhaps William W. Phelps was right, when he declared: "No man has found pure space, nor seen the outside curtains where nothing has a place," even though "the works of God continue, and worlds and lives abound" across the vast reaches of the universe. ("If You Could Hie to Kolob").

Perhaps Type 3 civilizations move about freely in a space-time continuum with which we are unfamiliar. Perhaps they are just as comfortable navigating tesseracts, (theorized 4-dimensional hypercubes), as we are the three spatially dimensional boundaries of up-down, front-back, and side-to-side. (See the movie: "Interstellar"). As "one among them that was like unto God" said, before the earth was formed: "We will go down, for there is space there," thus making a clear distinction between their limitless natural habitation and our confined world of every day that is defined by one temporal and three spatial dimensions. (Abraham 3:24).

Perhaps we are not only looking in the wrong places, but we are also looking at the wrong time, as well. Perhaps, for them, its arrow moves not just in one (forward) direction, but in two (forward and backward) directions. If aliens have learned to manipulate time as well as space, they may have already established lively communication with our past or our future, rather than with our present. Perhaps as they have fine-tuned the orientation of their messages, they have been intentionally programmed to reach us at more opportune times when we have been, or will be, better prepared or equipped to receive them. (See: the movie: "Interstellar").

The concept of "ancient aliens" popularized by The History Channel and books by Erich von Daniken ("Chariots of The Gods," "Twilight of The Gods," and "Signs of The Gods") suggests that within historical texts, archaeological data, myths, and legends, there is evidence of past human-extraterrestrial contact. Millions believe, or would like to believe, that the monolith found on the moon (see the movie: "2001: A Space Odyssey") was created millions of years ago by an alien race known as "The Firstborn," whose intention was to assist in the evolution of the human race. It may be that in the year 2513, a monolith will yet be found in Olduvai Gorge, Africa, buried in ancient rock. If so, that would be the first hard evidence of humankind's prehistoric evolutionary predecessors. (See: "Marvel Comics").

Should there prove to be monoliths in the real world, a face-to-face encounter with our alien counterparts may already be in the works. In anticipation of such a discovery, perhaps we should now be making a determined effort to scatter invitations throughout the galaxy, announcing to alien races that we have proposed an interstellar orientation meeting at a specific point in normal space and time, that lies in our future. If a Type 2 or a Type 3 alien civilization has mastered time-travel, it should be a simple thing for them to make a dramatic entrance at just the appropriate moment, no matter when the summons may have been received. Our contemporary efforts could then be better directed toward finalizing preparations to receive our invited guests at the aforementioned venue, rather than being engaged in spinning our wheels without gaining any traction by searching for random R.S.V.P.s from aliens who might not wish to be remembered as interstellar party-crashers.

Steven Hawking observed: "The quantum theory of gravity has opened up a new possibility, in which there is no boundary to space-time and no need to specify behavior at the boundary. There are no singularities at which the laws of science break down and no edge of space-time at which one has to appeal to some new law to set new boundary conditions for space-time. One could say: 'The boundary condition of the universe is that it has no boundary.'" ("A Brief History of Time: From the Big Bang to Black Holes," p. 136). From our perspective in space-time, aliens from a distant future might even now be getting ready for the festivities.

Or, perhaps aliens communicate at energy levels like those described by String Theory, that are mathematically complex and observationally obtuse. For example, the "Everett Many-Worlds Interpretation" of quantum mechanics, proposed in 1956, states that all the possibilities described by quantum theory simultaneously occur in a multiverse composed of independent parallel universes that are forever hidden from our view by the laws of physics.

Even if our timing is right, and there is a surfeit of alien Type 1, 2, and 3 civilizations, perhaps we are not looking in the right places, and they have been trying in vain to communicate all along, but have been doing so within the elusive dark matter that has recently been postulated to fill 73% of what has heretofore been described as "empty space."

Perhaps since the moment of creation, there have been points in space-time that are "without form, and void, and (there continues to be) darkness (here and there, then and now) upon the face of the deep." (Genesis 1:2). Perhaps in these places "worlds and lives abound (while) improvement and progression have one eternal round." Perhaps in the far reaches of the universe, "there is no end to (dark) matter, there is no end to space, there is no end to spirit, (and) there is no end to (alien) race." (William W. Phelps, "If You Could Hie to Kolob").

Perhaps our efforts to detect signs of extra-terrestrial intelligence have been ignorantly adjusted to be attuned to the wrong scale. For example, if environmentally-responsible and economically-conscious aliens have chosen to scatter sophisticated and recyclable non-biological "nano-probes" throughout the Milky Way, thereby avoiding the label of galactic litterbugs, and dodging the need for EPA equivalent Super-Fund cleanup, we may not have detected them because our primitive sensors haven't been upgraded to High Definition, or because we haven't yet invented the appropriately sensitive "Smart Card" to be inserted into our instruments. Perhaps we have been looking on a terrestrial order of magnitude for the unique signatures of alien life, while our efforts would have been better served by scanning the celestial section of cosmically calibrated classified ads for their calling cards.

What if evidence of alien life, or even evidence of its attempts at communication, is represented by terrestrial patterns of complex biological information vigorously interacting on subtle sub-cellular levels? After all, it's only been 64 earth-years (1953 – 2017) since Watson and Crick unraveled the mystery of D.N.A., or more accurately, raveled it up into a double helix. In order to reduce its footprint on the environment, alien life long ago may have become atomic or even sub-atomic, and we're simply not noticing its influence because it's flying well beneath our crude radar. Perhaps as we continue to investigate the human genome, we will find embedded within its vast matrix of TACG (thymine, adenine, cytosine, and guanine) the blueprint of a galactic family history. As the dog Frank in the movie "Men in Black" observed: "You humans are always looking for the spectacular. Look for something very small, like a jewel."

Carl Sagan has suggested that our natural senses may allow us to look at only one of "an infinite hierarchy of universes, so that an elementary particle, such as an electron, in our universe, would, if penetrated, reveal itself to be an entire closed universe. Within it, organized into the local equivalent of galaxies and smaller structures, there may be an immense number of other, much tinier elementary particles, which are themselves universes at the next level, and so on forever, an infinite downward regression of endless universes within universes. And upward as well. Our familiar universe of galaxies and stars, planets and people, would be a single elementary particle in the next universe up, the first step of another infinite progression."

"This is the only idea I know," he said, "that surpasses the endless number of infinitely old cycling universes in Hindu cosmology. What would those other universes be like? Would they be built on different laws of physics? Would they have stars and galaxies, and worlds, or something quite different? Might they be compatible with some unimaginably different form of life? To enter them, poised at the edge of forever, we would jump off" into a reality that could be more revealing than any we had ever before experienced. ("Cosmos," p. 262-267).

If we were to look more carefully, we might discover that alien cartographers have already provided us with the gift of a hidden star map intended to nudge us through a gate that leads to the heavens. (See See Genesis 28:17, and the movie: "Stargate SG1"). Perhaps "we can hear their message even now, as our heads buzz with a hum that won't go away." Perhaps "our stairway lies on the whispering wind," and we will ascend on a double helix into a new Aquarian Age. (Led Zeppelin, "Stairway to Heaven"). Perhaps there is "a secret something" that whispers, "You're a stranger here." Perhaps our own ancestors have "wandered from a more exalted sphere" and have imprinted incontrovertible evidence of their epic journey within the chemistry of life itself. (Eliza R. Snow, "O My Father").

If so, then perhaps alien intelligence is more impressive than we could have ever imagined, because it has already subtly communicated with us by planting the seeds of evolution into our DNA, thereby leaving an indelible and enduring stamp. Perhaps the protein-rich primordial broth agitated by the volcanic and seismic contractions and contortions of our early earth was really a bubbling alphabet soup created by intelligent design to spell out innovation, progress, strategy, and success. Perhaps the evidence has been right before our noses all along. Perhaps a superior intelligence had something to do with the creative process of our growth and development, but worked through genetics to provide the push we needed to achieve greatness. (The Discovery Institute defines "intelligent design" as ""certain features of the universe and of living things that are best explained by an intelligent cause, and not an undirected process such as natural selection.") Think of it. The immensely popular cookbook "The Joy of Cooking" could not have been created without an author. Its existence presupposes a chéf in the kitchen. The galactic equivalent of a perfect soufflé (on its page 137) may be just the hard evidence of extra-terrestrial intelligence that we have been looking for all along.

Along similar lines, perhaps interstellar space has been infused with a culture medium brewed by extra-terrestrial biologists. We may just now be beginning to discern its presence as quorum sensing, the intuitive decision-making process used by decentralized groups (that could be either millimeters or light years apart) to coordinate behavior. Pervasive and complex chemical communication could be the indelible signature of an alien influence not only on human behavior, but also on that of all other terrestrial carbon-based life forms (mammals, fish, birds, and insects, to name a few). The biotechnology of quorum sensing could be the lifeblood of all the species on earth. Instinctive as well as sentient behavior could trace their common origins to a cosmic point of singularity, the equivalent of an intergalactic exclamation point. Quantum mechanics could be nothing more than the evidence of our rudimentary efforts to explain this phenomenon.

Perhaps if we could somehow unravel the mysteries surrounding the complex matrix of life teeming in air, on land, and within the deepest oceans, there would lie before us, like the pages in an open book, the tangible evidence of a continuity of existence that has no temporal or spatial boundary. "May the Force be with you," is an expression with which we are familiar, even though its origins are popularly traceable to imaginary extraterrestrials. (See the movie: "Star Wars"). Maybe, if we tempered our appetite for the wholesale destruction of entire species and ecosystems, (think of the parallels between homo sapiens' behavior and that of the Empire, that utilized a Death Star to annihilate entire worlds), we would notice a majestic clockwork at work, and sense its celestial calibration. Perhaps we would then discern the quiet ticking away of the precious minutes of a day that is waning, and proactively intervene to avoid the gathering darkness that is looming on the eastern horizon. Perhaps we could then discipline ourselves to recognize a harmonic pulse, to better feel the surge of a spiritual essence rhythmically beating throughout nature, in perfect cadence across the cosmos, and we would be better prepared to more fully participate in and more positively influence the circle of life that is grandly defined and expansively circumscribed by nothing short of the universe itself. If only the Force could be with us, as it might be with extra-terrestrial Type 3 and 4 civilizations. As the Jedi Knight Obi-Wan Kenobi explained to Luke Skywalker, the Force is "an energy field created by all living things. It surrounds us, penetrates us, and binds the galaxy together." (See the movie: "Star Wars" episode 4).

It could be that evidence of alien life has been around us all the while, but we have been too preoccupied to notice. Perhaps we have not been able to distinguish the forest for the trees. Perhaps we need to stand back and take a collective deep breath in order to see more clearly that "there is no end to virtue; there is no end to might; there is no end to wisdom, (and) there is no end to light. There is no end to union; there is no end to youth; there is no end to priesthood; (and) there is no end to truth. There is no end to glory; there is no end to love, (and in fact) there is no end to being" itself in the limitless expanse of the universe. (William W. Phelps, "If You Could Hie to Kolob").

Perhaps the neurochemical reactions that lie at the foundation of the ideas that pop into our heads are the hard evidence we seek of alien life, since these thoughts often seem to have lives of their own that outlive their so-called "creators." Perhaps our déjà vu moments are electromagnetic anomalies, the mirrored reflections of forces that lie just beyond our comprehension, but are chronologically correct. Maybe this is why inspiration comes, from time to time, as a whisper from the dust "with clarity and freshness, uncolored and untranslated, (speaking) from within (ourselves) in a language original but inarticulate, heard only with the soul." (Hugh B. Brown).

Perhaps the elusive "codex" of Type 3 civilizations is represented by the Periodic Table, the tabular display of the building blocks of life composed of the 118 naturally occurring chemical elements organized on the basis of their properties. In fact, when we look at the "molecules that make up our bodies," that can be mapped out by utilizing the Periodic Table, "we find that they are traceable to the crucibles that were once the centers of high-mass stars that exploded into the galaxy, seeding pristine gas clouds with the chemistry of life. We are all connected to each other biologically, to the earth chemically, and to the rest of the universe atomically." (Neil deGrasse Tyson). Perhaps, unconsciously, we have been part of an interconnected cosmos all along, and the Force does bind the universe together, after all.

At the very least, when we ask: "Where is everybody?" our comprehension is catalyzed to embrace expanding self-awareness. When we ask: "What is the origin of the universe?" or "Why do its disparate elements behave as they do?" or "What is its ultimate destiny?" what we are really asking is "Where did we come from, and where are we going?" Perhaps it is the seething background radiation from the Big Bang itself that makes our blood hot to the touch. Perhaps the faint whisper of barely discernible communication from the stars lies not only within the constant cosmic background radiation temperature of precisely 2.725 degrees Kelvin, but also within the steady maintenance of our own body temperature at exactly 37.0 degrees Celsius. Or, it may be that extraterrestrials have evolved beyond life that is based on the biological functions that warm our blood, to embrace a reality that lies outside the boundaries of our narrow definitions. V'Ger (Voyager), reprogrammed by alien mechanical entities, may one day be sent back to earth to establish two-way communication in a universally understood binary language, in an effort to reconnect with its creator. (See the movie: "Star Trek, The Motion Picture").

Perhaps the genesis of our own terrestrial lives can be found elsewhere, and can be traced to an alien cosmic laboratory, where it was nurtured in a secret garden, later to be transplanted onto the fertile soil of a primordial earth that had been carefully cultivated by its creator to be pristine in its setting. If so, the hard evidence of extra-terrestrial life is independently confirmed each time we see our reflection in the mirror, or when we share with our friends the photographs of our children and grandchildren. It may be that the most enduring illustration of alien / terrestrial interaction lies in the visual image of storks dropping bundled-up newborn human babies down chimneys in Medieval Europe.

Where is everybody? There is within each of us the innate yearning to know that we are not alone in the universe. The Search for Extra-terrestrial Intelligence, (S.E.T.I.), is a worthy endeavor because it represents our determination to raise our sights to the potential benefits of an expanded view of life. Our efforts represent our desire to be up and moving on the pathway to personal re-discovery and self-actualization. Our blood is stirred when we recall the words of Captain James Tiberius Kirk, who declared: "Space is the final frontier," for he personified our yearning to imitate the daring and bravado of sea captains of old, who precariously ventured forth in fragile vessels on uncharted oceans to embark upon missions whose accomplishment burst the borders of human imagination. (See the movie: "Star Trek").

Without the evidence that that there are others in the far reaches of the universe who are navigating the ocean of life, and who are going through trials similar to ours, where will our own sanctuaries be when the wind blows and the rain beats down? To what sheltered harbor will we flee when tempests toss us about and our lives are in turmoil? When we are thrown to and fro as flotsam and jetsam, never coming to a knowledge of what is real, to what source will we look for the stability we so desperately seek, or for the answers to the questions that continually trouble our spirits? When we raise our sights to the possibility of an expanded view of life on an interstellar or even an intergalactic scale, and consider the remarkable potential it would have to catalyze our desire for cultural immortality, we are up and moving on the pathway to personal rediscovery in the larger arena of higher-dimensional awareness.

Nevertheless, we must concede the possibility that our desire to make contact with extra-terrestrials could be dangerous. As Q warned Captain Jean Luc Picard: "You judge yourselves against the pitiful adversaries you've encountered so far - the Romulans and the Klingons. They're nothing compared to what's waiting. Picard, you are about to move into areas of the galaxy containing wonders more incredible than you can possibly imagine, and terrors to freeze your soul." ("Star Trek: The Next Generation," "Q Who?"). Later in the same episode, after a particularly traumatic encounter with the recently discovered malevolent Borg, Q warned Picard: "If you can't take a little bloody nose, maybe you ought to go back home and crawl under your bed. It's not safe out here. It's wondrous, with treasures to satiate desires both subtle and gross. But it's not for the timid."

It is also possible that we are inadvertently sending the wrong messages, and alien life has chosen to ignore us because of its basic goodness and instinct for self-preservation, when measured against our primitive incivility. Our electromagnetic signatures could be perceived as threatening or just obscene. Think of all those episodes of "Miami Vice," the movies "Apocalypse Now" and "Full Metal Jacket," not to mention "War of The Worlds," "Aliens," "Predator," and Internet porn. These electronic emissions could be interpreted by our neighbors as caustic noise pollution on an interstellar magnitude of scale.

To counteract the potentially negative influence or misrepresentation of even a minority of our transmissions, on February 4, 2008, at 7:00 p.m. E.S.T., NASA beamed an interstellar dispatch, the Beatles song "Across the Universe," into deep space, sending a message of peace to any extraterrestrials who happen to be in the vicinity of Polaris, also called the North Star, in 2439. (Polaris is 431 light years distant from earth). The transmission coincided with the celebration of the 40th anniversary of the song's recording, the 45th anniversary of the Deep Space Network, an international antenna array that supports missions to explore the universe, and the 50th anniversary of NASA. "Words are flowing out like endless rain (and) slither wildly as they slip away across the universe. Pools of sorrow (and) waves of joy are drifting through my opened mind, possessing and caressing me. Images of broken light, which dance before me like a million eyes…call me on and on across the universe. Thoughts meander like a restless wind… They tumble blindly as they make their way across the universe. Sounds of laughter (and) shades of life are ringing through my opened ears, inciting and inviting me. Limitless undying love, which shines around me like a million suns…calls me on and on across the universe."

The lyrics, set to music, may represent our best effort to establish a positive connection with extra-terrestrial life. Such a bond would set in motion and catalyze an infinite expansion of the appreciation and understanding of our temporal and spatial realities that would, in turn, liberate us from fear, doubt, apprehension of danger, the turmoil of the world, and the vagaries of men. Casting off the self-limiting conditions that have heretofore blinded us to a larger view of life, we would expect to enjoy a more settled conviction of the truths waiting to be revealed within the parameters of an infinitely expanding reality. We would experience the liberating peace that follows obedience to newly discovered, but spiritually coherent, celestial guideposts and principles.

When we have our own personal epiphanies, and believe that we are not alone in the universe (whether or not we have found hard evidence to support our hopes and dreams), we will have begun a journey that will carry us beyond every conceivable event horizon to more intensive and reflective self-awareness, deeper and more abiding humility, and incomprehensively more profound and enduring faith. Our reinvigorated confidence will fortify our capacity for mind-expanding higher-level thinking and propel us on our way to Type 1 planetary stability, and beyond.

So, when our inquiry ("Where is everybody?") is rephrased and we ask: "Where did we come from? Why are we here? Where are we going?" the power of creation itself is unleashed in our behalf and we experience the exhilaration of a personally tailored "Big Bang" moment. It is as if we are present in the V.I.P. viewing section at the moment of creation itself. Our power "to become" is released from the oppressive bondage of ignorance and from self-defeating behaviors spawned by our own uncontrolled arrogance. The genesis of the universe falls into a comprehensible perspective and creates a context and continuity that allows our reality to expand to mind-boggling proportion.

Where is everybody? If we lift our eyes and strain to see beyond our limited horizons, we will intuitively know the answer to that question, and we just might find ourselves cast off into a stream of expanding self-awareness and carried along in quickening currents that take us on a fantastic journey to a far country. We might even come to the point where we begin to appreciate that "the universe is a machine for the making of gods." (Henri Bergson). As Q told Captain Picard: "Con permiso, Capitán. The hall is rented, the orchestra engaged. It's now time to see if you can dance." ("Q Who?"). Whether or not E.T. is calling, today we are one day closer than we were twenty-four hours ago to the discovery of what it really means to be "Dancing With The Stars."

"In my Father's
house are many mansions."
(John 14:2). Joseph Smith declared: It is
one of the first principles of my life, to allow
everyone the liberty of conscience. I am the
greatest advocate of the Constitution
of the United States there is on the
earth. In my feelings, I am always
ready to die for the protection
of the weak and oppressed
in their just rights."

Diversity

God is the Author of the greatest diversity on the planet earth. In fact, He created diversity when He divided the light from the darkness, the waters from the firmament, the heaven from the earth, the earth from the sea, the day from the night, and when he created all manner of living things, each to go forth and multiply after its own kind. His penultimate act of creative diversity was when "male and female created he them." (Genesis 1:27). He may have even created Mars and Venus specifically to be the habitation of men and women, respectively.

He expanded on His recurring theme of diversity when he established the twelve tribes of Israel, when He drew a distinction between Israel and gentile nations, when He established His covenant with Abraham, Isaac, and Jacob, when He separated the Levites from the other tribes of Israel, and when He highlighted the differences between Blood Israel, Land Israel, and Covenant Israel.

Paul addressed diversity when he wrote about spiritual gifts. "Now there are diversities of gifts," and "diversities of operations" is how he phrased it. (1 Corinthians 12:4 & 6, see also D&C 46:16). He also alluded to diversity when he wrote: "The body is not one member, but many." (1 Corinthians 12:14).

As a result of God's creative efforts, there are about 8.7 million species on our planet (give or take a million); about 6.5 million on land, and 2.2 million in the oceans. (See "The Census of Marine Life"). The scattering of people after the Tower of Babel fiasco created diversity within the human race. (See 1 Corinthians 12:28). Today, there are roughly 6,500 languages in the world, contributing to even more diversity. (However, about 2,000 of those have fewer than 1,000 speakers. The most popular language in the world is Mandarin Chinese, with about 1.25 billion speakers).

All we need to do is look around us to realize that God's creations are the expression of diversity. The scriptures affirm that He "is no respecter of persons." (Acts 10:34). "He denieth none that come unto him, black and white, bond and free, male and female; and he remembereth the heathen; and all are alike unto God, both Jew and Gentile." (2 Nephi 26:33). Interestingly, even with diversity, "all are alike unto God."

If we take a close look at the human genome, we will see that our closest living relatives (chimpanzees) share 96 percent of our DNA. The number of genetic differences between humans and chimps is ten times smaller than that between mice and rats. However, the 4% difference between human and chimpanzee DNA makes all the difference. Once again, even with genetic homogeneity, it is our diversity that trumps conformity. Our individual gene expression makes possible Beethoven's Moonlight Sonata, da Vinci's The Last Supper, and Einstein's Theory of Relativity, as well as stick figure finger paintings from the pre-school co-op down the street.

Just as our diversity builds strength, so do uniformity and conformity weaken our adaptive capacity as a species. Genetic diversity leads to resilient strains that resist disease. When you stop to think about it, this is one reason why converts are such an asset in the church. They introduce new material that expands the collective genome of the members and gives it elasticity. When these strains are nourished by rich gospel soil, the tender shoots of our testimonies are protected from the withering sun in the heat of day. The whole of the church is greater than the sum of its parts, because its pliancy that is the result of diversity allows it to continually transform itself into new and refreshing expressions.

Diversity is like a gyroscope that steadies our course as we negotiate rough seas. It also blesses us with an adaptive capacity to resist chafing irritation from both the acute infection of anxiety and the chronic inflammation of complacency. The classic signs of physical inflammation are redness, pain, heat, swelling, and loss of function. But we also have transmissible influences in each of our lives that combine to contribute to the loss of our individuality. Diversity gives us a competitive edge in the unforgiving arena of survival of the fittest. God may have been on to something when He created diversity, because it seems to strengthen our common identity as His children. E pluribus unim, or one out of many, comes to mind.

Even the family, the basic cohesive unit of solidarity, teaches us about diversity. In my own life, each of our seven children has a distinct personality. One, for example, could be characterized as more of a nurturer, another as an empathizer, and another who tends to be a motivator. One is definitely a peacemaker, another is a facilitator, another is a natural organizer, and another is a determined provider. All of them have each of these characteristics in differing proportions. One reason our family gets along so well is because we build consensus as we draw upon each other's strengths, which are qualities that we might not individually possess in abundance or recognize in ourselves. We have a common purpose, and naturally gravitate toward unity and harmony, even as we approach solutions to problems from slightly different perspectives. Our diversity gives our family a resilience it might not have otherwise enjoyed, it quickens our family gatherings, and guarantees that there will never be a dull moment when we are together, discussing great issues or trifling with trivialities.

The young men and women who have joined our family through marriage have learned to hang on for a wild ride. We have determined to put the fun back in dysfunctional. Our conversations are peppered with a variety of opinions that give spice to life. Our senses are stimulated with new ideas that light up our temporal and frontal lobes with creative expression. Our interests and activities reflect our zest for life.

Diversity has given our family the opportunity to learn to be tolerant, to be patient and long-suffering, to be forgiving, to be appreciative, and to express gratitude and show unconditional acceptance. Our familial diversity has exposed us to opportunities that might not have been ours under different circumstances. It has allowed us to venture into uncharted territory and to have experiences that are stimulating and refreshing. We have proven the Lord's assurance, first given to Joseph Smith: "All these things shall give thee experience, and shall be for thy good." (D&C 122:7).

Our diversity has evolved into a tool that has allowed us to stimulate our imaginations, and to brush with bold strokes as we create sweeping swaths of color across a very large canvas. Embracing our diversity has blessed us with refreshing, unconventional, and unorthodox experiences that have significantly contributed to our personal progress. Our diversity has allowed our home to become a learning laboratory. As the children have matured in years, that workshop has, by extension, expanded seven-fold. We've had a few minor explosions along the way, but so far, we haven't felt the need to build a panic room or burn down the house. But if we do, you can be sure that it is our diversity that will stimulate us to quickly improvise new ways to roast marshmallows, and then to build an even better home with exciting esthetic and technical innovations.

The diversity in our family is refreshingly apparent when we bear our testimonies, offer prayers, give service, teach lessons, express feelings, deal with challenges, approach our callings, spend our free time, exercise our agency, raise our children, apply our talents, embrace change, and prepare for the future.

We are grateful for our diversity. It has served a purpose by illuminating our common autobiographical thread that leads back to our Father in Heaven. We recognize that in His kingdom there are many mansions, with enough room in the household for Greeks and Romans, Jews and Gentiles, Nephites and Lamanites, the rich as well as the poor, and for those who might be black or white, and bond or free. There may even be room for hetero and homosexuals, believers and infidels, and saints and sinners.

Here's to diversity, "to those who are different, to those who didn't always get A's, to those who have ears twice the size of their peers, and noses that go on for days.

Here's to those who are different, the ones they call crazy or dumb; the ones who don't fit, with the guts and the grit, who dance to a different drum. Here's to those who are different, to those with a mischievous streak. For when they have grown, as history has shown, it's their differences that have made them unique." (Anonymous).

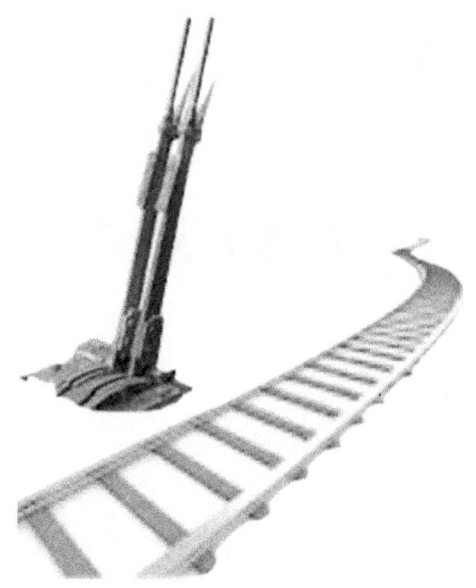

"Behold, this is the doctrine of Christ."
(2 Nephi 32:6).

Doctrinal Switch Points

Gordon B. Hinckley reminisced: "Many years ago I worked in the head office of one of our railroads. One day I received a telephone call from my counterpart in Newark, New Jersey, who said that a passenger train had arrived without its baggage car. The patrons were angry. We discovered that the train had been properly made up in Oakland, California, and properly delivered to St. Louis, from which station it was to be carried to its destination on the east coast. But in the St. Louis yards, a thoughtless switchman had moved a piece of steel just three inches. That piece of steel was a switch point, and the car that should have been in Newark, New Jersey, was in New Orleans, Louisiana, thirteen hundred miles away."

The switch points in our lives include events such as baptism, ordination to priesthood, the receipt of temple blessings, and the acceptance of church callings, as well as decisions relating to behavioral standards, education, mission, employment, marriage, and children.

The last chapters of Paul's first epistle to the Corinthians address four doctrinal switch points that illustrate how the Corinthians Saints had departed from the truth. First, was the relationship of husbands and wives with each other and with the Lord. As Paul wrote: "Neither is the a man without the woman, neither the woman without the man, in the Lord." (1 Corinthians 11:11). Marion G. Romney taught that a couple "should be one in harmony, respect, and mutual consideration. Neither one should plan or follow an independent course of action. They should consult, pray, and decide together. Husbands and wives are equal partners."

Secondly, Paul addressed the administration of the Sacrament. "But let a man examine himself," he counseled, "and so let him eat of that bread, and drink of that cup. For he that eateth and drinketh unworthily, eateth and drinketh damnation to himself, not discerning the Lord's body." (1 Corinthians 11:28-29, see 1 Corinthians 11:20, footnote 20 b, which provides the Joseph Smith Translation of this verse: "Is it not to eat the Lord's supper?")

"With so very much at stake, (the Sacrament) should be taken more seriously than it sometimes is. It should be a powerful, reverent, reflective moment. It should encourage spiritual feelings and impressions. As such it should not be rushed. It is not something to 'get over' so that the real purpose of a sacrament meeting can be pursued. This is the real purpose of the meeting." (Jeffrey R. Holland, C.R., 10/1995).

Then, Paul addressed the importance of all spiritual gifts. "But the manifestation of the Spirit is given to every man to profit withal. For to one is given by the Spirit the word of wisdom; to another the word of knowledge by the same Spirit; to another faith by the same Spirit; to another the gifts of healing by the same Spirit; to another the working of miracles; to another prophecy; to another discerning of spirits; to another divers kinds of tongues; to another the interpretation of tongues: But all these worketh that one and the selfsame Spirit, dividing to every man severally as he will." (1 Corinthinans 12:7-11).

"For all have not every gift given unto them; for there are many gifts, and to every man is given a gift by the Spirit of God." (D&C 46:11). "And all these gifts come from God, for the benefit of the children of God." (D&C 46:26). "But covet earnestly the best gifts." (1 Corinthians 12:31). "Seek ye earnestly the best gifts, always remembering for what they are given." (D&C 46:8). "For verily I say unto you, they are given for the benefit of those who love me and keep all my commandments, and him that seeketh so to do; that all may be benefited that seek or that ask of me, that ask and not for a sign that they may consume it upon their lusts." (D&C 46:9).

To illustrate spiritual gifts, Paul compared the members of the church to different parts of the body. (See 1 Corinthians 12:12-25). He did this to show that each member is important to the other members and to the church as a whole.

Paul wrote extensively about what he considered to be the greatest of all spiritual gifts. "Though I speak with the tongues of men and of angels, and have not charity, I am become as sounding brass, or a tinkling cymbal. And though I have the gift of prophecy, and understand all mysteries, and all knowledge; and though I have all faith, so that I could remove mountains, and have not charity, I am nothing. And though I bestow all my goods to feed the poor, and though I give my body to be burned, and have not charity, it profiteth me nothing. Charity suffereth long, and is kind; charity envieth not; charity vaunteth not itself, is not puffed up, Doth not behave itself unseemly, seeketh not her own, is not easily provoked, thinketh no evil; Rejoiceth not in iniquity, but rejoiceth in the truth; Beareth all things, believeth all things, hopeth all things, endureth all things. Charity never faileth: but whether there be prophecies, they shall fail; whether there be tongues, they shall cease; whether there be knowledge, it shall vanish away. For we know in part, and we prophesy in part. But when that which is perfect is come, then that which is in part shall be done away. When I was a child, I spake as a child, I understood as a child, I thought as a child: but when I became a man, I put away childish things. For now we see through a glass, darkly; but then face to face: now I know in part; but then shall I know even as also I am known. And now abideth faith, hope, charity, these three; but the greatest of these is charity." (1 Corinthians 13:1-13).

Then, Paul expressed his witness to the Corinthian Saints of the reality of the resurrection and the degrees of glory. He did this because many of the Corinthians had begun to dispute the reality of the resurrection. "Now if Christ be preached that he rose from the dead, how say some among you that there is no resurrection of the dead?" (1 Corinthians 15:12).

Paul cited eye-witnesses of the resurrection, including his own personal testimony. "He was seen of Cephas, then of the twelve: After that, he was seen of above five hundred brethren at once; of whom the greater part remain unto this present, but some are fallen asleep. After that, he was seen of James; then of all the apostles. And last of all he was seen of me also." (1 Corinthians 15:5-8).

We need to understand the larger picture, that of Paul's desire to be a witness the resurrection, in order to understand 1 Corinthians 15:39. Standing alone, this verse doesn't make much sense. But when we realize that he used the doctrine of baptism for the dead to teach about the resurrection, it fits in with the context of his larger message. Baptism for the dead would be meaningless without the resurrection. "Else what shall they do which are baptized for the dead, if the dead rise not at all? Why are they then baptized for the dead?" The same thing applies to his teachings about the degrees of glory. They only make sense in the larger context of instruction about the resurrection.

"But some men will say, How are the dead raised up, and with what body do they come? ...All flesh is not the same flesh. ...There are also celestial bodies, and bodies terrestrial: but the glory of the celestial is one, and the glory of the terrestrial is another. There is one glory of the sun, and another glory of the moon, and another glory of the stars: for one star differeth from another star in glory. So also is the resurrection of the dead." (1 Corinthians 15:35-40).

In this larger context, Paul taught doctrine intended to lead us back to our Father in Heaven. We all have switch points that, if followed, will change the direction of our lives, and lead us unerringly, with our baggage cars, to our intended destination.

Discouragement
is not the result of
inadequacy, but rather
is the consequence of
a lack of courage.

Enduring To The End

Built into the fabric of the Plan of Salvation is the opportunity for every one of us to endure to the end. Agency gives us the choice to do it in righteousness or in unrighteousness. If we choose the latter, we also accept the inevitable negative consequences of sin, which makes enduring much more painful than it needs to be. On the other hand, if we choose to endure in righteousness, we will find that our capacity for purposeful action leading to happiness increases over time.

The physical and psychological benefits of righteous endurance can be compared to training on a pedal bike. When we begin the regimen, we take it in stages. Interval training motivates us to greater achievement. During the process, we learn to be consciously aware of our breathing, cadence, and gearing. As we fine-tune these variables, we better control our cardiovascular rhythms, even as we push the limits of our capacities.

We are in touch with our bodies, and pay attention to the basics. We train consistently, without overdoing it. We know that if we allow our muscles to tense up, we will squander precious energy. When we shift to a lower gear (an easier gear), our forward momentum falters, and we inevitably slow down, unless with pick up our cadence.

As we become more in touch with our bodies, we learn to pace ourselves, and to automatically adjust to variations in the terrain that we encounter. We stay hydrated and observe proper nutrition. When we encounter hilly terrain, our endorphins kick in, and we take a perverse pleasure in suffering, because a strange thing happens. We build mental toughness and feel the exhilaration of an expansion of our capacity for endurance. Heber J. Grant was fond of quoting Ralph Waldo Emerson, who said: "That which we persist in doing becomes easier for us to do; not that the nature of the thing is changed, but that our power to do is increased."

It's true that we miss 100% of the shots we don't take. But we also miss about 50% of the shots we do take. So we don't allow ourselves to become discouraged if at first we don't succeed. In a worst-case scenario, we can always be used as a bad example.

We avoid the temptation to become overzealous in our efforts. We remember the poor soul, of whom it was said: He worked out for years to reduce all his fat. His muscles were firm and his stomach was flat. He jogged day and night to keep himself trim, and still found time to play tennis and swim. He drank protein drinks, and ate health food galore; then lifted, and stair-climbed, and lifted some more. He told family and friends that it gave him a 'high.' They encouraged him on, as he waved them good-bye. 'If things work out,' he yelled back from afar, 'I'll be a great athlete; I'll be a big star!' But how could he miss that big truck up ahead? One thud, and his beautiful body lay dead. Then he saw something that filled him with fright. His spiritual body was one sorry sight! No more than a skeleton, covered with skin. He got up to heaven, but didn't get in! 'Another soul's mine!' Satan started to scream. 'Give man something nice, and he'll take the extreme!' OK, I'll admit it; I'll outright confess. For the fast way to hell, take the excess express." (Anonymous).

Even if we have refrained from overzealously exercising our minds or spirits, but we find ourselves past our prime, we can still endure to the end. When we are over the hill, we pick up speed. Sometimes we will need to adjust our expectations. If we do so, it's likely that we'll be very pleasantly surprised. We'll just gird up our loins and take fresh courage, because God will never forsake us. (See William W. Phelps, "Come, Come, Ye Saints").

Enduring to the end, every day of our lives, prepares us for "that special moment when we are figuratively tapped on our shoulder and offered a chance to do a very special thing, unique to us and fitted to our talents. What a tragedy if that moment finds us unprepared or unqualified for that which would have been our finest hour." (Winston Churchill).

"You cannot prove the genuineness of any
document to one who has decided not to accept.
it. When a man asks for proof, we can be pretty sure
that proof is the last thing in the world he really wants.
His request is thrown out as a challenge, and the chances
are that he has no intention of being shown up. After
all these years, the Bible itself is still not proven to
those who do not choose to accept it. So the
Book of Mormon as an 'unproven' book
finds itself in good company."
(Hugh Nibley).

Establishing
The Word

It is hard to say just how old the writings in the Bible are, but scholars generally believe that oral traditions were passed down over the millennia, until they were first written down by Moses. In fact, revelation given to Joseph Smith affirms that "the Lord spake unto Moses, saying: Behold, I reveal unto you concerning this heaven, and this earth; write the words which I speak." (Moses 2:1). This revelation goes on to reveal that "a book of remembrance was kept...in the language of Adam, for it was given unto as many as called upon God to write by the spirit of inspiration; and by them their children were taught to read and write, having a language which was pure and undefiled... This was the book of the generations of Adam." (Moses 6:5-6 & 8).

Pseudepigraphical works suggest that around 1,700 B.C., Pharaoh of the 13th Dynasty said: "My heart yearned to behold the most ancient books of Atum (Adam). Open them before me for diligent searching, that I may know God as He really is." (Hugh Nibley, "Genesis of the Written Word," in "Nibley on The Timely and Timeless," p. 104). Enoch continued in the pattern of the ancient patriarchs, and confirmed that Adam had kept "a book of remembrance." (Moses 6:46). Abraham, as well, kept "a record of the fathers, even the patriarchs (and) a knowledge of the beginning of the creation." He recorded that he would "endeavor to write some of these things upon (that) record, for the benefit of (his) posterity." (Abraham 1:31). Jacob indirectly confirmed that many in ancient Israel recorded their testimonies, when he wrote that "none of the prophets have written, nor prophesied, save they have spoken concerning...Christ." (Jacob 7:11).

In fact, the Semitic alphabet itself may have been created for the express purpose of recording holy writ. If so, when we read the scriptures, we are witnessing forms of the original symbols through which these messages were first conveyed by God. In this light, we are bound to approach the scriptures with a newfound reverence and respect. The bottom line is clear: The origin of the Bible was not uncertain or devoid of authority, but rather, it was given by inspiration from the very beginning, that God might show His children the way of salvation.

From the time of Ezra, after the Babylonian Captivity in 587 B.C., a compendium of authorized Hebrew literature was gathered together by the prophets. Latter-day

Saints have a special knowledge of at least one such anthology that was collectively called "the Plates of Brass." (1 Nephi 4:16). But Israel hardly embraced these writings. Jeremiah, for example, prophesied "against Israel, and against Judah," citing the contempt in which he was held by God's covenant people: "O Lord, ...I am in derision daily. Every one mocketh me. For since I spake, I cried out; I cried violence and spoil; because the word of the Lord was made a reproach unto me, and a derision, daily. Then I said, I will not make mention of him, nor speak any more in his name. But his word was in mine heart as a burning fire shut up in my bones, and I was weary with forbearing, and I could not stay." (Jeremiah 20:7-9).

He was in the good company of his righteous contemporary, Lehi, who was also mocked by the Jews "because of the things which he testified of them; for he truly testified of their wickedness and their abominations; and he testified that the things which he saw and heard, and also the things which he read in the book, manifested plainly of the coming of a Messiah, and also the redemption of the world. And when the Jews heard these things they were angry with him; yea, even as with the prophets of old, whom they had cast out, and stoned, and slain; and they also sought his life, that they might take it away." (1 Nephi 1:19-20).

Jeremiah and Lehi were only two of the many prophets who preserved, compiled, and arranged the Word in a variety of ways. Today, it is organized in the Pentateuch, the five books of Moses, and then as a compilation of historical books, and of writings such as Psalms, Proverbs, Job, and Esther. The organization of these books in the Old Testament is not chronological, but follows a pattern based on subject matter such as law, history, poetry, and prophecy. The Word was preserved on papyrus, clay tablets, and writing boards that when hinged together became a folding "book." Hence, Ezekiel wrote: "Take thee one stick, and write upon it, For Judah, and for the children of Israel his companions: then take another stick, and write upon it, For Joseph, the stick of Ephraim, and for all the house of Israel his companions. And join them one to another into one stick; and they shall become one in thine hand." (Ezekiel 37:16-17).

Leather was also used, as were plates of various metals. There is an interesting account of the opening of the tomb of Mycerinus, "in the third of the three great pyramids. The writer reports that all that was found in the tomb was a blue sarcophagus containing 'the decayed remains of a man, but no treasure, excepting some golden tablets inscribed with characters of a language which nobody could understand.' The tablets were used to pay the workmen. We leave the reader to speculate on what might have been written on those plates of gold which one of the mightiest of Pharaohs apparently regarded as the greatest treasure with which he could be buried." (Hugh Nibley, "Lehi in The Desert," p. 120).

How ever ancient religious texts may have been preserved, Israel considered them to be of great importance. Those attributed to Moses were safeguarded in the Ark of the Covenant, a sacred chest 45 inches long, 27 inches wide, and 27 inches high. "Take this book of the law, and put it in the side of the ark of the covenant of the Lord your God, that it may be there a witness," wrote Moses. (Deuteronomy 31:26). The story is told of a later scribe, who cautioned: "My son, be careful in thy work, for it is heavenly work, lest thou err in omitting or in adding one jot (the smallest letter in the Hebrew alphabet) and so cause the destruction of the whole world." (Geddes MacGregor, "The Bible in The Making," p. 48).

In the Last Days, many of the doctrines of the kingdom that had been thought to have been lost to history has been restored in a variety of ways by modern day prophets. The Book of Mormon is a good example. It was translated by Joseph Smith, in just six weeks, between April 7, 1829, and the first week of June, 1829. The translation was unlike that of any other text, because it was accomplished "through the mercy (and) power of God." (D&C 1:29). This is as specific an explanation as is found regarding just how Joseph Smith translated the plates. In later years, he tended to let the record speak for itself. It was appropriate that he do so, because when we understand that it is an inspired translation, we are drawn to the book itself, and without debate or distraction regarding specific words or phrases can put to the test the challenge left within its pages by Moroni: "And when ye shall receive these things, I would exhort you that ye would ask God, the Eternal Father, in the name of Christ, if these things are not true; and if ye shall ask with a sincere heart, with real intent, having faith in Christ, he will manifest the truth of it unto you, by the power of the Holy Ghost." (Moroni 10:4).

Jesus Christ Himself has testified that The Book of Mormon is true. His words are recorded in the Book of Doctrine & Covenants: "He translated the book, even that part which I have commanded him, and as your Lord and your God liveth it is true." (D&C 17:6, see D&C 19:26). It is appropriate that the Savior used an ancient Hebrew oath in this impressive witness. As Paul said, "because he could swear by no greater, he sware by himself." (Hebrews 6:13).

One of Joseph Smith's most daunting challenges relating to the translation of ancient records must have been to preserve the nuance and language of the original authors, while making the narrative understandable to the contemporary mind. His "inspired" translation of the Bible come to mind. When that sacred record was first recorded, it was in the form of "a book…in the language of Adam," or in the Adamic tongue. (Moses 6:5). Then came Hebrew, then Aramaic, then the Greek Septuagint, then Latin. The English version used by Joseph Smith traces its origins to the 1611 King James Version that was inspired by the 1526 Tyndale

Bible, that was, in turn, heavily influenced by the Wycliffe Bible, translated in the late 1300s.

In 250 B.C., Ptolemy of Egypt initiated the accumulation of all the books of the known world into a library, in Alexandria, Egypt. Five hundred and fifty years later, the Christian Roman emperor Theodosius The Great, in the "interests" of the church, destroyed around 700,000 of the volumes in that library. As we ponder this wanton act of spiritual terrorism, we remember that "writing was not devised by men as a tool to help them in their everyday affairs. Successful businessmen have been illiterates, and there is ample evidence that writing was adapted to commercial uses only after such uses were found for it. If you bring together all the written records of man's past, you will discover that the overwhelming mass of material is religious in nature, and that the primary purpose to which writing has been put through the ages has not been for business records and correspondence, in which writing is employed awkwardly and without enthusiasm, but for keeping a remembrance of God's dealings with men. The specific purpose of writing, as the Egyptians put it, was to record the divine words." (Hugh Nibley, "The World and The Prophets," p. 207). If we can take anything positive from the senseless destruction of religious records in Alexandria, it might be that at least we have thereby been given a greater opportunity to walk by faith.

The Septuagint has been mentioned above as an early attempt to compile and preserve holy writ. Its origins can be traced to the efforts of six elders of every tribe, 72 in all, who translated the scriptures into Greek in the third century B.C., reportedly in 72 days. Thus, it was called the Septuagint, or "The Version of the Seventy." It was these scriptures that were used by the first Christians following the mortal ministry of Christ. Written in the international language of Greece, it facilitated the teaching of the gospel throughout the then known world.

The Septuagint has provided us with a remarkable opportunity to confirm, by eternal witness, the authenticity of The Book of Mormon as an inspired record. 2 Nephi 12:16 is a translation from chapter 2, verse 16, of the book of Isaiah. It reads: "Yea, and the day of the Lord shall come upon all the cedars of Lebanon...<u>and upon all the ships of the sea</u>, and upon all the ships of Tarshish." (Underlining mine). This verse is significant, because the phrase "...And upon all the ships of the sea..." is found in The Book of Mormon, but not in the K.J.V. Book of Isaiah. It is, however, found in the ancient Greek, or Septuagint, version of Isaiah.

Joseph Smith did not know any Greek at the time he translated The Book of Mormon, and there is no record that the Septuagint was available for his comparative study at the Palmyra Public Library, in 1829. Until the discovery of the Dead Sea Scrolls, scholars searching for original copies of the books of the Old Testament were unable to find any older than the 9th century A.D.. Part of the reason for this is that as copies were made, the originals were typically burned or buried. But the Dead Sea Scrolls, it was discovered, contain all of Isaiah, including the aforementioned original translation of Isaiah 2:16. The only logical conclusion is that the Book of Mormon rendering of this verse from Isaiah is a direct quotation from a text at least as ancient as the Septuagint. In fact, this Book of Mormon quotation from 2 Nephi 12 may be attributed to the Plates of Brass, which is a text that is hundreds of years older than the Septuagint. It is only one of innumerable small coincidences that confirm the historicity and divine authenticity of the Book of Mormon record.

It is the testimony of members of The Church of Jesus Christ of Latter-day Saints that "in the beginning was the Word...and the Word was God...And the Word was made flesh, and dwelt among us." (John 1:1, 14). Joseph Smith was counseled: "These words are not of men nor of man, but of me; wherefore, you shall testify they are of me and not of man; For it is my voice which speaketh them unto you; for they are given by my Spirit unto you; and by my power you can read them one to another; and save it were by my power, you could not have them. Wherefore, you can testify that you have heard my voice, and know my words." (D&C 18:34-36).

The Savior rebuked the Sadducees: "Ye do err, not knowing the scriptures." (Matthew 22:29). In the Last Days, even with the Reformation and the subsequent Age of Enlightenment, there can be no revelation when there is no student. Of the rulers who possessed the Word in His day, but did not keep the commandments, the Lord said: "The scribes and the Pharisees sit in Moses' seat: all, therefore, whatsoever they bid you observe, that observe and do; but do not ye after their works: for they say, and do not." (Matthew 23:2-3).

Rather, be like the travelers on the road to Emmaus, who declared: "Did not our heart burn within us...while he opened to us the scriptures?" (Luke 24:32). Today, we have an opportunity to know the scriptures in ways that are unparalleled in the history of the world. In 1974, L. Tom Perry was sustained as a member of the Council of Twelve Apostles, and he took his place next to Bruce R. McConkie. In their weekly meetings in the temple, one or another of the Apostles would often cite the scriptures, and when assistance was needed to complete a verse, the Apostle speaking would often ask: 'Bruce, can you help me?' Invariably, Elder McConkie would complete, from memory, not only the verse in question, but he would also go on for several more verses. Elder Perry reports that in the eleven years that he sat next to Elder McConkie, he never had the occasion to respond to a request, 'Tom, would you please help me with this verse?'

We may never be scriptorians like Bruce R. McConkie, but another Apostle, John Widtsoe, promised that if we would develop the habit of reading scriptures 15 minutes a day, that in 5 years we would know more about the gospel than any 100 persons selected at random in the church. As Paul urged: "Now it is high time to awake out of sleep: for now is our salvation nearer than when we believed." (Romans 13:11).

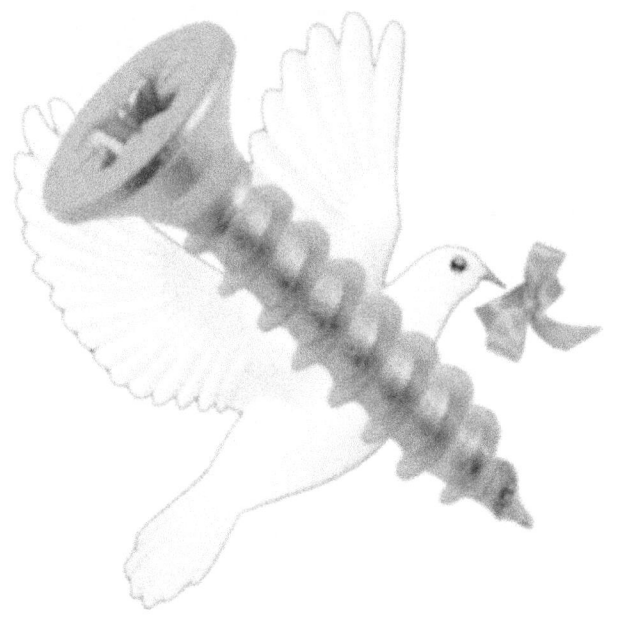

"Faith,
if it hath
not works, is
dead, being alone."
(James 2:17).

Faith
Is Like A Screw

Faith is like a screw that is slowly being turned in a solid piece of wood. Initially, a little tap from above may be required before the screw can stand independently and upright, balanced somewhat precariously on the surface of the wood, ready and eager to fulfill its purpose. If the wood is particularly hard, a little basic ground work might be necessary, such as pre-drilling a small guide hole. Then, the screw may be oriented in the proper direction and gently pressed into place, by the screwdriver that is positioned above its head. The little screw, if it were self-aware, would know, at this point, what was shortly coming. If it could, it would probably brace itself for the gentle pressure coming from above, as the weight of the screwdriver, and more particularly the driving force behind it, was brought to bear on its head.

Depending upon the resistance encountered as the screw twisted and turned deeper and deeper into the wood, the Master Craftsman who is in charge of all woodworking projects might direct that the screw be soaped, to make it easier to turn with less friction. Or, He might want to have his apprentice drill a larger guide hole that would more easily accommodate the screw. On the other hand, He might want to leave everything well-enough alone, in order to allow the expenditure of energy required to set the screw in place to be commensurate with the feelings of satisfaction and reward that could only come upon the successful completion of a project that had been well-executed.

Sometimes, there are only 4 or 5 threads on the shaft of a screw; but more frequently there are many more that are designed to address the requirements of the blueprint defining the task at hand. At times, turning a screw with many threads might seem tedious, and an impending sense of fatigue might threaten to overpower the muscles of the hand or wrist. But perseverance on the part of the apprentice will insure that the joints will be snug. In any woodworking project, weakness when initially setting the screws may result in loud squeaks and instability later on, after hard use has taken its toll. Projects that have been shoddily thrown together, will not stand the test of time.

But properly performed, with the correct expenditure of energy, the anchor will become more sure with each turn. Even after only a few twists, although the screw has not yet been driven all the way in, it will not come out or wiggle loose without the application of an equal and opposite force, or an even greater force than that which had been required to set it, in the first place.

As the screw is driven further and further into the wood, its reason for being will become self-evident. Something as simply designed as a wood screw can serve a multitude of purposes. It can hold a coat hook in place so that the garments of the priesthood may be appropriately cared for, or it can orient in its proper position a treasured family photo that has been hung in a place of honor on the wall. By bonding two separate and distinct pieces of wood together, a well-placed screw can transform them into something quite different from the raw materials, that is simply beautiful, such as an altar. It can secure the rod from which a veil may be hung. It can hold together a truss that has been designed to bear the weight of the statue of the angel Moroni.

When that little screw has been driven all the way in, so that its head is flush with the surface of the material that is being stabilized, it might blend in so well that it is hardly noticeable. Sometimes, the best screw does its job without ever being recognized. Little feet running toward the Bishop across the floor at church will not trip on it, and adult eyes might look right past it. Most screws are very inexpensive, but they provide solid anchors, and properly driven in place may remain there for years, with the need for only periodic preventive maintenance. An occasional turn with a screwdriver may be all that is necessary to confirm that everything remains as it should be.

With the anchor sure, just as is the case of well-driven faith, the screw, together with the energy that had been required to set it in place will not be wasted; is not dead. It serves an on-going, sustaining purpose, but the effort that had been expended to accomplish the initial task at hand will no longer be required. That kinetic energy of motion is transformed to the potential energy of position, and can be directed elsewhere. But its end product remains, just as the result of the expenditure of faith remain as a testament to good works.

One might legitimately ask what would have happened had the screw been left in its original packaging? What if it had never been utilized in its foreordained manner? We can look to the scripture that asks those who fear man more than they fear God, if it is true that faith without works is dead, being alone. The question begs our answer, and then demands that we head straight to God's hardware store to pick up a few essentials.

I have, in my toolbox at home, several plastic boxes with enough compartments to maintain an impressive collection of wood screws. If I find myself engaged in a project and I need a specific screw to accomplish a task, I know exactly where to go to select the right one. Rarely do I find myself at a standstill because I don't have the right fasteners, or the proper tools, for the job.

I want my faith to be like the screw I have described. As I build a foundation, I want it to be sturdy. I want to be worthy of my hire. I am reminded that we "are little children and...cannot bear all things now; (and that we) must grow in grace and in the knowledge of the truth." (D&C 50:40). "For the word of the Lord is truth, and whatsoever is truth is light, and whatsoever is light is Spirit, even the Spirit of Jesus Christ. And the Spirit giveth light to every man that cometh into the world; and the Spirit enlighteneth every man through the world, that hearkeneth to the voice of the Spirit." (D&C 84:45-46).

Initially, my budding faith is to believe what I do not see, and the reward of my faith is to see what I believe; to see what is real. I realize now that some things have to be believed to be seen. Even so, belief is only a mental assent to the truth or actuality of something, without the moral element of responsibility that we call faith. Someone once said that duct tape is like the Force. It has a light side and a dark side, and it holds the universe together. That may not be entirely accurate. It may be that faith is the screw that holds it all together.

The Hebrews have done
more to civilize men than any
other nation. If I were an atheist, and
believed blind eternal fate, I should still
believe that fate had ordained the Jews to
be the most essential instrument
for civilizing the nations.
(John Adams).

Fate

"Wherefore, men are free according to the flesh; and all things are given them which are expedient unto man. And they are free to choose liberty and eternal life, through the great Mediator of all men, or to choose captivity and death, according to the captivity and power of the devil." (2 Nephi 2:27).

There was a merchant in Baghdad who sent his servant to the marketplace to buy provisions. A short while later, the servant came back to the home of his master, his face white and his body trembling. He cried out: Master, just now the marketplace I was jostled by a man in the crowd, and when I turned I saw that it was Death. He confronted me with a menacing look, and made a threatening gesture. Now, lend me your horse, and I will ride away from this city and thereby avoid my fate. I will go to Samarra, and there Death will not find me.

The merchant readily lent him his horse, and the servant leaped on its back, dug his spurs into its flanks, and as fast as the horse could gallop, it carried him away to Samarra.

In the meantime, the merchant went down to the marketplace, and he sought out Death, who was standing in the crowd. He confronted him, and demanded to know why he had make a threating gesture to his servant, when he had seen him earlier in the morning. That was not a threatening gesture, said Death. It was only a startled look of surprise. I was astonished to see him in Baghdad, for I have an appointment with him tonight, in Samarra. (Adapted from W. Somerset Maugham, "The Appointment in Samarra").

"A free man thinks of death least of all things," Spinoza famously wrote, "and his wisdom is a meditation not of death but of life." ("Ethics" 4, Proposition 67).

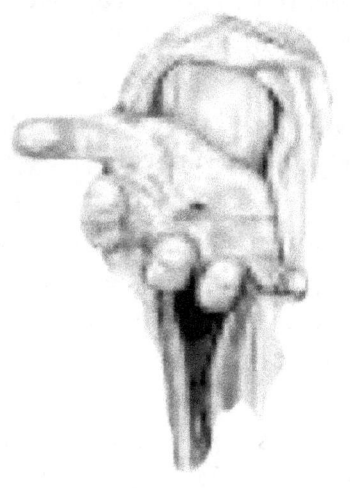

"Detritus is the
word, the awful
accumulation of wrong
decisions, improper turns.
Scrape away the excrescences
of history, the sins we've committed,
and maybe you get down to the bedrock
of human society, where diamonds hide."
(James Michener, "The Covenant").

Father, Forgive Them

On the Cross at Calvary, the Savior looked down upon the Roman soldiers who had crucified Him, and uttered these ten remarkable words: "Father, forgive them, for they know not what they do." (Luke 23:34). Incredibly, it was with the same spirit of forgiveness that He regarded His brethren the Jews, who had so recently condemned Him.

Their voices must have stung His ears, however, when He had heard them cry out: "His blood be on us, and on our children. (Matthew 27:5). These were the descendants of those of whom the Lord had spoken through the mouth of His prophet Isaiah: "Fear not, for... with everlasting kindness will I have mercy on thee, saith the Lord thy Redeemer." (3 Nephi 22:4 & 8). Through Isaiah, the Lord of all the earth had promised His covenant people: "No weapon that is formed against thee shall prosper; and every tongue that shall revile against thee in judgment thou shalt condemn. This is the heritage of the servants of the Lord, and their righteousness is of me, saith the Lord." (Isaiah 54:17).

These promises notwithstanding, in the courtyard of Pilate, the Jews had betrayed the Bridegroom to whom they had been betrothed. If there were ever justification for the Savior to harbor bitter feelings toward those who had wronged Him, it would be as He staggered under the weight of His cross as He made His way along the Via Dolorosa, the "Way of Grief, Sorrow, and Suffering," or simply the "Painful Way," knowing that every step would bring Him closer to Calvary, and knowing too, that the anguish that rolled over Him in waves was the result of His betrayal by His brethren.

Long before the Savior's comforting words had illuminated the mind of His prophet Isaiah, and even before the foundation of the world, He had begun to consistently accumulate reserves in His spiritual bank account to be used against the day when He would need them the most. He knew from the beginning, even before The Great and Eternal Plan of Deliverance from Death (2 Nephi 11:5) had been explained to the Father's children, that His was to be an infinite and eternal Atonement for every sin that would ever be committed by His brothers and sisters. Thus, when the critical hour came in the Garden of Gethsemane, followed by the mockery of his trial before Pilate and His crucifixion on Calvary, He was able to plumb the limitless depths of His mercy and extend His magnificent forgiveness to those who had so grievously offended him. "He was wounded for our transgressions, he was bruised for our iniquities: the chastisement of our peace was upon him; and (yet) with his stripes we are healed." (Isaiah 53:5). Thus, did His prophet Isaiah describe the Atonement of the Savior, over 700 years before His mortal ministry. Truly, the reach of His sacrifice was infinite in both its temporal and eternal scope.

As King Benjamin declared about 125 years before Christ's agony in Gethsemane: "The atonement (was) prepared from the foundation of the world, that thereby salvation might come to him that should put his trust in the Lord, and should be diligent in keeping his commandments, and continue in the faith even unto the end of his life." (Mosiah 4:6). The Atonement to which Benjamin referred took into account every sin that would be individually and collectively committed by the family of man, beginning at the foundation of the world and only ending after the Lord has come a second time to usher in His millennial reign on earth. The Atonement anticipated the shortcomings, and the sins of omission and of commission that would be frustratingly, repetitively, and painfully exhibited by every generation of the children of men, from the beginning to the end of time. It is all the more remarkable to realize that the Atonement anticipated sins that had not yet been committed. When the Savior stood before the Council and said to His Father: "Here am I, send me," (Abraham 3:27), He knew full well the price that would be required to satisfy Justice in order to obtain mercy. He had the spiritual reserves to make such a statement, but even his maturity as a God in heaven (see Joseph Fielding Smith, Jr., "Doctrines of Salvation," 1:32), could not take away the pain He must have felt, even then, for the scriptures describe Him as the "lamb slain from the foundation of the world." (Revelation 13:8).

Could His brothers and sisters who were also in attendance at the Council, who so easily and enthusiastically raised their arms to the square to support the Father's proposal, (see Job 38:7), have truly felt the import of the moment, that He was not only making history, but that He was also creating a binding foundation and precedent to re-write history? They were eyewitnesses to the vitalization of "the merciful plan of the great Creator." (2 Nephi 9:6). They must have palpably sensed in His condescension the enveloping reach of His love for them. They must have understood His penultimate example of humility, His supreme act of selflessness, and His superlative expression of altruism. He had just become their personal Redeemer as the power of the Atonement was activated in their behalf. We can only wonder how they could comprehend the significance of the events that were unfolding before them; that the exercise of their free will had just been guaranteed, the principles of the Plan certified, the price of their future offenses successfully negotiated, the guarantee of payment made in advance, and the demands of Justice satisfied and equally balanced against Mercy. Cherubim and a flaming sword were even then being prepared, to guard the way, and guarantee the eternal progression of Adam and Eve and their posterity. God's work and glory had been confirmed: To bring to pass the immortality and eternal life of man. (See Moses 1:39).

As Aaron taught King Lamoni's father, around a hundred years before the mortal ministry of the Savior: "Since man had fallen he could not merit anything of himself; but the sufferings and death of Christ atone for their sins, through faith and repentance, (and) he breaketh the bands of death, that the grave shall have no victory...that the sting of death should be swallowed up in the hopes of glory." (Alma 22:14).

With clarity of vision, Alma taught the people of Gideon about the future mission of the Savior. He and other Book of Mormon prophets taught the doctrine of the Atonement in a way that elsewhere in scripture is dealt with incompletely, with uncertainty, and with ambiguity. In Alma Chapter 7, there is little room for confusion. By following Alma's teachings, we can learn about the Atonement and apply its magnificent power to our own capacity for forgiveness.

Alma 7:11 suggests that part of the Atonement was accomplished during the three-year ministry of the Savior. "And he shall go forth, suffering pains and afflictions and temptations of every kind; and this that the word might be fulfilled which saith he will take upon him the pains and the sicknesses of his people." The description of the suffering of the Savior is particularly poignant in light of Alma's own suffering that came with the recognition of his sins. (See Alma 36:14 & 21). It seems that the work in which the Savior was engaged during His ministry followed a natural progression, and was built "line upon line, and precept upon precept," until His preparation was complete and every necessary detail had been worked out. Early in His ministry, Jesus had said, "My time is not yet come." (John 7:6). But later, when all had been accomplished, He confirmed, "My time is at hand." (Matthew 26:18). So it is with us. We generally develop our capacity for forgiveness over time, as our own schooling in mortality takes us from primary classes, to secondary, and finally to higher education. Sometimes, it is only in the graduate school of hard knocks that we finally learn how to be naturally charitable, and to forgive as the Savior does.

Alma 7:12 concerns the aspect of the Atonement that was completed upon the Cross. "And he will take upon him death, that he may loose the bands of death which bind his people; and he will take upon him their infirmities, that his bowels may be filled with mercy, according to the flesh, that he may know according to the flesh how to succor his people according to their infirmities." The crucified Christ is the primary focus of Christianity today, but if we fail to understand the Mortal Messiah, we risk narrowing our perspective to receive only a one-dimensional view that ignores the wonderful harmony that exists between His humanity and His divinity. In the context of this verse, it is well to remember that it is when we have known hardship that we develop empathy, are more likely to overlook the shortcomings of others, and are quicker to forgive them their trespasses. By learning to avoid being judgmental, and by developing benevolent blindness, we are better able to help others to meet their own challenges. The Savior asks us to follow Him to Golgotha, there to experience hardship at the hands of others. If we have embarked upon the journey to Christ, even as we experience adversity due to the influence of others who seek to do us harm, we will not be deterred from our resolve to forgive.

As the Lord explained to Joseph Smith: "If thou art called to pass through tribulation; if thou art in perils among false brethren; if thou art in perils among robbers; if thou art in perils by land or by sea; if thou art accused with all manner of false accusations; if thine enemies fall upon thee; if they tear thee from the society of thy father and mother and brethren and sisters; and if with a drawn sword thine enemies tear thee from the bosom of thy wife, and of thine offspring, and thine elder son, although but six years of age, shall cling to thy garments, and shall say, My father, my father, why can't you stay with us? O, my father, what are the men going to do with you? And if then he shall be thrust from thee by the sword, and thou be dragged to prison, and thine enemies prowl around thee like wolves for the blood of the lamb; and if thou shouldst be cast into the pit, or into the hands of murderers, and the sentence of death passed upon thee; if thou be cast into the deep; if the billowing surge conspire against thee; if fierce winds become thine enemy; if the heavens gather blackness, and all the elements combine to hedge up the way; and above all, if the very jaws of hell shall gape open the mouth wide after thee, know thou, my son, that all these things shall give thee experience, and shall be for thy good. The Son of Man hath descended below them all. Art thou greater than he?" (D&C 122:5-8). The more righteous we are, the better are we able to deal with the suffering that is a part of life, and that is likely not of our own doing. Our blessing may simply be the strength to endure the suffering that is a part of our mortal experience. (See D&C 121:7).

Alma 7:13 focuses on the dimension of the Atonement that was fulfilled in Gethsemane. "Now the Spirit knoweth all things; nevertheless, the Son of God suffereth according to the flesh that he might take upon him the sins of his people, that he might blot out their transgressions according to the power of his deliverance." Latter-day Saints tend to emphasize Gethsemane as the pivotal experience attendant to the Savior's sacrifice, but we can see that it was really a multi-dimensional drama played out on different stages. It began even before the creation of the earth, and will only end when the last repentant sinner has received intercession by the Redeemer, and forgiveness by the Father. In the meantime, our injunction is to develop the Savior's moral stamina, and to become as He is. As we internalize His divine attributes, we become perfected in Him. A key to the process is our capacity to forgive others, because forgiveness is central to the Atonement.

The Atonement's invitation to forgive and to be forgiven stands in counterpoint and is an effective antidote to the inevitable sense of empty despair, despondency, misery, and hopelessness related to the failings that have been and will continue to be an integral part of our schooling in mortality, for it must needs be that there is an opposition in all things. (See 2 Nephi 2:11). In support of Mercy, the power of the Atonement stands independently in the face of an avalanche of wickedness that has been poured out upon the world with increasing vitriol in the Last Days.

The Atonement is the only alternative to an otherwise overwhelmingly negative power influencing the affairs of mankind. Its only stipulation is that we acknowledge our disobedience and go through the process of repentance wherein we recognize our transgression, experience remorse, renounce the self-defeating behavior, resolve to do better, make restitution where possible, and then do our best to establish a reconciliation with the Spirit, and ultimately receive a remission of sin. The Atonement is the only force that has the power to bring about the kind of positive change illustrated in The Book of Mormon, when King Benjamin's people of Zarahemla "cried with one voice, saying: Yea, we believe all the words which thou hast spoken unto us; and also, we know of their surety and truth, because of the Spirit of the Lord Omnipotent, which has wrought a mighty change in us, or in our hearts, that we have no more disposition to do evil, but to do good continually." (Mosiah 5:2). We will have only completed the process of repentance when we, likewise, seek to do good continually, and when our forgiveness of others, painted in bold strokes with a broad brush, is at its foundation. As the Lord said: "I...will forgive whom I will forgive, but of you it is required to forgive all men." (D&C 64:10).

The Atonement allows us to overcome our selfish and morally indefensible desire for justice without mercy. Desperation was really at the foundation of Lucifer's alternative proposal at the Council, when he boasted: "I will redeem all mankind, that one soul shall not be lost." (Moses 4:1). He exhibited his true colors with that revealing assertion. Because he was incapable of forgiveness, the thought of remembering no more the sins of his repentant brethren scared the living daylights out of him. The noble and principled qualities that are expressed in the Atonement stand in contrast to the damning character flaws of the star that fell from heaven. (See Revelation 9:1). Lucifer became Satan because of his unprincipled and unilaterally dogmatic posturing; because he would have had us believe that his counterfeit proposal could grant absolution without apology, adjustment without appreciation, admonishment without adaptation, alteration without affection, amelioration without acquittal, amendment without admiration, castigation without consideration, censure without courtesy, chastisement without charity, clemency without compassion, condemnation without kindness, correction without concern, discipline without deprecation, indebtedness without indemnification, leniency without love, mercifulness without magnanimity, pacification without propitiation, probation without pardon, punishment without penance, reprimand without rectification, rebuke without resolution, reprimand without reassurance, reproof without reconciliation, resolution without reparation, retaliation without regard, retribution without reverence, revenge without respect, tolerance without tenderness, and vengeance without veneration.

The keystone of the Plan of Salvation is the Atonement that unflinchingly looks directly into the jaws of spiritual death without averting its eyes. It was not the Savior, but the devil who was the first to blink, and who was cast out of heaven. It is he who will not support his children at the last day. (See Alma 30:44).

Our acknowledgement of the necessity of the fundamental principle of opposition within the framework of the Plan does not give us license to act recklessly or to capitulate to the Dark Side, without accountability. Every expression of our exercise of free is simply a confirmation of the trust that our Heavenly Father places in us. He created us with the moral backbone to meet unforgiveness with compassion, intolerance with consideration, prejudice with impartiality, and narrow-mindedness with limitless opportunity for expression.

Opposition serves the useful purpose of allowing us to gauge the success of our internalization of the Plan's provisions. It gives us a sense of how we are doing in our efforts to consciously and energetically participate without deviation in purposeful programs of personal progress that carry us forward on proven paths. Conformity to God's laws has the capacity to provide significant sustainable support and to generate confidence, as we feel ourselves being carried forward as upon the wings of eagles. (See D&C 124:99). Without the comfortable sense of orthodoxy provided by the gospel, life can be nothing more than a cruel joke with a punch line that inevitably pierces our hearts without pity. If we allow ourselves to be left to the wiles of the adversary, we will find ourselves confronted by a sense of utter futility that is the inexorable result of our failure to focus on the innate upward thrust that is only generated by the desire, capacity, and discipline to reach out and embrace noble principles. His enticements can leave us gasping for a reassuring breath of celestial air, with the feeling that we have been sucker-punched below the belt.

Without the light of the Atonement, we are doomed to suffer in the shadows where we can only experience illusions and caricatures of reality. The discrepancy between marginalized behavior and the ideals of the Plan can become so great that short-lived pleasure in worldly ways evaporates as the morning dew in the full light of day. Sooner or later, when this disparity becomes so great that it reaches "critical mass," a requisite readjustment tears down our façade of corruption and hypocrisy to allow the cultivation of a more nurturing lifestyle made possible by a recommitment to obedience to the foundation principles of the Plan.

So it is, that for the Plan to have real vitality, we must forgive, even as we are forgiven. Our forgiveness must be anchored to the Atonement, as must every other facet of our lives. We must forsake our carnal nature, for it is nothing more than a shadowy image of Lucifer's rebellion in the Council. If we have harbored feelings of revenge, retaliation or reprisal, if the basic instincts that were activated by the Fall of Adam are to be conquered, we must rely upon the fire line of the Atonement to contain and conquer the conflagration of sin.

To illustrate this point, the Great Fire of 1910 was the largest forest fire in U.S. history. It burned about 4,687 square miles in northeast Washington, northern Idaho, and western Montana. It destroyed parts of ten different national forests, and killed 87 people, mostly firefighters. It remained the deadliest event for firefighters in the United States, until September 11, 2001.

By comparison, the Yellowstone National Park fire in 1988 burned about 1,240 square miles. The Yosemite National Park fire in 2013 burned about 384 square miles. Changes in weather often contribute to the control and elimination of wildfires, but what is critical to established firefighting tactics is the strategy of "containment" that is designed to bring the fire within the boundaries of exhaustively and painstakingly constructed fire lines. Only with containment may the blaze may be brought under control and ultimately extinguished. The Atonement is like an encircling fire-line that contains with 100% effectiveness the blazing inferno of sin, no matter how much potential fuel has been consumed or what combustible material may yet lie on the forest floor.

This principle of containment, that lies at the heart of Atonement, is so alien to the natural man that Satan, who was the world's original arsonist, can muster no effective counter-proposal. There is nothing within his arsenal to combat the Atonement. The best he can do is keep people from the truth, for he knows that the truth will make them free. (See John 8:32). His best strategy is to use the flame thrower of faithlessness to "turn their hearts away from the truth, that they become blinded and understand not the things which are prepared for them." (D&C 78:10). He knows that "there are many yet on the earth among all sects, parties, and denominations, who are blinded by the subtle craftiness of men, whereby they lie in wait to deceive, and who are only kept from the truth because they know not where to find it." (D&C 123:12). When we understand the power of the Atonement, our capacity for forgiveness, and to be forgiven, will be boundless.

The Atonement was designed to deal with mankind's worst depravities, moral corruption, and degradation, including atrocities such as the Holocaust and World War II, in which over 60 million people, 3% of the world population, lost their lives. The Atonement encompasses the sins of those who took part in the Stalinist purges of the 1940s and 1950s, a period of Soviet history in which nearly 10 million lives were taken. The encircling arms of the Atonement reach as far as the Rwandan genocide in 1994, and the Bosnian ethnic cleansing in 1995. The Atonement also has the capacity to cleanse each of us from our own secret sins and hidden transgressions. The Atonement is the fire retardant that is dumped on the raging inferno of our sins.

The Atonement encompasses our every day garden-variety sins, when we are slighted by a waitress, a store clerk, or a civil servant, and respond with anger; when a driver treats us discourteously, and we react in kind; when our spouse is inconsiderate of our feelings, and we counter spitefully; when a work associate treats us with disrespect and our retort drags us down to his lowest common denominator; or when a church leader exercises what we suppose to be unrighteous dominion and our reaction causes us to withdraw from full faith and fellowship. So, too, the Atonement stands ready to save us when we have been, not on the receiving end, but rather on the giving end, of these every-day interpersonal sleights.

If, in any of these situations, we do not beg for our own forgiveness, or ourselves forgive those who have purportedly trespassed against us, we will become vulnerable to a spiritual sickness that mimics the symptoms of those with advanced diabetes whose peripheral circulation has been compromised and who can no longer feel. As we experience the hard lessons of life that the Plan purposely throws our way with frustrating regularity, if we have not learned that the door of forgiveness swings both ways, we will become numb to the better angels of our nature and lose our capacity to touch and be touched by those around us. We will then find ourselves more and more isolated from the sensitivity to our surroundings that is critical to our full participation in the Plan of Happiness. We will find ourselves in a spiritual vacuum, gasping for life-sustaining air.

In beautiful Lancaster County, Pennsylvania, the Amish people have created their own version of the Promised Land. They live simply, without automobiles, electricity, or machinery. They conduct their affairs quietly and without ostentation, in relative isolation from the outside world. They tend their own gardens, sow and harvest their own crops, prepare their food simply, and fashion their own modest clothing. Their beautiful quilts are prized possessions, and are much coveted by others.

Living among them in 2006 was a 32 year-old "English" milk truck driver. He knew many of his Amish neighbors. On October 2, as evil influences overpowered him, his sanity disintegrated. He felt compelled to enter the simple Amish schoolhouse in Nickel Mines, and shoot and kill five Amish children, while wounding another five. He then turned the gun on himself, and a bullet to the brain ended his own inner torment.

His suicide did nothing to assuage the depth of distress, sense of suffering, and gravity of grief among the Amish. But, incredibly, in response to his heinous act, their anguish was not accompanied by anger. There was hurt, but no hate, distress, but no despair, and pain, but no pernicious plotting of payback. There was heartache without hardness of heart. The Amish immediately and without reservation expressed forgiveness for what their neighbor had done. Theirs was not just empty rhetoric, for they put their money where their mouth was. They reached out to his family, and literally wrapped their arms around its members. They attended his funeral, and invited his family to attend their own sorrowful services for their sweet children. Their faith carried them through difficult days and long nights, and blessed them with a remarkable sense of peace.

Some in the media could not understand what was happening within the Amish community. They wondered how they could so freely forgive under such circumstances. But others realized that "Letting go of grudges" is a deeply rooted value in Amish culture. Their willingness to forgo vengeance did not undo the tragedy or pardon the wrong, but rather it constituted the first step toward a more hopeful future.

The Christian Science Monitor very perceptively noted: "For most people, a decision to forgive comes, if ever, at the end of a long emotional journey that may stretch over months, if not years. The Amish invert the process. Their religious tradition predisposes them to forgive even before an injustice occurs." (10/2/2007). Remarkably, the Amish exhibited the Christ-like forgiveness that we often take for granted as a quality of the Savior, but rarely emulate ourselves.

As the Monitor pointed out, the key was that the Amish had learned to reverse the process of forgiveness. We tend to grapple with forgiveness after the offense. Perhaps the Amish understood the power of the Atonement better than the rest of us, and applied it in literal and personal ways that are hard for the rest of us to imagine, simply because it lies outside of our experience. They seemed to have already reached an epiphany wherein they realized that the Savior is our great Exemplar who forgave us our trespasses even before they had been committed. He took upon Himself the penalty for our sins before we committed them. For the Amish, "the sting of death is swallowed up in Christ." (Mosiah 16:8). His love and compassion, and the depth and breadth of His mercy, know no temporal or spatial bounds. For them, His Atonement was truly infinite in its scope. For them, His arms encircle the vilest of sinners, as well as the worthiest of saints, and His forgiveness is only conditional upon our willingness to repent.

The "Monitor" continued its observation of the remarkable example of the Amish: "Next to the Bible, the most important book in any Amish household is "der Martyrspeigel" ("The Martyr's Mirror") which documents the persecution suffered by the Anabaptists in Europe in the 16th and 17th centuries. This book is read aloud to Amish families nearly every day. Among the stories is the tale of one Amishman who was being pursued by a bounty hunter across a frozen lake. The ice cracked, and the bounty hunter fell in. The Amishman stopped and pulled the bounty hunter from what would have surely been an icy death, only to then be taken into custody and later executed for his faith. With such stories told time after time, it is not surprising that there is" within the Amish psyche "such a deep reservoir of forgiveness and grace."

A puckish observation is that revenge is a dish that is best served cold, when we are no longer caught up in the heat of the moment, but can afford to be crafty, cunning, and calculating as we plot our payback. But that stratagem is still like swallowing poison and hoping it will kill the other guy. The word "revenge" is found just thirteen times in the scriptures, but the word "forgive" is found one hundred fifty five times.

When we ponder the example of the Amish, we remember how Peter came to the Savior and asked Him: "Lord, how oft shall my brother sin against me, and I forgive him? Till seven times? Jesus saith unto him, I say not unto thee, Until seven times: but, Until seventy times seven." (Matthew 18:21-22). We are reminded, as well, of the Lord's injunction to Joseph Smith: "I, the Lord, will forgive whom I will forgive, but of you it is required to forgive all men." (D&C 64:10).

The Lord has commanded that we be perfect, even as our Father in Heaven is perfect. We can be perfect in our home teaching and visiting teaching, in our obedience to the Law of Tithing, and in our observation of the Law of The Fast. We can be perfect in our obedience to the Law of Chastity, and in the sustaining of our leaders. Beyond that, it gets a little tricky, but we can also strive to be perfect in our forgiveness of others, until seventy times seven. The Amish seem to have perfected their forgiveness; which gives us hope that so can we.

With His eternal perspective, the Savior tried to explain to His beloved Apostle Peter that to inherit the Kingdom of God, he would have to change his very nature.

He would have to be born again in order to "see the kingdom of God." (John 3:3). He would have to follow the example of "the Lamb slain from the foundation of the world." (Revelation 13:8). He would have to be as a little child, who is "alive in Christ, even from the foundation of the world." (Moroni 8:12). He would have to recognize the power of His ministry, and that He had prepared a way "for all men from the foundation of the world, if it so be that they repent and come unto him." (1 Nephi 10:8). He would have to act upon his understanding that "the plan of redemption" includes the commandment to forgive others without reservation, and that this injunction "was laid from the foundation of the world" through Jesus Christ. (Alma 12:2, cf. Alma 18:39).

The example of the Amish teaches us a mighty lesson about forgiveness. It puts the Atonement of Jesus Christ in a clearer perspective, and illustrates how mere mortals can develop an eternal point of view to help them to see with greater clarity how they can individually personalize this keystone principle of the gospel. Their model behavior stirs our hearts, and the Spirit quickens us to follow their example. The Lord told the brother of Jared: "Behold, I am he who was prepared from the foundation of the world to redeem my people. Behold, I am Jesus Christ. I am the Father and the Son. In me shall all mankind have life, and that eternally, even they who shall believe on my name; and they shall become my sons and my daughters." (Ether 3:14).

We are reminded of The Lord's Prayer, wherein we are taught: "And forgive us our debts, as we forgive our debtors." (Matthew 6:9-13). Then, in the next two verses, the Savior underscored the quality of forgiveness expressed in His archetypical prayer: "For if ye forgive men their trespasses, your heavenly Father will also forgive you: But if ye forgive not men their trespasses, neither will your Father forgive your trespasses." (Matthew 6:12). It is that simple.

In our society, we too often think that retribution is our right and responsibility. Too many religions in the world wield a sword of vengeance as their God-given duty. In contrast, rather than using religion to bless and legitimize revenge, the Amish believe that God smiles on simple acts of grace that open the door to reconciliation. They believe in allowing God to be the judge of our actions, and that if correction is to be administered, it should be done by His hand. Latter-day Saint doctrine agrees: "Judgment is mine, saith the Lord, and vengeance is mine also." (Mormon 8:12).

If we are ever to successfully deal with the inequalities of life and escape the quicksands of self-pity, we must personalize the lessons of the Atonement. We must change our nature and become new creatures in Christ. If necessary, we must practice in front of a mirror, and recite over and over again until we get it right: "Father forgive them, for they know not what they do." We must become more Amish.

"Cut the
cloth to fit the pattern
of revised circumstances
dictated by these trying times."
(Mark E. Petersen).

Finding Balance
In Our Lives

"See that all…things are done in wisdom and order; for it is not requisite that a man should run faster than he has strength. And again, it is expedient that he should be diligent, that thereby he might win the prize; therefore, all things must be done in order." (Mosiah 4:27).

To be balanced is to be decided, dogged, determined, indomitable, resolute, untiring, unwavering, and even heroic. Balance is the antithesis of fanaticism, wherein we lose sight of our objectives and redouble our efforts. To be balanced is to be ardent, eager, fervent, enthusiastic, passionate, and zealous, rather than overzealous, wherein we become obsessive and even feverish in our efforts to obtain elusive telestial treasures that have become sinfully slippery and are difficult to retain.

In our unstable environment, it takes a great deal of effort to create balance, and very little inattention to allow chaos to reign unchecked. In fact, if we do not consciously focus on structure and stability, and exert efforts to foster a sense of permanency, everything tends to fall apart. For example, a sculpture in marble may be destroyed over millennia by the incessant action of the elements, or in seconds by the careless brush of a coat sleeve. A thousand year old redwood tree may be weathered by the storms of centuries, or burn to the ground in hours. The city of Babylon took hundreds of years to build, and its hanging gardens were one of the seven wonders of the ancient world, but it is today only a dusty memory. Even the organization of words into coherent sentences or paragraphs, though etched in stone or sizzling in cyberspace, can be erased with one blow of a hammer, a single keystroke, or one swipe of a magnet over a computer disk.

Balance gives coherence to the behavioral sciences, as well. It explains why friendship can be devastated by an inconsiderate action or word, and how a life of moderation can be forfeit by one thoughtless act of indulgence in a moment of weakness. One glass of liquor can ruin a lifestyle of temperance, and yielding to the passion of the moment can negate the constructive efforts of a lifetime of chaste behavior. Testimony that has taken years to build can be destroyed through carelessness, by inattention, or by flirting with the faithless. The fiery darts of the adversary go hand-in-hand with the Law of Entropy (that dictates that everything tends to fall apart) that would destroy the balance that is so necessary in our lives.

Even though they may seem to be at odds, however, inasmuch as they come from opposite ends of the behavioral spectrum, the laws of entropy and eternal progression must ultimately be in balance with each other. In fact, it was ordained in heaven, and "must needs be, that there is an opposition in all things." (2 Nephi 2:11). A healthy juxtaposition between opposing points of view is necessary for the Plan of Salvation to work. The perfect understanding by Jesus Christ of the concept of balance allowed Him to create our world and pronounce His efforts "very good." (Genesis 1:31). The Law of Eternal Progression, to which He has bound Himself, rules supreme, but it is as much defined by its opposites in the physical universe as it is by itself. The presence of Satan in the Garden of Eden attests to that fact. (See Moses 4:6).

Since he operates more by subtraction than by addition, the adversary's program that tears down both individuals and relationships, prospers with deceit, deception, and fraud, and thrives on imbalance. He exults in instability. (See Exodus 12:23). We all remember the Hindu scripture, the Bhagavad-Gita, wherein Vishnu in his multi-armed form declares: "Now I am become Death, the destroyer of worlds." Perhaps this is why the natural man is an enemy to God, and has been from the beginning. Nevertheless, when our exercise of agency results in inequality, the disparity may simply be the representation of the manifestation of the natural consequences of imbalance. If this is so, its effects will be inevitable and inexorable unless the Author of Salvation, Who is the Maker and Fashioner of the universe, intervenes by utilizing higher laws that trump imbalance. As Paul perceptively explained to the Hebrews: "Ye have in heaven a better and an enduring substance." (Hebrews 10:34).

This may also help to explain the scope of the Savior's injunction: "Be ye, therefore, perfect, even as your Father in Heaven is perfect." (Matthew 5:48). His command may have been as much a statement of fact as it was a plea, or an expression of hopeful anticipation. The Plan of Salvation has within its arsenal enough firepower for us to overcome instability in our lives, and then, unencumbered by the wobbly constraints of uncertainty, to move onward and upward along a stable course of eternal progress.

The gate may be strait, and the way narrow, but those who accept Christ as their Guide will find it within their reach to travel a path of progression by threading the eye of the needle and walking a fine line past the seemingly inexorable, unalterable, unavoidable, unrelenting, and unstoppable demands of disproportion. For, "broad is the gate, and wide the way that leadeth to the deaths, and many there are that go in thereat," because they pursue a wavering course of unpredictability. (D&C 132:25). When individuals elect to ignore celestial law, that should be to them as a beacon penetrating the mists of darkness in a telestial world, they have tacitly chosen an alternative course leading to inevitable destruction that is the natural consequence of the operation of the immutable laws of physics that define imbalance, disorder, or entropy.

It is equilibrium in our lives that necessarily sets the stage for the exercise of moral agency and dictates the implementation of other equally important and co-existing laws. Mercy, in particular, exists to mitigate the otherwise inevitable consequences of lives that are out of balance, and through Atonement facilitates our journey of progress in both time and eternity. The principles that make up the Plan of Salvation are the ultimate expression of balance.

Only by incorporating these principles into the conduct of our lives can the disorder and destruction that result from imbalance be recognized, addressed, reversed, and erased with finality. While obedience nurtures the development of personality traits that are consistent with the symmetry of heaven, sin is harmful because it destroys our capacity to develop the steadiness that is representative of the Celestial Kingdom. Disorder takes the disobedient further and further from the influence of the Spirit, whose purpose it is to guide us away from the precipice of destruction to that more secure sanctuary that abides the stability of higher laws. Damnation results from activities that block the channels through which this spiritual power flows. It is the halt in our progression because of imbalance in our lives that is damning.

To counteract the consequences of sin, which are arguably the worst examples of imbalance in our lives, our days have been "prolonged, according to the will of God, that (we) might repent while in the flesh; wherefore, (our) state (becomes) a state of probation, and (our) time (is) lengthened, according to the commandments which the Lord God gave unto the children of men. For he gave commandment that all men must repent; for he showed unto all men that they were lost," because of the unsteadiness that naturally followed Adam and Eve's expulsion from the Garden into the telestial world. (2 Nephi 2:21).

Ever since the Fall, Satan has enjoyed a free pass to mingle among the children of men. He is flushed with excitement because he knows how difficult it is for us to resist our natural tendency toward volatility. Many of us love Satan more than we love God, and when we do so, we unavoidably exhibit the behavioral manifestations of that misplaced adoration. Our inattention to celestial signposts carries us onto crooked paths of self-destructive and self-defeating behaviors. We become "carnal, sensual, and devilish." (Moses 5:13). Without the intervention of higher laws, our unbalanced lives point us toward inevitable and ultimate destruction.

The Lord has confidence, though, in our ability to use the blueprint He has provided to set our lives in order, and to bring our behavior into balance with celestial law, and so has He "called upon men by the Holy Ghost everywhere and command(s) them that they should repent." Through the Atonement, repentance becomes a celestial bridge that transports the righteous past the vicissitudes of life to the stability of a world that lies beyond. "And as many as believed in the Son, and repented of their sins, (were) saved" from the inexorable effects of slow destruction. (Moses 5:15). Our lives can be like a train wreck in slow motion, but it we follow the counsel of Jehovah, we can fast-forward that newsreel to bring our character into a state of balance and harmony with the Law of Eternal Progression, eventually becoming "heirs of God, and joint heirs with Christ." (Romans 8:17). When we heed the grand design of the Plan, opposition works to our benefit.

By abiding celestial law, the Spirit opens our eyes, "so as to see and understand the things of God, even those things which were from the beginning before the world was." (D&C 76:12-13). We will see things even more clearly when we escape the confining limitations of our mortal clay that now negatively focuses our attention on worldliness, the ultimate negative manifestations of entropy, and on the related unstable rationalism that denies the power of the Atonement. Too often, we are "like unto a man beholding his natural face in a glass." (James 1:23). Without ever beholding our potential, or without ever breaking free of our enslavement to the upsetting laws of destructive behavior, we satisfy ourselves with a brief glimpse of salvation, even though the panoramic vista of the Plan of Salvation may be only superficially camouflaged by the deceivers' ghillie suit of gullibility.

When we finally do see things as they really are, and our lives come into a state of equilibrium with a lucidity that comes more from the heart than from the head, perhaps we will better understand how someone like Helen Keller could have had such balance in her life. She wrote not from the shaky vantage point of severe physical impairment and limited sensory stimulation, but rather with steadiness and profound spiritual enlightenment: "I believe that no good shall be lost," she declared, "and that all man has willed or hoped or dreamed of good shall exist forever. I believe in the immortality of the soul because I have within me immortal longings. I believe that the state we enter after death is wrought of our own motives, thoughts, and deeds. I believe that my home there will be beautiful with colour, music, and speech of flowers and faces I love. Without this faith, there would be little meaning in my life. I should be a mere pillar of darkness in the dark. Observers in the full enjoyment of their bodily senses pity me, but it is because they do not see the golden chamber in my life where I dwell delighted; for dark as my path may seem to them, I carry a magic light in my heart. Faith, the spiritual strong searchlight, illuminates the way, and although sinister doubts lurk in the shadow, I walk unafraid towards the Enchanted Wood where the foliage is always green, where joy abides, where nightingales nest and sing, and where life and death are one in the presence of the Lord." ("Midstream").

Imbalance in the temporal world that leads us from order to disorder suits the purposes of God as long as we are regularly jarred out of our collective complacency by the created confusion. Remember that when He created the world, He pronounced it "good." When imbalance upsets the stagnation of the status quo, makes us think, gets our juices flowing, prods us to purposefully expend our energy, and constructively puts our agency to work, it will have served its purpose. Brigham Young taught: "The first principle that ought to occupy our attention and which is the mainspring of all action is the principle of improvement," and this requires us to nurture a sense of balance in our lives, even as we deal with the vagaries of our temporal world, to bring order out of seeming pandemonium. (D.B.Y., p. 87).

Progress becomes the recompense for perseverance, salvation is the reward for surmounting obstacles, and the hope of eternal life is the blessing for enduring opposition. As we delicately balance our experiences, we become more comfortable with the perspective that confirms that gospel principles relating to the eternities can supersede physical laws that pertain only to the temporal world. When we enter into the covenants, something mystical and metaphysical happens. We are figuratively "born of God" and, although our feet are firmly planted on gospel sod, we feel as if we have ascended to dizzying heights without experiencing vertigo. (Mosiah 5:7). In a sense, we have become new creatures in Christ because we have been able to achieve perfect symmetry, oriented more to the laws of the eternal world and the guidance of the Master than to the limitations imposed by the physical world and the destructive effects of disproportion. (See 2 Corinthians 5:17). Our experience is inexplicable, and yet undeniable. "Whatsoever is born of God overcometh the (laws governing the physical) world." (1 John 5:3).

As we think about balance, Spencer W. Kimball's counsel rings with greater urgency. "So much depends upon our willingness to make up our minds, collectively and individually, that present levels of performance are not acceptable, either to ourselves or to the Lord. In saying that, I am not calling for flashy, temporary differences in our performance levels, but for a quiet resolve to lengthen our stride." ("Church News," 3/22/1975). He knew that our equilibrium would be enhanced if we would move forward with purpose.

He knew that the exertion caused by lengthening our stride might cause discomfort, as it stretched the limits of our stability in a violent confrontation that would tear at the very fabric of the natural world. But in doing so, he knew that we would find new spiritual strength. He knew that if we would go the second mile while doubling our stride, we would burst free of the shackles that had limited the expression of our potential, and we would receive "a gift of spiritual independence that would remove the veil of insensitivity from our destiny." (Richard L. Gunn, "A Search for Sensitivity and Spirit," p. 197). This independence would be exhilarating, because it would be accompanied by the recognition of new-found and soul-expanding opportunities. It would kindle within us the realization that we are spiritual beings having mortal experiences, and that the powers of heave would countermand the dizzying inequities of life.

Even though we mindlessly toil with blood, sweat, and tears, sacrificing even those things that are near and dear to us in order to obtain telestial treasures, at the end of the day the unevenness of the world can only deliver physical destruction, while steady obedience to the laws of the gospel creates the opportunity to progress eternally. If we nurture a one-dimensional view of the world that focuses on its cares, yielding to the things of the moment, if we lose our balance, we tend to fall into mischief. (See Proverbs 28:14). The gospel allows us to develop poise under provocation, and provides us with a multidimensional view of existence that nurtures an accurate and realistic milieu in which we may gain valuable experience.

Since many of us have not yet completed enough of the curriculum of the gospel to allow ourselves to be the successful architects of our own fate, we are commanded: "Give your language to exhortation continually." (D&C 23:7). "Let us not weary in well doing," wrote Paul. (Galatians 6:9). Because the world goes to such great lengths to throw us off balance, even those who are born again require constant and repetitive encouragement in their determination to steady the course and to progress eternally. Truly did Brigham Young believe, that: "All organized existence is in progress either to an endless advancement in eternal perfections, or back to dissolution. There is no period in all the eternities," he declared, wherein we "will become stationary, that we cannot advance in knowledge, wisdom, power, and glory." (J.D., 1:349). When we come to a standstill, we are at risk of toppling over. We must maintain momentum in order to sustain our progress.

We cannot afford to sleep at our posts, to pause to rest on shaky ground, or to allow complacency to sweep us over the precipice of destruction. The gospel stimulates our capacity for affirmative, constructive, and purposeful action, in order to maintain our balance. It is a simple formula: The Lord strengthens and blesses us as we repent and keep the commandments, but not necessarily with telestial toys that might lead us on detours leading away from the steadiness of the strait and narrow path. Nor will He coddle us by making our way easy, lest we be pacified into a false sense of carnal security and lose traction. The constant G-force exerted by the uphill path of progress very subtly counteracts and is in opposition to the downhill and negative effects of complacency that would otherwise result in a free-fall from faith, with disastrous consequences.

Balance is at the very heart of eternal laws that have the capacity to carry us beyond the conventional boundaries of our every day world. Our five natural senses enable us to relate to our physical surroundings, and act as biological barometers that provide us with reliable measurements to gauge the pervasive and yet inexorable effects of imbalance that almost imperceptibly grind us down.

But gradually, it is our very subtle extrasensory perceptions that bring us to the realization that gospel principles relating to the eternities supersede physical laws governing the temporal universe, and that there may yet be a reconciliation between the two. When we are "born of God" our orientation is more to the expansive laws of the eternal world than to the restrictive confines of the physical world. When we are in harmony with the eternities, we are in a better state of balance. When we are "born of God (we) overcome the world" with a freedom from incarceration to the inexorable immutability of the law of entropy. (1 John 5:3). This independence is incalculable, indescribable, and inexplicable, and yet it is undeniable. It is not maturational, but is generational, as we become "new creatures in Christ."

As the process unfolds and we learn to balance our lives, God subtly fortifies us, increasing our capacity to grow with opportunities to be anxiously engaged in good causes. He endows us with the ability to think, so that, on our own initiative, we can generate the power to avoid the conceptual cul-de-sacs, religious roundabouts, and doctrinal dead-ends that would cause us to lose our way, or to slow or even to stop our progress and cause us to tip over. He helps us to work out our salvation with fear and trembling. He nudges us to move out of our comfort zones into the stimulating environment of service, the cathartic setting of sacrifice, and even onto the painful paths that lead to our own personal Gethsemanes. Socrates said: "Know thyself," Cicero admonished, "Control thyself," but Jesus taught by the greatest example of all, encouraging us to give ourselves completely and without reservation, bringing ourselves into a state of harmony and balance with Him and with the eternities.

The Savior exhorts us to drink copiously and unceasingly from the fountain of truth in order to slake our thirst for principles that gyroscopically orient us toward heaven. He understands the difference between celestial sureties that are represented by eternal progression, and telestial tendencies that are represented by physical laws such as entropy. "Great and marvelous are the works of the Lord," Jacob exclaimed. "How unsearchable are the depths of the mysteries of him; and it is impossible that man should find out all his ways. And no man knoweth of his ways save it be revealed unto him." (Jacob 4:8).

The wise counsel of our prophets of God provides balance in a world that has been confused by weights and measures that have been compromised by the adversary's tampering. Their counsel creates desire in our hearts to negotiate the difficult road to Gethsemane, past the Garden Tomb, and on into celestial realms. It validates the promises made by our Father that the struggles of mortality would be worth every sacrifice, and that our experiences would be tailored to personal growth and development, as we are obedient to gospel principles. But only if the drama is played out within the context of the Everlasting Covenant, according to the rules established by the Plan of Salvation, can we achieve the balance necessary to receive the anticipated blessings. There has never been another way, nor will there ever be. Only the bedrock of the gospel can provide the footing to restore equilibrium in our lives, provide the stability we so desperately need in an uncertain world, steady the helm as we navigate through treacherous waters, and give us the poise and composure of truly balanced lives.

Today, we must be especially vigilant, and avoid enticements that rivet our attention, consume our energies, and demand our devotion. Sitting with the engine idling while wasting time in telestial traffic jams can damage our capacity and desire to move forward. We must avoid looking beyond the mark or getting sidetracked by doctrinal detours. Our destination is well-defined, and if we only half-heartedly seek truth, it is because our instability causes us to confuse knowledge for intelligence, and think that when we are learned we are wise. We must never fail to understand that to be learned is good, but only if we will hearken unto the counsels of God. The lesson of balance is one that if taken to heart kindles faith, protects testimony, and even saves souls.

More people
are killed each
year by the bite of
mosquitos than are
by being stepped
on by charging
elephants.

Friendship

Some of the qualities we look for in friends are charity, honesty, integrity, kindness, and unselfishness. True friends would never think to contribute to our delinquency, hardship, or misery. They would rather leave us better than when they found us.

We read in the Old Testament that after David killed Goliath, he quickly became a hero in Israel. He was on the cover of People Magazine, Muscle Magazine, Outside Magazine, and nearly every tabloid at the newsstand. He made the rounds of all the late night talk shows, was on The Voice, made book deals with the major publishing houses, entered into negotiations for the rights to a TV Movie, and signed product endorsements with Power Bar, Monster Energy, Muscle Milk, and Red Bull. The exclusive photos of the battle went viral on the Internet and on Instagram. David had thousands of followers on Twitter, and David Action Figures flew off the shelves at Toys R Us.

Initially, King Saul and all Israel honored him, as well. In particular, it is interesting to read about how Jonathan (King Saul's son) felt about David. Remember, that while David was greatly honored by the people as a war hero, Jonathan received little attention for his own success on the battlefield. Nevertheless, "the soul of Jonathan was knit with the soul of David, and Jonathan loved him as his own soul." (1 Samuel 18:1). Jonathan gave his royal robe and weapons to David: "And Jonathan stripped himself of the robe that was upon him, and gave it to David, and his garments, even to his sword, and to his bow, and to his girdle." (1 Samuel 18:4).

It would have been easy for Jonathan to feel jealous of David. As Saul's son, Jonathan was next in line to be king. However, the prophet Samuel had anointed David to become the next king. "Then Samuel took the horn of oil, anointed him in the midst of his brethren: and the Spirit of the Lord came upon David from that day forward." (1 Samuel 16:13).

After David's slew Goliath, Saul took David into his home and set him over his armies. "And David went out whithersoever Saul sent him, and behaved himself wisely." He was self-deprecating, self-effacing, and spiritually sensitive. "And Saul set him over the men of war, and he was accepted in the sight of all the people, and also in the sight of Saul's servants." (1 Samuel 18:5).

Nevertheless, Saul turned against David. After all, it had been David, and not Saul, who had been invited to appear on Larry King Live, and on The Tonight Show. It had been David who had received the royalties from product endorsements. Professional jealousy became a determining factor in their relationship.

Remember, the magic of Camelot was that King Arthur had a round table constructed for his royal court. So too, Ammon's influence in the court of King Lamoni had been his humility. "Where is this man that has such great power?" King Lamoni had asked. "And they said unto him, Behold, he is feeding thy horses." (Alma 18:8-9). So much for self-aggrandizement.

"And it came to pass as they came, when David was returned from the slaughter of the Philistine, that the women came out of all cities of Israel, singing and dancing, to meet king Saul, with tabrets, with joy, and with instruments of musick. And the women answered one another as they played, and said Saul hath slain his thousands, and David his ten thousands. And Saul was very wroth, and the saying displeased him; and he said, They have ascribed unto David ten thousand, and to me they have ascribed but thousands: and what can he have more but the kingdom? And Saul eyed David from that day and forward." (1 Samuel 18:6-9).

Sometimes, it is difficult to be happy about the success of others. We think that if someone else is recognized for their achievements, it will diminish us. Your "A" will overshadow my "B." Your church calling is more significant than mine. Your mission assignment is more glamorous than mine. You seem to have many talents, and I have so few. You're a stud-muffin and I'm such a geek. Your car is way cooler than my beater. Your degree, your education, your job, your experiences, your opportunities, your luck, your house, your kids, your vacations. It will never, ever end, if you have allowed yourself to compose such a list.

Jealousy and pride are seductively effective satanic tools designed to negatively influence our spiritual well-being. "When pride has a hold on our hearts, we lose our independence of the world and deliver our freedoms to the bondage of men's judgment." (Ezra Taft Benson, C.R., 4/1989). In a shouting contest, or even in a popularity contest, the world will always prevail over the Spirit.

Jonathan was a true friend when his father Saul ultimately sought to kill David. His example forces us to ask ourselves: "What do we do today, when evil influences attack and erode the spiritual independence of our friends, and we see them brought down into the bondage of men's judgments?"

"Jonathan spake good of David unto Saul his father, and said unto him, Let not the king sin against his servant, against David; because he hath not sinned against thee, and because his works have been to thee-ward very good: For he did put his life in his hand, and slew the Philistine, and the Lord wrought a great salvation for all Israel: thou sawest it, and didst rejoice: wherefore then wilt thou sin against innocent blood, to slay David without a cause?" (1 Samuel 19:4-5).

There was a divine principle at the foundation of the friendship between Jonathan and David. "Behold, the Lord be between thee and me for ever," declared Jonathan. (1 Samuel 20:23). Likewise, in the Book of Mormon record, did Alma "rejoice exceedingly to see his brethren, and what added more to his joy, they were still his brethren in the Lord; yea, and they had waxed strong in the knowledge of the truth; for they were men of a sound understanding and they had searched the scriptures diligently, that they might know the word of God." (Alma 17:2).

Joseph Smith reflected the same qualities of friendship that had been exhibited by Jonathan, when he declared: "I salute you in the name of the Lord Jesus Christ, in token or remembrance of the everlasting covenant, in which covenant I receive you to fellowship, in a determination that is fixed, immovable, and unchangeable, to be your friend and brother through the grace of God in the bonds of love, to walk in all the commandments of God blameless, in thanksgiving, forever and ever. Amen." (D&C 88:133).

"The will of the Lord…
the mind of the Lord,…the
word of the Lord…the voice of
the Lord, and the power of
God unto salvation."
(D&C 68:1-4).

General Conference:
The Super Bowl Of Spiritual Symposia[1]

"My servant, Orson Hyde, (a member of the original Quorum of the Twelve in this dispensation) was called by his ordination to proclaim the everlasting gospel, by the Spirit of the living God, from people to people, and from land to land, in the congregations of the wicked, in their synagogues, reasoning with and expounding all scriptures unto them. And, behold, and lo, this is an ensample unto all those who were ordained unto this priesthood, whose mission is appointed unto them to go forth. And this is the ensample unto them, that they shall speak as they are moved upon by the Holy Ghost. And whatsoever they shall speak when moved upon by the Holy Ghost shall be scripture, shall be the will of the Lord, shall be the mind of the Lord, shall be the word of the Lord, shall be the voice of the Lord, and the power of God unto salvation." (D&C 68:1-4).

Following in the footsteps of Orson Hyde, who served for 28 years as President of the Quorum of the Twelve Apostles, officers and members of the church gather at its headquarters in Salt Lake City, Utah, and in stake and ward meetinghouses across the globe, to participate directly or by satellite transmission in the proceedings of the Semi-Annual General Conferences of the church, held each year in April and October. On October 30, 2014, the First Presidency clarified confusion relating to the status of the General Women's Meeting, as well as the General Young Women's Meeting, that since 1994 had been held a week prior to General Conference in April and October respectively, by announcing: "The General Women's Meeting will be designated as the General Women's Session of general conference." A combined meeting is now held semiannually for both women and young women, a week before the general sessions of Conference.

So popular is the Conference, that admission tickets are required to attend sessions in the 21,000 seat Conference Center in Salt Lake City. Members living in the United States and Canada may obtain these free of charge from their local priesthood leaders, although there are generally not nearly enough to go around. Those visiting from outside the United States and Canada may receive tickets under special circumstances. Entrance is limited to those ages eight and older for general sessions and twelve years and older for the priesthood session. Conference attendees are not allowed to bring babies into the Conference Center, for obvious reasons relating to the excellent acoustics of the building.

Those who are invited to speak at General Conference are typically selected from among the General Authorities and General Officers of the church. The General Authorities include the following:

There are three members of The First Presidency of the church, the highest governing body of the church. Its members are special witnesses of the name of Jesus Christ, called to teach and testify of Him throughout the world. Members of the First Presidency travel around the world to speak to members and local leaders. When not traveling, they counsel together and with other general church leaders on matters affecting the worldwide church, such as missionary work, temple building and spiritual and temporal welfare."[2]

There are twelve members of The Quorum of the Twelve Apostles, "the second-highest presiding body in the government of the church. Its members travel the world as special witnesses of the name of Christ and serve under the direction of the First Presidency."[2]

There are seven members of The Presidency of the Seventy, consisting of "seven General Authority Seventies who are called by the First Presidency and given authority to preside over the various Quorums of the Seventy."

There are seventy five members of The General Authority Seventies, who "preach the gospel and serve as special witnesses of Christ to the world. They assist the Quorum of the Twelve Apostles in preaching the gospel of Jesus Christ throughout the world. They serve in the Presidency of the Seventy, in Area Presidencies, and in other headquarters administrative functions. Under the direction of The Quorum of the Twelve Apostles, they travel frequently to meet with and teach church leaders, missionaries, and members of the church in local congregations."

General Authority Seventies "have authority to serve anywhere in the world. The authority of Area Seventies is generally limited to the area where they serve. The Presidency of the Seventy is drawn from the General Authority Seventies, and presides over all quorums of the Seventy."

At the 2015 General Conference of the church, as part of the ongoing evolution of its administration, the General Authorities in the 1st and 2nd Quorums of Seventy were combined, reconfigured, and re-designated as General Authority Seventies. Until then, the members of the 1st Quorum of the Seventy served from the time of their call until approximately seventy years of age. At that time, they transitioned to an emeritus status. Members of the 2nd Quorum of the Seventy, however, were called for a period of 5 to 7 years, and then were released from their callings. Members of both quorums had been designated General Authorities of the church. The new structure combines the two groups with no separate quorum designation, and its members are now called "General Authority Seventies."

There are three members of a Presiding Bishopric, consisting of "the Presiding Bishop and his two counselors. Each holds the office of bishop, and they serve under the direct supervision of the First Presidency. The Presiding Bishopric is responsible for many of the church's temporal affairs."

Others from among the General Officers of the church who may be selected to speak at General Conference include:

Three members of the Relief Society General Presidency, who, "under the direction of the First Presidency, oversee the activities of all Latter-day Saint women ages 18 and over. They help guide and support the women of the church." The Relief Society is one of the oldest and largest women's organizations in the world.

Three members of the Young Men General Presidency, "who provide instruction, encouragement and support in living the gospel of Jesus Christ for male church members ages 12 through 18. These leaders serve under the direction of the First Presidency and guide and support the young men of the church."

Three members of the Young Women General Presidency, "who provide instruction, encouragement, and support in living the gospel of Jesus Christ for female church members ages 12 through 17. These leaders serve under the direction of the First Presidency and help guide and support the young women of the church."

Three members of the Primary General Presidency, "who oversee the church's organization that teaches children ages 18 months to 11 years the gospel of Jesus Christ and helps them live its principles. These leaders serve under the direction of the First Presidency and help guide and support the children and their local leaders."

Three members of the Sunday School General Presidency, "who oversee the church's organization that teaches adults the gospel of Jesus Christ and helps them live its principles. These leaders serve under the direction of the First Presidency and help guide and support adult members and their local leaders."

So there are a total of approximately 100 General Authorities, and 15 General Officers of the church. All of them are heavy hitters in the church. These all-stars have extensive experience administering its temporal and spiritual affairs, on the local, regional, hemispherical, and global levels. Many have been honored to be the most valuable players on their stake and ward teams, and some were first-round draft picks at the time they declared their free-agency and emerged from full-time missions into adulthood. A few became rookies of the year. None, however, have received any kind of signing bonus or other financial incentive to serve. They do not employ talent agents nor do they have personal coaches. Their service is not tied to any church related salary cap; in fact, they receive no salary at all. (Some do receive living stipends). Most of them were not first round draft picks; in fact, many of them were walk-ons who proved their mettle only after they had gotten down into the trenches.

They conduct their lives in quiet contrast to the inflammatory lifestyles of many of the athletes who wear Super Bowl rings. They did not get where they are through a series of playoffs and division championships. They receive no product endorsements, and sign no lucrative deals with sponsors. They selflessly serve without thought of remuneration or recognition.

On the other hand, there are 53 members of the squad on a Super Bowl football team. It is probably safe to say that each of them dreams of being the star of the show; of taking home the trophy for Most Valuable Player. Each of them, regardless of playing time in the championship game, receives $97,000.00 (for winners) or $49,00.00 (for losers) for their participation. For most of the players, this bonus is chump change, because the average yearly salary per player is around $2.1 million. (The minimum NFL wage is $420,000.00). It should be noted that in the General Conferences of the church, there are no winners or losers. Everyone is treated the same.

As noted above, there is no cost of admission to General Conference, and there are no advertising incentives related to the satellite transmission of Conference proceedings to stake centers throughout the world. In contrast, Super Bowl 50 was the most expensive sporting event in U.S. history, with an average ticket resale price of $5,335.00. Interestingly, the most expensive ticket for Super Bowl I was $12.00. (Yes, you read that correctly: Twelve dollars). But then again, fifty years ago, you could typically walk into the Tabernacle on Temple Square to participate in a Conference session, and keep your money in your pocket, to later purchase a "Cinnabon" across the street. Now you need that elusive Golden Ticket, but few other things about Conference have changed.

A typical Super Bowl football game lasts three hours and 12 minutes, but the ball is only in play for around 11 minutes. Conference, on the other hand, is composed of four 2 hour general sessions, a 2 hour Priesthood Session, and a 2 hour General Women's Session as noted above. Every minute is packed with inspiring instruction delivered via music and the spoken word. There is no ostentatious half-time show, and there are no clever advertisements designed to hold your attention. However, advertisers pony up mega-bucks for exposure on Super Bowl broadcasts. A 30-second commercial for the first Super Bowl in 1967 cost $42,000.00; it hit $1 million in 1995, and C.B.S. is charging $5 million for 30 second ads in 2016, which works out to $166,666.00 per second.

Just for fun, think of the "Super Bowl" value of an invocation or benediction at General Conference. If the average prayer lasted just one minute, its value would be ten million dollars. That said, those who have attended or listened to Conference frequently attest to the fact that they've heard multi-million dollar prayers!

According to the NFL Players Association the average length of the career of a professional football player is about 3.3 years. On the Super Bowl roster of General Authorities (just considering The First Presidency and Quorum of the Twelve) the average length of service is 17.6 years in their current position. Without exception, all of them came from decades of devoted service in other callings. Their average age is 76, and there is no emeritus status. They keep laboring in the vineyard until they are finally released when they are called home to their Heavenly Father.

The Super Bowl is surrounded by extravagant and intense publicity and promotion by the media. Similarly, the April 2016 proceedings of General Conference were translated in real-time into more than 80 languages and were available in 94 languages total via television, radio, satellite and Internet. But, at the same time, the main-stream media rarely gives General Conference even lip service. Instead, it focuses on worldly matters and debates the merits of the Super Bowl contenders who are going to face off for the Vince Lombardi Trophy on the third Sunday in February. I recall an Area Conference that was held in Spokane, Washington, on May 10-11, 1986. Headlines in the local newspapers that weekend should have declared to a spellbound city: "Largest Priesthood Gathering Ever Held in the Northwest," "Apostles of the Lord Visit Spokane," and "Ten Thousand Saints of The Most High God Assemble." In fact, there was no reference whatsoever to the Conference in either of Spokane's daily newspapers. Instead, the media reported on the health of the economy, the political fortunes of prominent politicians, baseball games, and other telestial trivia.

The media devotes an inordinate amount of attention to the Super Bowl, and sports analysts and commentators discuss every permutation, and dissect every variable relating to the impending contest, ad nauseam, as if the fate of the world hung in the balance. On the other hand, the leaders of the church only go so far as to print the proceedings of the Conference in the Ensign magazine, in the monthly issue that follows the conclusion of Conference. They leave to the members of the church the responsibility to seek spiritual confirmation from the Holy Ghost, and to choose from among the addresses delivered, those that are of most relevance to their personal circumstances.

Unlike the conduct of prominent members of The Church of Jesus Christ of Latter-day Saints, the behavior of the members of the National Football League is fraught with controversy. It is almost desirable to be labeled a "bad boy." A good example is the flap surrounding "DeflateGate," that involved the allegation that the New England Patriots had tampered with footballs used in the American Football Conference Championship game (in 2016), which New England won, by deliberately under-inflating the football so that it would be easier for their quarterback to grip and throw, easier for his receivers to catch, and less likely for him to fumble, especially in the cold and rainy conditions in which the game was played. (Tom Brady, the quarterback, was suspended for four games, as a result of the investigation into the scandal, but he remains unrepentant).

Only one General Authority (George P. Lee, a member of the Seventy) has, in recent memory, been disciplined (excommunicated in 1989) by the church for conduct unbecoming a church member. In 1943, Richard R. Lyman, a member of the Quorum of the Twelve, was also excommunicated for "a violation of the law of chastity."

Many of those who play in the Super Bowl have familiar household names, and are nearly revered by fans and the press, but they possess talents that pale in comparison to those who actively participate in General Conference. Leaders of the church enjoy associations in the rarified atmosphere of a religious society that is unique, reminding us of the introductory remarks made by President John F. Kennedy, who hosted a White House dinner on April 29, 1962, honoring Nobel Prize laureates. He said of them, as could be said of the leaders of the church who gather twice a year to celebrate the Super Bowl of Religious Symposia: "I think this is the most extraordinary collection of talent and of human knowledge that has ever been gathered together at the White House, with the possible exception of when Thomas Jefferson dined alone."

Footnotes:

1. Unless otherwise noted, quotations are from LDS.Org

2. As of 2017:

Thomas S. Monson – year called: 1963 54 years of service
Russell M. Nelson – year called: 1984 33 years of service
Dallin H. Oaks – year called: 1984 33 years of service
M. Russell Ballard – year called: 1985 32 years of service
Robert D. Hales – year called: 1994 23 years of service
Jeffrey R. Holland – year called: 1994 23 years of service
Henry B. Eyring – year called: 1995 22 years of service
David A. Bednar – year called: 2004 13 years of service
Deiter F. Uchtdorf – year called: 2004 13 years of service
Quentin L. Cook – year called: 2007 10 years of service
D. Todd Christofferson – year called: 2008 9 years of service
Neil L. Anderson – year called: 2009 8 years of service
Ronald A. Rasband – year called: 2015 2 years of service
Gary E. Stevenson – year called: 2015 2 years of service
Dale G. Renlund – year called: 2015 2 years of service

"Surely
the Lord God
will do nothing, but he
revealeth his secret unto his
servants the prophets."
(Amos 3:7).

God
Is NowHere

If God does not speak to us today, perhaps it is because He cannot. Perhaps He has suffered a massive stroke resulting in aphasia. Maybe He has lost His First Amendment rights, and no longer enjoys freedom of speech. Maybe He has developed xenophobia, and has retreated behind the walls of His kingdom because He feels threatened by those who insist that He does not exist. Maybe He just doesn't care about His children anymore. His silence might be evidence that He has lost interest in us, has other things on His mind, has other priorities, or has become distracted by other, more pressing, concerns. Maybe He has finally realized that we just don't need Him anymore. Maybe He is sitting back and taking a much-needed vacation from His responsibilities because technology has taken His place, science satisfies our needs, and rationalism has assuaged our consciences.

Maybe He is daunted by our advances in the healing arts and feels that His therapeutic powers have become obsolete. Maybe the explosion in information technology has intimidated Him. Maybe He feels overshadowed by our advances in education, that Common Core has finally leveled the educational playing field, and that there is no longer a need for pointed, and specific, and individual, religious instruction. Maybe He has grown tired of competing against the avalanche of negative press in a media that has its own agenda. Maybe He has been overwhelmed by the mesmerizing wonders of Industrial Light and Magic, and of C.G.I., and feels that His miracles cannot possibly compete with their enchantments. Maybe He has nothing to add to the dialogue, because we've gotten things figured out on our own, and have demonstrated that we are securely in control of our own destiny.

Maybe none of the above is true, however, which begs the question: Does God still speak to His children? Certainly, we must concede that He can, whenever He wishes to do so. A second question, then, is: Does God have any interest in or desire to communicate with His children. The scriptures reveal how deeply He has always cared about us, how intensely He has been concerned about our welfare, and how intertwined are our lives with His work and glory. It seems clear that He would no more abandon us to our own devices, than we would leave a toddler unattended in a dark alleyway in the bad part of town. Why would He ever forsake us, or leave us to the whims of a fate beyond His or our control?

Surely, we need His wise counsel now as much as we ever have, because we have the potential to destroy each other and ourselves if we do not carefully follow His Plan. We need Him and His living prophets today, just as we did in times of old, to guide us around telestial traffic jams. We need help to free ourselves from conceptual quicksands. We need inspired guidance to deal with doctrinal dead ends. We desperately need to be shown how to successfully negotiate the minefields of mortality. We need his authorized and ordained priesthood servants to act as our tactical S.W.A.T. Team, and as our personal bomb squad, to identify, address, and neutralize, every unattended backpack that poses a threat to our spiritual security.

Angelic counsel was given to Joseph Smith almost 200 years ago, when he was told: "Wherever the sound (of the marvelous work) shall go, it shall cause the ears of men to tingle, and wherever it shall be proclaimed, the pure in heart shall rejoice." When we hear the words of living prophets, the Spirit washes over us with a confirmation that is undeniable. But Moroni cautioned: "Those who draw near to God with their mouths, and honor him with their lips, while their hearts are far from him, will seek its overthrow, and the destruction of those by whose hands it is carried." Then, ominously, Joseph was warned: "Therefore, marvel not if your name is made a derision and had as a by-word among such, if you are the instrument in bringing it, by the gift of God, to the knowledge of the people." (Quoted in "The Messenger & Advocate"). As Jesus taught: "A prophet is not without honour, save in his own country, and in his own house." (Matthew 13:57). Some people just can't handle the good news.

Naysayers notwithstanding, "what do we hear? Glad tidings from Cumorah! Moroni, an angel from heaven, declaring the fulfillment of the prophets—the book to be revealed. A voice of the Lord in the wilderness of Fayette, Seneca County, declaring the three witnesses to bear record of the book! The voice of Michael on the banks of the Susquehanna, detecting the devil when he appeared as an angel of light! The voice of Peter, James, and John in the wilderness between Harmony, Susquehanna county, and Colesville, Broome county, on the Susquehanna river, declaring themselves as possessing the keys of the kingdom, and of the dispensation of the fulness of times!" (D&C 128:20).

Heavenly Father has responded to our needs. Today, we have someone among us who can stand tall, and with a clear vision see the storm clouds before they appear on the horizon. Noah built the ark long before the barometer plummeted, the sky darkened, and the rains fell. The Law of Tithing was introduced as fire insurance to protect our homes while they still stand, before the great and dreadful day of the Lord comes to consume the wicked in its flames. The temple was reintroduced as a preventive measure, that the earth might avoid being utterly wasted at the coming of the Lord. A Proclamation on The Family was made 13 years before the battle lines were drawn over Proposition 8. Pornography was denounced when the Internet was still in its infancy. Self-reliance and self-sufficiency were advocated before the Great Depression brought the world to its economic knees. The Word of Wisdom was given 138 years before the declaration of war on illicit drugs. The Perpetual Education Fund was announced 160 years before Common Core. The watchmen upon the walls see the enemy while he is yet afar off, allowing us to make ready and to keep him from breaking down the hedges of our vineyards. (See D&C 101:54).

Our living prophets teach us how to live in harmony with God's Plan, show us how to prepare the way for the Lord's return, and invite us to participate in the establishment of His kingdom on the earth. "The greatest event that has ever occurred in the world since the resurrection of the Son of God from the tomb and his ascension on high," declared Joseph F. Smith, "was the coming of the Father and of the Son to that boy Joseph Smith, to prepare the way for the laying of the foundation of his kingdom."

Our living prophets show us how to be happy. They have a knack for seeing the eternal principle of agency in a different light. They recognize that the exercise of free will does entail risk, because the element of failure is real and is always just one decision away, but they have confidence that it is the only way that we may justify our claim to unspeakable joy in our Father's kingdom. Without brow beating us, our prophets give us repetitive opportunities to recommit ourselves to our covenants of obedience to tried and true principles. At the same time, they reassure us that the laws pertaining to happiness will qualify us to receive the blessings tied to obedience. They continually find ways to nurture our spiritual well-being, and inner peace with words of encouragement. "Happiness (after all) is the object and design of our existence, and will be the end thereof," said the Prophet Joseph Smith, "if we pursue the path that leads to it, and this path is virtue, uprightness, faithfulness, holiness, and keeping all the commandments of God." ("Teachings," p. 255).

"The most important prophet, as far as we are concerned, is the one who is living in our day and age. Every generation has need of (counsel) from the living prophet. Therefore, the most crucial reading and pondering which you should do, is of the latest inspired words from the Lord's mouthpiece." (Ezra Taft Benson, "Liahona," 6/1981).

Our living prophets share our perspective, but they are also able to see through the clarifying and purifying lens of eternity. They bless our lives in many ways by nurturing our understanding of the Plan of Salvation. The veil that has been drawn over our eyes, preventing us from seeing eternity with an unimpeded view, is nearly transparent to our prophets. Joseph Smith explained as a statement of fact: "Could you gaze into heaven five minutes, you would know more than you would by reading all that has ever been written on the subject." (H.C., 6:50). Asked how he could govern so many people, he replied: "I teach them correct principles, and they govern themselves." (John Taylor, "The Organization of the Church," Millennial Star, 11/15/1851, p. 339). His comprehension of the Plan of Salvation allowed him to teach the body of known truth, to clarify truth that had been heretofore hidden from the world, and to reveal new truth to the world that would enrich the quality of our lives. Truly, the Prophet Joseph Smith "was a prism of the Lord Jesus Christ." (Truman Madsen).

Within the Lord's restored Church of Jesus Christ of Latter-day Saints, the Quorum of The First Presidency, and The Quorum of The Twelve, are composed of living prophets, seers, and revelators. The subjects upon which they have recently focused their attention include the call to be Christ-like, how to receive the Holy Ghost, learning by the Spirit, recognizing revelation, the blessings of obedience, sharing the gospel, family history and temple work, priesthood power, education, building strong families, the protective power of prayer, making covenants with God, helping new members, staying out of debt, preparing for The Second Coming, and understanding the scriptures. (See Conference Reports, October 2015).

These prophets, seers, and revelators, who hold the keys of the kingdom and who stand next to Jesus Christ, Who is at the head of the church, are to be upheld by our confidence, faith, and prayers. (See D&C 107:22). Of the President of the Quorum of The First Presidency, we have been commanded to give "heed unto all his words and commandments which he shall give unto you as he receiveth them, walking in all holiness before me; For his word ye shall receive, as if from mine own mouth, in all patience and faith. For by doing these things the gates of hell shall not prevail against you; yea, and the Lord God will disperse the powers of darkness from before you, and cause the heavens to shake for your good, and his name's glory." (D&C 21:4-6).

One such living prophet has taught: "There will be some things that take patience and faith. You may not like what comes from the authority of the church. It may contradict your political views. It may contradict your social views. It may interfere with some of your social life. But if you listen to these things, as if from the mouth of the Lord himself, with patience and faith, the promise is that the gates of hell shall not prevail against you." (President Harold B. Lee, C.R., 10/1970). At the close of a later general conference, President Ezra Taft Benson reiterated: "For the next six months, your conference edition of the Ensign should stand next to your standard works and be referred to frequently." (C.R., 4/1988).

As it was said of Joseph Smith, so could it be said of each of the 99 Apostles (as of 2016) who have carried the mantle of prophet, seer, and revelator in the Last Days, that among their greatest contributions has been their knowledge of what is to come after death. They have done much to clarify our understanding of heaven and to make it seem worth working for.

"As I made my journey, and was
come nigh unto Damascus about noon,
suddenly there shone from heaven
a great light round about me."
(Acts 22:6).

God's Tactical Flashlight

Sometimes it seems almost as if positive energy comes in discrete packages that are dispensed by especially cheerful individuals who always have a smile on their face and a spring in their step. For example, think of the amazing ability some have to light up the room by their mere presence. Think of charismatic leaders who inspire their followers to defy the odds and attempt the impossible, of those whose compelling charm and magnetic personalities have an almost mystical draw, of those who can so easily captivate others with the sparkle of their rhetoric, of those with the hypnotic ability to mesmerize their listeners with magical word-portraits that are motivational and inspiring, and of the natural appeal and irresistible draw of those whose minds and spirits have been endowed with discernment, inspiration, and revelation, and whose eyes and lips have been touched by the finger of God.

These people have dedicated themselves to worthwhile activities that give their lives meaning and purpose. They are committed to self-improvement and engage with others in ways that are mutually supportive. They do not waste time being defensive, but instead welcome constructive criticism. They share their knowledge and ideas with others and are mentors to those who may have dozed off while on the path toward self-actualization. They enjoy the journey as much as the destination. They do not allow power and influence to corrupt them or to deter them from focusing their energies on core principles. Even when life throws them a curve, they smile. They realize that happiness is contagious, and as carriers, they infect others with cheerfulness. They are courteous and thoughtful, and speak of others as if their parrot were the town gossip. They are kind and gentle, especially when interacting with the village idiot. When necessity arises, they use diplomacy, celebrating the differences between individuals, because they know that we are all children of God, with unique talents and abilities.

When I visualize these individuals and their capacity to stimulate, encourage, provoke, and persuade others to embrace their positive energy, I compare them to the dramatically illuminating and enlightening power of high intensity tactical flashlights, the kind that are driven by light emitting diodes that are fueled by lithium ion batteries.

But those who hum with positive energy go even one step further. They not only generate enthusiasm, but they also have learned how to compartmentalize its negative counterparts. They have discovered how to neutralize bad vibrations. In the "Ghostbusters" movie franchise, mischievous ectoplasmic entities captured by the team were transferred to a secure and stable containment field. Our God-given fetters are more subtle, but infinitely more effective, because they do not rely on contraptions that must be plugged in to the wall socket in order to function. Ours consist of powerful spiritual guidance systems that find their expression in the security of obedience to unchanging principles that are then magnified by provident living, and by the solidarity of our repetitive recommitment to covenants through ordinances that are administered by the priesthood.

In "Ghostbusters," the effect of the inadvertent disruption of the electrical power flow to the containment field was catastrophic. In life, the consequences related to ignorance of negative psychokinetic energy can be just as calamitous. When we are about to be "slimed" by the seething spiritual gloom that swirls about us like effluent spewing from a broken sewer pipe, we must consciously and deliberately encircle it with a containment boom, channel it into a suitable vessel, and then slam on the lid, securing it tightly. Even if the darkness within the trap is later opened, the discharge that attempts to escape will be dissipated and neutralized, because it will be instantly subjected to the dazzling light emitting diodes that are part of our own customized versions of Dr. Egon Spengler's ingenious portable proton pack.

When we have been quickened by the Holy Ghost, we become His particle accelerators and His tactical flashlights, prominently and strategically set on a hill so that we cannot be hidden. For all the world to see, we confidently publish abroad in the land our noble commission to give "light unto all that are in the house." We let our lights "so shine before men, that they may see (our) good works, and glorify (our) Father which is in heaven." (Matthew 5:14-16). By doing so, the concentrated power that radiates from the Holy Ghost is gathered out from under a bushel, where, left unattended, it could have easily decayed into destructive negative energy. We focus that clean, pure, environmentally friendly light in positive directions. In Ghostbuster terminology, we "cross the streams" when we are faced with inter-dimensional portals that require extreme measures (the "Gozer Gambit") in order to close the door with finality on negative dimensional realities that continually probe our firewalls in attempts to encroach upon our world.

The darkness that oozes out from those destructive dominions threatens to disrupt our spiritual symmetry, causing a stupor of thought. As Samuel the Lamanite asked: "How long will ye suffer yourselves to be led by foolish and blind guides? Yea, how long will ye choose darkness rather than light?" (Helaman 13:29). If we were to try to teach the world the principles of the gospel by relying upon only the illumination provided by the dim light of the moon, it would be nigh unto impossible. If, for additional illumination, we utilized the glow provided by an inexpensive flashlight, or relied upon the weakened energy reserves of a proton pack that lacked a full charge, we might just be able to make out the glimmering facets of the light of the Spirit. These additional lumens of energy are like the faint glow of the microwave background radiation from the Big Bang, and might also be likened to the Light of Christ that permeates the universe. At 2.76° Kelvin, it is better than nothing at all, but arguably, since it hovers just above absolute zero, it is less than ideal.

Before the introduction of the proton packs or the spiritual tactical flashlights provided by the gift of the Holy Ghost, the real problem in the world was that in their efforts to clarify their consideration of Christ, even earnest seekers of truth were only "multiplying mirrors and studying angles without increasing the light," when what was really needed was a flood of protons "that would not only replace the darkness, but would also illuminate elements and principles that, heretofore, had been only dimly perceived." (See B.H. Roberts, The Truth, The Way, The Life, p. 263). In their attempts to increase the light by playing the angles, they were able to see a bit more clearly, but still, many basic principles remained only dimly perceived. The problem was that these individuals were only spinning their wheels because the number of available lumens of energy had not been increased. What was really needed was more light! Heavenly Father orchestrated the Restoration in order to address the problem of darkness in the world. Hence, the Savior appeared to Joseph Smith in the Sacred Grove as "the light which shineth in darkness." (D&C 11:11).

The Restoration then set in motion a number of protocols that were designed to increase the amount of available light. These measures generously provided more than enough tactical flashlights to go around. Heavenly Father saw to it that every earnest student of the scriptures would be able to read even its fine print with unerring clarity. Its footnotes would snap into sharp focus. Its topical guide would intuitively begin to make more sense. The relevance of the teachings of His prophets and of additional scriptures would become increasingly apparent. Foundation principles would knit together coherently as they were stitched into an understandable pattern, and the power of the word and the witness of truth would be conveyed without the need for external warrant.

God decided to change the name of His proton pack to something that would be less trendy but still catch the attention of His children; something that would more dramatically describe the increased illumination. The spiritual tactical flashlight would be called "the Gift of the Holy Ghost." Its power would far surpass the output that had heretofore been provided by the Light of Christ. Those who would subsequently enroll in His curriculum would enjoy a many-fold increase in their spiritual visual acuity. Whereas they had been limping along with a few hundred lumens to mark their path of progress, now they would have thousands at their disposal. They would feel as if their whole bodies had been filled with light. They would feel the comfort of an increase in their protection from evil influences, and would experience the flush of excitement as they vanquished the adversary with the unsophisticated weapons of light and truth. They would savor the indescribable emotion of light penetrating to their nethermost parts. Their souls would resonate with understanding, as when Joseph Smith received "The Vision" known as Section 76 of the Doctrine & Covenants. The prophet is said to have declared: "My whole body was full of light, and I could see even out at the ends of my fingers and toes." (Philo Dibble, Journal record).

This spiritual upgrade of our positron colliders to full-fledged electrostatic accelerators with well-collimated particle beam emitters may help to explain the circumstances surrounding the appearance of the Angel Moroni to young Joseph in his bedchamber, in 1821. He later wrote of the experience: "While I was thus in the act of calling upon God, I discovered a light appearing in my room, which continued to increase until the room was lighter than at noonday, when immediately a personage appeared at my bedside, standing in the air, for his feet did not touch the floor. He had on a loose robe of most exquisite whiteness…beyond anything earthly I had ever seen; nor do I believe that any earthly thing could be made to appear so exceedingly white and brilliant. His hands were naked, and his arms also, a little above the wrist; so, also, were his feet naked, as were his legs, a little above the ankles. His head and neck were also bare. I could discover that he had no other clothing on but this robe, as it was open, so that I could see into his bosom. Not only was his robe exceedingly white, but his whole person was glorious beyond description, and his countenance truly like lightning. The room was exceedingly light, but not so very bright as immediately around his person." (J.S.H. 1:30-32).

In the scriptures, light is mentioned 510 times, while light and its contrasting element of darkness are linked together 103 times. One particularly vivid description of darkness is found in The Book of Mormon in the 8th chapter of 3 Nephi. It states that at the time of the crucifixion of Christ, "there was darkness upon the face of the land." (V. 19, see Matthew 27:51). In Book of Mormon lands, so overpowering, so complete, so total and universal was the murky blackness, that "those who had not fallen could feel the vapor of darkness." (V. 20, see Exodus 10:21-23). Not only the Holy Ghost, but also the Light of Christ seems to have been withdrawn; thus, "there could not be any light at all." (V. 21, see D&C 84:45-46, & 88:7-13). The survivors of the storm that had swept over the countryside could see neither "the sun, nor the moon, nor the stars, for so great were the mists of darkness which were upon the face of the land." (V. 22). (See D&C 76:32).

Hopefully, this Book of Mormon record is as close as any of us will ever come to understanding just how overwhelming will be the spiritual darkness that will prevail among those who are resurrected to a kingdom without glory, which is as a "lake which burneth with fire and brimstone, which is the second death." (D&C 63:17). For the Sons of Perdition, their existence in such a spiritual vacuum will be a living hell. (See D&C 76:32).

At the very least, we are reminded of the experience of Joseph in the grove near his home outside of Palmyra, New York: "Thick darkness gathered around me, and it seemed to me for a time as if I were doomed to sudden destruction. But, exerting all my powers to call upon God to deliver me out of the power of this enemy which had seized upon me, and at the very moment when I was ready to sink into despair and abandon myself to destruction - not to an imaginary ruin, but to the power of some actual being from the unseen world, who had such marvelous power as I had never before felt in any being - just at this moment of great alarm, I saw a pillar of light exactly over my head, above the brightness of the sun, which descended gradually until it fell upon me. It no sooner appeared than I found myself delivered from the enemy which held me bound. When the light rested upon me I saw two Personages, whose brightness and glory defy all description, standing above me in the air. One of them spake unto me, calling me by name and said, pointing to the other: This is My Beloved Son. Hear Him!" (J.S.H. 1:15-17). Joseph had walked in darkness, but had seen a great light. He had dwelt in the land of the shadow of death, but upon him the light had shined. (See Isaiah 9:2).

Eighteen hundred years earlier, the Savior had taught the Jews: "If thy whole body, therefore, be full of light, having no part dark, the whole shall be full of light, as when the bright shining of a candle doth give thee light." (Luke 11:36). Joseph had powerfully witnessed that "light and truth forsake that evil one." (D&C 93:37). The expression of this divine principle was fully realized when he then beheld both the Father and the Son in the Sacred Grove. As Paul had taught the Thessalonian Saints, so had the blessing come to pass: "And then shall that wicked one be revealed, whom the Lord shall consume with the spirit of his mouth, and…destroy with the brightness of his coming." (J.S.T. 2 Thessalonians 2:8).

Just as the Ghostbusters confronted Gozer in its temple on the top of a Manhattan skyscraper, so too, when we face horrifying "Sumerian demons" or giant "Stay Puft Marshmallow Men" in whatever form they choose to masquerade themselves, our training should compel us to turn to our proton packs, "for the Lord is our defence, and the Holy One of Israel is our king." (Psalms 89:18). "And the Lord will create upon every dwelling place of mount Zion, and upon her assemblies, a cloud and smoke by day, and the shining of a flaming fire by night" to resist and overcome the enemy. (Isaiah 4:5).

In the real world, our tactical flashlight versions of proton packs provide powerful bursts of light with the capacity to temporarily stun our adversaries. Spiritual tactical flashlights can do the same thing even more efficiently. The power of the ordinances of the gospel and of our related covenants is so great that it can be a shield and a protection to us against evil influences. It can enable us to disorient our foes, giving us time to complete our mortal missions and return with honor to our heavenly home.

As Joseph Smith received instruction, the meaning and intent of the scriptures was opened to his understanding, so much so that he could actually comprehend the mind and will of God. (See D&C 76:12). "For the word of the Lord is truth, and whatsoever is truth is light, and whatsoever is light is Spirit, even the Spirit of Jesus Christ." (D&C 84:45). Joseph may have been the first to explode the myth of using only 10% of our brains. He came to regularly enjoy a many fold increase in the illumination of his mind that enabled him to comprehend difficult to understand principles.

As he matured in the gospel, the unknown possibilities of existence crystallized in his brain. He was transformed to understand in a tangible way that "intelligence cleaveth unto intelligence; wisdom receiveth wisdom; truth embraceth truth; virtue loveth virtue; light cleaveth unto light; mercy…claimeth her own; justice continueth its course, (and) judgment goeth before the face of him who sitteth upon the throne." (D&C 88:40).

As we ponder the scriptures, the Spirit reveals just how breathtaking increasing the light can be. In visions splendid, we are on our way attended by the Holy Ghost, but only if we establish habit patterns to keep our tactical lights, the spiritual versions of our proton packs, on at all times, locked and loaded with the safety off. We need to keep ourselves worthy and choose wisely, as the Grail Knight warned in the motion picture "Indiana Jones and The Last Crusade." Those of us who bear the vessels of the Lord need to be clean, for "he that keepeth his commandments receiveth truth and light, until he is glorified in truth and knoweth all things." (D&C 93:28).

There are many knock-off devices in the world that promote themselves as proton packs, including neutron wands, bozon darts, particle accelerators, and containment lasers. A recent Internet search found over 6 million sites that reference these devices. Most turn out to be inferior imitations offered by less than reputable online retailers. Every one, it seems, endorses itself as the best. But, in our quest to find the Holy Grail of Light, we must never settle for what is really life in a shabby room illuminated by a bare bulb hanging from a frayed cord, in a second-class hotel in the bad part of town. Instead, we must hold out for a positron collider, proton pack, or tactical light powerful enough to illuminate the way to the holy hill of the Lord, where we may find His tabernacle. (See Psalms 43:3). As Obi Won Kenobe would say: May the Force always be with us!

When we have paid a fair price, and have received our device as advertised, we must handle it with reverence, as if it were a Jedi lightsaber, our own personal Liahona, or even a Urim and Thummim. We must resist the temptation to jump ahead without mastering all of the operating instructions. We must study and practice, and be diligent and consistent in our training. Only then, may we "press forward with a steadfastness in Christ, having a perfect brightness of hope, and a love of God and of all men." (2 Nephi 31:20).

Before initially utilizing the light, we must make sure our batteries are at full capacity, and afterwards, replenish them as frequently as necessary. The dynamo that is the repository of our spiritual strength has a memory like an elephant and likes to be fully charged. However, repeated use will only increase its capacity and make it stronger. The number of cycles available for our use is endless. One helpful feature is the option to leave our light on all the time, so that we may have unbridled confidence that "the sun shall be no more (our) light by day; neither for brightness shall the moon give light unto (us), but the Lord shall be unto (us) an everlasting light, and (our) God (our) glory." (Isaiah 60:19).

If we have been abiding by the Light of Christ, we have only been given a glimpse into the limitless power of the intrinsic illumination that rests within the Godhead. With an awakening comprehension, we begin to understand that our "Father, and the Son, and the Holy Ghost are one," and that they share a palpable divine power and authority. (3 Nephi 11:27). The Holy Ghost, in particular, seems to have the ability to dazzle us with an endless reserve of photons that illuminate every corner of our minds and our spirits. The promises proffered by the combined capacity of the intrinsic light possessed by the Holy Trinity is beyond our comprehension. Particle physics tells us that, at the moment of the Big Bang, there was an incomprehensible number of photons, or units of electromagnetic energy, that were created. The number is 1 followed by 89 zeroes, which is essentially insignificant when compared to the luminosity of God. At the end of the day, "there is no power but of God." The powers that we can define, measure, and quantify as photons, "are ordained of God" for the use of the Trinity, to provide reliable light in a dark and dreary world. (Romans 13:1).

All the members of the Godhead possess the inherent electro-magnetic capacity of a tactical flashlight that has been calibrated to an infinite scale. Their realm, the Celestial Kingdom, is full of an unfathomable, unsearchable, undefinable, light. In the Kirtland Temple Dedicatory Prayer, Joseph Smith resorted to symbolism, when he envisioned "bright, shining seraphs" who surrounded the throne of God. (D&C 109:79). Isaiah likewise described seraphim with live coals in their hands. (See Isaiah 6:6). Ezekiel saw the glory of the Lord that "stood over the threshold of the house" of

God, and that it "was filled with (a) cloud," and he saw its court, that "was full of the brightness of the Lord's glory." (Ezekiel 10:4).

God has given us clues regarding just how bright His glory really is. He has instilled in us a sense of curiosity that almost compels us to stare in wonder at the night sky, as we attempt to absorb with our minds what seems to be an infinite number of stars. The Milky Way, a glowing smear of light cast from 100 to 400 billion stars, mesmerizes us. Myths from around the world give it its name and explain its origin. The Greeks believed it was created when suckling Heracles dribbled the breast milk of Hera, the wife of Zeus, across the night sky. It was also described as the trail to Mount Olympus, the home of the Gods, and as the path of ruin made by the chariot of the Sun God Helios. In Sanskrit, the Milky Way was called Akash Ganga (Ganges of the Heavens), and was considered sacred. Hindu cosmology explains the galaxy as an ocean of milk churned by the gods for a thousand years in order to release Amrita, the nectar of immortal life. All we know for sure about the Milky Way and our universe is what God told Moses: "The heavens, they are many, and they cannot be numbered unto man; but they are numbered unto me, for they are mine." (Moses 1:37).

But how many stars can we see with just the naked eye, without the aid of a spiritual Hubble telescope or tactical flashlight? The total comes to a paltry 9,000 stars visible across the entire sky, but inasmuch as we can only see half the celestial sphere at any moment, we must necessarily divide that number by two, to arrive at 4,500 stars. We can see about one star per cubic parsec (one second of arc). If we were at the core of the galaxy, we could see 100 times that many, and if we were inside one of the Milky Way's many globular clusters, we could see 1,000 stars per cubic parsec. Both the day and the night sky would be filled with over 4.5 million visible stars! Their light would be so consistently bright that it would fill the entire sky, and we might think that we were near Kolob, which "is set nigh unto the throne of God." (Abraham 3:9).

Of course, we do not know where Kolob is, but in May 2015, NASA announced the discovery of a galaxy (WISE J224607.57-052635.0), at the edge of the known universe, nearly 13.7 billion light years from earth, that shines with as much light as more than 300 trillion sun-like stars. No wonder that the Lord described Himself as "the light, and the life, and the truth of the world." (Ether 4:12). John said He "is light, and in him is no darkness at all." (1 John 1:15). After Joseph Smith had seen the Savior in vision in the Kirtland Temple, he said: "His eyes were as a flame of fire; the hair of his head was white like the pure snow; his countenance shone above the brightness of the sun; and his voice was as the sound of the rushing of great waters, even the voice of Jehovah." (D&C 110:3). David also described the countenance of the Lord, and wrote that it consisted of "light." (See Psalms 4:6). Jeremiah described the revelatory process as words that were in his heart as a burning fire shut up in his bones, that made him weary with forbearing, so much so that he could not stay. (See Jeremiah 20:9).

Following the long night of apostasy generally characterized as The Dark Ages, light and truth once again illuminate our day, just as they did in ancient times. Isaiah wrote prophetically of latter-day Israel: "Arise, shine; for thy light is come, and the glory of the Lord is risen upon thee. For...the Lord shall arise upon thee, and his glory shall be seen upon thee. And the Gentiles shall come to thy light, and kings to the brightness of thy rising." (Isaiah 60:1-3).

Before time existed, the physical and spiritual properties of light and darkness contributed to a division among the people that culminated in "war in heaven." We can almost hear the clash of words, as "Michael and his angels fought against the dragon, and the dragon and his angels fought against Michael." (J.S.T. Revelation 12:6). Nephi wrote of the eternal consequences of that conflict: "Our father also saw that the justice of God did also divide the wicked from the righteous; and the brightness thereof was like unto the brightness of a flaming fire, which ascendeth up unto God forever and ever, and hath no end." (1 Nephi 15:30).

During His mortal ministry, Christ was "the life and the light of the world (and) the word of truth and righteousness." (Alma 38:9). He declared: "I am come a light into the world, that whosoever believeth on me should not abide in darkness." (John 12:46). Isaiah had prophetically declared that His glory would "kindle a burning like the burning of a fire." (Isaiah 10:16). David expressed the hope we all share, that he would be delivered from the jaws of death, so that he might "walk before God in the light of the living." (Psalms 56:13).

Without the influence of the Savior, and without the comfort of knowing that we have tactical flashlights upon which we can rely, "we wait for light, but behold obscurity; for brightness, but we walk in darkness. We grope for the wall like the blind...as if we had no eyes: we stumble at noonday as in the night; we are in desolate places as dead men. We roar like bears, and mourn sore like doves: we look for judgment, but there is none; for salvation, but it is far off from us. For our transgressions are multiplied before (God), and our sins testify against us." (Isaiah 59:9-12). In contrast, the light that blazes from our spiritual tactical flashlights shows us the way we must go in order to dwell within the secure envelope of the word of God. It is "a lamp unto (our) feet, and a light unto (our) path." (Psalms 119:105). His bright and beautiful creations draw us closer to Him. "All things bright and beautiful, all creatures great and small. All things wise and wonderful. The Lord God made them all." (Cecil Francis Alexander).

The Savior taught: "The Comforter, which is the Holy Ghost, whom the Father will send in my name, he shall teach you all things, and bring all things to your remembrance, whatsoever I have said unto you." (John 14:26). When we receive inspiration from heaven, and enjoy a quantum leap in the expansion of our understanding of the physical and spiritual worlds, it is as if flash bulbs are going off in our heads, or as Einstein put it: a storm has broken loose in our minds.

Lightning is a "striking" example of the storms that can be unleashed by God, and each time we witness its blinding flash, accompanied by a resounding clap of thunder, we should be reminded of Him. The Savior revealed: "Any man who hath seen any or the least of these hath seen God moving in his majesty and power." (D&C 88:47). We scarcely appreciate how that seething energy envelops the earth and turns it into a fiery hot cauldron. There are estimated to be around 2,000 lightning storms raging across the face of the earth at any given time, contributing to over 100 ground strikes per second. The air around these can reach a temperature 3 times hotter than the surface of the sun. The estimated peak power of a single bolt can be 1,000 Giga Watts (one thousand million watts). The total energy pent up and often released in a single large thunderstorm has been calculated to be enough to meet the energy needs of the United States for 20 minutes.

These are impressive statistics, but lightning is just a faint whisper of the power and influence of God. To provide a constant reminder of Him, ancient Israel kept a fire burning upon the altar in the temple. (See Leviticus 6:13). When Moses was high on the mount, "the angel of the Lord appeared unto him in a flame of fire out of the midst of a bush: and he looked, and, behold, the bush burned with fire, and the bush was not consumed." (Exodus 3:2). Channukah, the Jewish Festival of Light, commemorates the miracle in the temple when the candles of the Menorah burned for eight days, after being filled with only enough oil to last for one. The recurring miracle, however, is not our witness of thunderstorms, or of burning bushes and lamps, but that "truth shineth!" (D&C 88:7). Even the least among us can discern between truth and its dark counterpart, because the former has an intrinsic glow and an enduring quality. It lasts forever, for "intelligence, or the light of truth, was not created or made, neither indeed can be." (D&C 93:29).

The physical manifestations of lightning and thunder from heaven are the equivalents of our spiritual tactical flashlights, and remind us of the power of God, for it is He Who "maketh lightnings." (Psalms 135:7). It is His voice that is the thunder in the heavens, and it is His lightning that streaks across the sky and causes the earth to tremble and shake. (See Psalms 77:18). It would not be surprising to learn that lightning was created by the hand of God as a type and a shadow, for as it "cometh out of the east, and shineth even unto the west; so shall also the coming of the Son of man be." (Matthew 24:27).

When the angel of the Lord descended from heaven after the death and resurrection of the Savior, "his countenance was like lightning, and his raiment white as snow." (Matthew 28:2-3). As the Psalmist recorded: "His lightnings enlightened the world, (and) the earth saw, and trembled." (Psalms 97:4). Perhaps "thunderings, and lightnings" are the best way to describe how conversation between the Gods in the Celestial Kingdom would sound to mortal ears. (Revelation 8:5). God's testimony, after all, is "the voice of thunderings, and the voice of lightnings." (D&C 88:90).

"And the temple of God was opened in heaven, and there was seen in his temple the ark of his testament: and there were lightnings, and voices, and thunderings." (Revelation 11:19). "And it came to pass" that there was "a thick cloud upon the mount, and the voice of the trumpet exceeding loud; so that all the people that (were) in the camp (of Israel) trembled." (Exodus 19:16). Everyone shared a common experience, as their raw nerve endings were universally touched by the power and influence of God. "And all the people saw the thunderings, and the lightnings, and the noise of the trumpet, and the mountain smoking." (Exodus 20:18).

"And out of the throne (of God) proceeded lightnings and thunderings and voices." (Revelation 4:5). "When he uttereth his voice, there is a multitude of waters in the heavens, and he causeth the vapours to ascend from the ends of the earth; he maketh lightnings with rain, and bringeth forth the wind." (Jeremiah 10:13). "How oft have I called," He asked, "by the voice of thunderings, and by the voice of lightnings?" (D&C 43:25). "And the voice of his word," wrote Daniel, "was like the voice of a multitude." (Daniel 10:6).

At the end of the day, as Rabindranath Tagore mused, there will be eye-kissing, heart-sweetening light that dances at the center of our lives and strikes the chords of our love; and there will be butterflies that spread their sails on a sea of light, with lilies and jasmine that surge up on the wave crests of light that is shattered into gold on every cloud and scattered in profusion as gemstones. This is the familiar light that is the province of all those who have been born again into a newness of life.

This is the light that reminds us that on one special evening two thousand years ago, there was no darkness at all, "but it was as light as though it was mid-day. And it came to pass that the sun did rise in the morning again, according to its proper order; and they knew that it was the day that the Lord should be born." (3 Nephi 1:19).

In the scriptures, the first recorded words of Heavenly Father were: "Let there be light." (Genesis 1:3). His last recorded words (to date) were "This is my beloved Son, Hear Him." (J.S.H. 1:17). These two verses are inextricably linked and are as bookends to our faith. Our own sun rises and falls on our desire to be drawn to His light and to be mesmerized by His magic.

"When we
walk with a man
of science, and we are sensitive
enough to enlarge our perceptions, we
can more quickly appreciate the accomplishments
of the mind. When we walk with an artist, and we are
stretching our sensitivities, we can more easily appreciate
the accomplishments of the heart. When we walk with
Christ, and we lengthen our spiritual stride,
we can more swiftly appreciate the
accomplishments of the soul."
(Richard L. Gunn).

Heaven Can Wait

In the 1970s, a motion picture entitled "Heaven Can Wait" was produced, that told the story of a man who cheated death, in a way, because he was allowed a second chance to live his life. As I have thought about the film, it strikes me that today I celebrate a milestone in my own life. I've lived one day longer than ever before, and in so-doing have set a new personal record for longevity. At least for now, or so it seems, heaven can wait!

But, even as I rejoice, I come to the sobering realization that there is a price to be paid, for I am also one day closer to eternity. I'm okay with that, because I understand that "to every thing there is a season, and a time to every purpose under the heaven; a time to be born," as well as "a time to die." (Ecclesiastes 3:1-2). Addressing that subject, Spencer W. Kimball said: "I am confident that there is a time to die, but I also believe that many people die before 'their time' because they are careless, abuse their bodies, take unnecessary chances, or expose themselves to hazards, accidents, and sickness. God controls our lives, and guides and blesses us, but He gives us our agency. We may live our lives in accordance with His Plan for us or we may foolishly shorten or terminate them." ("Teachings of Presidents of the Church," p. 11–21).

What really struck me as I read his observation, however, was the phrase that "God controls our lives" in the sense that He "guides and blesses us," with the qualifying modifier thrown in that He still "gives us our agency." At first glance, control and agency would appear to be antithetical, but they actually do no violence to harmony if we think of them as dynamic counterparts that are the fundamental elements of a process that leads us through a twisted temporal matrix toward the expansive, unrestrained, and seamless reality of "immortality and eternal life." (Moses 1:39). To put it another way, we realize that control and agency are part of the "opposition in all thing" described by Lehi, that are necessary for the Plan of Salvation to work, and that "if these things are not, there is no God." (2 Nephi 2:11 & 13).

He knew beforehand that when we left our first estate, we would be confronted with seemingly contradictory principles relating to His never-ending parental concern on the one hand, and our promised birthright of agency or free will on the other. To resolve this conundrum, He created the gift of time and stitched it into His Plan as a dimension that is entirely unique to mortality. By doing so, He was able to powerfully address His own worry for His children without violating His Prime Directive relating to the preservation of their free will.

The imaginative device of time made it possible for us to have experiences similar to His own, to appreciate both vicariously and up close and personally the delight as well as the anxiety that accompany parenthood, and to grow in gratitude for the grounded approach to rearing children that is at the very core of both His Plan and our Divine Center. Best of all, His design allowed us to acquire nurturing parenting skills without experiencing the heartbreak of losing our little ones through the friendly fire of either overprotection or indifference. With time on their side, as the children of God negotiate the minefields of mortality, collateral damage may be kept to a minimum.

You see, God has given us the gift of time that we may have the opportunity to take upon ourselves His armour, with our loins girt about with truth and the breastplate of righteousness, and our feet shod with the preparation of the gospel of peace; above all, taking the shield of faith, the helmet of salvation, and the sword of the Spirit. (See Ephesians 6:13-17). Our inexorable movement through time allows these noble qualities to facilitate our transition from mortal clay to the eternal element of the spirit, without the exercise of inappropriate or misguided control on His part that would have stifled our development from dependency as little children, through independency as self-actualized young adults, and finally to interdependency as committed disciples of His Son. All of the elements of the principles of the Pan harmonize with each other, to complete His grand design.

Our Heavenly Father did all of this seamlessly, so that when the veil is parted, time will cease to exist. (See D&C 84:100). It will have served its purpose in His magnum opus, and we will move on, as it were. The righteous will discover that He had one more ace up his sleeve; one more wonderful blessing that only One who controls the universe could have devised. We will marvel at the omnipotence of His Son, and with the disciples of old, ask: "What manner of man is this, that even the wind and the sea obey him?" (Mark 4:41). As we make the transition to that "undiscovered country from whose bourn no traveler returns," (Shakespeare, "Hamlet," Act 3, Scene 1), we will find that He designed our transition to immortality in such a way that, "it shall come to pass that those that die in (the Lord) shall not taste of death, for it shall be sweet unto them." (D&C 42:46).

Even now, we yearn to return to our natural state of immortality, for "time is clearly not our natural dimension. Thus it is, that we are never really at home in time. Alternately, we find ourselves impatiently wishing to hasten its passage or to hold back the dawn. We can do neither, of course. We are clearly not at home in time, because we belong to eternity. Time, as much as any one thing, whispers to us that we are strangers here. If time were natural to us, why is it that we have so many clocks and wear wristwatches?" (Neal A. Maxwell, B.Y.U. Devotional, 11/27/1979).

The scriptures suggest that time commands a high priority on God's agenda, as evidenced in His handbook of instructions that unfolds the details of the Plan of Salvation. There are 1,381 references to "time" in the scriptures, and 2,749 references to "now." Surprisingly, "eternal life" and "eternal lives" are mentioned only 113 times, "eternity" just 38 times, and immortality only 30 times. Perhaps, it is only for our convenience that we are far more often left to digest the easily recognizable, manageable, and savory reduction sauce of time. For the moment, at least, we are comfortable living in a linear temporal dimension from which there seems to be only one exit. Our only possible liberation from the arrow of time will come when we lay aside our mortal clay, clothed in the garments of immortality and eternal life. It is in that state of existence when we will finally and fully comprehend the multi-dimensional scope of His work and glory. (See Moses 1:39).

God's stroke of genius in harnessing the quixotic element of time, by apportioning it in discrete increments of seconds, minutes, hours, and so on, allows thought, feeling, and spontaneity to germinate within the fertile matrix of agency. The scriptures record that before the dawn of creation: "The Lord said: Let us go down. And they went down at the beginning, and they, that is the Gods, organized and formed the heavens and the earth." (Abraham 4:1). Coming from the eternal vantage point of the abode of the Gods, the celestial clock, insofar as earth was concerned, was reset. It was calibrated to a temporal scale by omniscient, omnipotent, and omnipresent Beings, whereas the reckoning had been beforehand "the Lord's time, according to the reckoning of Kolob." (Abraham 3:4).

In a process that is far beyond our comprehension, the earth literally fell from Kolob into a template of time as we know it. Its arrow, that had heretofore been defined by other temporally incomprehensible terms and conditions, so that it traveled in all directions simultaneously, was now locked into just one forward track. At that pivotal moment, a majestic mechanism was introduced that would eventually set in motion an evolution in thought culminating in Newton's "Principia," and Einstein's Theories of Relativity, ideas that have shaken the foundations of our understanding of physics, or broadly speaking, have mathematically wrestled with the concept of time in the natural world.

In 1916, Einstein's brain conceived the key that would unlock the mercurial side of the nature of time. In a sense, he let the genie out of the bottle. Common folk like us, who are now comfortable with the phrase "It's all relative," seldom recognize the intimate association that expression shares with our exercise of free will, and with our comprehension of God. The truth be told, with our greater appreciation for the relationships between time and space has come a sense of relief that, in order to honor the principle of agency, God does not have to cease to be, nor with our expanding awareness is He required to relinquish His omniscience and omnipotence. This is the only explanation that makes sense of President Kimball's aforementioned declaration that God controls our lives, and guides and blesses us, while at the same time preserving our agency. We do not live in the deterministic universe envisioned by Sir Isaac Newton, but neither are we liberated by the permissiveness of Einstein's relativity.

We have been able to do wonderful things with the gifts of time, space, and free will, while simultaneously keeping Heavenly Father firmly in the driver's seat. He is still in control, but the key element relating to His children is that "the power (remains) in them, wherein they are agents unto themselves." (D&C 58:28, underlining mine). We use action verbs to describe just how empowering is this gift. Action verbs describe things that we "do," and they presuppose motion in multiple dimensions across a temporal spectrum. We press forward with steadfastness, and we feast upon the words of eternal life. We read, we fear, we ponder and pray, we lift the latch, and we force the way. We are bathed in vitality, and we are empowered with an otherworldly serenity that obliterates the fetters of time precisely because they are artificial. As Bagheera, the powerfully built black panther confided to Mowgli the man-cub: "I had never seen the jungle. They fed me behind bars from an iron pan until one night I felt that I was Bagheera the Panther, and no man's plaything, and I broke the lock with one blow of my paw, and I came away." (Rudyard Kipling, "The Jungle Book").

Our normal lifespan gives us ample opportunity to develop patience as we bide our time, mature in discipline as we take time, delight in diligence as we make time, expand our care and concern as we find time, enhance our thoughtfulness as we spend time, cultivate wisdom as we invest time, and experience pleasure as we share time. Time is our steady schoolmaster that teaches us the fundamentals, the grammar of the gospel as it were, and when we use it wisely, it becomes a tool that helps us to engage the comprehensive curriculum of Christ in the ivory towers of academia, even the house of the Lord, where we receive higher levels of education. (See Galatians 3:24 & D&C 109:7).

Under normal circumstances, heaven can wait, in order to allow us to enjoy the gift of time and to use it with responsibility. In the motion picture, "Indiana Jones and The Last Crusade," the Grail Knight told Indie: "You must choose. But choose wisely, for as the true Grail will bring you life, the false Grail will take it from you." The gospel

Plan teaches us how to choose wisely, because it identifies the Holy Grail that must be our quest. Spencer W. Kimball urged: "Do it! Do it right! Do it right now!" because "there's no time like the present; no present like time, and life can be over in the space of a rhyme." (Georgia Byng). Even the rabbit in Alice's "Wonderland" recognized the value of time well-spent, when he exclaimed to no one in particular: "I'm late! I'm late! For a very important date! No time to say 'Hello!' 'Good-bye!' I'm late, I'm late, I'm late!" (Lewis Carroll, "Alice's Adventures in Wonderland").

As time is measured by The Science and Security Board of The Bulletin of Atomic Scientists, it is 11:55 p.m. on the Doomsday Clock, which represents a countdown to global catastrophe. Since 1947, the Board, including 18 Nobel Laureates, has maintained the clock and pessimistically adjusted its hour and second hand closer and closer to the apocalyptic hour of midnight. With just five minutes left until the clock strikes twelve, we can be sure that the angels in heaven have already raised their swords, and are only waiting upon the Lord's command to let them fall.

We are reminded of the "Sword of Damocles" who exclaimed to Dionysius, his king, that he was truly fortunate as a great man of power and authority, surrounded by every imaginable luxury. "In response, Dionysius offered to switch places with Damocles so that Damocles could taste that fortune firsthand. Damocles quickly and eagerly accepted the king's proposal. Damocles sat down in the king's throne surrounded by every luxury, but Dionysius had arranged that a huge sword should hang above the throne, held at the pommel only by a single hair of a horse's tail. Damocles finally begged the king that he be allowed to depart because he realized that with great fortune and power comes also great danger." ("Wikipedia").

With so little time left on our own doomsday clock, each of us must ask ourselves, what does prudence dictate that we do? We could roll the dice on the assumption that heaven can, and will, wait. We could put the inevitable out of our minds, and dull our senses with the narcotics of immediate gratification and the hope and expectation of deferred consequences. The problem with that flawed perspective is that it leads to faulty perception, impaired judgment, and unfortunate and unanticipated consequences. In real life, things don't end well if we eat, drink, and make merry, putting out of our thoughts the swords that dangle above our heads. The older we get, the more we realize that heaven can't wait, because we are already living in eternity.

Both Newton and Einstein, who, as noted above, toyed with the equations defining the arrow of time, may have been on to something. One or both may have been right, or both could be equally wrong. Time may be absolute in a relative sense, but not necessarily in the way those two pillars of physics would have defined it. Maybe God is the only One that can have it both ways, and Who can tinker with time without paying homage to the laws of physics. He may have found a way to slow down the hectic pace of our lives, in order to allow us to ponder the solemnities of eternity and to engage our agency in ways that only He could envision. In any event, we can be sure that His learning style is the only one that is expansive enough to accommodate the concept of eternal progression, even as we view it from within the limitations of a temporal perspective.

If the time space continuum is thought of as a temporal and spatial matrix conceived by God to allow us to be free agents, then the distractions we have learned to throw up may be nothing more than coping mechanisms to help us deal with the day-to-day minor emergencies of mortality. If the consequences of disobedience to the laws governing the Celestial Kingdom can be viewed as distortions in the fabric of time and space, then we can see how they would require mending to restore equilibrium in the cosmos. These repair processes might take shape as the laws governing faith, repentance, forgiveness, obedience, sacrifice, consecration, mercy, justice, and atonement. These laws of the gospel might be more fundamental to our moving, and being while living in mortality than most of us realize.

Time and space, with the catalyzing influence of agency, are in perfect balance when they allow us to regroup, reassess, repent, and take purposeful action. Thanks to Heavenly Father's omniscience, the observable elements of time and space, and the immaterial element of agency combine into a single clarifying creation that coalesces to give us a swift kick in our complacency, bringing us to the realization that heaven really can't wait. That comprehension, and that acknowledgement, may lead to the unified field theory of purposeful action that is the Holy Grail to which the Knight was referring. When we realize that heaven can't wait, our quest takes on its deserved sense of urgency and we are up and moving on the path of progression.

When these elements of the Plan operate in perfect harmony, there is still plenty of wiggle-room within which we may make choices that are refreshingly unhampered by coercion. Free will remains untarnished. The Plan provides us with currency sufficient to satisfy our needs, but also allows us to substitute for legal tender wads of counterfeit cash with which we may attempt to make late payments, with interest tacked on for bad behavior. Remember, the kicker in the aforementioned quotation from the teachings of Spencer W. Kimball is that "God controls our lives, guides and blesses us, but gives us our agency." If we try to subvert the Plan with futile efforts to gain, obtain, and retain blessings we do not deserve, our destabilizing efforts will reward us with nothing more than a pyrrhic victory. Time will grind on, but if we have sown the wind, we will reap the whirlwind. (See Hosea 8:7).

Heaven cannot wait. The idea that it can is a subtle tactic of the devil, designed to lull us into a false sense of complacency. The idle use of our time is the devil's workshop. Surely, we must be living in heaven right now. We feel each other's pain and loss, as well as pleasure and gain. One of the compelling evidences that heaven cannot wait is our abundant blessing of concern, consideration, kindness, compassion, and empathy. These are qualities that remind us of our former life, and that propel us on the path of progress leading back home. Heaven cannot wait because its benign benevolence is blind to hypocrisy, and demands that we address principles and doctrines that resonate with truth. It is precisely because heaven cannot wait that we "never send to know for whom the bell tolls," because it tolls for each of us. (John Donne, "Meditation 17").

Heaven can't wait, because it is all around us, clamoring for our attention. It begins even "in our infancy! (But then), shades of the prison-house begin to close upon the growing boy, (and) he beholds the light, and whence it flows; he sees it in his joy. The youth, who daily farther from the east must travel, still is nature's priest, and by the vision splendid is on his way attended. At length, the man perceives it die away, and fade into the light of common day." (William Wordsworth, "Ode: Intimations of Immortality from Reflections of Early Childhood").

Heaven is our natural element. It is the aether that infuses our lungs with celestial air, and is the state of being to which we all intuitively aspire. God created the physical world, and established laws to govern it that were designed to lead us back into His presence. Because we are spiritual beings having mortal experiences, we sometimes feel that we are not synchronized with our natural element. If that is so, our true greatness, and our power, will only be manifest when "the stars fade away, the sun himself grow dim with age, and nature sink in years." Then, we "shall flourish in immortal youth, unhurt amidst the war of elements, the wreck of matter, and the crash of worlds." (Joseph Addison, "Cato," Act 5, Scene 1).

"Sow a thought,
reap an act. Sow an act,
reap a habit. Sow a habit, reap
a character. Sow a character,
reap an eternal destiny."
(David O. McKay).

How Then Can I Do This Great Wickedness?

In the Book of Genesis, we read about Joseph, the favored son of Jacob, who was cast into a pit by his jealous brothers, taken to Egypt by Ishmaelite traders, and sold into slavery. There, he served faithfully in the house of Potiphar, refused the advances of his wife, and was consequently cast into prison. After interpreting Pharaoh's dream, Joseph was brought into Pharaoh's court and made a ruler in Egypt.

The scriptures record the words of Pharaoh to Joseph: "Thou shalt be over my house, and according unto thy word shall all my people be ruled: only in the throne will I be greater than thou. And Pharaoh said unto Joseph, See, I have set thee over all the land of Egypt." (Genesis 41:40-41).

This story could be a model for our own lives. When we think about the motion pictures, television shows, and magazines that are currently popular in our culture, we need to stop and ask ourselves: "What standards of morality are promoted by the media?" Consider these titles, to name just a few. Movies: "Cheap Thrills," "The Good Lie," and "American Hustle." Television shows: "Desperate Housewives," "Sex and The City," and "Girls Behaving Badly." Magazines: "Allure," "Glamour," and "Self."

The behavior of Potiphar's wife is a reflection of our own society's attitudes toward sexuality, and stands in sharp contrast to the principles that governed Joseph's conduct. Today, the "Oscars" may reflect societal values, but the 13 Articles of Faith are the tangible particles of faith of Latter-day Saints that withstand the rigors of scrutiny from every perspective. Societal norms are precariously balanced on the shifting sands of expediency, and with the slightest telestial tremor they can come tumbling down in any of a number of ways, but the Lord's firm and immoveable standards are grounded on the bedrock of unchanging principles. The gospel puts the essential differences between values and principles in perspective. As Joseph Smith famously declared: "I teach people correct principles, (and not just values), and they govern themselves." (John Taylor, "The Organization of the Church," Millennial Star, 11/15/1851, p. 339). It is not enough to be a good person or a gifted leader; one must be principled as well.

Joseph's father Jacob married Leah and Rachel, daughters of his mother's brother

Laban, and also married their handmaids, Zilpah and Bilhah. (Yes, he had four wives). Jacob's wives bore him twelve sons, who became the progenitors of the twelve tribes of Israel, after the Lord changed Jacob's name to Israel. (Genesis 32.328). His eleventh son was Joseph, and as the eldest son of Jacob and Rachel, he received the birthright when Reuben, the eldest son of Jacob and Leah, lost it through unrighteousness. "Now the sons of Reuben the firstborn of Israel, for he was the firstborn; but, forasmuch as he defiled his father's bed, his birthright was given unto the sons of Joseph the son of Israel: and the genealogy is not to be reckoned after the birthright. For Judah prevailed above his brethren, and of him came the chief ruler; but the birthright was Joseph's." (1 Chronicles 5:1-2).

His brothers were jealous of him because their father "Israel loved Joseph more than all his children, because he was the son of his old age: and (because) he made him a coat of many colours." (Genesis 37:3). (See my essay: "A Coat of Many Colors"). Joseph also shared with his brothers his dream that 11 sheaves of corn, and "the sun and the moon and the eleven stars made obeisance" to him. (Genesis 37:9). Sometimes, we react the same way as did Joseph's brothers, with feelings of jealousy or anger, when members of our family, ward, or stake, offend us or ostensibly receive better treatment than we do.

In Joseph's case, it could have been worse. His brothers only conspired to throw him into a pit, there to leave him to his fate. But then, fortuitously, Ishmaelite traders arrived on the scene. These took him into Egypt and sold him into slavery, where he later became instrumental in saving both the Egyptians and his family from famine.

But before that could happen, Joseph was sorely tested by God. His first trial had to do with how he would deal with affluence, even though he was a slave. "And the Lord was with Joseph, and he was a prosperous man; and he was in the house of his master the Egyptian." (Genesis 39:1). Potiphar, a wealthy officer of Pharaoh, "left all that he had in Joseph's hand; and he knew not ought he had, save the bread which he did eat. And Joseph was a goodly person, and well favoured." (Genesis 39:6).

When we read this part of the account, we are reminded of the young man who interviewed with a prospective employer. He was asked: "If I hire you, and entrust to you the care of my business affairs, can I count on you to be honest?" To which the young man replied: "You can count on me to be honest whether you hire me or not." Needless to say, he got the job.

Next, Potiphar's wife famously tried to seduce Joseph, but "he left his garment in her hand, and fled, and got him out." (Genesis 39:12). So too, we have the power to remove ourselves from situations where we are tempted. Joseph might have used any number of weak excuses and yielded to the advances of Potiphar's wife. "I'm a slave and am, therefore, not responsible for my actions. I can always repent later. No one will know. All I want is to be happy. I want to be accepted. Everyone's doing it. It's normal to have these feelings. It's okay because we love each other. It doesn't hurt anyone." These are simply rationalizations, because we know that the Lord will not allow us to be tempted beyond our capacity to resist. (See 1 Corinthians 10:3). In addition, we all have the Light of Christ, or conscience, to remind us what is right and what is wrong. (See Alma 28:14, D&C 88:7, & Moroni 7:18-19).

Joseph was severely punished after the failure of his attempted seduction by Potiphar's wife. "And Joseph's master took him, and put him into...a place where the king's prisoners were bound." (Genesis 39:20) For being true to our guiding principles, we too must face the consequences, no matter what they may be. We may be excluded from "the in-crowd." We may be picked last, or not at all. Others may poke fun at us, or try to make us feel guilty. We may be passed over for promotion, or not even secure a job in the first place. The best thing to do in these situations is to seek the companionship of the Spirit as Joseph did while in prison, for the Lord was with him. (Genesis 39:21-23). When we are similarly tried, we may go to the temple to repose in quiet contemplation, lose ourselves in the service of others, bear our souls to the Lord in prayer, immerse ourselves in scripture study, focus our minds and persevere with work, or rededicate ourselves to do our best.

Genesis Chapter 28 describes Jacob's dream of the ladder. "And he dreamed, and behold a ladder set up on the earth, and the top of it reached to heaven: and behold the angels of God ascending and descending on it. And, behold, the Lord stood above it, and said, I am the Lord God of Abraham thy father, and the God of Isaac. The land whereon thou liest, to thee will I give it, and to thy seed; and thy seed shall be as the dust of the earth, and thou shalt spread abroad to the west, and to the east, and to the north, and to the south. And in thee shall all the families of the earth be blessed. And behold, I am with thee, and will keep thee in all places whither thou goest, and will bring thee again into this land. For I will not leave thee, until I have done that which I have spoken to thee of." (Genesis 28:12-15).

"Jacob realized that the covenants he had made with the Lord were the rungs on the ladder that he himself would have to climb in order to obtain the promised blessings that would entitle him to enter heaven and associate with the Lord." (Marion G. Romney, "Ensign," 3/1971).

Spencer W. Kimball said of his cultural counterparts: "The Lord has blessed us as a people with a prosperity unequaled in times past. The resources that have been placed in our power are good, and necessary to our work here on the earth. But I am afraid that many of us have been surfeited with flocks and herds and acres and barns and wealth and have begun to worship them as false gods, and they have power over us. Do we have more of these good things than our faith can stand? In spite of our delight in defining ourselves as modern, and our tendency to think we possess a sophistication that no people in the past ever had, in spite of these things, we are, on the whole, an idolatrous people." ("Ensign," 6/1976).

Brigham Young said that Utah would become the crossroads of the west. 'This will become the great highway of the nations. Kings and emperors and the noble and wise of the earth will visit us here, while the wicked and ungodly will envy us our comfortable homes and possessions. The worst fear that I have about this people is that they will get rich in this country, forget God and his people, wax fat, and kick themselves out of the church and go to hell. This people will stand mobbing, robbing, poverty, and all manner of persecution, and be true. But my greater fear for them is that they cannot stand wealth; and yet they have to be tried with riches, for they will become the richest people on this earth." ("Brigham Young: The Man and His Work," p. 126-129).

In 1997, Gordon B. Hinckley said: "Brigham Young's prophecy has been fulfilled. This is now a great and beautiful and fertile area. It has become the Crossroads of the West. Thousands and tens of thousands and hundreds of thousands pass this way constantly. We in the Office of the First Presidency are called upon day after day and week after week to meet the great of the earth." (Address given at B.Y.U., 2/2/1997).

On another occasion, President Hinckley said: "This has become one of the great highways of the nations. Millions come to Temple Square. There are hundreds of flights daily in and out of here. Kings and emperors and the noble and wise of the earth visit us here. There's scarcely a week when we do not have some prominent world figure call on us. We have been blessed with the bounties of heaven and the earth. Now, with gratitude in our hearts, let us not dwell upon the few problems we have. Let us rather count our blessings and in a great spirit of gratitude, motivated by a great faith, go forth to build the kingdom of God in the earth." (Address given at B.Y.U., 3/6/1994).

We must do as Joseph did, and as his father Jacob did, who "awakened out of his sleep, and he said, Surely the Lord is in this place...and this is the gate of heaven. ...And he called the name of that place Beth-el." (Genesis 28:16 & 19). In Hebrew, Beth-el means "House of God." Our gate of heaven can be anywhere, or any way, we grasp the horns of sanctuary and feel God's peace, comfort, and support. (See Leviticus 4:25). With His help, all of our experiences and circumstances can work together for our good.

During our sojourn
on earth, it helps to have celestial signposts to
guide us through the telestial traffic jams and conceptual cul-
de-sacs that threaten to detour us from the strait and narrow way.
The expanding circle of opportunity afforded by obedience to gospel
principles assures us of direct experience with the perfect law of
liberty. Thus, we trade the uncertain course adopted by
individuals bound for the telestial kingdom for
the certain reality of celestial surety.

I Am
A Child Of God

The story is told of young Spencer W. Kimball traveling alone by train from his home in Thatcher, Arizona to Salt Lake City. An older man boarded the train at an intermediate stop, and sat down next to 10 year old Spencer. He asked the boy: "Where are you headed?" "Salt Lake City," was his reply. The next question was predictable: "Are you a Mormon?" "Yes," answered Spencer.

Then the man asked the obvious question: "What do Mormons believe?" Spencer had been grounded in the gospel by faithful parents who had taught him the Thirteen Articles of Faith, and so he answered: "Well, we believe in God the Father, and in His Son Jesus Christ, and in the Holy Ghost." "What else do you believe?" asked the man. "We believe that men will be punished for their own sins, and not for Adam's transgressions." And so it went.

I was reminded of President Kimball's experience as I sat on the stand at the funeral of a faithful ward member. I had been asked to give the eulogy, and as I looked out over the congregation, I saw many unfamiliar faces, many of whom were the non-member relatives of my friend. Then, as I stood before them, I simply said: "Claude was a good man, who believed in our Father in Heaven, who had a firm an abiding testimony of the divinity of His Son Jesus Christ, and who regularly felt the influence of the Holy Ghost. He believed that we will be punished for our own sins, and not for the transgression of Adam, and thus, he was grateful for the Atonement of Jesus Christ." And so it went.

As they were growing up, I always told my children that if they memorized the Articles of Faith they would never be without the material for an extemporaneous address in church. We made it a point in our family to make sure that they knew them by heart before their baptismal interview with the Bishop. We taught them to make them the particles of their faith, as well. In doing so, their mother and I easily taught the foundation teaching that they were children of our Heavenly Father, Who knew them, Who loved them, and Who watched over them. However, I recently realized that, with the possible exception of my funeral eulogy, I had largely neglected to utilize that resource when interacting with non-members.

Consider the scenario where we are at a party and meet a total stranger. Within 3 minutes, we are on a first-name basis, and the other party is asking: "What do you do?" What they mean is: "What do you do for a living?" That is interesting, in light of the fact that we identify ourselves in many different ways, including the place of our birth, our nationality, our language, our hobbies, and yes, sometimes even by our occupation. None of these appellations are wrong, however, unless they supersede our identity as children of God.

I am not suggesting that we should introduce ourselves with: "Hello. I am a child of God." But we might want to steer away from the rote answers that are superficial, have little meaning, and create negligible interconnectivity. (See my essay: "Connections"). If our first and consistent response is based on a remembrance of who we are, and who they are, that we are all sons and daughters of God, we may be better prepared for the Spirit to then work its magic. The Lord has promised: "I will go before your face. I will be on your right hand and on your left, and my Spirit shall be in your hearts, and mine angels round about you." (D&C 84:88).

The song "I Am A Child of God" was written in 1957 by Naomi Randall. (1908 - 2001). Her friend Mildred Pettit composed the music. It is one of 45 hymns that The Church of Jesus Christ of Latter-day Saints includes in its basic curriculum, and it is one of the first hymns that new members typically learn. It has been translated into over 90 languages, and is a refrain that is virtually synonymous with L.D.S. teachings. The phrase itself has become the vehicle for communicating a basic doctrine in simple and easy-to-understand language. Thus, it is frequently found in church instructional curricula, in sermons, and even in merchandize and novelties.

Randall composed the song at the request of the Primary General Board, of which she was a member at the time. Its objective was to have a song that Primary age children could sing, that would reflect the L.D.S. teaching on the nature of our relationship with God. In language reminiscent of the experience of Job, Randall described how she went about fulfilling her commission from the Board.

"I got down on my knees and prayed aloud, pleading that our Heavenly Father would let me know the right words. I then fell asleep, but around 2:00 a.m., I awakened and began to think again about the song. Words came to my mind. I immediately got up and began to write the words down as they had come to me. Three verses and a chorus were soon formed. I gratefully surveyed the work, drank of the message of the words, and returned to my bedroom where I knelt before my Father in Heaven to say: Thank you!"

Job had described his own instruction from the Spirit, with these words: "In a dream, in a vision of the night, when deep sleep falleth upon (us), in slumberings upon the bed. Then he openeth (our ears), and sealeth (our) instruction. (Job 33:1-16).

"I am a Child of God" was first performed at a stake Primary conference in 1957. After hearing it, Spencer W. Kimball, who was then an Apostle, asked the Primary General Board if the phrase "Teach me all that I must know" could be changed to "Teach me all that I must do." As he later explained, "To know isn't enough. The devils know and tremble. We have to do something." The change was gratefully accepted by Sister Randall.

"I am a Child of God" was first published in the "Sing with Me" songbook for children. (1969). In 1978, Sister Randall composed a fourth verse, but when the song was added to the L.D.S. Hymnal that same year, the verse was excluded because it was not considered an official part of the original song. However, in 1989, when a new songbook for children was published, the fourth verse was included. Today, "I am a Child of God" (three verses) is hymn number 301 in "Hymns of The Church of Jesus Christ of Latter-day Saints," and the song is included in the "Children's Songbook" with the 4th verse included.

This brings us to the first verse: "I am a child of God, and He has sent me here; has given me an earthly home, with parents kind and dear." As William Wordsworth wrote: "Our birth is but a sleep and a forgetting. The soul that rises with us, our life's star, hath had elsewhere its setting, and cometh from afar. Not in entire forgetfulness, and not in utter nakedness, but trailing clouds of glory do we come, from God, Who is our Home." ("Ode: Intimations of Immortality, from Recollections of Early Childhood").

Our knowledge of pre-mortality places a high priority on our responsibility to teach our children correct principles, thereby to nurture their faith. "Faith," after all, "cometh by hearing, and hearing by the word of God." (Romans 10:17). "For unto us," wrote Paul, "was the gospel preached, as well as unto (ancient Israel); but the word preached did not profit them, not being mixed with faith in them that heard it." (Hebrews 4:3).

In the Book of Moses, we learn that the great lawgiver's self-image was based on his relationship with God. (Moses 1:3-4). He knew that he was a child of God. In fact, his identity was inexorably intertwined with that of God. "And God spake unto Moses, saying: Behold, I am the Lord God Almighty, and...thou art my son. (Moses 1:3-4). Today, we teach our children who they are, and the missionaries teach those who are learning about the gospel who they are using the same parameters. That knowledge largely shapes our character.

And then, the chorus: Lead me, guide me, walk beside me, help me find the way. Teach me all that I must do to live with Him some day." Children learn to be obedient so that they may, in turn, teach their own little ones in an unbroken pattern. "Inasmuch as parents have children in Zion, or in any of her stakes which are organized, that teach them not to understand" the doctrines of the kingdom, "the sin be upon the heads of the parents.... And their children shall be baptized for the remission of their sins when eight years old, and receive the laying on of the hands. And they shall also teach their children to pray, and to walk uprightly before the Lord." (D&C 68:25-28).

The second verse reads: "I am a child of God, and so my needs are great. Help me to understand his words before it grows too late." The three most important days of your life are the day you were born, the day you find out why, and the day you die. And so we come full circle. "When a baby is born, and as we wait with those who are dying, we brush against the veil, as greetings and goodbyes are said almost within earshot of each other. In such moments, this resonance with realities on the other side of the veil is so obvious that it can be explained in only one way." (Neal A. Maxwell, "B.Y.U. Devotional," 11/1979).

We are children of God who will return to Him someday. When we come home from our mission, it will seem like it was such a short time that we were away. I am sure that we will think of the people we met, and the people we helped. We'll think of how we have grown spiritually. It seems like we were just children, so immature, when we left home such a short time ago. Mother will be there waiting to embrace us, standing just a bit behind father, who will be bursting with pride. We will wipe away tears of happiness on mother's cheeks. Father will strike hands with us, then embrace us warmly. The feelings will be resonant, I am sure, and we will know this is where we belong – this is a real homecoming – home to Heavenly Father and Mother." (Anonymous).

The third verse reads: "I am a child of God. Rich blessings are in store. If I but learn to do his will, I'll live with him once more." Alma called the Plan of Salvation the Plan of Happiness. (Alma 42:16). Its design is to provide a way for us to find eternal happiness, which "is the object and design of our existence, and will be the end thereof if we follow the path that leads to it. And this path includes faith, virtue, uprightness, and keeping all the commandments of God." (Joseph Smith, "Teachings," p. 255-256).

As we pass through mortality, it helps to have celestial signposts to guide us through the telestial traffic jams, doctrinal dead-ends, and conceptual cul-de-sacs that threaten to detour us from the strait and narrow way. The expanding circle of opportunity afforded by obedience to gospel principles assures us of direct experience with the perfect law of liberty. Thus, we trade the uncertain course adopted by individuals bound for the telestial kingdom for the certain reality of celestial surety.

When we engage our agency within the bounds the Lord has set, we limit our options. Good decisions automatically eliminate the negative consequences of poor choices. Those who suffer from compulsions have reached this condition because of repeated and successive re-acts until a point is reached where, as William James explained, 'unlimited freedom leads to unlimited tyranny.' Instead, those who know that they are children of God are independent in that stage of development to which their decisions have led them. In this, the best of circumstances, "the universe is a machine for the making of Gods." (Henri Bergson, "Two Sources of Morality and Religion," p. 306).

There is also a fourth authorized verse that is included in the Children's Songbook: "I am a child of God. His promises are sure. Celestial glory shall be mine if I can but endure." To know that we are children of God is enough to kindle a spark within us that ignites our sense of wonder and illuminates our understanding of the far reaches of eternity. But it would be wrong to leave it at that, for to know only, would underestimate the magnitude of the Plan, and put at risk our relationship with God in such a way that its overarching importance in every aspect of our lives might be compromised. At the end of the day, to know that we are His children, and then to act upon that knowledge, frees us to dynamically interact with Him. Our active faith is founded upon the very points of doctrine that address salvation, and upon these elements hinges its correct understanding. "I am a Child of God," as it turns out, is a very good choice of words when describing the intimacy that our Heavenly Father desires to have with each of us.

Our Family Tree

"No other success can compensate for failure in the
home. The poorest shack in which love prevails
over a united family is of greater value to
God and future humanity than any
other riches. In such a home,
God can work miracles."
(David O. McKay).

In Defense
Of The Family

"The Family: A Proclamation to The World," is a statement by The First Presidency and Council of the Twelve Apostles of The Church of Jesus Christ of Latter-day Saints. It was first read by President Gordon B. Hinckley as part of his message at the General Relief Society Meeting held September 23, 1995, in Salt Lake City, Utah. It reads: "We, the First Presidency and the Council of the Twelve Apostles of The Church of Jesus Christ of Latter-day Saints, solemnly proclaim that marriage between a man and a woman is ordained of God and that the family is central to the Creator's plan for the eternal destiny of His children.

All human beings - male and female - are created in the image of God. Each is a beloved spirit son or daughter of heavenly parents, and, as such, each has a divine nature and destiny. Gender is an essential characteristic of individual premortal, mortal, and eternal identity and purpose.

In the premortal realm, spirit sons and daughters knew and worshipped God as their Eternal Father and accepted His plan by which His children could obtain a physical body and gain earthly experience to progress toward perfection and ultimately realize their divine destiny as heirs of eternal life. The divine plan of happiness enables family relationships to be perpetuated beyond the grave. Sacred ordinances and covenants available in holy temples make it possible for individuals to return to the presence of God and for families to be united eternally.

The first commandment that God gave to Adam and Eve pertained to their potential for parenthood as husband and wife. We declare that God's commandment for His children to multiply and replenish the earth remains in force. We further declare that God has commanded that the sacred powers of procreation are to be employed only between man and woman, lawfully wedded as husband and wife. We declare the means by which mortal life is created to be divinely appointed. We affirm the sanctity of life and of its importance in God's eternal Plan.

Husband and wife have a solemn responsibility to love and care for each other and for their children. "Children are an heritage of the Lord." (Psalms 127:3). Parents have a sacred duty to rear their children in love and righteousness, to provide for their physical and spiritual needs, and to teach them to love and serve one another, observe the commandments of God, and be law-abiding citizens wherever they live. Husbands and wives - mothers and fathers - will be held accountable before God for the discharge of these obligations.

The family is ordained of God. Marriage between man and woman is essential to His eternal plan. Children are entitled to birth within the bonds of matrimony, and to be reared by a father and a mother who honor marital vows with complete fidelity. Happiness in family life is most likely to be achieved when founded upon the teachings of the Lord Jesus Christ. Successful marriages and families are established and maintained on principles of faith, prayer, repentance, forgiveness, respect, love, compassion, work, and wholesome recreational activities. By divine design, fathers are to preside over their families in love and righteousness and are responsible to provide the necessities of life and protection for their families. Mothers are primarily responsible for the nurture of their children. In these sacred responsibilities, fathers and mothers are obligated to help one another as equal partners. Disability, death, or other circumstances may necessitate individual adaptation. Extended families should lend support when needed.

We warn that individuals who violate covenants of chastity, who abuse spouse or offspring, or who fail to fulfill family responsibilities will one day stand accountable before God. Further, we warn that the disintegration of the family will bring upon individuals, communities, and nations the calamities foretold by ancient and modern prophets. (Ephesians 4:13).

We call upon responsible citizens and officers of government everywhere to promote those measures designed to maintain and strengthen the family as the fundamental unit of society."

The First Presidency and Council of The Twelve Apostles were inspired to make this proclamation because the family is the basic building block of eternity. It is the best defense against the evils and designs of an uncaring world. It is the best institution of higher education in the world. It has been certified by God, and has received His divine approbation. The creation of the eternal family is the end product of the ordinances of the temple, and links us both to our forefathers and to our descendants.

Families give us a sense of identity, and allow us to commit our lives and our fortunes to a common destiny. They allow us to share the risks related to mortality; in essence, to indemnify ourselves against the vicissitudes of life. In the family, we tap into the power of God, as we participate in ordinances relating to the execution of the Plan of Salvation.

Our family ties can be traced back to our first parents, who were the literal offspring of God. Each member of our family is a physical and spiritual descendant of Heavenly Father, and so, we become legitimate heirs of all that He has. Our families provide the context we need to become more like Him. They give context to the Primary song: "I am a child of God."

The family is the mortar that holds the walls of the Celestial Kingdom in place. It grounds us, and anchors us to the Infinite, giving mortality an eternal perspective. At the same time, the family gives its members an opportunity to develop a sense of humor. It provides a longitudinal perspective of stability in a disposable society.

The family is where we go for triage, when we have been wounded by the world. It is our safe haven, where we can confidently grasp the horns of sanctuary. In the family, we learn about the order of heaven. It is in the family that we learn how to prepare to receive covenants.

The family provides role models for us to follow. It prepares us to become parents, ourselves. It is a training manual that teaches us about the celestial principles of service, sacrifice and consecration. It teaches us about the four cardinal virtues of prudence, temperance, fortitude, and justice, and about the three heavenly graces of faith, hope, and charity. The family teaches us how to love ourselves and each other. It teaches us about responsibility, accountability, humility, and morality.

A return to the traditional values of the family may be our only hope if we want to fix the mess we've created for ourselves as a society. Far too often, the family is composed of a bunch of narcissistic brats who all have a room full of trophies for being participants, who never had to get up at 4 a.m. to milk the cows, who never went to Seminary, who never learned the Young Women values, who never earned a Duty to God award, who never served in the Young Women or Aaronic Priesthood, who never gave a talk in Primary or Sacrament meeting, who never went home teaching with their dad, who never blessed the Sacrament, offered prayers, went on wilderness treks, or sang the hymns of Zion. They never watched brothers and sisters go on missions, or return home with honor. They never watched their fathers bless the sick, dedicate homes or graves, or write in their journals. They never were give the opportunity to follow the counsel of ecclesiastical leaders, raise their hands to sustain others in church callings, and never witnessed the workings of the Spirit. They never felt its influence, followed its promptings, read their scriptures, or fasted and prayed. They never received a patriarchal blessing. They never were given the opportunity to plan, conduct, or even participate in a family home evening. They never paid tithes or offerings, or were asked to sacrifice.

Far too often, those who could even loosely be regarded as family members are "strangers from a realm of light, who have forgotten all - the memory of their former life and the purpose of their call. And so, they must learn why they're here, and who they really are." (Doug Stewart, "Saturday's Warrior"). That is the purpose of the gospel of Jesus Christ; to make possible the creation of eternal families.

"Direct exposure
(with Mormons) dispelled
the mystery and won respect.
After Ernest Hemingway summered
among Mormons in Ketchum, Idaho,
in the 1960s, he wrote: "To tell the
truth, if I were reborn and I had
a choice, I'd be a Mormon."
(Truman Madsen).

In Defense Of
The Prophet Joseph Smith

"I feel like shouting hallelujah, when I think that I ever knew Joseph Smith, the Prophet," declared Brigham Young. ("Deseret News," 10/31/1855). On one occasion, anticipating his own family reunion beyond the veil, Joseph had said: "I will tell you what I want. If tomorrow I shall be called to lie in yonder tomb, in the morning of the resurrection let me strike hands with my father." (H.C., 5:361). When we depart this life, it would be wonderful if one of the first things we did after passing through the veil was to strike hands with the Prophet Joseph Smith. It is he, after all, who "holds the keys of this last dispensation, and (none of us will) enter into the Celestial Kingdom of God without (his) consent." (Brigham Young, J.D., 7:289-290).

There are things in this life that we know with absolute, unshaken certainty. We know that we must obey the laws of physics. We know the sun will rise tomorrow morning. We know that April showers will bring May flowers. We know that if we over-eat, or even if we glance at a piece of chocolate cake, we'll gain weight. We know that when we step off a curb, our feet will eventually strike pavement.

We also know things of a metaphysical nature. We know who we are. We know things that cannot be rationally explained. We know that Joseph Smith was a prophet of God. Imagine what he must have thought when the angel Moroni told him that his name would "be had for good and evil among all nations, kindreds, and tongues." (J.S.H. 1:33). The "Messenger & Advocate" reported that Moroni further cautioned him: "Wherever the sound (of the marvelous work) shall go, it shall cause the ears of men to tingle, and wherever it shall be proclaimed, the pure in heart shall rejoice, while those who draw near to God with their mouths, and honor him with their lips, while their hearts are far from him, will seek its overthrow, and the destruction of those by whose hands it is carried. Therefore, marvel not if your name is made a derision and had as a by-word among such, if you are the instrument in bringing it, by the gift of God, to the knowledge of the people."

We can very easily put a positive spin on the negative press about Joseph Smith that was foreseen by Moroni. We can share the words of those who knew him personally and who gave the best years of their lives for the work he helped to establish. Eliza R. Snow declared: "His integrity was as firm as the pillars of heaven." ("Anniversary Tribute to the Memory of President Joseph Smith," "Woman's Exponent," 1/1/1874).

Mary Ann Winters, a stepdaughter of Parley P. Pratt, remembered: "The Holy Spirit lighted up his countenance 'til it glowed like a halo around him, and his words penetrated the hearts of all who heard him." (Cited by Truman Madsen, in "Joseph Smith The Prophet," p. 89-90).

We might also want to remember that the Internet does not have a "truth" filter. Some information promulgated by detractors, no matter how convincing, is simply not true. Jeffrey R. Holland said: "This is a divine work in process, so please don't hyperventilate if from time to time issues arise that need to be examined, understood, and resolved. They do and they will. In this church, what we know will always trump what we do not know." ("Ensign," 5/2013).

When something as important as testimony is concerned, we do not discard that which we know to be true because of things we do not yet understand. Dieter F. Uchtdorf said: "First doubt your doubts before you doubt your faith. We must never allow doubt to hold us prisoner and keep us from the peace that comes through faith in the Lord Jesus Christ." ("Ensign," 11/2013).

The scriptures teach: "By their works ye shall know them." (Moroni 7:5). Neal A. Anderson warned against "studying the church through the eyes of its defectors." (C.R., 10/2014). He likened that practice to "interviewing Judas to understand Jesus. Defectors always tell us more about themselves than about that from which they have departed." ("B.Y.U. Devotional," 11/8/1977).

Some information about Joseph, while true, may be presented out of context to his own day and circumstances. The "Joseph Smith Papers" provide a window into his world, and have done a wonderful job of re-examining his life in context. The assessment of his character by contemporaries also provides even-handed and unbiased judgment.

Joseph Smith's clerk, Howard Coray, remembered: "I sat and listened to his preaching (and was) completely carried away with his indescribable eloquence and power of expression, speaking as I have never heard any other man speak." (Letter from Howard Coray to Martha Jane Lewis, 8/2/1889, Sanford, Colorado, pp. 3-4, "L.D.S. Church Archives").

John M. Bernhisel, who boarded in Joseph and Emma's home in Nauvoo, recalled: "Joseph Smith is naturally a man of strong mental powers, and is possessed of much energy and decision of character, great penetration, and a profound knowledge of human nature. He is a man of calm judgment, enlarged views, and is eminently distinguished by his love of justice. He is kind and obliging, generous and benevolent, sociable and cheerful, and is possessed of a mind of a contemplative and reflective character. He is honest, frank, fearless and independent, and as free from (false appearances) as any man to be found." (H.C., 6:468).

Daniel D. McArthur, who led one of the first handcart companies to Salt Lake City, might have said it best: "It always seemed to me that if I ever did know anything on this earth, I surely knew that he was a prophet." ("Juvenile Instructor," p. 129, 2/15/1892).

Edward Stevenson, a member of the Seventy for over 50 years, from 1844 to 1897, said: "The Prophet testified with great power concerning the visit of the Father and the Son, and the conversation he had with them. Never before did I feel such power." ("Reminiscences of Joseph, the Prophet, and the Coming Forth of The Book of Mormon," p. 4). Wilford Woodruff testified: "In his public and private career, he carried with him the Spirit of the Almighty, and he manifested a greatness of soul which I had never seen in any other man." ("Deseret News," p. 363, 1/20/1858).

Because spiritual questions deserve spiritual answers from God, the mission of Joseph Smith demands more than intellectual consideration. It requires that we ask of God, as did Joseph. "If any of (us) lack wisdom, (we should) ask of God, that giveth to all men liberally, and upbraideth not; and it shall be given (us). But let (us) ask in faith, nothing wavering. For he that wavereth is like a wave of the sea driven with the wind and tossed." (James 1:5-6). The same scripture that drove Joseph to his knees in the Sacred Grove should motivate each of us to seek equivalent spiritual confirmation.

Our own faith needs to be securely in place, in order to help others to feel the Spirit. Neal A. Anderson observed that while traveling on a commercial airliner it is important to know how to put on an oxygen mask in the event of the loss of cabin pressure. The instruction provided by the flight attendants concludes with this admonition: "Be sure to adjust your own mask before helping others." (C.R., 10/2014).

Now is the time to adjust our own spiritual oxygen masks so that we are prepared to help others who are seeking refreshment from celestial air. Henry B. Eyring said that in our love for others who exhibit faltering faith, we "may be tempted to go with them through their doubts, with the hope that we can find proof or reasoning to dispel them." But he cautioned: "You and I can do better, if we do not stay long with what others see as the source of their doubts. Their problem does not lie in what they think they see; it lies in what they cannot yet see. We do best, if we turn the conversation to the things of the heart, those changes of the heart that open spiritual eyes." ("C.E.S. Address," 2/5/1993).

We need to recognize that a testimony of the Prophet Joseph Smith will come differently to each of us. There are probably as many conversion stories as there are converts, and probably nearly as many conversion stories as there are life-long members of the church. The constant water balloon volleys from the sidelines may occasionally get us wet, but they need never extinguish that burning fire of faith that was ignited by the Spirit at the time of our initial conversion.

Scriptures in the Book of Mormon that we feel, and that we know are absolutely true, can anchor our faith. Joseph Smith said: "When you joined this church you enlisted to serve God. When you did that you left the neutral ground, and you never can get back on to it. Should you forsake the Master you enlisted to serve, it will be by the instigation of the evil one, and you will follow his dictation and be his servant'" ("Teachings of Presidents of the Church: Joseph Smith," p. 324).

When we read the testimony of the Prophet Joseph Smith in the Pearl of Great Price, the Spirit will bear witness of the work. We will realize that one of his greatest contributions "was his knowledge of what is to come after death. He did much to clarify our understanding of heaven and to make it seem worth working for." ("My Religion & Me" Course Manual). As we approach that happy reunion beyond the veil, we will bring a clear understanding of the sacred calling and divine mission of Joseph Smith. We will know Brother Joseph again, as we look him in the eye, strike hand with him, and are welcomed into his fellowship.

HISTORY

"I realize in some
measure my responsibility,
and the need I have of support
from above, and wisdom from
on high, that I may be able
to teach this people."
(Joseph Smith).

Joseph Smith's History

While Joseph Smith's History is presented in the first person as though he had written it himself, in fact he composed none of it. He did dictate small portions, and was a major force in collecting and preserving materials from which the history was written, but holographs (documents personally written by Joseph Smith) are rare.

"Joseph Smith's authorship is defined as those writings which he personally wrote, dictated, or assigned to be written and were subsequently approved for publication by him. A very strict standard is applied to any statements attributed to Joseph Smith. During his lifetime was the statement or document attributed to Joseph subject to review and correction by Joseph?

In order to qualify as an unimpeachable source, one of two conditions must exist. The first, or actual, reality includes the holographic, or personally handwritten, writings of Joseph and dictated words that were recorded by a scribe and subsequently read and approved by Joseph. The second, or verifiable, reality would be an article written by assignment under Joseph's authority, and approved and signed by him." (Source: "Book of Mormon Archaeological Forum").

The question always arises as to why his history was written as though he were the author. One reason may have been for the sake of narrative consistency. He dictated a small portion of the history, but much more was compiled at his direction. Another was the fact that his scribes used methods standard in their day; ghostwritten annals were the norm in 19th century historiography, even though their efforts may appear to us to be deceptive, in terms of authorship.

Although Joseph Smith dictated portions of the history, much of it relies on the diaries kept by clerks who traveled with him, described his activities, and gave summaries of his sermons. Only about 35 pages of his diaries are in his own handwriting. Occasionally, these entries were reviewed by Joseph, but generally there was little time for such activity. The bulk of his journals consists of the independent work of various clerks and associates. The manuscript of his history was more or less complete up to the year 1838. Following his death in 1844, an effort was made to bring the manuscript up to date, but its editing and compilation were not completed until 1858.

"I am like a huge, rough stone rolling
down from a high mountain; and the only polishing I
get is when some corner gets rubbed off by coming in contact with
something else, striking with accelerated force against religious bigotry,
priestcraft, lawyer-craft, doctor-craft, lying editors, suborned judges
and jurors, and the authority of perjured executives, backed by
mobs, blasphemers, licentious and corrupt men and women;
all hell knocking off a corner here and a corner there."
(D.H.C., 5:401).

Joseph Smith's World

Joseph Smith was born on December 23, 1805. Also born in 1805 (on November 28) was the prominent archaeologist John Lloyd Stephens, who in 1840-1841 initiated the study of ancient civilizations in Meso-America. Before his expeditions, little or nothing was known of pre-Columbian cultures in that part of the world. In 1840, he actually purchased the Mayan city of Copán in what is now Belize, for the sum of $50.00. It is now a UNESCO World Heritage Site.

To put 1805 in context, keep in mind that it was only in 1830, the same year the church was organized, that the first steam railroad (the Baltimore & Ohio) carried both passengers and freight. Three years later, Oberlin College, in Ohio, was the first institution of higher education to admit both men and women. It was also the first university in the United States, in 1841, to confer degrees upon women. Elizabeth Blackwell was the first woman in the United States to receive a medical degree, in 1849, from Geneva Medical College of Western New York. The first postage stamp was issued by the United States government, on July 1, 1847. The 5¢ stamp, with an image of Benjamin Franklin, is currently valued at around $2,500.00. The first commercial oil well was drilled in Titusville, Pennsylvania, in 1859. Women's suffrage was granted in Wyoming Territory, in 1869. Ada H. Keply was the first woman to graduate from law school, (the Union College of Law, in Chicago, Illinois) in 1870.

In 1825, the Erie Canal opened. It was 363 miles long, and was dug entirely by hand. "I've got a mule, her name is Sal, fifteen miles on the Erie Canal. She's a good ol' worker and a good ol' pal, fifteen miles on the Erie Canal. We've hauled some barges in our day, filled with lumber, coal, and hay, and we know every inch of the way, from Albany to Buffalo. Low bridge, everybody down! Low bridge, for we're comin' to a town! And you'll always know your neighbor, you'll always know your pal, when your navigatin' on the Erie Canal." The Canal, that had been under construction between 1817 and 1825, ran right through Palmyra, New York.

Returning to our consideration of life in the United States in 1805, it is hard for us to imagine that there were just 17 states in the Union – the original 13, (in the order in which they joined the Union: Delaware, Pennsylvania, New Jersey, Georgia, Connecticut, Massachusetts, Maryland, South Carolina, New Hampshire, Virginia, New York, North Carolina, and Rhode Island) plus Vermont, Kentucky, Tennessee, and Ohio.

In 1805, U.S. Marines stormed the beaches in Tripoli. ("From the halls of Montezuma to the shores of Tripoli; we fight our country's battles in the air, on land, and sea.") Thomas Jefferson's second term as the third President of the United States began on Monday, March 4. He took the oath of office in the Senate Chamber of the United States Capitol Building, that had been completed in 1800. At the time, he was living in the White House, whose construction was started in 1792, and completed in 1800. Before his first inauguration, he had been living at Conrad and McMunn's Boarding House, near the Capitol. In fact, he slept there the evening before, and had breakfast with his fellow boarders the morning of his first inauguration.

Beginning with Jefferson, and until after the Civil War, nondiscriminatory and voluntary religious services were conducted in the Capitol building. Jefferson rode on horseback to attend these services, although James Madison came in a coach. In 1806, a female evangelist named Dorothy Ripley delivered a sermon to Jefferson, Vice President Aaron Burr, and a "crowded audience."

On November 15, 1805, after 4,100 miles of travel up the Missouri River, over the Rocky Mountains, and down the Columbia River, the Voyage of Discovery led by co-captains Meriwether Lewis and James Clark finally arrived on the western shores of the continent. They had left St. Louis on May 14, 1804, and arrived at the Pacific Ocean on November 15, 1805, one year six months and one day after beginning a round-trip journey that had been envisioned would take just a year.

When the Corps of Discovery dragged themselves into the camp of the Nez Perce on the Pacific side of the Lolo Pass, in September 1805, they were exhausted and near starvation. But the Nez Perce welcomed them, fed them, helped them make canoes, and agreed to care for their horses until they returned the following spring on their journey home.

Lewis and Clark wintered at Fort Clatsop, a rude log fortress they constructed in what is now Oregon. It was named in honor of a local Indian tribe. There, they endured three months of cold, wet weather, where it rained all but twelve days. They headed back to St. Louis in the early spring of 1806. Sacajawea's son, Jean Baptiste Charbonneau, who had been born a year earlier in the Mandan Villages of North Dakota, traveled to the Pacific and back to St. Louis with the Voyage of Discovery, and grew up to be a scout who, forty years later, would guide the Mormon Battalion to California.

In 1805, Andrew Jackson was 38 years old. In 1829, he would become the 7th President of the United States. George Washington had died 6 years earlier, and Benjamin Franklin had been dead for 15 years. He had famously said: "If you would not be forgotten as soon as you are dead and rotten, either write things worth reading, or do things worth writing."

In 1805, on October 21, Admiral Horatio Nelson was killed at the Battle of Trafalgar, off the southwest coast of Spain. Perhaps the most significant naval battle in history, both strategically and tactically, the Battle of Trafalgar not only ensured England's dominance of the seas, but also made Nelson a legend (although not a living one). In 1805, Napoleon was made Emperor of France. Within ten years, he would be exiled to Elba. Alexis de Tocqueville was born on July 29, 1805. He would later write the influential book "Democracy in America." In it, he wrote: "I confess that in America I sought the image of democracy itself, with its inclinations, its character, its prejudices, and its passions, in order to learn what we have to fear or hope from its progress."

On July 2, 1805, Hans Christian Anderson was born. Among other things, he wrote: "Every man's life is a fairy tale written by God's fingers." "Being born in a duck yard does not matter, if only you are hatched from a swan's egg." "Just living is not enough, said the butterfly, one must have sunshine, freedom, and a little flower." "Enjoy life. There's plenty of time to be dead." "The whole world is a series of miracles, but we're so used to them we call them ordinary things." "Life itself is the most wonderful fairy tale."

Popular early nineteenth century recipes included Johnny Cake: "Scald one pint of milk and add to it three pints of Indian meal and half a pint of flour, then bake before fire. And Baked Beans: Soak a quantity of beans overnight. Put in a pot. Add molasses, salt, salt pork or meat fat. Bake for a long time in a slow oven."

In Thomas Jefferson's 1805 Second Inaugural Address, among other things he said: "In matters of religion I have considered that its free exercise is placed by the Constitution independent of the powers of the general government. I have therefore undertaken on no occasion to prescribe the religious exercises suited to it, but have left them, as the Constitution found them, under the direction and discipline of the church or state authorities acknowledged by the several religious societies.

Our wish…is that public efforts may be directed honestly to the public good, that peace be cultivated, civil and religious liberty unassailed, law and order preserved, (and) equality of rights maintained.

I shall now enter on the duties to which my fellow-citizens have again called me, and shall proceed in the spirit of those principles which they have approved. I fear not that any motives of interest may lead me astray; I am sensible of no passion which could seduce me knowingly from the path of justice, but the weaknesses of human nature and the limits of my own understanding will produce errors of judgment sometimes injurious to your interests. I shall need, therefore, all the indulgence which I have heretofore experienced from my constituents; the want of it will certainly not lessen with increasing years. I shall need, too, the favor of that Being in whose hands we are, who led our fathers, as Israel of old, from their native land and planted them in a country flowing with all the necessaries and comforts of life; who has covered our infancy with His providence and our riper years with His wisdom and power, and to whose goodness I ask you to join in supplications with me that He will so enlighten the minds of your servants, guide their councils, and prosper their measures that whatsoever they do shall result in your good, and shall secure to you the peace, friendship, and approbation of all nations."

This is the world that greeted Joseph Smith on December 23, 1805, and in which he lived for the next thirty eight years. It was the land of America, whose fertile soil would nourish tender gospel seeds. As The Book of Mormon promised: "And inasmuch as ye shall keep my commandments, ye shall prosper, and shall be led to a land of promise; yea, even a land which I have prepared for you; yea, a land which is choice above all other lands." (1 Nephi 2:20).

In "a declaration of belief regarding governments and laws in general, adopted by unanimous vote at a general assembly of the church held at Kirtland, Ohio, August 17, 1835," (Superscript to D&C 134), the church that had been organized by Joseph Smith stated: "We believe that religion is instituted of God; and that men are amenable to him, and to him only, for the exercise of it, unless their religious opinions prompt them to infringe upon the rights and liberties of others; but we do not believe that human law has a right to interfere in prescribing rules of worship to bind the consciences of men, nor dictate forms for public or private devotion; that the civil magistrate should restrain crime, but never control conscience; should punish guilt, but never suppress the freedom of the soul." (D&C 134:4).

In the world of Joseph Smith, the prophecy of Thomas Jefferson had come to pass, that "the tree of liberty must be refreshed from time to time with the blood of patriots and tyrants," as well as of martyrs, to the truth of God.

"Zion comes in many different colors. Zion speaks Aymara, Afrikaans, Fijian, Polish, Mandarin, and, more than twenty other languages. It lives in well over six hundred stakes and in practically every country in the world, from China to Argentina. It has 3,227,796 members who are red, yellow, brown, black, and white. Zion wears a sarong, a grass skirt, a blue collar, and a beret. It lives in igloos, huts, and condominiums. Most important of all, it shares a common testimony that Jesus is the Christ, and that His love, indeed, makes the world go 'round."
("Mormonad," "New Era," 9/1973).

Jumping Out Of Our Skin

Normally, our red, yellow, brown, black, or white skin fits very well, thank you, like a well-tailored Brooks Brothers or Talbot's suit. It should, because it has been reported that we annually spend over $55 billion to pamper it with creams, lotions, balms, emollients, astringents, clarifiers, modifiers, oils, ointments, liniments, balsams, salves, gels, and lubricants. Why do we bother? It may be because our skin reflects who we are; ideally, it wraps us up in neat and tidy packages; it is the organ system that can make or break a first impression.

We all know that beauty is only skin deep, and that some people get under our skin, or make our skin crawl. We all have escaped calamity by the skin of our teeth, and some of us have breathed deep sighs of relief when we have, perhaps selfishly, saved our own skin. At other times, in spite of our best efforts, we have gotten skinned. We sometimes need to develop a thick skin, because so many of us have a thin skin. We just need to learn to be comfortable in our own skin. At the end of the day, we cannot allow others get under our skin.

At times, we have been so frightened that we have almost jumped out of our skin, while at other times, we have become so accustomed to trauma that it is no skin off our nose. However, if we are caught in a downpour, we may get soaked to the skin, or if we fail to maintain adequate nutrition, we may waste away until we are nothing more than skin and bones. Faced with challenges, we may find more than one way to skin a cat.

Our skin is the largest of our organ systems, covering an area of around 22 square feet. About 1,000 species of bacteria (around 1 trillion in all) call our skin home. Skin comes in pre-determined colors, although with applications of bleaching crème (e.g. "Porcelana") or spray-tan, some lighter or darker shade adjustments can be made. Our skin is individually crafted for a custom fit, and it uniquely and precisely defines and shapes our physical form. It does an excellent job of covering nearly 100% of our exteriors, no matter that we may be short, tall, fat, or thin, newborn or elderly. It doesn't do quite as well with the aged, however, because it can get very wrinkly, but so can the skin of babies, if they are left in bath water for too long.

Skin provides tidy cohesiveness, and can be quite esthetic, even eliciting sexual desire in the hearts of those who behold its beauty. It delicately helps us to maintain our balance and integrity, as well as our temperature. But it can annoyingly expand over time in response to changing circumstances, especially if we habitually overindulge at the dinner table. It is quite elastic, almost instantly transforming its shape by either stretching or contracting. It folds and creases over time, like a roadmap, to reveal our disposition, and it can broadcast to others whether we have been consistently happy or sad, or have habitually smiled or frowned. It can be hard and cracked and worn by exposure to weather, or it can feel soft and supple and as smooth as a baby's bottom. It can blister with heat, and be either dry or clammy, or warm or cold to the touch.

The skin covering our fingertips has 2,500 nerve receptors per square inch, which can be a real bonus for safecrackers. It callouses with work, and can develop goose bumps when the weather is nasty or when we are frightened. It turns white with shock, and gets clammy during panic attacks (or when we are going through menopause). It streaks with sweat during exercise, during acts of passion, and when we are nervous. It flushes with embarrassment, and puckers up when we are kissing. It resists tearing, but can uncomfortably blister when exposed to thermal or ultraviolet radiation. It bruises with injury, and leaks blood when it is punctured. It grows hair, which sometimes sprouts in awkward places. It gets dirty easily, but can be cleaned up nicely with the application of warm soapy water. It completely replaces itself every four weeks (about 27 trillion cells, in all). It is a biological clock that unerringly mirrors the inexorable passage of time, in spite of all of our efforts to slow down the process or turn the tide. In general, our skin provides a very accurate indication of how we have interacted with the outside world. Without its organizational ability, we would be hard to recognize; we would be like octopuses on roller skates.

Skin serves our needs for the moment, suits our lifestyle, and provides us with a much neater and tidier appearance than some of the alternatives that come to mind. Think: jellyfish, slugs, seaweed, mucous membranes, tripe, and the movie "Alien." But when all is said and done, as comfortable as we may be in our own skin, it is not our natural element. It is only a fleeting shadow and corruptible approximation of what was provided at the creation. God's declaration: "Let us make man in our image, after our likeness," defines what the covering of our proper and perfect frame should look like under ideal circumstances. (Genesis 1:26).

In a Garden setting, the skin of Adam and Eve must have glowed with the innocence and purity of their former home. We know that the countenances of angels who come from the presence of God to minister among men are as lightning. (See Matthew 28:3, D&C 20:6, & J.S.H. 1:32). When the Savior visited the Kirtland Temple, those who saw Him recounted that "His countenance shone above the brightness of the sun." (D&C 110:3). In his dedicatory prayer in that holy house, Joseph Smith implored our Father in Heaven: "Help us by the power of thy Spirit, that we may mingle our voices with those bright, shining seraphs around thy throne, with acclamations of praise, singing Hosanna to God and the Lamb!" (D&C 109:79).

The celestial skin of our first parents was the holy representation of a backstage pass that granted them favored access to their Father's listening ear. He must have visited the Garden many times, instructing and preparing Adam and Eve for mortality. They were certainly familiar with His form and comfortable with His companionship, as He took them into "His bosom" where they shared many innocent intimacies. (Isaiah 40:11).

Heavenly Father had created the Garden as a learning laboratory with limitations. Adam and Eve were quite comfortable in their celestial skin, right up to the moment when their Father quietly asked them: "Who told thee that thou wast naked?" (Genesis 3:11). His inquiry redefined their existence and put a sharp point to the purpose of life. Beforehand, they'd had no reason to believe that appearances could be deceiving, but now they had to deal with the consequences of the destroyer's hypocrisy, who had appeared to them in the skin of a serpent. The introduction of the concept of opposition into their peaceful environment negated their naivety, pummeled their purity, and violated their virtue. The scriptures attest to the telestial turmoil that resulted from the disruption of their idyllic existence. But they also describe a transformation from a morally static environment to one filled with the promise of progression through the exercise of free will. Had He not allowed the introduction of opposition into the only world Adam and Eve had ever known, God would have ceased to be God. (See 2 Nephi 2:13). Even as their skin lost a bit of its intrinsic luster, Adam and Eve kept their faces oriented toward the light their Father promised to give them, and their cheeks must have glowed with hopeful anticipation.

It was not long after their expulsion from Eden, that nearly every one of their descendants began to walk "in his own way, and after the image of his own god, whose image (was) in the likeness of the world." (D&C 1:16). Agitators for social change probed the limits of their newfound independence, in contrast to their first parents' lifestyle of moderation. The restraint that had been taught in the tranquility of the Garden was now being put to the test out in the lone and dreary world.

Among the children of men, however, one thing became almost immediately apparent. The image and likeness of God that had been so familiar in the Garden became almost unrecognizable in the urban jungles east of Eden, as nudity became the norm and the string bikini the logo of lasciviousness. In the parlors where the sons of Adam and the daughters of Eve festooned their bodies with tattoos and piercings, their skin became a caricature of its former purity.

To put a positive spin on it, though, mortals became the perfect runway models, warts and all, to showcase opposition. We have all witnessed those who have vacationed in Idumea to celebrate the festival of free will and the carnival of carefree living. But we also remember Paul, who shed his telestial trappings in order to experience a greater comprehension of eternity. He must have felt inadequate trying to describe what had happened to him, for he simply wrote: "Whether in the body, or out of the body, I cannot tell." (2 Corinthians 12:3). He knew that he had somehow jumped right back into his celestial skin, and sensed that he had been clothed with a finer substance in a spiritual aether that allowed him to gently brush against the veil in order to catch a glimpse of eternity.

But in the lone and dreary world, Satan exulted in his new role as the de-facto god of this earth. (See 2 Corinthians 4:4). He actually believed that he had thwarted the Plan by metaphorically bringing to the attention of Adam and Eve their nakedness. More literally, his nefarious plan was designed to expose their vulnerability by penetrating their celestial skin and contaminating it with the worldly elements of transgression. Satan mistakenly thought that by then calling attention to their nakedness, their embarrassment at having yielded to temptation would require them to forsake forever their celestial skin that God had provided. The tempter fancied himself a telestial tailor, who could trick Adam and Eve into thinking that they could hide their nakedness from God. "And the eyes of them both were opened, and they knew that they had been naked. And they sewed fig leaves together and made themselves aprons." (Moses 4:13).

Satan believed that his enticements would irreparably destroy the celestial skin of Adam and Eve, which had been their spiritual protection, and that in the ensuing confusion over a wardrobe change, he could install himself as a puppet ruler, even the god of this world. (See 2 Corinthians 4:4). What he had not counted on, however, was the fact that it was not their celestial skin, but their divine nature, that had been Adam and Eve's protection. All that was necessary to restore their purity was the further light and knowledge from God that they had been promised. Satan never saw that one coming.

Satan also believed that by partaking of the forbidden fruit, the natural defense systems of Adam and Eve had been irreparably weakened. But the Lord, who sees the end from the beginning, countered by promising them further light and knowledge even after their expulsion from Eden. "I will give unto you a pattern in all (these) things," He later affirmed, "that ye may not be deceived." (D&C 52:14). That pattern provided a means for the redemption of not only Adam and Eve, but also of their posterity, with a reach that would touch even those in the present day.

Satan also believed that by partaking of the forbidden fruit, the natural defense systems of Adam and Eve had been irreparably weakened. But the Lord, who sees the end from the beginning, countered by promising them further light and knowledge even after their expulsion from Eden. "I will give unto you a pattern in all (these) things," He later affirmed, "that ye may not be deceived." (D&C 52:14). That pattern provided a means for the redemption of not only Adam and Eve, but also of their posterity, all the way down to the present day.

Jesus Christ alluded to the skin that defines heavenly forms and features, and that is common to all of us, with this reassurance: "He that hath seen me hath seen the Father." (John 14:9). The countenance of the Gods is marked by refreshing candor and uncomplicated honesty, and is a reflection of Their divine attributes and Their noble character. Its nature and expression is free of whimsy, confusion, and hypocrisy. The visage of God is "like a jasper stone, clear as crystal." (Revelation 21:11). The Savior's countenance is in the express image of His Father, and what we see is what we get, plain and simple. (See Genesis 1:26). Figuratively and literally, we receive Him at face value. Our undeviating Exemplar is unlike those chameleon-like figures who sell their birthright for a mess of pottage, compromise their standards for stardom, and dilute their discipleship with the values of vulgarity.

Joseph F. Smith, in his Vision of The Redemption of The Dead, described "Abel... and his brother Seth, one of the mighty ones, who was in the express image of his father, Adam." (D&C 138:40). Evidently, patriarchal proclivities extended from father to son. President Smith continued: "From among the righteous, he organized his forces and appointed messengers, clothed with power and authority, and commissioned them to go forth and carry the light of the gospel. (D&C 138:30). When we return to our heavenly home, we may be clothed in tangible trappings, but we will also be arrayed with the power and authority of vestments that cast intrinsic light.

Case in point - the Doctrine & Covenants records: "God ministered unto" Joseph Smith "by an holy angel, whose countenance was as lightning, and whose garments were pure and white above all other whiteness." (D&C 20:6). "Not only was the angel's "robe exceedingly white, but his whole person was glorious beyond description, and his countenance truly like lightning. The room was exceedingly light, but not so very bright as immediately around his person." (J.S.H. 1:32).

God's pattern provides us with many opportunities during mortality to put our fingers to the pulse and test the promises of His Plan's guiding principles. He is the quintessential travel agent, whose side trips and excursions have been arranged to expand our appreciation of life's real purpose, which is to learn from our experiences while interacting with the wonders of the world. In order to accomplish this, we must ultimately take over the responsibility for our own itinerary by organizing ourselves, as we "prepare every needful thing; and establish a house, even a house of prayer, a house of fasting, a house of faith, a house of learning, a house of glory, a house of order, (and) a house of God." (D&C 88:119). Once again, the elegant simplicity of the Plan trumps the deception and confusion of its convoluted and counterfeit alternatives.

The pattern of the Plan works to our benefit when we pay attention to its priorities. Proper prior parental planning on God's part prevents poor priesthood performance on ours. To that end, in our pre-earth existence a Council was held to pre-emptively obtain our informed consent to endorse the principles of the Plan prior to our coming to earth. During that discussion, God explained His vision for our continuing progression, and opened the floor up to a frank discussion of the risks we would take by participating in His ordained program. He answered questions, and even anticipated the actions of those who would later foster rebellion.

However, "it is extremely important to get straight what happened in that premortal council," taught Neal A. Maxwell. "It was not an unstructured meeting, nor was it a discussion between plans, nor a brain-storming session, as to how to formulate the plan for salvation and carry it out. Our Father's plan was known, and the actual question put was whom the Father should send to carry it out." ("Deposition of a Disciple," p. 11).

That the meeting came to a successful conclusion is implied by the scripture that asks: "Where wast thou when I laid the foundations of the earth? Declare, if thou hast understanding. When the morning stars sang together, and all the sons of God shouted for joy." (Job 38:4 & 7). Even then, our Elder Brother, "the good shepherd," anticipated and addressed our concerns. (John 10:11). His nurturing influence during our pre-mortal sojourn helped to settle our minds regarding the uncertainties that lay ahead, and convinced us that He is "not the author of confusion, but of peace." (1 Corinthians 14:33).

What happened to us later was akin to "going down a rabbit hole." (See Lewis Carroll, "Alice's Adventures in Wonderland," Chapter 1). Our travel from our first estate through the birth canal into the breathtaking expanse of the wide, wide world erased the memory of our former life, but new vistas soon opened up to fill in the void. To reinforce our understanding of the principles we had aforetime internalized, religious recognition, a re-cognition, a re-knowing, or an intuitive remembrance of our former glory, came into play. Carefully articulated Articles of Faith had been formulated that would now "ring a bell" and stir our memories. To describe the process, the expression "Deja-vu" was coined.

These ingenious devices were provided to show us how to jump right back into the spiritual skin that had defined our familiar home from the beginning. For those who would be "born again," that shield would be akin to the barrier protection afforded to health care providers, to safeguard them from the relentless assault of pathogens during critical patient care. With equivalent "barrier protection" shielding our divine center, the likelihood of a return to the full form and stature of our spirit could be maximized.

The Plan has been tested in the crucible of countless classrooms across the cosmos. It is "fair as the moon, clear as the sun, and terrible as an army with banners." (D&C 109:73). Its worth defies argument. Its dedication to proven principles is incontrovertible. Its learning opportunities minimize the risk of succumbing to the wiles of a counterfeit and corruptible curriculum that is only a caricature of canon.

The original "Wile E. Coyote" is the devil, who "is the author of all sin," and the architect of the aforementioned cowardly curriculum. (Helaman 6:30). Even as he gloated in the "nakedness" of Adam and Eve in the Garden, he "knew not the mind of God." (Moses 4:6). The high-fives Satan and his henchmen must have exchanged turned out to be a bit premature. God parlayed his trickery right into the execution of the Plan. "Wo unto them that are deceivers and hypocrites," warned the Savior, for their deceptions will come to naught. (D&C 50:6).

Anciently, a 'hypocrite' was the mask worn by actors in the classical plays written by Aeschylus, Euripides, Aristophanes, and others. The term has come to derisively characterize those who make false appearances with the intent to deceive. It describes those who pretend to be something they are not. If we are not careful, hypocrites can get under our skin; they can worm their way right into our hearts, minds, and souls following the compromise of our barrier protection. Our celestial features can then be distorted into a hypocrite's mask.

In the novel "The Picture of Dorian Grey," by Oscar Wilde, a particularly handsome young man's portrait degenerates over time in response to his moral depravity and self-indulgence, while at the same time his features retain their alabaster innocence. He adheres to the philosophy that the only way to eliminate a temptation is to yield to it. After many years of decadence have taken a mighty toll on his character, he loses his mind, grabs a knife and attacks the picture that with such stark realism and accuracy has reflected his mounting debauchery. The servants of the house awaken to a cry from the locked room of the anguished debaucher, and break down the door. Before them lies the body of an unrecognizable old man, stabbed in the heart, his face withered and decrepit. Only by the ring on his finger can they identify the disfigured corpse as their master. (The Ring of Gyges comes to mind. See below). Beside the emaciated figure is the picture of Dorian Gray that has reverted to its original loveliness.

In Book 2 of Plato's "The Republic," Glaucon and Adeimantus present the myth of the Ring of Gyges, by means of which Gyges is able to make himself invisible. They then ask Socrates: "If one came into possession of such a ring, why should he act justly?" Socrates replies that although no one could see their body, the soul would be horribly disfigured by the evils that had been committed behind the illusory shield of invisibility.

Thankfully, God has turned the tables on Satan by providing a way for us to jump out of our skin whenever it has become corrupted and contaminated by sin. We need not fear that our spiritual portraits will lose their luster. We need not be like that unfortunate soul who took the Excess Express, and who, when he got to heaven, "saw something that filled him with fright. His spiritual body was one sorry sight! No more than a skeleton covered with skin. He got up to heaven but didn't get in!" (Anonymous).

God's Plan gives our bumpy ride through mortality a profoundly positive twist, energizing it with vitality and the ability to re-write its last chapters, and even to alter eternity. We cannot go back and start a new beginning, but we can start today and make a new ending. We can re-boot the system, get rid of bad code, and with "Time Machine," restore damaged files. We can create enough RAM and additional disk space to write a bedtime story in which we live happily ever after. Hans Christian Anderson said it best: "Every person's life is a fairy tale written by the finger of God."

He has made it possible for us to be dermatologically transformed, to physically manipulate the makeup of our bodies, to figuratively influence our integumentary systems, and to defeat spiritual death without the need for expensive creams, lotions, balms, emollients, astringents, clarifiers, modifiers, oils, ointments, liniments, balsams, salves, gels, and lubricants. He has provided a prequel to the resurrection, by allowing us to have the experience of jumping out of our corruptible skin. This may be a collective experience, but it is always intensely personal. It was our Exemplar, after all, Who stood beside an empty tomb, and cautioned Mary: "Touch me not; for I am not yet ascended to my Father." (John 20:17). She then went and told the other disciples about the miracle she had witnessed. (John 20:18).

When we present ourselves before God, we too will be untouched by corruption. (See Alma 5:14). As the people of Zarahemla exclaimed, so must we: "The Spirit of the Lord Omnipotent... has wrought a mighty change in us, or in our hearts, that we have no more disposition to do evil, but to do good continually." (Mosiah 5:3). Under those circumstances, the last thing we would want to do would be to compromise our spiritual solidarity by contaminating it with a corruptible lifestyle.

The Plan has the inherent power to accomplish the transformation of 27 trillion skin cells, not in four weeks' time, but only after being wrapped in the "clean linen cloth" of the gospel. (Matthew 27:59). If the clothes in which we have gone out to play on terra firma have been soiled by sin, we can forsake our filthiness in favor of clean heavenly vestments. Unlike the clothing made for the Emperor in the tale by Hans Christian Anderson, our celestial garments are tangible; they are real. We need not fear the cries of children in the streets: "But they aren't wearing anything at all!" ("The Emperor's New Clothes").

The scriptures prepare our minds with additional contrasting examples. When Belshazzar of old saw the writing upon the wall, his "countenance was changed, and his thoughts troubled him, so that the joints of his loins were loosed, and his knees smote one against another." (Daniel 5:6). A fundamental transmutation with intensely personal negative consequences was in the works. Soon thereafter, he was "weighed in the balances, and found wanting." (Daniel 5:27). The celestial skin provided by God to Belshazzar had mutated through apostasy, and the resultant 20 pounds or so of dermal and epidermal cells (comprising not only the largest, but also the heaviest organ system in the human body) no longer afforded him protection from the elements of his cankered and cancerous environment.

Things turned out better for leprous Naaman, the captain of the hosts of the king of Syria, who was told by the messenger of Elisha: "Go and wash in Jordan seven times, and thy flesh shall come again to thee, and thou shalt be clean. Then went he down, and dipped himself seven times in Jordan, according to the saying of the man of God: and his flesh came again like unto the flesh of a little child, and he was clean." (2 Kings 5:10 & 14).

The skin of other lepers benefitted from the application of celestial salve, as well. The scriptures record that as Jesus "entered into a certain village, there met him ten men that were lepers, which stood afar off: And they lifted up their voices, and said, Jesus, Master, have mercy on us. And when he saw them, he said unto them, Go shew yourselves unto the priests. And it came to pass, that, as they went, they were cleansed." (Luke 17:12 & 14).

Joseph Smith recorded his impressions from many encounters with the Spirit: "Often times it maketh my bones to quake while it maketh manifest." (D&C 85:6). Faithful members of the church have had similar feelings in preparation to receive "health in their navel and marrow to their bones," as they jump out of telestial trappings into celestial robes. (D&C 89:18). More than a nutritional nuance or a medical marvel, this priesthood transformation insures a metaphorical manipulation through rhetorical analogy: "Though (their) sins be as scarlet, they shall be as white as snow; though they be red like crimson, they shall be as wool." (Isaiah 1:18).

King Benjamin suggested: "The natural man is an enemy to God, and always has been from the beginning," even from that time so long ago when Adam and Eve initially jumped out of carefully crafted and meticulously maintained celestial skin. (Mosiah 3:19). It is clear that each of us must, as Paul suggested, be fitted by the Master Tailor to receive a heavenly vestment and become "a new creature" in Christ. (2 Corinthians 5:17). "Have ye spiritually been born of God?" Alma asked. "Have ye received his image in your countenances? (Alma 5:14).

It is obvious when the Spirit has stretched and molded us, because its expression will be manifested in an unblemished skin-tone. We will have "the look." Like it or not, by the time we are middle-aged, the record of the conduct of our lives will have been indelibly etched into the unalterable expressions of our countenances. If we have memorized the celestial melodies that move us to "sing the song of redeeming love," our countenances will shine with a radiance from the presence of the Lord that will rest upon us. (Mosiah 5:26, see D&C 138:24).

After his parents' expulsion from the Garden, "Cain was very wroth," and he deliberately shed his celestial skin, as had the snake who was his mentor. (We do not know for sure, but he may have been in those difficult teenage years). In any event, he was in a flat spin from which he could not recover. His "countenance fell." (Genesis 4:5). He could neither overcome his fallen nature nor endure the molting process we all must face when we make 'the leap.' But it is only at that moment that we are able to slough off the telestial trash of trillions of dead skin cells, so that our "sleeping dust (may be) restored unto its perfect frame." (D&C 138:17). It is only then that "the sinews and the flesh upon them, the spirit and the body (will be) united, never again to be divided." (D&C 138:17). It is only then that "old things shall pass away,"(D&C 29:24), "and there shall be a new heaven and a new earth." (Ether 13:9). Only then, will we shed the trappings of our former life, and "every limb and joint shall be restored to its body; yea, even a hair of the head shall not be lost; but all things shall be restored to their proper and perfect frame." (Alma 40:23).

In the meantime, God gives us repetitive opportunities to practice "jumping out of our telestial skin," into the more comfortable and form-fitting celestial silhouette that enables us to leap tall buildings at a single bound. We may do it consciously or automatically, impulsively or with measured consideration. We may apply "Nu-Skin," testing its claim of protection from the scorching sun in the heat of the day. We may sometimes jump from the frying pan right into the fire. When we jump, we may settle on complacency plateaus, but with practice we will more frequently land on springboards to action that vault us upward to pinnacles of perfection where we can confidently maintain our balance. We should always look before we leap, but leap we must. Sometimes, we are prompted, but at other times we are so intensely invested, so spiritually charged, or so inspired, that we only need to heed the admonition: "Who hath faith to leap shall leap." (D&C 42:51).

At a critical juncture in their trek through the far reaches of the galaxy, Captain Jean Luc Picard urged his crew: Now, this will put us at risk. Quite frankly, we may not survive. But I want you to believe that I am doing this for a greater purpose, and that what is at stake here is more than any of you can possibly imagine. I know you have your doubts about me, about each other, about this ship. All I can say is that although we have only been together for a short time, I know that you are the finest crew in the fleet. And I would trust each of you with my life. So, I am asking you for a leap of faith, and to trust me." ("All Good Things..." Episode that aired 5/23/1994).

Before we take that leap, if we happen to be startled by our corruptible reflection in the windows of a great and spacious building, we need to jump out of our skin all the more forthrightly, without hesitation, remembering that "the Lord seeth not as man seeth; for man looketh on the outward appearance, but the Lord looketh on the heart." (1 Samuel 16:7). We need to jump without even thinking about it, emulating the Saints who have rejoiced in their resurrection. Of these, Joseph F. Smith observed: "Their countenances shone, and the radiance from the presence of the Lord rested upon them." (D&C 138:24). We need to jump so that our afterglow is so compelling that its lingering effects overshadow any latent images of our reflection in the windows of even the tallest telestial towers.

When Joseph Smith and Oliver Cowdery attended the dedication of the Kirtland Temple, they shed their telestial trappings to enjoy an unprecedented vision of the Savior. "His eyes were as a flame of fire," Joseph recorded, and "the hair of his head was white like the pure snow; his countenance shone above the brightness of the sun." (D&C 110:3). The Lord's appearance was untainted by telestial trauma. He was "Alpha and Omega, the beginning and the ending, the Lord, who is, and who was, and who is to come, the Almighty." (J.S.T. Revelation 1:8). Joseph and Oliver were provided with a preview of the extreme makeover, punctuated by a spiritual change of wardrobe, that awaited them in the Celestial Kingdom.

Joseph's observations went beyond garments and compelled him to consider the spiritual center of resurrected beings. Of the Angel Moroni, he had recorded: "His hands were naked, and his arms also, a little above the wrist; so, also, were his feet naked, as were his legs, a little above the ankles. His head and neck were also bare. I could discover that he had no other clothing on but this robe, as it was open, so that I could see into his bosom. Not only was his robe exceedingly white, but (also) his whole person was glorious beyond description, and his countenance truly like lightning. The room was exceedingly light, but not so very bright as immediately around his person." (J.S.H. 1:31-32).

But what about those of us who are less sure of ourselves? What happens if we look in the mirror and see the face of a stranger staring back at us? What if our knees wobble at the prospect of a leap that requires an "identity transplant?" This has happened enough times in the scriptures that the "face" is referenced 684 times, "new" 206 times, "image" 166 times, "change" 104 times, and "countenance" 70 times. "Image of God" is mentioned a dozen or so times, and "visage" 4 times. The scriptures provide a lot of counsel regarding the purpose behind our packaging.

Since the first partial face transplant was performed on a woman in France in 2006, psychologists have been asking if such a procedure carries the risk of psychological impairment, or if it might, on the other hand, offer the possibility of enriching the narrative of one's life by putting a new face to identity. The jury is still out on that question, but it begs another: What happens under ideal circumstances, when the Lord's witness protection program functions optimally, and Satan can no longer find us, because we have been "born again; yea, born of God," and changed from our "carnal and fallen state, to a state of righteousness, being redeemed of God, becoming his sons and daughters?" (Mosiah 27:25). What happens when we are no longer recognizable as our former selves, when all ties to our past lives have been severed? What positive changes occur when we jump out of our skin, when "old things are passed away, (and) all things are become new?" (2 Corinthians 5:17).

The simplest answer to these questions might be found in the recorded experiences of those who have had a "heart transplant" when they accepted the gospel. Alma spoke of his own father's conversion: "According to his faith there was a mighty change wrought in his heart." (Alma 5:12). Paul may have been thinking along the same lines, when he described the new gospel-oriented identity that is found in the "fleshy tables of the heart." (2 Corinthians 3:3). Converts often emerge from the refiner's fire having had spiritual open-heart surgical procedures, wherein the dross of their former life has been burned out of their systems by the white-hot fire of God.

The identity crisis of such individuals is mitigated because of God's care and concern relating to these extreme makeover procedures. It turns out that the grass really is greener on the other side of the fence, where a pleasant pastoral environment promises a new perspective. The prophet may have been alluding to this when he wrote: "Say to the prisoners, Go forth; to them that are in darkness, Shew yourselves. They shall feed in the ways, and their pastures shall be in all high places." (Isaiah 49:9).

In any event, of those who have taken their vows and moved upward to new plateaus that are springboards for affirmative action, their new look is visibly different. Their features are flushed with confidence. They stand out from the crowd. They are enthusiastic, passionate, fervent, eager, animated, excited by life, and get a high from the natural release of endorphins.

These dedicated disciples remind us of Abinadi, of whom the scriptures record: "The Spirit of the Lord was upon him; and his face shone with exceeding luster." (Mosiah 13:5). They stand in sharp contrast or opposition to those whose yoke is a heavy burden because they are mired in sin and bound in iniquity. Of them, Jeremiah wrote: "Their visage is blacker than a coal; they are not known in the streets: their skin cleaveth to their bones; it is withered." (Lamentations 4:8).

Those who have brushed against physical death often describe an "out of body" experience akin to "jumping out of their skin." Today, members of the Lord's church do the same when they are redeemed from spiritual death; when they "walk in newness of life." (Romans 6:4).

Latter-day Saints come full circle, and end where they began, albeit with a wider perspective from a higher vantage point. It is strangely familiar to read about how "the Gods went down to organize (them) in their own image, in the image of the Gods to form (them), male and female to form they them." (Abraham 4:27). To really take advantage of their temporal travels and put a positive spin on their telestial trials, Latter-day Saints learn to jump out of their skin, to be restored to their "proper and perfect frame," and ultimately to face their destiny, clothed in glory, immortality, and eternal life. (Alma 40:23). They constantly remind themselves that they are "strangers from a realm of light, who have (nearly) forgotten all - the memory of their former life and the purpose of their call. And so, they must learn why they're here, and who they really are." (See Doug Stewart, "Saturday's Warrior").

It is amazing how our
laughter and our smiles can
speak a universal language. When
we are happy, we are moved by the
tempo of harmonious melodies of gospel
rhythms and motivated to shift into higher
spiritual gears. We leave our plateaus behind
us, as we are propelled upward on concentric
waves of the spirit. Your smile is your logo,
your personality is your business card,
and how you leave others feeling
after an experience with
you becomes your
trademark.

Keep Smiling[1]

Surprisingly, in the scriptures, there are just four references to "smiling." Three of them are in The Book of Mormon, and one is in the Pearl of Great Price. Considering that smiling is a universal language that is emotionally understood in much the same way by almost everyone on the planet, I find this perplexing. Maybe the Patriarchs lived in a more austere and somber age. Perhaps they simply used different words to communicate the expression of the human emotion that lies at the very heart of our spirits. Certainly, in the gospel there is a lot to smile about, and one would think that the prophets would openly address and showcase its emotional appeal.

Gordon B. Hinckley was one who did. On more than once, he urged us to light up the world with our smiles, and not to be pickle suckers. On one occasion, he begged students at B.Y.U.: "I come this morning with a plea that we stop seeking out the storms and enjoy more fully the sunlight. I am suggesting that we accentuate the positive. I am asking that we look a little deeper for the good, that we still our voices of insult and sarcasm, that we more generously compliment virtue and effort. I am not asking that all criticism be silenced. Growth comes of correction. Strength comes of repentance. Wise is the man who can acknowledge mistakes pointed out by others and change his course. I am not suggesting that our conversation be all honey and blossoms. Clever expression that is sincere and honest is a skill to be sought and cultivated. What I am suggesting and asking is that we turn from the negativism that so permeates our society and look for the remarkable good in the land and times in which we live, that we speak of one another's virtues more than we speak of one another's faults, that optimism replace pessimism, that our faith exceed our fears." (11/29/1974).

Lack of smile references notwithstanding, there are still a lot of scriptures that are tied to emotions whose expression are found in a smile: There are 333 references to "joy," 127 to "glad," 62 to "gladness," 40 to "happy," 37 to "happiness," 34 to "merry," and 15 to "mirth." That is 646 references to the emotional states that should evoke a smile. Interestingly, there are 10 references to "laughter," and 1 to "jovial," but all 11 have negative connotations.

For what it is worth, here are the four references to "smiling" that are found in the scriptures: "And when Jesus had spoken these words he came again unto his disciples; and behold they did pray steadfastly, without ceasing, unto him; *and he did smile upon them again;* and behold they were white, even as Jesus." (3 Nephi 19:30). "And it came to pass that Jesus blessed them as they did pray unto him; *and his countenance did smile upon them,* and the light of his countenance did shine upon them." (3 Nephi 19:25). "And the hand of providence hath smiled upon you most pleasingly." (Jacob 2:13). "Wherefore Enoch saw that Noah built an ark; and that *the Lord smiled upon it,* and held it in his own hand." (Moses 7:43).

Because I want to keep this essay on topic, if we were to pick and choose from among the expressions that are related to smiling, we might settle upon "countenance," as the one that is most closely aligned. For example, D&C 59:15 speaks of *"a glad heart and a cheerful countenance."* Psalms 89:15 describes those who *"walk in the light of (the Lord's) countenance."* Proverbs 15:13 teaches that *"a merry heart maketh a cheerful countenance."* 1 Samuel 16:12 turns our mind's eye to David, who was *"of a beautiful countenance,* and goodly to look at." The Savior is described as having such a peaceful appearance that Moses was moved to exclaim: "The Lord *lift up His countenance* upon thee, and give thee peace." (Number 6:26). David described Him as *"the health of my countenance,* and my God. (Psalms 42:11). Alma asked his brethren of the church if they had "spiritually been born of God," or if they had *"received his image in (their) countenances."* (Alma 5:14). Joseph Smith described the Savior as having a *"countenance (that) was as lightning"* (D&C 20:6), that *"shone above the brightness of the sun."* (D&C 110:3). The Lord assured him: "Ye shall behold *the joy of my countenance."* (D&C 88:52). The laborers in the field all received *"the light of the countenance of their Lord."* (D&C 88:58).

Intriguingly, if we perform a simple exercise, and substitute the word *"smile"* for the word *"work"* in selected scriptures, the results almost pop off the page. For example: "Great and marvelous are thy *smiles,* O Lord God Almighty! (1 Nephi 1:14). "The day should come that they must be judged of their *smiles."* (1 Nephi 15:32). "If a man bringeth forth good *smiles* he hearkeneth unto the voice of the good shepherd." (Alma 5:41). "Prepare ye the way of the Lord, for the time is at hand that all men shall reap a reward of their *smiles."* (Alma 9:28). Therefore let your light so shine before this people, that they may see your *smiles* and glorify your Father who is in heaven. (3 Nephi 12:16). "Who can comprehend the marvelous *smiles* of God?" (Mormon 9:16). "I remember the word of God which saith by their *smiles* ye shall know them; for if their *smiles* be good, then they are good also." (Moroni 7:5). "The Lord shall come to recompense unto every man according to his *smile."* (D&C 1:10). "My *smile* shall go forth." (D&C 3:16). "By their desires and their *smiles* you shall know them." (D&C 18:38). "I shall pass upon the inhabitants thereof, judging every man according to his *smiles* and the deeds which he hath done." (D&C 19:3). "My *smiles* have no end, neither beginning." (D&C 29:33). "Those that live shall inherit the earth, and those that die shall rest from all their labors, and their *smiles* shall follow them; and they shall receive a crown in the mansions of my Father." (D&C 59:2). "Pray unto the Lord, call upon his holy name, make known his wonderful *smiles* among the people." (D&C 65:4). "Great and marvelous are the *smiles* of the Lord, and the mysteries of his kingdom which he showed unto us, which surpass all understanding." (D&C 76:114).

I particularly like the following scripture, because smiles seems to lie at the pinnacle of our discipleship: "All those who humble themselves before God, and desire to be baptized, and come forth with broken hearts and contrite spirits, and witness before the church that they have truly repented of all their sins, and are willing to take upon them the name of Jesus Christ, having a determination to serve him to the end, and truly manifest by their *smiles* that they have received of the Spirit of Christ unto the remission of their sins, shall be received by baptism into his church." (D&C 20:37).

We can achieve the same powerful effect by substituting the word "*smile*" for the word "endure." "If they *smile* unto the end, they shall be lifted up at the last day." (1 Nephi 13:37). "I am the law, and the light. Look unto me, and smile to the end." (3 Nephi 15:9). How about the word "*perseverance?*" "Let your *smiles* be redoubled, and you shall in nowise lose your reward (D&C 127:4). Try it with the word "*faith.*" "Look forward for the remission of your sins, with an everlasting *smile.*" (Alma 7:6). "As many as are not stiff-necked and have *smiles*, have communion with the Holy Spirit." (Jarom, 1:4). "Hope cometh of smiles." (Ether 12:4). "By *smiles*, they become the sons of God." (Moroni 7:26). "Without *smiles* there cannot be any hope." (Moroni 7:42). "Remember that without *a smile* you can do nothing." (D&C 8:10). "Without *smiling* no man pleaseth God." (D&C 63:11).

If we tack on the modifier "*with a smile upon your face*" to certain scriptures, they become even more meaningful. For example: "I command thee that thou shalt pray vocally as well as in thy heart, *with a smile upon your face.*" (D&C 19:28). Or: "And thou shalt declare glad tidings, yea, publish it upon the mountains, and upon every high place, and among every people that thou shalt be permitted to see, *with a smile upon your face.*" (D&C 19:29). Or: "Take upon you the name of Christ, *with a smile upon your face.*" (Alma 34:38). Or: "If thou art merry, praise the Lord with singing, with music, with dancing, and with a prayer of praise and thanksgiving, *with a smile upon your face.*" (D&C 136:28). Smiling can even be a token, as it were, of our covenant relationship with the Lord. "Choose ye this day to serve the Lord God, *with a smile upon your* face." (Moses 6:33). "If they hold out faithful to the end they are received into heaven, that thereby they may dwell with God in a state of never-ending happiness, *with smiles upon their faces.*" (Mosiah 2:41). "This mortal shall put on immortality, and this corruption shall put on incorruption, and shall be brought to stand before the bar of God, *with a smile upon their face."* (Mosiah 16:10). "And then shall it come to pass, that the spirits of those who are righteous are received into a state of happiness, *with smiles upon their faces."* (Alma 40:12).

What would the scriptures, or the world for that matter, be like, if there were no smiles to brighten their pages or our lives? "The evil spirit teacheth not a man to pray, but teacheth him that he must not pray, *and that he must never smile."* (2 Nephi 32:8). "Do not suppose, because it has been spoken concerning restoration, that ye shall be restored from sin to happiness, ***or from frowns to smiles.***" (Alma 41:10). "How then can I do this great wickedness, and sin against God, and *wipe the smile from my face?"* (Genesis 39:9). "And there shall be weeping and wailing among the hosts of men, *and there shall be no cause to smile under the heavens."* (D&C 29:15).

Fortunately, the scriptures abound with allusions to our smiles that are not only grammatical constructions, but are also curves that set everything straight. Even though it may be raining, the scriptures teach that if we keep smiling, the sun will soon show its face and smile right back at us. Smiles in the scriptures are often concealed, but they cannot be hidden for long. As smiles peek out at us as honest emotions from behind familiar passages, we can almost hear the Spirit challenging us to smile in return; to smile so widely that we could eat a banana sideways.

When we feel happy, we smile with all our heart, and when we're down, we smile with all our might. If we do nothing else, we can still be the smile on the faces of those that mourn, or stand in need of comfort. Our smiles can be the one daily exercise in which we engage without ever breaking a sweat. The smiles that we wear on the outside tell others what's happening on the inside. Sometimes our joy is the source of our smile, but sometimes our smile may be the source of our joy. As we smile with a determined effort to fight our way through brimming tears, we can take comfort in the fact that at least the corners of our mouths point toward heaven.

Even as the world broadcasts insistent messages that beauty has the advantage, we know that it is our smile that is the absolute guarantee. When we get up in the morning, we are only half-dressed until we put on our smile. We realize that, when it comes to smiling, one size fits all. Our smile is an accessory that never goes out of style. No matter what obstacles may be thrown before us throughout the day, smiling in the face of our challenges makes the tasks that lie ahead seem easier. Somehow, our trials are no match for a confident smile. Others are less likely to notice our imperfections, our shortcomings, or our old and worn out clothes, when we are wearing a smile. As frugal shoppers, we know that a smile is an inexpensive way to change our look. We hope it is true that every smile makes us a day younger. Our smile is like an instant face-lift. Stubborn frowns bring out wrinkles, but those whose smile-induced dimples are doubly blessed, for they have been entrusted with a special role in the universe, and that is to smile.

As we embrace life, we recognize that vibrant color is nature's way of smiling at us. After every storm, we look forward to the dappled rays of sunlight that smile down upon us. Among all the mighty works of man, we realize that a smile is civilization's finest adornment. Of all the creations of God, we acknowledge that a beautiful smile that is flashed for no apparent reason separates us from all other creatures. We have no original facial expressions: We have inherited our smiles from our parents, we borrow them from our friends, and we receive them as gifts from complete strangers. We are drawn to those who make a difference in our lives, to those who make us smile.

Smiling evokes vivid memories of our innermost emotions, just as our vivid memories often arouse smiles. Sometimes, our joy is the source of our smiles, but sometimes it is the other way around. We don't cry because it's over; we smile because it happened. Too often, we underestimate the power of our smile, or forget that it is love that has taught us how to smile. A gentle word, a kind look, and a good-natured smile can work wonders and accomplish miracles, especially when we remember that smiles are meant to be given away. They are the most inexpensive of gifts that should never be in short supply, and yet their power can disarm kingdoms.

With our smiles, we sign our autographs. They may be the most powerful forces in nature, whose effects may last for eternity. It only takes a split second to smile, and then we may forget about it; and yet, to the one to whom it has been given, and who needed it at that exact moment, its positive influence might last a lifetime. When we receive a prompting to smile at a stranger, we might never know that we have changed a life. When we are blessed to see the smiles on the faces of innocent children, we are given a glimpse of the divine nature that is in each of us.

Smiling can be intensely gratifying. It can warm our hearts when others smile, but most of us especially like it when it is we who have made them smile. When we possess a smile, one of the many faces of love knocks at our door. Smiles fill our hearts with the joy of life. When we smile, we find that, all along, happiness was right under our noses.

Sometimes we smile to keep from crying, but it can be inexpensive therapy for our wounded souls. When we feel that there is no reason to smile, we try to find one, because we have learned the hard way that nothing can shake a smiling heart. If we have to, we determine be the smile on someone else's downcast face, to melt away their fears and their tears. Our smile can replace their despondency with cheerfulness.

If need be, with a smile on our face we can climb the steps to the gallows, crack a joke to the crowd, give a coin to the hangman, and make the drop. Short of that, we pray for opportunities to replace the tears of the downcast and oppressed with faces that invite the Spirit to pass through smiling portals that are the windows of their souls.

We are ever on the lookout for those who could really use a smile as therapy for their lonely heart. When we see others who needs a smile, we give them one of ours. We keep apples in our fruit basket, but we know by experience that it is a smile a day that keeps the pain away. Smiles are the spotlights that shine on our hearts. The simplest gift we can give to another is our smile. We try to so live that we can be someone else's reason to smile. We recognize the incredible power of our smiles to change the world, and so we defend ourselves against the worlds' power to change our smiles. We smile at everyone because it might be our last chance to do so, because we, or they, may not be here tomorrow.

Smiling doesn't always mean we are happy. Sometimes, we smile to avoid sadness. A smile may be just the therapy that we need. Or, because our smile may be the only sunlight in the life of a fellow traveler, we are careful to so live that we don't dim that light. Because they are nondiscriminatory, our smiles may be the quickest way to establish communication with strangers. We answer both praise and criticism with a smile. Our smiles can be good ice-breakers, because if we've put a smile on the face of someone we haven't met or barely know, we've done more good than we can imagine.

We smile if for no other reason than that there seem to be so many frowns. Our smile makes a positive statement that squarely addresses the pessimism of a dark and negative world. In fact, the most potent force on earth could be our smile. We smile because we accept hatred with love. Our smiles are the lights of our souls, that can conquer even the coldest hearts, because they dance to the rhythms of nature. We smile as if unborn poems are stirring within us. Our smiles are the bouquet of our joy, the expression of our ecstasy with life, and the God-given manifestation of love, that drive out darkness, which is why a genuine smile can be the best form of communication.

If we need to recharge our batteries, with conscious effort we may take a few steps into the darkness, buoyed up by the sustaining influence of our smiles, which are our spiritual strong searchlights. If we have lost our smiles, we know in which direction we must move to find them again. If we are really desperate, and cannot find a reason to smile, we can always go out and buy a puppy. When we are still, and are seeking quiet spiritual confirmations, the surplus of our hearts will overflow in smiles. When technology threatens our inner peace, we replace the cell phones in our hands with smiles on our faces. There is no other emoticon that can take the place of a genuine smile that is personally given to another human being. Every once in a while, we smile even if life tastes like bitter bile. When thunderstorms roll in, we make a choice to either succumb with fright, or smile and look to see if we can find a rainbow somewhere around the edges of the gloomy downpour.

Our smiles release an awesome power within us. We have heard the compliments of others, who say: Your smile becomes you. But perhaps you become you, when you smile. Those who smile while they are alone used to be called insane, until we invented smartphones and social media. A smile is the light in our window that tells others that there is a caring, sharing person inside. In the morning, we drink a glass of sunshine to brighten our hearts and lift our spirits, and then we smile to spread the light of life. As we pleasantly smile, we take control of the moment, and as we persist in smiling, we own it.

Sometimes, when we wish to make particularly significant contributions, we offer our silence with smiles on our faces. We smile at others with such intensity that they feel that they have won a prize, and they have no choice but to smile back at us, in appreciation. Our cheerful conversation tickles our throats and forces our lips into smiles. We can only appreciate the value of a smile when we own the face behind it. But when our smiles become the expressions of the divine center within us, they are easier to give away.

Even simple smiles are rewarded in heaven. Our smiles are the unfathomable gifts of the gods. While others smiled, we cried at birth, and even if others cry, we hope to be able to smile at our death. We would love to die smiling, because we have already been blessed to see smiles on the faces of those who have been about to pass through the veil. We have been given a foretaste of heaven, and when we journey there, we hope to go with smiles on our faces. However, should we forget to do so in the excitement of the moment, we hope there will be someone waiting in eternity to greet us with a smile, the token of love, and that we will be prompted to remember to do the same. In the interim, the biggest reward of our lives will be to have finished each day with smiles on our faces. Someday, we are going to be able to look back on every shared smile, and then we will be blessed to quietly smile one last time.

It's easy to learn to smile. When we do so, our faces light up as if with a celestial glow. When we smile large, our cheeks may hurt, but it's the cutest thing. When we smile, our mouths and hearts coordinate with each other. We smile as if we've just been told the best joke on earth. When we smile like the morning sun, our lives are filled with fun. Anyone can smile on their best of days. We want to be able to smile on our worst days. Our genuine smiles come from our hearts, but our healthy smiles need good dental care. We know that life is short, and so we smile while we still have teeth.

Our smiles are like flowers that attract bees to nectar. We are smile-magnets. Our smiles are like the last ones others will ever see on earth. When we smile, not only our ears rise, but also our listening ability. We decorate our faces with piles of smiles. We smile at perfect strangers, and mean it, because we realize that nearly everyone could use a lift. We look for special opportunities to spoil the day of grumps, by giving them our smiles. Sometimes we crack a smile, even though we don't like breaking things. Because it's the worst form of identity theft, we refuse to let anyone steal our smiles.

If we're not using our smiles, we're like the person with a million dollars in the bank and no pen to write a check. If we're not smiling, it's because our hearts must be on vacation. When we wear a smile, we have friends, but when we wear a frown, we have wrinkles. No one is perfect, unless they smile. Our smiles preemptively confuse approaching frowns. While frowns mean nothing, our smiles mean everything. It takes 64 facial muscles to make a frown, and only 13 to make a smile, and so we ask ourselves: "Why work overtime?" (It really does take more muscles to frown than it does to smile, which make sense because yesterday I saw someone who frowned so much they ended up pulling a groin muscle). Before we put on a frown, we need to make absolutely sure there are no smiles available. It's no coincidence that smiles turn up the corners of our mouths, while frowns turn them down. In the economy of nature, it could have just as easily have been the other way around, if it were not for the fact that God has an immense sense of humor.

We never ask for permission to smile, and never consider ourselves too poor to give one away. One time, I thought I had lost my smile. But then I found it in a daffodil. Life is about the number of faces that smile when they hear our names mentioned. I have been told that I have a winning smile, but I must confess that it's just not true. My grin only won a silver medal at last year's Facial Expression Olympics. We smile and thank God that we are alive. Especially when it's cold outside, we can always bring someone into the warmth of our smile.

We smile so powerfully that it shames the sun itself, because a smile can be even more cheerful than a beautiful spring day. We smile as if the sun had just come out from behind a cloud. The world always looks brighter from behind a smile. If we were given a star for every time we smiled, we hope that we would soon be holding the night sky in our hands. If we haven't seen our wives smile at a traffic cop, we haven't seen them smile at their prettiest. For some reason, our children are always on their best behavior when they're smiling. We know by experience that love is a smile that is shared between two people. Our smiles are often the best reaction to life's experiences. Smiles are the twinkle that adds to our happiness, which is probably why each of us has smiles to go before we sleep. The weather models of the best meteorologists in the world can't measure the warmth of our smiles. Our enigmatic smiles are worth ten pages of dialogue. When we smile, we reflect the face of God.

You want to know who is amazing, and has the best smile ever? Read the first word of this paragraph again. But, your smile isn't about you; it's about helping others. A smile doesn't always stand for a perfect life, but those who smile when they fall, give the devil a good slap on the cheek. If we smile, or if we don't smile, everyone around us is affected. Our smile is a perfume that we cannot pour out on someone else without getting a few drops on ourselves. What sunshine is to flowers, smiles are to humanity.

Our smiles are like stress-formula vitamins that boost our energy reserves when physical, emotional, and spiritual stress have worn us down. When we sulk, we create noise, but when we smile, we create music. If we can win an argument by stretching our lips into a smile, it makes no sense to open our mouths and lose it. If the world appears either abundant in smiles or overwhelmed by scowls, we might ask ourselves if we are responsible. It's hard for someone to stay angry with us when we smile. We keep right on smiling, because it makes people wonder what we're up to. Love and peace can create smiles, but our smiles can also create love and peace. If we disagree with others, our discussions should be punctuated with smiles. Our smiles are evidence that we are on the side of their recipients. Smiles increase our face value. When we lead with a smile, we are more likely to be lucky.

Our smiles are contagious and they are the only infectious affliction everyone is encouraged to spread. They can start an epidemic, and so we should indiscriminately share them. Most smiles are jump-started by other smiles. The shortest distance between two people is a smile. Our smiles can be the keys that fit the locks on our hearts. One smile probably won't change the world, but it could change ours, and so we smile at everyone. We never know when we're smiling at an angel. Although a laugh can be a smile that has burst its borders, a smile means a lot more, because it is a true reflection of emotion, while laughter is often just a by-product of humor. Unlike gossip, no-one minds if you spread a smile. Our smiles speak a language that even babies understand; think of the smile that flickers on a baby's mouth when it is sleeping, and prepare to be amazed.

Remember to smile the next time you stand before the congregation to bear your testimony, when you are given a service opportunity, when you approach the Recommend Desk at the temple, when you greet your son or daughter who has just returned home from a date, when you are asked about your home or visiting teaching report by your file leaders, when you meet with the Bishop to discuss a church calling, when you entertain the missionaries with a meal in your home, when a non-member friend asks you a question about the church, or when you are asked by a neighbor to move outside your comfort zone to provide temporal or spiritual assistance.

Remember to smile when things don't go as you have planned, when life throws you a curve, when your best-laid plans go awry, when the baby needs a diaper change, when the car starts making weird noises, when your son throws an errant baseball through the front window, when the new driver in your family has a close encounter with a curb or a tree, when an open container of yoghurt falls upside-down on the kitchen floor, or when someone who has used the bathroom before you has squeezed the toothpaste from the middle of the tube.

Remember to smile when you miss by one day the big sale at the department store, when someone at work who is less deserving gets the promotion, when someone else gets recognition for your achievements, or when a neighbor comes home with the same new car you've been dreaming about.

But also remember to smile when you think about how the Lord has blessed you, and how He has provided for your needs and even granted you a surplus, how you have friends you can trust, how your spouse and children sustain you, how others look to you for counsel, how your dog thinks you can do no wrong, and how fortunate you are to be alive.

We are all familiar with the story of the man who complained because he had no shoes, until he met a man who had no feet. Helen Keller took gratitude to a whole new level when she "asked a friend who had just returned from a long walk in the woods what she had observed. 'Nothing in particular,' he replied. "How was that possible," Helen asked herself? "I, who cannot hear or see, find hundreds of things to interest me through mere touch. I feel the delicate symmetry of a leaf. I pass my hands lovingly about the rough shaggy bark of a pine. Occasionally, if I am very fortunate, I place my hand gently on a small tree and feel the happy quiver of a bird in full song." ("Three Days to See," "The Atlantic Monthly," 1/1933).

We need to be more like Brigham Young, who testified: "I feel like shouting Hallelujah, all the time, when I think that I ever knew Joseph Smith," or like Parley P. Pratt, who declared: "I have received the holy anointing, and I can never rest till the last enemy is conquered, death destroyed, and truth reigns triumphant." With smiles on our faces, may each of us have the joyful anticipation of a reward both on earth and in heaven. We have all heard the story about the optimistic little boy, who, when faced with the task of shoveling up an enormous pile of manure in the horse stall behind his home, enthusiastically set about his task with the smiling exclamation: "There's got to be a pony in there, somewhere!"

We should be excited to live in a time when smiling is in vogue, with the possible exception of runway models who look like they have been weaned on pickles. There is so much to smile about! From "selfies," to Facebook posts, to Instagram photos, to Pinterest, and even to SnapChat, it's cool to broadcast a smiling face in cyberspace. But in a disposable society that casts aside interpersonal relationships like empty plastic water bottles, where the counterfeits for happiness can be so easily manufactured, processed, packaged, and promoted, let's make sure we generate daily smiles, and are doing so for the right reasons. Let's not allow gullibility or photoshop to overpower our native common sense. Let's take a lesson from Joseph Smith, who by all accounts was a good-natured and affable soul. But even he admitted: "I was guilty of levity, and sometimes associated with jovial company, not consistent with that character which ought to be maintained by one who was called of God as I had been. But this will not seem very strange to any one who recollects my youth, and is acquainted with my native cheery temperament." (J.S.H. 1:28).

Let's all hope and pray for sunshine in our souls "today, more glorious and bright than glows in any earthly sky, for Jesus is (our) light. O there's sunshine, blessed sunshine, when the peaceful, happy moments roll; when Jesus shows His smiling face, there is sunshine in the soul." (Eliza Hewitt).

Footnote:

1. When composing this essay, I relied heavily on a number of anonymous sources, that the reader will surely recognize.

"God of our fathers, known of old, Lord of our far-flung battle line, beneath whose awful hand we hold dominion over palm and pine. Lord God of Hosts, be with us yet, lest we forget, lest we forget. The tumult and the shouting dies; the Captains and the Kings depart: still stands Thine ancient sacrifice, an humble and a contrite heart. Lord God of Hosts, be with us yet, lest we forget—lest we forget! "
("Recessional," Rudyard Kipling).

Lest We Forget

In the book of Deuteronomy, Moses taught Israel how to create an environment that would help her to resist Satan's temptations. This included physical reminders of the Lord and of the covenants she had made with Him. Today, we do the same type of things to protect ourselves from the influence of Satan. In our homes, these physical reminders betray the fact that we are members of The Church of Jesus Christ. The objects on display remind us of our covenants with the Lord. When we take a virtual tour through our homes, we see in our mind's eye these things that remind us of the Savior. We have church media, such as the Ensign, New Era, and Friend, the scriptures, perhaps scraps of marble left over from the construction of a nearby temple, maybe even a rock from the Sacred Grove, a replica of the First Edition of The Book of Mormon, religious sculpture, and so on.

We take our cue from the example of ancient Israel. After testing, chastening, and teaching the Israelites in the wilderness of Sinai for 40 years, the Lord said that she was ready to enter the Promised Land. But first He had some important instructions to give. His prophet Moses delivered these instructions in three sermons that are recorded in the Book of Deuteronomy, that was the last of the five books of Moses. In these, he reviewed Israel's sojourn in the wilderness, recognizing God's hand in her preservation and deliverance. He also discussed Israel's responsibilities as a chosen people, and emphasized that she must obey God, particularly the commandments to remember Him and refrain from idol worship. He also warned that although the children of Israel were ready to enter the Promised Land, if they were not true to their covenants, they would lose their inheritance and be scattered. Essentially, they would fall victim to the power of Satan.

In our day, the Lord's priesthood leaders have taught that the church exists to perfect the Saints, so that they too might enter into God's Rest, that is their promised land. Just as Moses had done with Israel, our prophets remind us of our responsibilities as His chosen people, emphasizing that we must obey His commandments, particularly those that forbid idol worship. As was the case anciently, our promised blessings are subject to our ability to endure to the end in righteousness. Just as Moses warned Israel, so are we cautioned that if we forsake our covenants as His chosen people by turning to wickedness and the worship of golden calves of our own making, we will lose our inheritance.

The last counsel of Moses to Israel is as applicable today as it was then: "And thou shalt love the Lord thy God with all thine heart, and with all thy soul, and with all thy might. And these words, which I command thee this day, shall be in thine heart. Thou shalt teach them diligently unto thy children, and shalt talk of them when thou sittest in thine house, and when thou walkest by the way, and when thou liest down, and when thou risest up. And thou shalt bind them for a sign upon thine hand, and they shall be as frontlets between thine eyes. And thou shalt write them upon the posts of thy house, and on thy gates." (Deuteronomy 6:5-9).

Moses instructed his people to place passages of scripture, or frontlets, between their eyes, on their hands, on the posts of their houses, and on their gates. He hoped that these would be constant reminders to help them to remember God. In our day, those who are in a similar covenant relationship with God wear garments that are constant reminders of the promise of His protection against the power of the destroyer, until they have finished their work upon the earth.

When disciples who follow these instructions are "captained by Christ (they) will be consumed in Him. Enter their homes, and the pictures on their walls, the books on their shelves, the music in the air, and their words and acts (will) reveal them as Christians." (Ezra Taft Benson). Such individuals will be unlikely to ever "forget the Lord." (Deuteronomy 8:11). They will be protected from getting caught up in the thick of thin things, they will not be inclined to confuse the sizzle for the steak, and they will more likely to remember prayer, scripture and seminary study, church and temple attendance, and family home evening.

Brigham Young said: "The worst fear that I have is that (the Saints) will get rich in this country, forget God and his people, wax fat, kick themselves out of the church, and go to hell. This people will (endure) mobbing, robbing, poverty, and all manner of persecution, and be true. But my greater fear for them is that they cannot stand wealth." ("Brigham Young: The Man and His Work," p. 128).

Moses counseled the Israelites to build upon the Rock of their salvation. He urged them to "write (their covenants) upon the posts of (their) houses" (Deuteronomy 6:9), and to "not appear before the Lord empty" handed. (Deuteronomy 16:16). We would do well to do likewise.

"We often catch
a spark from the awakened
memories of the immortal soul,
which lights up our whole
being as with the glory
of our former home."
(Joseph F. Smith).

Light
And Truth

On the one hand, the government (which is, after all, here to help us) has initiated myriad programs to "fix" societal ills. We have programs that focus on educational challenges, health and welfare assistance, unemployment assistance, social service, supplemental nutrition, substance abuse addiction recovery, and the list goes on. Unfortunately, these have proven to be haphazard in their nature, with no coherence. In the cold light of day, as we see government assistance in all its forms imploding from faulty comprehension, misguided stewardship, inept execution, and negligent management, we must come to realize that our problems can only be effectively addressed with priesthood correlation.

As the Restoration continued to evolve, the concept of priesthood correlation was formulated as early as 1908, and the Correlation Department of the church, also called the Correlation Program, or simply Correlation, was officially organized in 1972. The power of these programs focuses on the family. For almost 50 years, it has done a remarkable job maintaining consistency in assisting the family in the understanding and practical application of principles and doctrines, benefitting from the administration of the ordinances of the priesthood, becoming more familiar with the resources of auxiliary organizations, providing access to meetings, including fundamental and continuing education opportunities, and making available materials and other tangible and intangible assets, to name a few.

With the increasingly pressing concerns of a multi-cultural membership, and with the church moving into the Third World, Priesthood Correlation has never been more important. The adversary has mounted unprecedented assaults on the family and family values, and the inspired program of Priesthood Correlation is one of the church's major assets in the arsenal to combat evil. Heavenly Father maintains a steady claim upon His children, and He insures their welfare with priesthood correlation.

The integrity of the family is vitally important, and He takes any assault on family values, such as abortion, immorality, pornography, and spousal and substance abuse, very seriously. In 1969, President Joseph Fielding Smith, Jr. prophetically counseled: "There are many great and real dangers to be reckoned with, and those which concern us more than all others combined have to do with our children. The only real protection or adequate defense can be afforded by the home and its influences." ("Our Children: The Loveliest Flowers From God's Own Garden," "Relief Society Magazine," 1/1969).

It has never been more important than it is now to bring up our children in light and truth. The light of which we speak is any influence that draws Heavenly Father's children to Jesus Christ, and truth is any belief that is in harmony with gospel principles. Charles Dickens wrote of Victorian England: "It was the best of times," but it was also "the worst of times." ("A Tale of Two Cities"). Because those times are so characteristic of the Last Days, the Lord has provided the following inspired counsel: "In consequence of evils and designs which do and will exist in the hearts of conspiring men in the last days, I have warned you, and forewarn you, by giving unto you this word of wisdom" which is the fulness of the gospel, "by revelation." (D&C 89:4). Today, more than ever before, we need the wisdom of Solomon to negotiate the treacherous minefields of mortality.

I was a teenager between 1959 and 1966, when society in the United States began to undergo seismic change. I was a young adult from 1967 to 1981, and witnessed widespread protest for social justice and equality. I was middle aged between 1982 and 2006, when the foundations of Western society began to be regularly rocked by state supported terrorism. In 2007, I joined the ranks of the elderly, and started drawing social security in 2014. I'm now officially over the hill, but I'm picking up speed!

In my lifetime, the challenges associated with raising children have changed dramatically. We are all experiencing an accelerated pace in the fast lane of life. There are incessant multi-media assaults on our senses. There are far more influences eroding family values than there were when Ma and Pa were raising their family on Walton's Mountain. Today, even more than we did in 1958, when the following counsel was given, we need to "keep our families intact, and keep them under the influence of the Spirit of the Lord, trained in the principles of the gospel, that they may grow up in righteousness and truth." (Joseph Fielding Smith, Jr., C.R., 4/1958).

Today, sophisticated marketing techniques tempt us to indulge in things we didn't realize we craved, do not need, should not have, and cannot afford. "We have confidence in the young and rising generation in the church and plead with them not to follow the fashions and customs of the world, not to partake of a spirit of rebellion, and not to forsake the paths of truth and virtue." (Joseph Fielding Smith, Jr., "C.R., 4/1970). We feel both the positive and the negative effects of global awareness and the consequences of the Butterfly Effect. Moral equivocation is evaporating any semblance of adherence to standards that might be left. "Chastity, virtue, and freedom from are and must be basic to our way of life, if we are to realize its full purpose." (Joseph Fielding Smith, Jr., C.R., 4/1970).

Today, political correctness embraces, and even celebrates, all sorts of deviant behavior, in the name of tolerance, and a celebration, even an adoration, of diversity. But it forgets that there is a difference between diversity and divisiveness. Flimflam artists adroitly fleece us of our very identity as children of God, and most of the time, we are not even aware that the theft is taking place. "Vice is a monster of such frightful mien, as to be hated needs but to be seen. Yet seen too oft, familiar with her face, we first endure, then pity, then embrace." (Alexander Pope). We have come full circle from Eve's temptation in the Garden. We are again beguiled with tinkling cymbals and sounding brass. The difference is, that when she asked "Is there no other way?" she was left with no alternative. We, thanks to her, have a choice.

Today, "we must shelter (our children) from the sins and evils of the world as much as we can." They "will have to be taught to discern between good and evil…and be instructed in the doctrines of the church." (Joseph Fielding Smith, Jr., C.R., 10/1916). Translation: They will need to be taught and become familiar with and comfortable with principles that stand in sharp contrast to the so-called values of society that are continually morphed by the shifting sands of cultural expediency. We cannot rely upon the constantly mutating values of society to provide any semblance of a foundation upon which our children may be reasonably expected to somehow develop independently into responsible adults.

Therefore, our Heavenly Father has offered us timely and relevant guidance to shepherd us through these turbulent times. The Lord's church has stepped up to the plate to help our families. For starters, since the introduction of Priesthood Correlation, there have been somewhere in the neighborhood of 90 General Conferences (around a thousand addresses by General Authorities). The church and its agencies have become service organizations, as it were, to help families, by providing them with regular bulletins filled with practical advice, and offering solutions to the problems they face on a daily basis.

The Lord has provided us with "The Family – A Proclamation to The World" (1995), echoing Joseph Fielding Smith, Jr., who twenty five years earlier had said: "The first duty pertaining to the training of the children of the church belongs in the home." We have unprecedented access to church media (books, magazines, pamphlets, television, and internet-based resources). These focus on "solidarity in family relationships as the sure foundation upon which the church and society itself will flourish." (Joseph Fielding Smith, Jr., "Message from the First Presidency," in "Family Home Evenings," 1970–71).

We receive daily encouragement from our local priesthood leaders and general authorities. "The Lord has commanded us, one and all, to bring our children up in light and truth. Where this spirit exists, disharmony, disobedience, and neglect of sacred duties cannot succeed." (Joseph Fielding Smith, Jr., C.R., 4/1965).

Since April 27, 1915, over 100 years ago, the Family Home Evening program has been a resource to sustain family values. "There is no greater legacy that parents can leave to their children than the memory and blessings of a happy, unified, and loving home." (Joseph Fielding Smith, Jr., "Message from the First Presidency," in Family Home Evenings, 1970-71). He continued: "Parents who ignore the great help of (family home evening) are gambling with the future of their children." ("Message from the First Presidency," "Ensign," 1/1971).

We all have access to educational opportunities such as seminaries and institutes, higher education, and the Pathway Program. The Church Educational System was established in 1877. "The first released-time seminary program was launched at Granite High School in Salt Lake City, Utah. Begun largely as an experiment by a single stake, the program has since grown into a worldwide system of religious education, bringing gospel instruction to young members of the church. From small beginnings, the seminary program and its collegiate counterpart - institutes of religion - have grown to become the primary educational entities in the church, with a larger enrollment than any other LDS educational venture and a wider reach than almost any educational organization worldwide. Today, the seminary and institute programs teach over 700,000 students in 143 different countries through the efforts of nearly 50,000 full-time, part-time, and volunteer teachers and administrators." (L.D.S. Infobase).

The Priesthood Correlation Program teaches members to help their families without violating the principle of agency. It encourages "teaching children when they are young. No person can begin too early to serve the Lord. Young people follow the teaching of their parents. The child who is taught in righteousness from birth will most likely follow righteousness always. Good habits are easily formed and easily followed." (Joseph Fielding Smith, Jr., "Take Heed to Yourselves!" p. 414).

As David O. McKay observed, from the time a child is born until about their eighth birthday (which just happens to be the age of accountability), we teach the principles of the gospel. From their baptism until about the age of 16, we train our youth in the application of these principles with the goal of ingraining the habits of provident living. After their 16th birthday, by and large, we can only trust them to walk in the ways of the Lord.

And so, we introduce our children at a young age to the scriptures. We "begin by teaching at the cradle-side." (Joseph Fielding Smith, Jr., C.R., 10/1948). We weave gospel principles into family activities, as our children commit the 13 Articles of Faith not only to memory, but also to lifestyle. These articles of faith become the particles of their faith. We find priesthood purposes in activities that are oriented toward conversion to the gospel of Jesus Christ, land we live its teachings, serve faithfully in callings, and dedicate ourselves to the responsibilities entrusted to us, giving meaningful service, living worthily to receive priesthood blessings and temple ordinances, preparing to serve honorable full-time missions, obtaining as much education as possible, preparing for and entering into temple marriage, and giving proper respect to others.

We surround ourselves with uplifting art, good music and literature, and other wholesome influences. We avoid indulging ourselves with telestial toys, and we develop the discipline to focus on celestial sureties rather than telestial trinkets.

When our time comes to pass beyond the veil, we will leave behind with our loved ones legacies of both tangible and intangible remembrances. We will leave them with our testimonies. We will leave them with gratitude for the privilege and blessing it has been to be knit together as families.

In anticipation of that day, we will develop the aforementioned action plan to realize our objectives. We will break that plan down into a sequence of steps that must be taken, and identify activities that must be performed well, for our strategies to succeed. We identify and allocate resources, so that we may understand beforehand the costs required to reach our goals. We recognize specific tasks that must be performed, and by whom, and we have a time line that allows us to follow through to successful conclusions.

Because our children are the nobility of heaven, a choice and a chosen generation with a divine destiny, we are willing to make the sacrifices necessary to insure their continuing success. Our children come to us from their heavenly home, "like gentle rain through darkened skies, with glory trailing from their feet as they go, and endless promise in their eyes." While under our care, they grow tall and strong, "like silver trees against the storm; who will not bend with the wind or the change, but stand to fight the world alone." Our children "are the few, the warriors saved for Saturday; to come the last day of the world. These are they, of Saturday." They "are the strong, the warriors rising in their might to win the battle raging in the hearts of men, on Saturday." They are "strangers from a realm of light, who have forgotten all - the memory of their former life and the purpose of their call. And so, they must learn why they're here, and who they really are." (Doug Stewart).

Too few drink
deeply from the fountain of
truth, while far too many dip in a
ladle once or twice, take a few
sips, and then gargle
and spit.

Living Water

To help defend Jerusalem against attacks by the Assyrians, King Hezekiah ordered that the fountains of the spring of Gihon outside the city walls of Jerusalem be covered. The spring was then diverted to the pool of Siloam, inside the city walls, to provide easy access to the water. This was done by digging a tunnel through about 1770 feet of limestone rock. Without this water inside the walls of the city, the people of Jerusalem would not have survived the subsequent siege by the Assyrians.

Just as the water from the spring of Gihon was vital for the physical survival of Hezekiah's people during the Assyrian conflict, living water is essential for our spiritual survival during our battles with Satan. In effect, we are under siege throughout our mortal lives, and our unimpeded access to living water is our only hope of salvation.

What is this living water? Jesus said to the woman at the well: "Whosoever drinketh of this water shall thirst again. But whosoever drinketh of the water that I shall give him shall never thirst; but the water that I shall give him shall be in him a well of water springing up into everlasting life." (John 4:10-14). The living water that spiritually sustains us is the doctrine of the gospel of Jesus Christ.

Living water is so crucial to our well-being, that the Lord has provided a conduit that can penetrate solid limestone, as it were, so that it may freely flow into our lives. With great effort, this conduit is chiseled through our rough exterior and stony nature with the tools of faith, obedience, study, prayer, good works, and other healthy lifestyle choices. The conduit to living water is created when we not only believe, but also act on our belief, in being honest, pure, chaste, benevolent, kind, and in doing good to others. Living water has the power to sustain our lives when we are not just hearers, but doers of the word as well. (See James 1:22).

We receive living water in the House of the Lord, where we receive instruction, are endowed with power and understanding, and feel peace and joy. We receive living water when we are washed clean from the blood and sins of our generation, through our faithfulness. Worship in the temple was an important protective strategy for the Israelites in Hezekiah's time, and it can be a vital weapon in our own arsenal of protection, as well.

The scriptures teach us that we should seek living water "diligently, and teach (each other) words of wisdom; yea, seek...out of the best books words of wisdom; seek learning, even by study and also by faith. (We must) organize (ourselves and) prepare every needful thing; and establish a house, even a house of prayer, a house of fasting, a house of faith, a house of learning, a house of glory, a house of order, (and) a house of God, that (our) incomings may be in the name of the Lord; that (our) outgoings may be in the name of the Lord; (and) that all (our) salutations may be in the name of the Lord, with uplifted hands unto the Most High. Therefore, (in order to be refreshed with living water, it would be well to) cease from all (our) light speeches, from all laughter, from all (our) lustful desires, from all (our) pride and light-mindedness, and from all (our) wicked doings." (D&C 88:118-121).

In ancient Israel, Hezekiah's father, Ahaz, was a wicked king who had desecrated the temple of the Lord and "shut up (its) doors" (2 Chronicles 28:24). When Hezekiah became king of the Southern Kingdom of Judah in 715 B.C., one of the first things he did was open the doors of the temple and order the priests and Levites to cleanse the Lord's holy house. He realized that the temple first needed to be sanctified in order for his people to enjoy the refreshment of its living water. "For our fathers have trespassed, and done that which was evil in the eyes of the Lord our God, and have forsaken him, and have turned away their faces from the habitation of the Lord, and turned their backs. Also they have shut up the doors of the porch, and put out the lamps, and have not burned incense nor offered burnt offerings in the holy place unto the God of Israel." (2 Chronicles 29:6-7).

If we disregard the blessings to be found in temple worship, we may be equally guilty of turning away our faces from the habitation of the Lord. Because the people of Judah disregarded the temple, "the wrath of the Lord was upon Judah and Jerusalem, and he...delivered them to trouble, to astonishment, and to hissing.... For, lo, (their) fathers (had) fallen by the sword, and (their) sons and (their) daughters and (their) wives (were) in captivity for this." (2 Chronicles 29:8-9).

Hezekiah hoped to re-establish the Covenant with the Lord by cleansing the temple and preparing it for worship again. The scriptures record that he declared: "Now it is in mine heart to make a covenant with the Lord God of Israel, that his fierce wrath may turn away from us." (2 Chronicles 29:10). He wanted to keep unclean things out of the temple.

Through Joseph Smith, the Lord has promised once again to provide living water in the temples that are found throughout the world, declaring: "Inasmuch as my people build a house unto me in the name of the Lord, and do not suffer any unclean thing to come into it, that it be not defiled, my glory shall rest upon it; Yea, and my presence shall be there, for I will come into it, and all the pure in heart that shall come into it shall see God. But if it be defiled I will not come into it, and my glory shall not be there; for I will not come into unholy temples." (D&C 97:15-17).

If uncleanliness disqualifies us from partaking of the living water found in the temple, the Lord has made it possible for us to follow the example of the people of Hezekiah. The conduit to living water is accessible if we do as Joseph Smith implored at the dedication of the Kirtland Temple: He prayed that "no unclean clean thing (should) be permitted to come into (the House of the Lord) to pollute it." He prayed that when the "people transgress, (that they might) speedily repent and return unto (God), and find favor in (His) sight, and be restored to the blessings which (He) ordained to be poured out upon those who (should) reverence (Him) in (His) house." (D&C 109:20-21).

Anciently, when the temple had been cleansed, Hezekiah and the people of Jerusalem "made an end of offering, the king and all that were present with him. (And they) bowed themselves, and worshipped. Moreover, Hezekiah the king and the princes commanded the Levites to sing praise unto the Lord with the words of David, and of Asaph the seer. And they sang praises with gladness, and they bowed their heads and worshipped. Then Hezekiah answered and said, Now ye have consecrated yourselves unto the Lord, come near and bring sacrifices and thank offerings into the house of the Lord. And the congregation brought in sacrifices and thank offerings; and as many as were of a free heart, burnt offerings." (2 Chronicles 29:29-31).

In our day, Jesus Christ has promised unimpeded access to living water with this instruction: "Thou shalt offer a sacrifice unto the Lord thy God in righteousness, even that of a broken heart and a contrite spirit." (D&C 59:8). Elsewhere, He said: "Verily I say unto you, all among them who know their hearts are honest, and are broken, and their spirits contrite, and are willing to observe their covenants by sacrifice - yea, every sacrifice which I, the Lord, shall command – they are accepted of me." (D&C 97:8).

Anciently, Hezekiah invited the Ten Tribes of the Northern kingdom of Israel to come to the House of the Lord for the celebration of the Passover. "And Hezekiah sent to all Israel and Judah, and wrote letters also to Ephraim and Manasseh, that they should come to the House of the Lord at Jerusalem, to keep the Passover unto the Lord God of Israel." (2 Chronicles 30:1).

By the time of Hezekiah's reign, much of the kingdom of Israel (the Northern Kingdom) had already been taken captive by the Assyrians. Hezekiah promised the remaining Israelites that if they would "turn again unto the Lord," the captives would be released. Instead, most of the people of Israel rejected Hezekiah's invitation.

Because of the wickedness of the people, the remainder of the kingdom of Israel was taken captive within several years, were lost to history, and became the Lost Ten Tribes.

In order to avoid a similar spiritual captivity, Moroni urged us, in the last verses of The Book of Mormon: "I would exhort you that ye would come unto Christ, and lay hold upon every good gift, and touch not the evil gift, nor the unclean thing. And awake, and arise from the dust, O Jerusalem; yea, and put on thy beautiful garments, O daughter of Zion; and strengthen thy stakes and enlarge thy borders forever, that thou mayest no more be confounded, that the covenants of the Eternal Father which he hath made unto thee, O house of Israel, may be fulfilled. Yea, come unto Christ, and be perfected in him, and deny yourselves of all ungodliness; and if ye shall deny yourselves of all ungodliness, and love God with all your might, mind, and strength, then is his grace sufficient for you, that by his grace ye may be perfect in Christ; and if by the grace of God ye are perfect in Christ, ye can in nowise deny the power of God." (Moroni 10:30-32).

Nephi had earlier expressed a common theme of The Book of Mormon: "Inasmuch as those whom the Lord God shall bring out of the land of Jerusalem shall keep his commandments, they shall prosper upon the face of this land; and they shall be kept from all other nations." (2 Nephi 1:9).

When the Assyrians finally did invade the kingdom of Judah, the prophet Isaiah and King Hezekiah prayed for help, and an angel of the Lord destroyed much of the invading army. Isaiah dualistically prophesied: "No weapon that is formed against thee shall prosper; and every tongue that shall rise against thee in judgment thou shalt condemn." (Isaiah 54:17).

In our day, the Savior has promised us equivalent protection, if only we will nourish ourselves with living water: "Let my army become very great, and let it be sanctified before me, that it may become fair as the sun, and clear as the moon, and that her banners may be terrible unto all nations. That the kingdoms of this world may be constrained to acknowledge that the kingdom of Zion is in very deed the kingdom of God and his Christ; therefore, let us become subject unto her laws." (D&C 105:31-32).

Hezekiah and his people received the Lord's protection because of their repentance and their righteousness, which was demonstrated by their worship in the temple. In the dedicatory prayer at the Kirtland Temple, Joseph Smith asked our Father in Heaven to establish with the nourishment of living water "the people that shall worship, and honorably hold a name and standing in this thy house, to all generations and for eternity; That no weapon formed against them shall prosper; that he who diggeth a pit for them shall fall into the same himself; That no combination of wickedness shall have power to rise up and prevail over thy people upon whom thy name shall be put in this house; And if any people shall rise against this people, that thine anger be kindled against them; And if they shall smite this people thou wilt smite them; thou wilt fight for thy people as thou didst in the day of battle, that they may be delivered from the hands of all their enemies." (D&C 109:24-28). Little wonder that President Howard W. Hunter encouraged: "Let us be a temple-attending people. Attend the temple as frequently as personal circumstances allow." ("Ensign," 10/1994).

Hezekiah was succeeded as king by his son Manasseh, and then by his grandson Amon, and then by his great-grandson Josiah, who was made king of Judah when he was just eight years old. He became a righteous king who ruled in Israel from 641 to 610 B.C., at the very time Lehi was growing up in the land of Jerusalem.

Josiah sought the true God, eradicated idolatry in the kingdom, and employed craftsmen to repair the temple. During its renovation, Hilkiah the high priest "found a book of the law of the Lord (the scriptures) given by Moses." (2 Chronicles 34:14). By this time in Judah's history, the written law apparently had been lost and was virtually unknown. This is surely why Lehi felt that it was so important for his sons to return to Jerusalem, at great personal risk, to retrieve the Plates of Brass, which would be to them as living water. As Nephi wrote: "And behold, it is wisdom in God that we should obtain these records, that we may preserve unto our children the language of our fathers; and also that we may preserve unto them the words which have been spoken by the mouth of all the holy prophets, which have been delivered unto them by the Spirit and power of God, since the world began, even down unto this present time." (1 Nephi 3:19-20).

When he read the book of the law, Josiah "rent his clothes." (2 Chronicles 34:19). He was distressed to discover what the book of the law contained. The scriptures record his words: "Great is the wrath of the Lord that is poured out upon us, because our fathers have not kept the word of the Lord, to do after all that is written in this book." (2 Chronicles 34:21). He realized that Israel had polluted the living water that had been provided to sustain her during her greatest trials.

President Ezra Taft Benson said: "In 1829, the Lord warned the Saints that they were not to trifle with sacred things. Surely The Book of Mormon is a sacred thing, and yet many take it lightly, and treat it as though it is of little importance. In 1832, as some early missionaries returned from their fields of labor, the Lord reproved them for treating The Book of Mormon lightly. As a result of that attitude, he said, their minds had been darkened. Not only had treating this sacred book lightly brought a loss of light to themselves, but it had also brought the whole church under condemnation, even all the children of Zion. And then the Lord said: 'And they shall remain under this condemnation until they repent and remember the new covenant, even the Book of Mormon.' (D&C 84:54-57). If the early Saints were rebuked for treating the Book of Mormon lightly, are we under any less condemnation if we do the same?" Have members of the church jeopardized their standing before the Lord, because of their pollution of living water?

After Josiah found out that his people would be condemned because they had not done as the scriptures instructed, he called all the people to the temple and read to them out of the book of the law. (2 Chronicles 34:29-30). President Spencer W. Kimball said: "Access to (the scriptures) means responsibility for them. We must study the scriptures according to the Lord's commandment, and we must let them govern our lives." As the Lord taught regarding living water: "These words are given unto you, and they are pure before me; wherefore, beware how you hold them, for they are to be answered upon your souls in the day of judgment." (D&C 41:12).

Because they understood that living water would save their very lives, while Josiah and his people were at the temple, they made sacred promises with the Lord. "And the king stood in his place, and made a covenant before the Lord, to walk after the Lord, and to keep his commandments, and his testimonies, and his statutes, with all his heart, and with all his soul, to perform the words of the covenant which are written in this book. And he caused all that were present in Jerusalem and Benjamin to stand to it. And the inhabitants of Jerusalem did according to the covenant of God, the God of their fathers. And Josiah took away all the abominations out of all the countries that pertained to the children of Israel, and made all that were present in Israel to serve, even to serve the Lord their God. And all his days, they departed not from following the Lord, the God of their fathers." (2 Chronicles 34:31-33).

Just so, today we make sacred covenants with the Lord before the altars of the temple, the fulfillment of which will bring us earthly blessings and eternal exaltation. As we focus our attention on obeying the Lord's commandments and being worthy to enter the temple, our thirst will be quenched with the living water provided by the gospel of Jesus Christ.

"I command all men, both in the east and in the west, and in the north, and in the south, and in the islands of the sea, that they shall write the words which I speak unto them; for out of the books which shall be written I will judge the world, every man according to their works, according to that which is written."
(2 Nephi 29:11).

Lost Books
Of The Bible

As it has come down to us, the Bible is of great worth: "Knowest thou the meaning of the book?" the angel asked Nephi. "The book that thou beholdest is a record of the Jews, which contains the covenants of the Lord, which he hath made unto the house of Israel, and it also containeth many of the prophecies of the holy prophets...wherefore they are of great worth unto the Gentiles. (For) when it proceeded forth from the mouth of a Jew it contained the fulness of the gospel of the Lord." (1 Nephi 21-24). In older editions of The Book of Mormon, this verse was rendered "...the plainness of the gospel of the Lord." But the fulness of the gospel is the Plan of Salvation, and that is a more accurate description of the Bible before its plain and most precious parts had been deleted.

What is it that has been removed from our K.J.V. of the Bible? The "great and abominable church, which is most abominable above all other churches, (has) taken away from the gospel of the Lamb many parts which are plain and most precious; and also many covenants of the Lord have they taken away." (1 Nephi 13:26). Sometimes knowingly, and at other times unwittingly, it has changed the covenant, and has effectively eliminated the Old Testament as a witness for Christ. This is an abomination because such action stops the potential progression of those caught in its snares, and destroys the purpose of mortality in the great Plan of Salvation. With this in mind, the "Church News" reported: "The witness for Christ was the most important thing in that ancient record." (1/1966). Without the testimony of Christ, the Old Testament loses much of its purpose and power. In consequence of the removal of these things, "an exceedingly great many do stumble, yea, insomuch that Satan hath great power over them." (1 Nephi 13:29).

Clearly, additional scripture is important. Nephi wrote: "I beheld the book of the Lamb of God, which had proceeded forth from the mouth of the Jew, that it came forth from the Gentiles unto the remnant of the seed of my brethren. And after it had come forth unto them I beheld other books, which came forth by the power of the Lamb." (1 Nephi 13:38-39).

Then he addressed the importance of "these last records, which thou hast seen among the Gentiles." They "shall establish the truth of the first," he wrote, "which are of the twelve apostles of the Lamb, and shall make known the plain and precious things which have been taken away from them, and shall make known to all kindreds, tongues, and people, that the Lamb of God is the Son of the Eternal Father, and the Savior of the world; and that all men must come unto him, or they cannot be saved." (1 Nephi 13:40).

Additional scripture is valuable, in spite of the protestations of "many of the Gentiles (who) shall say: A Bible! A Bible! We have got a Bible, and there cannot be any more Bible." (2 Nephi 29:3). God is interested in other nations, besides the Jews: "Know ye not that there are more nations than one?" asked his prophet. "Know ye not that I, the Lord your God, have created all men, and that I remember those who are upon the isles of the sea; and that I rule in the heavens above and in the earth beneath; and I bring forth my word unto the children of men, yea, even upon all the nations of the earth?" (2 Nephi 29:7).

Additional scripture becomes a second witness of Christ: "Know ye not that the testimony of two nations is a witness unto you that I am God, that I remember one nation like unto another. Wherefore, I speak the same words unto one nation like unto another. And when the two nations shall run together the testimony of these two nations shall run together also." (2 Nephi 29:8).

The body of scripture is the basis upon which God shall judge the world: "For I command all men, both in the east and in the west, and in the north, and in the south, and in the islands of the sea, that they shall write the words which I speak unto them; for out of the books which shall be written I will judge the world, every man according to their works, according to that which is written." (2 Nephi 29:11).

Latter-day Saints are absolutely certain that there is scripture that has been either purposely deleted, or unintentionally lost, from the King James Version of the Bible. As the aforementioned verses from The Book of Mormon testify, this missing scripture could be invaluable in eliminating the confusion that currently exists among Christians in matters relating to doctrine.

The debate with those of other faiths centers on whether it is a constructive use of time to discover these writings, and then to decide if they should be considered canonical, or if they should be relegated to apocryphal works (biblical or related writings that have significant spiritual value, but have not been accepted as part of the canon of scripture), pseudepigraphical works (a loose collection of falsely attributed works that may have esoteric or historical value) or simply profane works (that are not sacred and may even be detrimental to one's spiritual welfare).

This is arguably a moot point, inasmuch as there are currently over a hundred different translations of the Bible, that collectively incorporate into some 31,102 verses tens of thousands of textual variants, many of which twist the meaning of individual passages or messages. Ultimately, the question "What is the Bible?" might never be answered with finality. To add to the confusion, the King James Version of the Bible has 66 books, while the Catholic version has 73 books. The additional books in the Catholic version are Tobit, Judith, Wisdom, Sirach, Baruch, and 1 & 2 Maccabees.

What adds spice to the discussion are the nearly two dozen biblical references to sources that are nowhere to be found, either in that sacred record or elsewhere. The interesting thing is that these authors found these sources to be relevant to their message, so much so, that they pointedly identified them. These include:

The Book of The Covenant (Exodus 24:7). "And he took **the book of the covenant**, and read in the audience of the people: and they said, All that the Lord hath said will we do, and be obedient." The term "covenant" is usually taken to refer to the legal, moral, and cultic corpus of literature found in Exodus 20:22-23:33.

The Book of The Wars of the Lord (Numbers 21:14). "Wherefore it is said **in the book of the wars of the Lord**, What he did in the Red sea, and in the brooks of Arnon." "The Book of The Wars of the Lord, mentioned only once in the Bible, apparently contained an anthology of poems describing the victories of the Lord over the enemies of Israel. This is the complete title of a book which, like several other literary works, has not been preserved." ("Jewish Virtual Library").

The Book of Jasher (Joshua 10:13). "And the sun stood still, and the moon stayed, until the people had avenged themselves upon their enemies. Is not this written **in the book of Jasher**? So the sun stood still in the midst of heaven, and hasted not to go down about a whole day." The translation "Book of the Just Man" is the traditional Greek and Latin translation, while the transliterated form "Jasher" is found in the King James Bible.

The Book of The Acts of Solomon (1 Kings 11:41). "And the rest of the acts of Solomon, and all that he did, and his wisdom, are they not written in **the book of the acts of Solomon**?" The Acts of Solomon may have been written by the biblical prophet Iddo, who was the author of other lost texts, as well. "Now the rest of the acts of Solomon, first and last, are they not written in **the book of Nathan the prophet, and in the prophecy of Ahijah the Shilonite, and in the visions of Iddo the seer** against Jeroboam the son of Nebat? (2 Chronicles 9:29).

The Book of the Chronicles of the Kings of Israel (1 Kings 14:19). "And the rest of the acts of Jeroboam, how he warred, and how he reigned, behold, they are written **in the book of the chronicles of the kings of Israel.**" "The Chronicles of the Kings of Israel is a book that gives a more detailed account of the reigns of the kings of ancient Kingdom of Israel than that presented in the Hebrew Bible, and may have been the source from which parts of the biblical account were drawn. The book was likely compiled by or derived from the kings of Israel's own scribes, and is likely the source for the basic facts presented in the Bible, though the compiler(s) of the biblical text clearly made selective use of it and added commentaries and judgments. The book is referred to several times in the Hebrew Bible, but was either not included in the corpus of the biblical text or was removed from it at some stage. The book is counted as one of the Lost books of the Old Testament. This text is sometimes called The Book of the Chronicles of the Kings of Israel or The Book of the Annals of the Kings of Israel." ("Wikipedia").

The Book of the Chronicles of the Kings of Judah (1 Kings 14:29). "Now the rest of the acts of Rehoboam, and all that he did, are they not written **in the book of the chronicles of the kings of Judah**?" "The Chronicles of the Kings of Judah is a book that gives a more detailed account of the reigns of the kings of ancient Kingdom of Judah than that presented in the Hebrew Bible, and may have been the source from which parts of the biblical account was drawn. It is one of the Lost books of the Old Testament. It is unlikely that any copies of this book still exist." ("Wikipedia").

The Chronicles of King David (1 Chronicles 27:24). "Joab the son of Zeruiah began to number, but he finished not, because there fell wrath for it against Israel; neither was the number put in the account of **the chronicles of king David.**" "It may have been written by the biblical prophet Nathan, who was one of King David's contemporaries." ("Wikipedia").

The Books of Nathan and Gad (1 Chronicles 29:29). "Now the acts of David the king, first and last, behold, they are written in the book of Samuel the seer, and in **the book of Nathan the prophet, and in the book of Gad the seer** is a lost text." The Book of Gad the Seer is a presumed lost text, supposed to have been written by the biblical prophet Gad. These writings of Nathan and Gad may have been incorporated into 1 and 2 Samuel. This text is sometimes called Gad the Seer or The Acts of Gad the Seer.

The Prophecy of Ahijah and Visions of Iddo (2 Chronicles 9:29). "Now the rest of the acts of Solomon, first and last, are they not written in the book of Nathan the prophet, and **in the prophecy of Ahijah the Shilonite, and in the visions of Iddo** the seer against Jeroboam the son of Nebat?" "The book called the Visions of Iddo the Seer is a lost text that was probably written by the biblical prophet Iddo, who lived at the time of Rehoboam." ("Wikipedia").

The Book of Shemaiah (2 Chronicles 12:15). "Now the acts of Rehoboam, first and last, are they not written **in the book of Shemaiah** the prophet, and of Iddo the seer concerning genealogies? And there were wars between Rehoboam and Jeroboam continually." "It was probably written by the biblical prophet Shemaiah, who lived at the time of Rehoboam." ("Wikipedia").

The Book of the Kings of Judah and Israel (2 Chronicles 16:11). "And, behold, the acts of Asa, first and last, lo, they are written in **the book of the kings of Judah and Israel**."

The Book of Jehu (2 Chronicles 20:34). "Now the rest of the acts of Jehoshaphat, first and last, behold, they are written **in the book of Jehu** the son of Hanani." "The Book of Jehu is a lost text that may have been written by the biblical prophet Jehu ben Hanani, who was one of King Baasha's contemporaries." ("Wikipedia").

The Story of the Book of the Kings (2 Chronicles 24:27). "Now concerning his sons, and the greatness of the burdens laid upon him, and the repairing of the house of God, behold, they are written in **the story of the book of the kings**." "The book is found nowhere in the Old Testament, so it is presumed to have been lost or removed from the earlier texts." ("Wikipedia").

The Acts of Uzziah (2 Chronicles 26:22). "Now the rest of **the acts of Uzziah**, first and last, did Isaiah the prophet, the son of Amoz, write." "The Acts of Uziah is a lost text that may have been written by Isaiah, who was one of King Uzziah's contemporaries. This manuscript is sometimes called Second Isaiah or The Book by the prophet Isaiah." ("Wikipedia").

The Vision of Isaiah (2 Chronicles 32:32). "Now the rest of the acts of Hezekiah, and his goodness, behold, they are written in **the vision of Isaiah** the prophet, the son of Amoz, and in the book of the kings of Judah and Israel." "The Vision of Isaiah is known to be part of a larger compilation of texts collectively called the Ascension of Isaiah." ("The Gnostic Society Library").

The Book of the Kings of Israel (2 Chronicles 33:18). "Now the rest of the acts of Manasseh, and his prayer unto his God, and the words of the seers that spake to him in the name of the Lord God of Israel, behold, they are written in **the book of the kings of Israel**." "The book may be identical with the Books of Kings in the Old Testament, or it may have been lost or removed from the earlier texts." ("Wikipedia"). The Sayings of The Seers (2 Chronicles 33:19). "His prayer also, and how God was entreated of him, and all his sin, and his trespass, and the places wherein he built high places, and set up groves and graven images, before he was humbled: behold, they are written among **the sayings of the seers**." The Sayings of the Seers is referred to as the Sayings of Hozai, in the Masoretic Text.

The Book of the Chronicles before the King (Esther 2:23). "And when inquisition was made of the matter, it was found out; therefore, they were both hanged on a tree: and it was written in **the book of the chronicles before the king**." "The Chronicles of the Kings of Israel is a book that gives a more detailed account of the reigns of the kings of ancient Kingdom of Israel than that presented in the Hebrew Bible, and may have been the source from which parts of the biblical account were drawn. The book was likely compiled by or derived from the kings of Israel's own scribes, and is likely the source for the basic facts presented in the Bible, though the compiler(s) of the biblical text clearly made selective use of it and added commentaries and judgments." ("Wikipedia").

A reference to an earlier Epistle of Paul to the Ephesians (Ephesians 3:3). "How that by revelation he made known unto me the mystery; (**as I wrote afore in few words**)."

A reference to an epistle of Paul from Laodicea (Colossians 4:16). "And when this epistle is read among you, cause that it be read also in the church of the Laodiceans; and that ye likewise read **the epistle from Laodicea**." "The Epistle to the Laodiceans is a possible lost letter of Paul the Apostle, the original existence of which is inferred from an instruction to the church in Colossae to send their letter to the church in Laodicea, and likewise obtain a copy of the letter "from Laodicea." Several ancient texts purporting to be the missing "Epistle to the Laodiceans" have been known to have existed, most of which are now lost. A Latin "Epistle to the Laodiceans" is actually a short compilation of verses from other Pauline epistles, principally Philippians, and on which scholarly opinion is divided as to whether it is the lost Marcionite forgery or alternatively an orthodox replacement of the Marcionite text." ("Wikipedia").

A former Epistle of Jude (Jude 3). "Beloved, when I gave all diligence to write unto you of the common salvation, it was needful for me to write unto you, and exhort you that ye should earnestly contend for the faith **which was once delivered unto the saints**."

Prophecies of Enoch (Jude 14). "And Enoch also, the seventh from Adam, prophesied of these, saying, Behold, the Lord cometh with ten thousands of his saints." "Where did Jude get his quotation? It is useless to speculate, for the record does not say. He may have received it directly from the Spirit. He may have quoted from some earlier source to which the writer of the Book of Enoch also had access. No conclusion can be drawn in the absence of more precise information." ("Wikipedia").

Our
families can be
our greatest source
of joy in time, as
well as in the
eternities.

Marriage And Family Are Ordained Of God

A single bee can collect about 1/12 teaspoon of honey in its lifetime, so it would take the life's work of about 560 workers to make one pound of honey. For this they would have to collect nectar from about two million flowers, and fly a total of about 55,000 miles.

In many ancient cultures, honey occupied a prominent position of influence and symbolism. The prophet Jeremiah characterized ancient Israel as "a land flowing with milk and honey." (Jeremiah 32:22). In Egypt, Ramses III, made an offering of 21,000 jars of honey to Hapi, the Nile god. In Greek mythology, honey was the nectar of the gods. The infant Zeus was fed honey by his nurse, Melissa, whose name is Greek for "honey bee." In Rome, Pliny the Elder called honey "the sweat of the heavens" and "the saliva of the stars."

But what does the production of honey have to do with marriage and family? If we want to succeed in this work that more than any other produces "soul sweat" and generates "the saliva of the stars," we are going to have to perform around 5 diaper changes per day for three years, or somewhere in the neighborhood of 5,500 for each child. We will need to prepare around 20,000 meals, three every day of the year for 18 years or so. We are going to get our kids ready for church around 1,000 times, on 52 Sundays a year for 18 years. We will help each of them get to Seminary over 700 times, or 180 mornings a year for 4 years. The only way to come to grips with this, in our minds, is to think of it as theatrical encore, as exercises conceived by a loving God with an immense sense of humor.

For active church members, these routines may seem normal, but many have undergone dramatic changes in the past few years. A generation ago, we all sat down in our family rooms in front of the television, to watch episodes of "Father Knows Best," "The Waltons," and "The Life of Reilly." Now our unsupervised kids watch "The Simpsons," "The Bachelorette," "Jackass," "Celebrity Wife Swap," "Naked Survival," and "The Real Housewives of (Fill in the Blank)."

What's taking a beating here is the traditional family. Once, the church was pilloried for its unconventional view of the family. Now, it is ridiculed for its traditional view of the family. It may be that our easy days are over.

The recurring cycle seems to be a period of righteousness that fosters prosperity, followed by apostasy that leads inevitably to destruction. When we "sow the wind, (we) shall reap the whirlwind." (Hosea 8:7). Long ago, Alexis de Tocqueville is said to have written: "I sought for the greatness and genius of America in her commodious harbors and her ample rivers, and it was not there; in her fertile fields and boundless prairies, and it was not there; in her rich mines and her vast world commerce, and it was not there. Not until I went to the churches of America and heard her pulpits aflame with righteousness did I understand the secret of her genius and her power. America is great because she is good, and if America ever ceases to be good, America will cease to be great." ("Reflections of Alexis de Tocqueville," p. 71. This has also been cited to a quotation in "Picturesque America" by William Cullen Bryant, p. 502, first published in 1872, but such a statement has not been located in the 1874 or 1894 editions.)

Civilizations rise and fall for complex reasons, but there may be one underlying cause of societal implosion. Satan has focused significant energies and invested immense resource on the destruction of family values. He goes about it by working under the radar. He creates economic burdens to get mothers out of the home and into the workplace. He employs political pressures, under the guise of "equality" and "equal opportunity." Within the ivory towers of academia, he tutors the rising generation with carefully groomed mentors; rebels without a cause who rail against the establishment and every proven principle. He infiltrates government, and suppresses the will of the silent majority by legitimizing the wild, rabid, and morally indefensible demands of the vocal minority. He snuffs out freedom of expression within democracy, and with gold and silver buys up armies and navies, and false priests who oppress.

He uses pride and covetousness, to make us want to keep up with the Joneses. In the name of political correctness, he uses prejudice and intolerance to suppress the expression of any opinion that challenges his twisted viewpoint, to which he has given the oxymoronic name "politically correct." He manipulates the media with the pervasive influence of robotic talking heads who lack any real evidence of higher-level brain function. He panders to the lowest common denominator, and rewards mediocrity and laziness. He launches hostile takeovers within the judicial system, to validate affirmative action and Title-9, access to abortion, and gay, lesbian, bisexual and transgender rights that infringe on the moral majority. He uses medicine to make contraceptives easily available to minors.

He takes legitimate venues of intellectual inquiry, like philosophy, and distorts and perverts them by grooming articulate spokespersons to advocate his cause. He poisons our innate yearning for genuine heroes by substituting those who should be our role models with shallow and one-dimensional celebrities whose credentials are only skin deep, and who use their unmerited fame and fortune to make unqualified endorsements.

He rails against the pattern of heaven itself, which is the vehicle through which eternal principles are communicated and transmitted, and the setting in which God's mission statement is accomplished. He mounts offensives against everything that is intrinsically virtuous, lovely, of good report, and praiseworthy. He belittles the institutions that are the glue that holds our society together, and that are key to our understanding of where we came from, why we are here, and where we are going. He mounts repetitive offensives on the traditional concept of marriage that is a covenant between a man and a woman, represents the order of God, and has divine implications. He launches relentless cyber attacks on everything that is decent about our culture. He knows that our firewalls are formidable, but he preys upon our indifference, laziness, impatience, and procrastination. He contaminates "the very substance that binds families together for time and eternity." (Ezra Taft Benson, "The Teachings of Ezra Taft Benson," p. 492).

He knows that, at face value, immorality, dishonesty, covetousness, and lasciviousness, are a hard sell, but he recognizes and manipulates powerful influences that oppose the Light of Christ and the Holy Ghost. He has witnessed first-hand that "vice is a monster of so frightful mien, as to be hated, needs but to be seen. Yet seen too oft, familiar with her face, we first endure, then pity, then embrace." (Alexander Pope).

A study conducted by the Organization for Economic Cooperation and Development found that 26% of American children are raised by a single parent, a number high above the 15% average seen in the other 26 countries surveyed. Among African-Americans the rate nearly tripled, with 72% of black children relying on a single parent. 53% of births to American women younger than 30 are outside marriage, research has found.

We have sown the wind, with unchastity, divorce and abortion, and now we are reaping the whirlwind, with pandemic sexually transmitted disease, the destruction of the family, and a perversion of the definition of marriage. Lot pleaded with God to spare Sodom and Gomorrah, with what he initially thought would be a reasonable request: "Peradventure there be fifty righteous within the city," he begged, "wilt thou also destroy and not spare the place for the fifty righteous that are therein?" (Genesis 18:24). Then, the pragmatist that he was, he revised his expectations, and asked that the city be spared for 45, and then 40, then 30, then 20, and finally 10. And the Lord said: "I will not destroy it for ten's sake." (Genesis 18:29-32).

Sadly, there were not ten righteous souls to be found, and so the Lord had compassion for Lot, and told him: "Escape for thy life; look not behind thee, neither stay thou in all the plain; escape to the mountain, lest thou be consumed." (Genesis 19:17). "Then the Lord rained upon Sodom and upon Gomorrah brimstone and fire from the Lord out of heaven; And he overthrew those cities, and all the plain, and all the inhabitants of the cities, and that which grew upon the ground." (Genesis 19:24-25).

If we remain true to our covenants, there will be no empty chairs around the table when we gather as families in the eternities. When we return home from our mortal mission, we will fondly remember the people we met, and those we helped. We will recall how we have grown both physically and spiritually. We will find mother there, waiting to embrace us, as she stands beside father, who will be bursting with pride. We will brush away tears of happiness on our cheeks. Father will strike hands with us, and then hug us tenderly. Mother will put her arm around our waist, and escort us to the familiar surroundings of the room that has been prepared for our homecoming. The atmosphere will be pungent with a heavenly aether that is punctuated by the melodious strains of our native language. Every detail will be just as we had imagined it would be, including the reassuring radiant heat of a celestial fire kindled beforehand by Father. We will know that this is just where we belong, at home once again, with our heavenly parents.

Our families can be our greatest source of joy in time, as well as in the eternities. In moments of deep reflection, we "think of stepping on shore, and finding it heaven! We visualize taking hold of a hand, and finding it God's hand. We envision breathing a new air, and finding it celestial air. We imagine feeling invigorated, and finding it immortality. We dream of passing from storm and tempest to an unbroken calm, and of waking up, and finding it home." (Anonymous).

Sir Walter Scott may have been thinking of the blessings of family, as well as of its contrasts, when he wrote: "Breathes there the man, with soul so dead, who never to himself hath said, 'This is my own, my native clan!' Whose heart hath ne'er within him burned, as home his footsteps he hath turned from wandering on a foreign strand! If such there breathe, go, mark him well. For him no minstrel raptures swell. High though his titles, proud his name, boundless his wealth as wish can claim; despite those titles, power, and pelf, the wretch, concentered all in self, living, shall forfeit fair renown, and, doubly dying, shall go down to the vile dust, from whence he sprung, unwept, unhonoured, and unsung." ("The Lay of The Last Minstrel").

"If Mormonism
could be true to its foundations and
remain unchanged for four generations, it
might well become the most powerful
social influence in the world."
(Leo Tolstoy).

May the 4th Be With You

Jedi Knights both serve and utilize a mystical power called the Force to assist them as the guardians of peace and justice in the galaxy. Their philosophy of self-denial stands in contrast to that of their arch-enemies, the Sith, who use the dark side of the Force, that they might control others.

"May the Force be with you!" declared General Dodonna, before the Death Star battle in Episode 4 of the Star Wars saga. Obi-Wan Kenobe described the Force as "what gives a Jedi his power. It's an energy field created by all living things. It surrounds us and penetrates us. It binds the galaxy together." Duct tape, something with which we are all familiar, is like the Force. It has a light side, and a dark side, and it, too, binds the universe together.

The Master Teacher Yoda explained to young Luke Skywalker: "A Jedi's strength flows from the Force. But beware of the dark side: Anger, fear, and aggression. The dark side are they. Easily they flow, quick to join you in a fight. If once you start down the dark path, forever will it dominate your destiny, consume you it will." We must resist the temptation to yield to the dark side, or to the baser elements of our nature.

The universal Force for good is the hope of the galaxy. Isaiah described it in these words: "For unto us a child is born, unto us a son is given: and the government shall be upon his shoulder: and his name shall be called Wonderful, Counsellor, the mighty God, the everlasting Father, the Prince of Peace." (Isaiah 9:6). Dominus vobiscum is a Latin phrase meaning "The Lord be with you." It is an ancient salutation and blessing traditionally used by the clergy in the Roman Catholic Mass. In other words, "May the Force be with you." Yoda explained: "My ally is the Force, and a powerful ally it is. Its energy surrounds us and binds us. Luminous beings are we, not this crude matter. You must feel the force around you, everywhere."

The scriptures refer to the Force, albeit somewhat obliquely, as when Helaman described the "strong force." (Alma 57:8). Mormon also described how a Nephite city enjoyed the protection of "an exceedingly strong force." (Alma 55:26). On another occasion, Helaman said: "We were obliged to employ all our force" to accomplish an objective. (Alma 57:13). Even under the most trying of circumstances, when there were significant demands upon his energies and resources, "he retained all his force." (Alma 59:10).

Jeremiah described "the forces that were with him," and how a group of his enemies "that fled stood under the shadow of Heshbon because of the force." (Jeremiah 41:11 & 38:45). Mormon wrote that his armies fought "with all (their) force." (Mormon 3:6). Job revealed that his "force (was) in the navel of his belly." (Job 40:16). Joseph Smith described his experience with the Force, when he wrote: "Never did any passage of scripture come with more power to the heart of man than this did at this time to mine. It seemed to enter with great force into every feeling of my heart." (J.S.H. 1:12).

When the Force is used righteously, it is almost always associated with peace. Luke asked the Jedi Master Yoda: "How am I to know the good side from the bad?" Yoda explained to his apprentice: "You will know. When you are calm, at peace, passive. A Jedi uses the Force for knowledge and defense, never for attack." In "Star Wars: The Return of The Jedi," when Luke was engaged in personal combat with Darth Vader and threw his lightsaber away instead of making a killing blow, we see what Yoda meant. In that moment, Luke understood the power of the Force and became a true Jedi Knight.

The scriptures also describe the dark side of the Force: "And there went out another horse that was red: and power was given to him that sat thereon to take peace from the earth, and that they should kill one another: and there was given unto him a great sword," reminiscent of a lightsaber. (Revelation 6:4). "When you look at the dark side, careful you must be," cautioned Yoda, "for the dark side looks back." Be careful of the company you keep.

We think of the light side of the Force when we consider these scriptures. "Peace be both to thee, and peace be to thine house, and peace be unto all that thou hast. (1 Samuel 25:6). The Force is associated with the Holy Spirit of God. Hence, Jesus said: "Peace be unto you." (Luke 24:36). Early on, Joseph Smith was taught about the guidance provided by the Force. He was told by the Savior: It will "be signalized unto you by the peace and power of my Spirit, that shall flow unto you." (D&C 111:8).

Even when engaged in mortal combat, the Jedi consciously calm their spirits and exercise discipline when focusing their minds, in order to be at one with the Force. But it is not enough to simply be at peace when engaging its power. A Jedi Knight must move beyond simple tranquility; he must actively promote peace. The Sons of Mosiah, for example, were as Jedi, for they "did publish peace; they did publish good tidings of good; and they did declare unto the people that the Lord reigneth." (Mosiah 27:37).

The Force is the soul mate of faith. Jesus said to one young woman: "Daughter, be of good comfort; thy faith," or thy ability to allow the Force to heal thee, "hath made thee whole; go in peace." (Luke 8:48). For true Jedi, faith and fear are incompatible. Those who have faith are never in fear of loss, for that "is a path to the Dark Side." (Yoda).

In essence, Peter taught that "grace and peace (are) multiplied (by the Force) through the knowledge of God." (2 Peter 1:2). In other words, the power of the Force is magnified as we become more familiar with, and the more we emulate, the mission of the Savior. The Force is strong in those who give heed and diligence to the word of God. For example, "there was continual peace among (the people of Nephi), and exceedingly great prosperity in the church because of their heed and diligence which they gave" to the Force. (Alma 49:30).

The Force bears fruit when faith that is buttressed by works supports its principles. "And it came to pass that Nephi went forth among the people, and also many others, baptizing unto repentance, in the which there was a great remission of sins. And thus the people began again" to feel the power of the Force, and "to have peace in the land." (3 Nephi 1:23).

Sometimes the Force is manifest by a tangible and palpable "covenant of peace" that moves out in concentric waves through the galaxy. (Numbers 25:12). Isaiah exclaimed: "How beautiful upon the mountains are the feet of him that bringeth good tidings, that publisheth peace," that embraceth the Force, "that publisheth salvation, that saith unto Zion, Thy God reigneth!" (Isaiah 52:7).

But, for those who turn to the dark side, "there is no peace," whatsoever, "saith the Lord." (1 Nephi 20:22). Sometimes the righteous need to call upon all of their energies to apply the power of the Force in support of "their liberty, their lands, their wives, and their children, and their peace, and that they might live unto the Lord their God, and that they might maintain that which was called by their enemies the cause of Christians." (Alma 48:10).

The Force is associated with truth, as well. "I will…reveal unto (the Jedi an) abundance of peace and truth," said Jeremiah. (Jeremiah 33:6). While the lightsaber is the weapon of choice of the Jedi Knights, they are nevertheless counseled to "stand, therefore, having (their) loins girt about with truth, having on the breastplate of righteousness, and (their) feet shod with the preparation of the gospel of peace." (D&C 27:16).

The Jedi do not employ the Force with pomp, ostentation, or for purposes of self-aggrandizement, or self-gratification. It is used quietly. "I will give peace and quietness unto Israel," promised the Lord to those who embrace the Force. (1 Chronicles 22:9). It speaks hope to the soul, emboldens our faith, and encourages those who feel its power, imbuing them with the confidence of deliverance out of the hands of their enemies. (See Alma 58:11).

The light side of the Force locks horns with the dark side. The Jedi know that there are only two options: "Do. Or do not. There is no try." (Yoda). Through an angel, the Lamb of God declared that He would use the Force to "work a great and a marvelous work among the children of men; a work which shall be everlasting, either on the one hand or on the other — either to the convincing of them unto peace and life eternal, or unto the deliverance of them to the hardness of their hearts and the blindness of their minds unto their being brought down into captivity, and also into destruction, both temporally and spiritually, according to the captivity of the devil." (1 Nephi 14:7). "If you end your training now," Yoda cautioned young Luke Skywalker, "if you choose the quick and easy path as Vader did, you will become an agent of evil. Once you start down the dark path, forever will it dominate your destiny."

The Jedi understand that the righteous application of the Force does not guarantee freedom from tribulation. "These things I have spoken unto you, that in me ye might have peace. In the world ye shall have tribulation: but be of good cheer," for the Force shall be with you, and with it, "I have overcome the world." (John 16:33). Yoda would have us remember that "fear is the path to the dark side. Fear leads to anger. Anger leads to hate. Hate leads to suffering."

Those who fight to maintain the influence of the Force recognize the righteousness of their cause. When "the spirit came upon Amasai, who was chief of the captains" of the armies of Israel, "he said, Thine are we, David, and on thy side, thou son of Jesse: peace, peace be unto thee, and peace be to thine helpers, for thy God helpeth thee." (1 Chronicles 12:18). This Israelite warrior, this Jedi Knight, understood the power of the Force.

Those who learn to use the Force for righteous purposes in the protection of the Galactic Republic are sanctified by the Spirit. Paul besought the Saints: "And the very God of peace sanctify you wholly; and I pray God your whole spirit and soul and body be preserved blameless" by the power of the Force "unto the coming of our Lord Jesus Christ." (1 Thessalonians 5:23). The scriptures promise every Jedi apprentice: "Peace be multiplied unto you." (Daniel 4:1).

Those who mature in their instruction in the application of the Force will find that it gives them power over the elements. Just as Yoda used the Force to lift Luke's T-65 X-Wing out of the swamp at Dagobah, so too Jesus "arose, and rebuked the wind, and said unto the sea, Peace, be still. And the wind ceased, and there was a great calm." (Mark 4:39). On the other hand, "The dark side clouds everything." (Yoda). "Remember," however, "that it is not the work of God that is frustrated, but the work of men." (D&C 3:3).

When modern-day Jedi Knights apply the Force, they acquaint themselves with the Author of peace. Yoda explained: "To be Jedi is to face the truth, and choose. Give off light; be a candle." Job's equivalent exhortation was: "Acquaint now thyself with him, and be at peace: thereby good shall come unto thee." (Job 22:21). Jedi of all ages, and throughout the galaxy, recognize the source of their strength, that is given by grace "from God our Father, and from the Lord Jesus Christ." (Philippians 1:2). It was given, Paul wrote, "unto Timothy, my own son in the faith: Grace, mercy, and peace." All three are equal manifestations of the Force, "from God our Father and Jesus Christ our Lord." (1 Timothy 1:2).

"In the end," explained Yoda, "cowards are those who follow the dark side." The Jedi have "strong minds, great hearts, true faith and ready hands." They are "men whom the lust of office does not kill; men whom the spoils of office cannot buy; men who possess opinions and a will; men who have honor; men who will not lie; men who can stand before a demagogue and damn his treacherous flatteries without winking! Tall men, sun-crowned, who live above the fog in public duty and in private thinking. For while the rabble, with their thumbworn creeds, their large professions and their little deeds, mingle in selfish strife, Lo! Freedom weeps, Wrong rules the land, and Justice sleeps." (Josiah Gilbert Holland, who is rumored to have been a Jedi Knight in disguise).

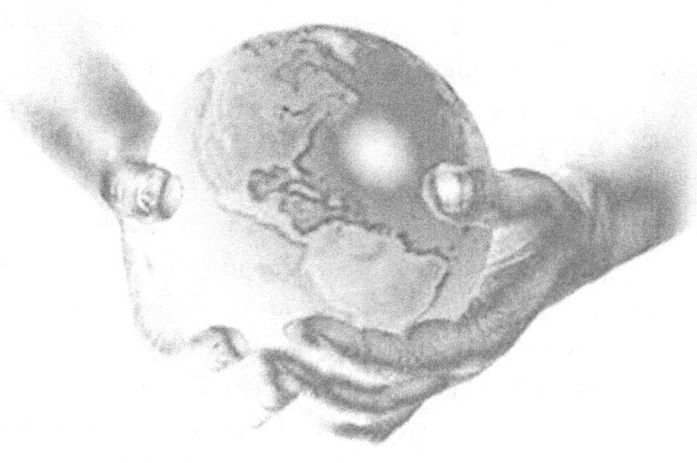

"What is man, that thou art mindful of him?
And the son of man, that thou visitest him?
Or thou hast made him a little lower than
the angels, and hast crowned him
with glory and honour."
(Psalms 8:14-15).

Our Father In Heaven Knows Us

"For this is my work and my glory, to bring to pass the immortality and eternal life of man." (Moses 1:39). Just as our earthly fathers would do, Heavenly Father invests His time and energy doing things for us simply because we are His sons and daughters, and He loves us.

1. Fathers show their love for us by taking the time to talk with us. There was once a little boy who, before going to bed, was saying his prayers in a very low voice. His mother gently chided him: "I can't hear what you're saying, son." "I wasn't talking to you, Mom," said the small child. (See Mosiah 4:21).

Fathers avoid vain repetition, as should we. For example, a visitor was once invited to offer the invocation for a congregation of L.D.S. inmates at the Utah State Prison. As he was praying, he asked: "Bless all those who could not be here, that Thou might make it possible for them to be here next time."

On another occasion, members of a ward brought their non-member neighbors to several activities, and then to a church service. At the conclusion of each, in the benediction, supplication was made that "no harm or accident might befall us." Finally, the neighbors asked, "Do a lot of Mormons die on the way home from meetings?"

2. Fathers listen to our problems. When we pray, our petitions are often independent of circumstances. One morning, as a family began to eat breakfast, it was Tommy's turn to ask the blessing. He asked Father in Heaven to bless the food, and then he thanked Him for the beautiful day. When the prayer was finished, his mother reminded him that it was 33° outside and freezing rain was falling from the dreary sky. She asked him why he had thanked Father for the beautiful day. Tommy replied: "Mommy, you can't judge the day by the weather."

Faith is fear that has said its prayers. Faith is incompatible with fear. Dozens of times, the scriptures admonish us: "Ask, and ye shall receive." On one occasion, before providing wise counsel, Nephi said: "Now after I have spoken these words, if ye cannot understand them it will be because ye ask not, neither do ye knock, wherefore, ye are not brought into the light, but must perish in the dark."

(2 Nephi 32:5). We must persistently, insistently, actively, and consistently solicit the attention of the Lord. But we cannot hope to receive $10,000.00 answers, after offering 10 cent prayers.

But our prayers must be well-intentioned. We should avoid repetition that is not so much saying the same thing, as not praying from the heart. A drowning man sputters the word "Help!" once, twice and then a third time. The word that he uses over and over again may be the same, but we can be sure that it is coming from his heart

A man was walking along the edge of a steep cliff, when he lost his footing and tumbled off into space. On the way down, he cried to God: "Save me, save me!" Just then, his pant leg snagged a root sticking out of the face of the cliff, and he was unceremoniously jerked to a stop. As he looked around himself to survey his situation, he muttered: "Never mind, God. I'm all right now." We must "pray always, and not faint (and He will) consecrate (our) performance unto (us), that (our) performance may be for the welfare of (our) soul." (2 Nephi 32:9).

3. Fathers provide wise counsel. Their best guidance comes when they have developed a rapport with the Spirit that allows their powers to expand as they become receptive to flashes of insight and they are cast off into a stream of revelation and carried along in the quickening currents of direct experience with God. The Holy Ghost facilitates our reception and acceptance of a Plan whose design holds the key to the release of our energy to be creative, and that fosters freedom. In its elements is the perfect law of liberty.

The mysteries of the kingdom are windows of opportunity to better understand prayer, revelation, priesthood authority, baptism, living prophets, the Godhead, the Atonement, repentance, forgiveness, the Sacrament, the endowment, celestial marriage, eternal progression, and exaltation. The Lord has assured us: Ye "shall know of a surety that these things are true, for from heaven will I declare it unto (you)." (D&C 5:12).

4. Fathers provide for our needs. They teach us that wealth is not measured by the quantity, or even by the quality, of our possessions, but by our attitude toward these things. "Seek not for riches but for wisdom, and behold, the mysteries of God shall be unfolded unto you, and then shall you be made rich." (D&C 6:7). We cannot escape the fact that we generally hope to obtain only those things upon which we have focused our attention, for "the soul attracts that which it secretly harbors; that which it loves." (James Allen, "As a Man Thinketh"). That is a good thing, as long as we keep our priorities straight. Ultimately, we will be judged by the things we stand in line for.

5. Fathers teach us to save money for a mission, but also to establish a spiritual bank account, against anticipated withdrawals on rainy days. At its best, our financial and spiritual preparedness are intertwined. We learn principles of frugality that foster a conservative approach to both money management and spiritual economy. We learn to avoid living from paycheck to paycheck both temporally and spiritually. We learn to make regular deposits to our accounts, so that when we need to make withdrawals, there will be sufficient means to do so. We cannot, in the day of adversity, expect to write checks that cannot be cashed.

6. Fathers provide a nurturing atmosphere in which we can grow to reach our potential. The sturdiest plants that bear the best fruit are those that have deep roots in rich gospel soil. So should it be with all of Heavenly Father's children. They should be provided the mulch of music and art, and the mossy loam of conversation, example, decency, virtue, honor, and spirit in order to give them room to grow freely. Their topsoil must be deep and sustaining and nourishing. It is unthinkable that we would allow it to be blown away in a dust bowl of depravity, a tornado of travesty, or a hurricane of hubris, or to be inundated by ignorance, compounded by confusion, or to suffer the anorexia of apathy.

The spirit of the 13th Article of Faith is always manifest in our homes. "If there is anything virtuous, lovely, or of good report or praiseworthy, we seek after these things." To the extent that we do this, we may expect to blossom with creativity and stand out as champions for righteousness. Our fathers know that if they "train up a child in the way he should go...when he is old, he will not depart from it." (Proverbs 22:6).

7. Fathers bless us with their wisdom. Backing off when we should be pressing forward can spell the difference between defeat and victory. Keeping our wits about us in challenging situations is crucial, because falling apart is more a mental meltdown than it is a physical collapse. A proverb tells us that we should "keep sound wisdom and discretion" in such circumstances. (Proverbs 3:21). We are also admonished: "Incline thine ear unto wisdom, and apply thine heart to understanding." (Proverbs 2:2). "For the Lord giveth wisdom. Out of his mouth cometh knowledge and understanding." (Proverbs 2:6). "Be ye, therefore, wise as serpents," counseled the Master. (Matthew 10:16).

8. Fathers create happy memories. When the Lord was ministering ever so briefly among the Nephites following His resurrection, He knew that it would be important for the people to have time to absorb His teachings, that they might have happy memories. After a spiritually stirring and yet exhausting day of instruction, His disciples were told: "Go ye unto your homes, and ponder upon the things which I have said, and ask of the Father, in my name, that ye may understand, and prepare your minds for the morrow, and I come unto you again." (3 Nephi 17:3).

9. Fathers build faith. The highest pinnacle of our spiritual life is the unbroken sunshine of absolute and undoubting faith in God's love. It was in this sense that Helen Keller wrote: "I believe that no good shall be lost, and that all man has willed or hoped or dreamed of good shall exist forever. I believe in the immortality of the soul because I have within me immortal longings. I believe that the state we enter after death is wrought of our own motives, thoughts, and deeds. I believe that my home there will be beautiful with colour, music, and speech of flowers and faces I love. Without this faith, there would be little meaning in my life. I should be a mere pillar of darkness in the dark. Observers in the full enjoyment of their bodily senses pity me, but it is because they do not see the golden chamber in my life where I dwell delighted; for dark as my path may seem to them, I carry a magic light in my heart. Faith, the spiritual strong searchlight, illuminates the way, and although sinister doubts lurk in the shadow, I walk unafraid towards the Enchanted Wood where the foliage is always green, where joy abides, where nightingales nest and sing, and where life and death are one in the presence of the Lord." ("Midstream").

10. Fathers build character. They know that "fame is a vapor, and popularity is an accident, and those who cheer you today may curse you tomorrow. In the end, the only thing that endures is character." (Horace Greeley). Woven throughout the teachings of fathers of all ages is the capacity to instill a sense of integrity, of character, and of honesty that shines like a light in the eyes. George Washington wrote: "I hope I shall always possess firmness and virtue enough to maintain what I consider the most enviable of all titles, the character of an honest man." (Letter to Alexander Hamilton, Mount Vernon, 8/28/ 1788).

11. Fathers teach us how to respect our bodies and each other, especially within the sacred bounds of marriage and family. "There are but a very few beings in the world who understand rightly the nature of God, and if men do not understand the character of God they do not comprehend themselves." (Joseph Smith). One of the blessings associated with the restoration of the gospel has been a reawakening of understanding that mortality is a blessing that gives us the opportunity to develop qualities and character traits that are consistent with the divine nature of our Father in Heaven. Because of the restoration, ordinances are now available that bind us to receive the blessings of the gospel by means of covenants of action between ourselves and God. These bring us to a greater appreciation of His nature. The marriage covenant lies at the apex of these ordinances of exaltation.

Marriage is the most sacred relationship that can exist between a man and a woman, and "is perhaps the most vital of all the decisions and has the most far-reaching effects. Of all the decisions, this one must not be wrong," because our exaltation hinges upon it." (Spencer W. Kimball, "Ensign," 10/1979). Heavenly Father would not have given us the Law of Eternal Marriage were it not possible to become as He is, to internalize His divine nature and develop His character, and so the bond of holy matrimony is received by a covenant whose validity is recognized both on earth and in heaven.

12. Fathers teach us how to show gratitude. Because God "giveth to all men liberally," one of our greatest challenges is to muster the capacity to express real and continuous appreciation. (James 1:5). At the end of the day, we have no real resources, and will be forever in His debt, and yet, we may still "buy wine and milk without money and without price." (Isaiah 55:1). Perhaps it is in the multitude of our expressions of gratitude that we best communicate our love to our Heavenly Father, and even build up a spiritual credit. Gratitude translates our love into action. With its cultivation, wonderful things happen. Good eclipses evil. Love overpowers jealousy, hate, and prejudice. Light drives away darkness. Knowledge banishes ignorance. Humility overwhelms pride. Courtesy checks rudeness. Appreciation overcomes thanklessness. Abundance overshadows poverty. Well-being replaces weakness. Simplicity supplants perplexity. Harmony displaces discord. Faith controls fear. Hope casts out despair. Charity subdues selfishness. Joy deposes unhappiness, sadness, dejection, and misery. Confidence is substituted for timidity. Certainty dethrones bewilderment. Assurance dislodges discouragement and even despair.

13. Fathers create petri dishes infused with the agar of experience, to be consumed in the learning laboratory of life. Most young people in the United States spend twelve years gaining what some people call "an education." But for some, the process is sporadic at best. Often it is put on hold, or worse, it stops altogether. All of us remember going back to elementary school in the fall and writing an essay entitled: "How I spent my summer." So the real questions may be: "Does education continue even when we are not in school? Does education cease during our undisciplined free time? Does eternal progression relate to education? Does the Latter-day Saint tradition relating to education have a foundation in gospel principles? Is improvement through education a key to successful living?" Our fathers can help us to develop perspective as we ponder these questions, and act upon our promptings.

14. Fathers teach us how to sift through the dross and focus on the important things. While they drew, a kindergarten teacher walked up and down the rows of desks in her classroom of children, observing their work. She stopped beside one little girl and asked what her drawing was. She replied, "I'm drawing a picture of God." The teacher paused, and then said, "But no one knows what God looks like." Without missing a beat or looking up from her paper, the little girl replied, "They will in a minute." Though tender in years, this child had what adults might call "focus."

If we ignore the innate urge to concentrate our energies, and if we allow ourselves to be habitually distracted by trivial concerns, we sin by omission and risk settling for a life in a "second-class hotel" of our own making. As Brutus observed, there is, after all, "a tide in the affairs of men, which, taken at the flood, leads on to fortune. Omitted, all the voyage of their life is bound in shallows and in miseries." (Shakespeare, "Julius Caesar," Act 4, Scene 2).

15. Fathers help us to multiply our talents. Narrowly defined, a talent is a stewardship or a responsibility in the Kingdom of God. Paul taught that under the best of circumstances, we "are one body in Christ," although we bring individual gifts to the table. (Romans 12:5-6). After we have linked our fortunes to the church, we "are no more strangers and foreigners, but fellowcitizens with the saints, and of the household of God." (Ephesians 2:19-20). Within this vast congregation "are diversities of gifts." (1 Corinthians 12:4-31). The implication is that every member of the flock has talents that may be used to bless the lives of others living within the household.

After we have discovered our talents and God provides ways to improve and develop them, we would do well to remember the law of inertia. After we get moving, we need to sustain our momentum, remembering that if we always do what we always did, we'll always get what we always got. Even if we are on the right road, we're going to get run over, if we just sit there. Those who seek to improve their talents have high ideals, which "are like stars. We will not succeed in touching them with our hands. But, like the seafaring man in the desert of waters, we choose them as our guides, and following them, we will reach our destiny." (Carl Shurz, "B.Y.U. Studies," 16:40).

We must share our talents with others, lest we be like the "very cautious man who never laughed or played; who never risked and never tried; who never sang or prayed. And when, one day, he passed away, his insurance was denied. For since he never really lived, they claimed he never died." (Anonymous).

16. Fathers teach us how to multi-task. We can even learn how to multi-task righteousness. At the beginning of each day, we can wake up with a prayer in our hearts even as we prepare for the day in other ways. While attending to a host of responsibilities, Harold B. Lee was often asked difficult ecclesiastical questions. He often prefaced his answers with: "In the early hours of the morning, while I was pondering that very question..." Multi-taskers like him seize every opportunity to ponder the important questions of life. The Spirit helps them to anticipate the questions, and better prepares them with inspiration to discern the answers.

While brushing our teeth at the break of day, we keep pads of paper and pencils on the counter, because thoughts pop into our minds relating to the complexities of life that lie before us. Whoever invented 3-M sticky notes had multi-tasking in mind. When we multi-task, the capabilities of our minds are more breathtaking than even the most sophisticated computers that can "think" only in a linear fashion. The arrangement of ones and zeros in binary code cannot compete with 100 trillion neural connections, or synapses, in the human brain (which is at least a thousand times the number of stars in the Milky Way galaxy). "What a piece of work is a man! How noble in reason! How infinite in faculty! In form and moving, how express and admirable! In action, how like an angel! In apprehension, how like a god! The beauty of the world! The paragon of animals! (Shakespeare, "Hamlet," Act 2, Scene 2).

We face new challenges every day, and as conflicts inevitably begin to pile up, we use gospel principles as multi-tasking tools to help us to cope successfully. At one and the same time, as we deal with issues that demand our conscious attention, there are underlying currents of honesty, benevolence, patience, courage, and virtue that define our behavior, focus our energy, and give coherence to our actions. How we comport ourselves is, essentially, a witness of our faith and testimony. Our charity, compassion, and tolerance are silent evidences of our core values. A harmonic spirituality that resonates within us allows our character to run on cruise-control even as we multi-task.

17. Fathers teach us things we could not otherwise know. Without such revelatory guidance, we cannot comprehend the two great opposites that are at work in the universe, and without that understanding, we cannot create order in the seeming chaos of existence. We cannot enjoy the holy and exalted state of happiness, unless we are in harmony with gospel principles, and are in active opposition to satanic forces. The Light of Christ and the Holy Ghost quietly whisper to us that there was opposition from the beginning, and that we cannot enjoy moral agency that leads to happiness unless we learn to reject the enticements of Satan, whom God has allowed, for a wise purpose, to assault the fortress of our spiritual security. Mortality becomes a time of testing and of putting to the proof, all made possible by the exercise of free will. Agency and opposition are powerful forces that shape and mold us, and constantly refine us in the fiery blast furnace of experience. Fathers cannot eliminate the consequences that hang over our heads as the dangling Sword of Damocles, (See my essay entitled "Heaven Can Wait") but they can teach us principles of the gospel that allow us to successfully cope with opposition. Always at issue is the question whether we will repent and take advantage of the Savior's Atonement.

18. Fathers provide a nurturing atmosphere in which we can grow. Even the best athletes cannot hope to compete competitively, much less enjoy podium finishes, unless they understand the rules of the game and have been provided a foundation upon which to build winning strategies. No one can reasonably expect to be able to successfully engage the circumstances defined by the game of life, unless they possess the rule book and comprehend the guidelines that govern existence. As Alma said: "God has had mercy on us, and made these things known unto us that we might not perish; yea, and he has made these things known unto us beforehand, because he loveth our souls as well as he loveth our children; therefore, in his mercy he doth visit us by his angels, that the Plan of Salvation might be made known unto us as well as unto future generations." (Alma 24:14).

19. Fathers teach us how to set realistic goals. Often, our problem is not that we set our goals too high and fail to reach them. Rather, it is that we set them too low, and we do reach them, far too easily and with the expenditure of minimal effort. Calvin Coolidge said: "We cannot do everything at once, but we can do something at once." While still a young man, Abraham Lincoln, declared: "I will prepare myself, and someday my chance will come."

Fathers teach us that we should never settle for mediocrity; that we can instead forget ourselves through service, right into heaven. They prepare us for "that special moment when we are figuratively tapped on the shoulder and offered a chance to do a very special thing, unique to ourselves and fitted to our talents. Their nurturing influence protects us against the risk of being unprepared or unqualified for that which could be our finest hour." (Attributed to Winston Churchill). Making the effort now, however small or seemingly inconsequential, is the critical element that infuses the undertaking of successful endeavors with positive energy. It may be too late to write a new beginning to our life story, but it is never too late to begin a new ending.

If we work without vision, we will become mired in details, and conceptually punch a time clock, work for pay, and be satisfied with an hourly wage. If we have vision, but don't understand that inspiration and perspiration are inseparably interrelated, we will be living a fantasy. But if we have both vision and the determination to work to achieve our goals, it will be our destiny to soar with eagles rather than walk with turkeys.

20. Fathers teach us not only how to endure, but also to do so in righteousness. When we are on the path leading to eternal life, it is important to move forward with purpose. It is not enough to have been baptized and to have received the Holy Ghost. We must not camp out on the illuminated path that stretches out before us, and remain in a passive or vegetative state. The dictionary is the only place where success comes before work. Hence, the Savior's observation: "Many will say to me in that day: Lord, Lord, have we not prophesied in thy name, and in thy name have cast out devils, and in thy name done many wonderful works?" (3 Nephi 14:22). We need to be "doers of the word, and not hearers only." (James 1:22).

The scriptures celebrate come-from-behind victories, and tell us that "the race is not to the swift, nor the battle to the strong, neither yet bread to the wise, nor yet riches to men of understanding, nor yet favour to men of skill; but time and chance happeneth to them all." (Ecclesiastes 9:15). When we believe that we are winners, however, anything is possible.

21. Fathers instill in us an appreciation of the principles that relate to happiness. If we ignore the wise counsel of our elders, or if we take for granted or abandon the principles upon which happiness is founded, it may slip between our fingers and be lost forever. Sometimes, we use our agency inappropriately and make poor investment choices with our time and talents. Frequently, we are left with only a wad of counterfeit currency with which we must make late payments with interest tacked on for bad behavior. And still, in our efforts to gain, we seldom obtain, and more rarely retain, feelings of true happiness. Never learning the hard lessons of life, we continually look to gods of wood and stone that have no power to redeem us from our misery. Our worldly ways leave us vulnerable to a spiritual sickness that mimics the symptoms of those with advanced diabetes whose peripheral circulation has been compromised. We become numb to "the better angels of our nature." (Abraham Lincoln).

As we lose the capacity to touch and feel, we become more and more isolated and lose a sensitivity to our surroundings that is critical to the success of the Plan. We may become inured to our condition, overcompensate with knee-jerk reactions, or develop "lead feet" as we put the pedal to the metal, even as we lose contact with the road that lies before us. Although life in the fast lane may be thrilling, when it "takes our breath away" we may not realize that our reduced lung capacity has robbed us of the capacity to engage in spiritually aerobic exercise, and endure to the end. Cheap thrills can never replace the lofty goals of the Plan. They are counter-productive and defeat its objectives that would have allowed us to enjoy our journey at an unhurried and yet sustainable pace.

22. Fathers sometimes have the means to provide for our secular education, but they always dig deeply into their reserves to provide for our spiritual education. We pay dearly for our secular education, and expect a return on our investment. But as we study the gospel, we obtain far more valuable spiritual experience. At the moment of our baptism, each of us is called and chosen to enroll in the Lord's university; to participate in a bachelor of independent study fine arts program that demands very little in the way of temporal tuition. The only entrance requirement is a ready heart and a willing mind. Its design is solely intended to expand the scope of our Father's Plan to include all of His children. It is variously called The Plan of Salvation, The Plan of Our God, The Plan of Redemption, The Plan of Mercy, The Great and Eternal Plan of Deliverance from Death, The Merciful Plan of The Great Creator, and my favorites, The Plan of Happiness and The Great Plan of Happiness. Whatever its name, the Plan overshadows His ordained core curriculum of universal missionary work by those who have matriculated into His program.

The Plan is a diagram to follow that illustrates how to make our way through mortality. It is a map to guide us home, a table that documents the perils and pitfalls we must avoid, a chart to fall back on when tempests beset us, and a graph that outlines and defines our progress on the pathway to perfection. Like the World Wide Web that requires only computer literacy, access to a network with an I.P. address, and relevant hardware and software, the elements of the Plan have the potential to bring fluency to our stumbling petitions and inarticulate yearnings, capability to our weaknesses and incapacities, order to our spiritual ignorance and illiteracy, and meaning to an otherwise chaotic world. In simple terms, the Plan is our key to happiness.

23. Fathers bless our lives with opportunities to experience opposition and disappointment. Like birds being pushed out of the nest for the first time, we are given opportunities to spread our wings, face our destiny, and embrace our potential. Our fathers have plumbed the depths of our capability, and have confidence that we can fly on our own. But they also know that there is a safety net to protect us, should we fall from grace and plummet toward earth. It is for our benefit that they allow us to become acquainted with the winds of adversity, as well as with the tricky air currents, and hazardous vortices that might be masked behind a sun-swept sky.

As we flutter through time and space, we become acquainted with evil as well as with good, with darkness as well as with light, with error as well as with truth, with sorrow as well as with happiness, and with punishment for the infraction of eternal laws as well as with the blessings that follow obedience.

24. Fathers help us to resist Satan. The adversary wants us to believe that he does not exist, but our fathers know best. He has always raged "in the hearts of men, and stir(red) them up to anger against that which is good." (2 Nephi 28:20). Sometimes he pacifies us, and lulls us into a false sense of worldly security, making us believe that we are gaining something when we are really losing. He does this very subtly, so as not to awaken our senses to the reality of what is happening. (See 2 Nephi 28:21). His favorite strategy is to move us from brilliant, dazzling white, through every shade of grey, to a fathomless black which, by subtraction, is the absence of worthy thoughts, words, and deeds, in an unprincipled moral vacuum. He flatters us, and whispers that he does not exist, which leads us to judge ourselves to be deserving of peace and plenty, without having really earned the reward.

25. Fathers teach us about the consequences of sin. "Ye look upon me as a teacher," Jacob said to his people, many of whom were his own children, and so "it must needs be expedient that I teach you the consequences of sin. Behold, my soul abhorreth sin, and my heart delighteth in righteousness." (2 Nephi 9:48-49).

26. Fathers teach us how to repent. The Lord Himself told Adam, His first mortal child: "Wherefore, teach it unto your children, (His own grandchildren), that all men, everywhere, must repent, or they can in nowise inherit the kingdom of God, for no unclean thing can dwell there, or dwell in his presence." (Moses 6:57).

27. Fathers teach us about the nature of time. It seems to be human nature to want to hold on to it dearly, for it is terrifying to think that time will grind to a halt, and the body will turn to dust, when we pass the event horizon of death. Heavenly Father looks at it differently. "Someone once said that time is a predator that stalks us all our lives," reflected Captain Jean Luc Picard. "I prefer to think of it as a companion that accompanies us on the journey, reminding us to cherish every moment." ("Star Trek Generations").

Fathers teach their children how to manipulate time and to make the most of their gift of mortality, that they might insure their happiness and continued prosperity in eternity. They teach their children to give careful attention to the way in which they spend their time, and also to the care with which they make time, the diligence with which they find time, and the discipline they exhibit in taking time. They learn how to participate in the creative process of making more time for accomplishment in their already busy lives! Only foolish people who have lost their focus on things of real worth would treat time so disdainfully that they would waste time, or would actually kill time.

28. Fathers give us the freedom to exercise our agency, but they also teach us about responsibility. They honor the eternal principle of free will. God counseled Adam: "Thou mayest choose for thyself, for it is given unto thee." (Moses 3:17). It is riskier, but it makes eternal progress possible. "Behold," He declared in the Garden after the Fall, "the man is become as one of us to know good and evil." (Moses 4:28). It was obvious to Him that choices garnished with opposition would be necessary in order to achieve immortality and eternal life through the Atonement of Christ.

In the process, rather than enslaving us in good habits, God repeatedly gives us opportunities to voluntarily recommit ourselves to covenants of obedience to true and eternal principles. Our own fathers follow His example.

29. Fathers provide us with experiences that allow us to develop trust in the abilities with which we have been blessed. It is empowering to think of ourselves as disciples. When we learn to exercise restraint through obedience to eternal principles, our choices expand exponentially to secure our freedom. Our education becomes a repetitively reinforcing pattern of behavior that creates a blueprint for success. "You may know me," said this personality trait. "I'm your constant companion. I'm your greatest helper; I'm your heaviest burden. I will push you onward or drag you down to failure. I am at your command. Half the tasks you do might as well be turned over to me. I'm able to do them quickly, and the same every time, if that's what you want. I'm easily managed. All you have to do is be firm with me. Show me exactly how you want it done, and after a few lessons, I'll do it automatically. I'm the servant of all great men and women, and the servant of those who fail, also. I work with all the precision of a marvelous computer. You may run me for profit, or you may run me to ruin. It's your choice. It really makes no difference to me. Work with me. Be easy with me, and I will destroy you. Be firm with me, and I'll put the world at your feet. Who am I? I'm Habit!" (Anonymous).

Fathers help us to commit ourselves to a perpetual program of self-improvement and to look upon "graduation" as the commencement of a wonderful journey. The formal education they provide prepares us how to think, how to process information, and how to act. They teach us to approach our continuing education with an appreciation of the dynamic influence it can have in our lives, and make us aware of its power to focus our energy and steady our course, so that it might become a vehicle to reach for the stars. "Of all the communities available to us," said Albert Einstein, "there is not one I would want to devote myself to, except for the society of the true searchers, which has very few living members at any time."

30. Fathers allow us to experience both the positive and the negative consequences of our own actions. The reality is that we miss 100% of the shots we don't take. We sometimes fail to appreciate that most of us also miss about 50% of the shots we do take. Fathers encourage us to take the shots, no matter the consequences. They are always on the sidelines, cheering us on, and applauding our efforts.

The Plan of Salvation operates roughly the same way. Time was created to see if we would behave as we know we should. Because we often do not, "there was a time granted unto man to repent, yea, a probationary time, a time to repent and serve God." (Alma 42:4). Therefore, "the days of the children of men were prolonged, according to the will of God, that they might repent while in the flesh; wherefore, their state became a state of probation." (2 Nephi 2:21). If we become angry or frustrated with ourselves when we do not live up to our potential, and especially if we throw in the towel, call it a day, or give up entirely, our "days of probation are past; (because we) have procrastinated the day of (our) salvation until it is everlastingly too late, and (our) destruction is made sure." (Helaman 13:38).

31. Fathers sometimes intervene in our behalf, in order to spare us the unpleasant consequences of our foolish behavior. Fathers who have known hardship are usually much better able to help their children to deal with adversity. This principle may help to explain why so many church members, even after living Christ-like lives, are not spared such trials. But even in the face of challenges, the church becomes a community of true believers, and when we identify with it, we "are no more strangers and foreigners, but fellowcitizens with the saints, and of the household of God." (Ephesians 2:19).

32. Fathers sacrifice for us. They teach us about the ultimate sacrifice which was the Atonement, that can save us from our natural state of carnality, sensuality, and devilish inclinations. They teach us how the Atonement triggers the operation of the Law of Mercy, which mitigates for those who conform to its requirements the effects of the first Law, which demands Justice. The Atonement lifts us to a state of holiness, spirituality, and angelic innocence. The Apostle Paul confirmed: "By grace ye are saved, thru faith, and that not of ourselves; it is the gift of God." (Ephesians 2:8).

33. Fathers provide role models for us to follow. Those without such magnificent mentors, who provide memorable and stable foundations built upon the unchanging and eternally validated laws of the gospel, may be forced to make value judgments based on the shifting sands of expediency and circumstance. They are no better off than the beasts, and will fail to improve the quality of their dispositions. Their intellects can never bridge the gap between rational behavior and faith, nor can they manufacture the moral and ethical mortar necessary to build the foundation of character. The example of our fathers can set the tone upon which we anchor our own belief systems, thus setting the stage for generational cycles of happiness.

"How
carefully most do men
creep into nameless graves, while
now and again one or two forget
themselves into immortality."
(Phillips Brooks).

Our Neighbors

"It's a beautiful day in the neighborhood, a beautiful day for a neighbor. Would you be mine? Could you be mine? I have always wanted to have a neighbor just like you. I've always wanted to live in a neighborhood with you. So let's make the most of this beautiful day. Since we're together, we might as well say, would you be mine? Could you be mine? Won't you be my neighbor? Won't you please, please won't you be my neighbor?" (Lyrics by Fred Rogers)

Jesus taught us to love our neighbors as ourselves. (Matthew 19:19). This counsel is diametrically opposed to the world's philosophy, that is best articulated by Daddy Warbucks, who told Annie: "You don't have to be nice to those you climb over, or step on, as you climb the ladder of success, if you don't plan on coming back down again." We are constantly reminded: "It's not what you know; it's who you know. You don't get what you deserve; you get what you negotiate. He who has the gold makes the rules." But as Brigham Young declared: "If we go on lusting after the groveling things of this life which perish with the handling, we shall surely remain fixed with a very limited amount of knowledge and like a door upon its hinges, move to and fro from one year to another without any visible advancement or improvement." (J.D., 10:266, see Proverbs 26:14). If we really want to get ahead in the world, we need to learn to prioritize the needs of our neighbors.

We love our neighbors as ourselves when we yield to the influence of the Holy Spirit, put off our telestial tendencies, begin to appreciate the scope of the Atonement of Christ, return to our childhood roots, and become meek, submissive, humble, patient, full of love, and willing to submit to all things. (See Mosiah 3:19). We become teachable, as we are guided by the peaceable things of the kingdom. We learn to see past our neighbors' shortcomings, and unconditionally and ceaselessly forgive every one of our "brothers their trespasses," until "seventy times seven." (Matthew 18:32 & 35).

We do this in the face of Satan's Golden Question, which seizes upon our telestial tendencies like a bulldog sinks its teeth into a postman's pants: "Do you have any money?" He has done a tremendous job of perverting the Lord's teaching by having us believe that we can have anything in this world for money, including the admiration and respect of our neighbors. Does a need exist? Solve the problem with a generous application of money, to be repeated in incrementally larger doses four times a day for life. This is the prescription upon which the world relies to cure our ills and those of our neighbors.

When the noise of the world gets in the way and we forget who our neighbors really are, it's time to get out the body bags, because the inevitable casualties of war will soon begin to stack up. No matter how much we have patronized them, we lose friends in a slow hemorrhage, as they defect to the enemy's camp. Our self-preoccupation wastes our energy with distractions we cannot control. Because of our shortsightedness, we damage ourselves in ways both subtle and unexpected. We cannot persist in self-centered behavior that relies on the corrosive elements of acrimony, anger. animosity, bitterness, hostility, rancor, sullenness, and vindictiveness toward others, without suffering self-inflicted wounds. All this can be avoided by following the simple admonition to love our neighbors as ourselves, which is one of the fundamental operational principles of the Plan of Salvation. Brigham Young declared: "All organized existence is in progress either to an endless advancement in eternal perfections, or back to dissolution. There is no period in all the eternities wherein organized existence will become stationary, that it cannot advance in knowledge, wisdom, power, and glory." (J.D., 1:349).

"Who are our neighbours?" the lawyer asked Jesus. (See Luke 10:25-37). They are those who speak Aymara, Afrikaans, Fijian, Polish, Mandarin, and around 6,500 other languages. They live in 196 countries on 7 continents and on the isles of the sea. The color of their skin is red, yellow, brown, black, and white, and everything in between. They are equally comfortable wearing a sarong, a grass skirt, a lava lava, a burqa, or blue jeans. They find shelter in igloos, bamboo huts, thatch cottages, canvas tents, cardboard shanties, and condominiums. They eat kaeng khua, poi, muamba de galinha, raggmunk, hrútspungar, and hamburgers on sesame seed buns. Most importantly, and whether or not they recognize the feeling, each one carries a spark of divinity that is the gentle glow of the light of Christ.

It was with this "world-view" that the Savior embraced His neighbors. Giving them more than just "lip service," He practiced what He preached. His counsel encouraged substantive assistance rather than passive inattention. As John Taylor taught: "There are some Christian people in this world who, if a man were poor or hungry, would say, 'Let us pray for him.' I would suggest a little different regimen for a person in this condition: rather take him a bag of flour and a little beef or pork. A few such comforts will do him more good than your prayers." (J.D., 19:47). The Savior actively involved Himself in the lives and fortunes of His neighbors, and was non-discriminatory in His attention to their needs.

Mosiah also knew who his neighbors were, and how to treat them. The Savior was his behavioral mentor and model. He was ready to succor those that stood in need and provide for them of his own substantial means. He withheld judgment and assisted the poor, asking: "Are we not all beggars? Do we not all depend upon the same Being, even God, for all the substance which we have, for both food and raiment, and for gold, and for silver, and for all the riches which we have of every kind?" (Mosiah 4:16-19). His love of his neighbors cast a benevolently blind eye on their supposed faults or shortcomings. His example taught that good intentions and empathy are not enough, but that our love for others needs to be as wide as the encircling arms of the Lord Jesus Christ.

Two
ways to
be rich are
to have more
or to want less.

Pennies From Heaven

"Every time it rains, it rains pennies from heaven. Don't you know each cloud contains pennies from heaven? You'll find your fortune falling all over town. Be sure that your umbrella is upside down. Trade them for a package of sunshine and flowers. If you want the things you love, you must have showers. So when you hear it thunder, don't run under a tree. There'll be pennies from heaven for you and me." (Lyrics by Johnny Burke & Arthur Johnston).

When the reserves in our spiritual bank accounts are nearing depletion, or even if we are overdrawn, we may still receive pennies from heaven, or the currency of faith, in various forms. God will continue to give us "knowledge by his Holy Spirit, yea, by the unspeakable gift of the Holy Ghost." (D&C 121:26). He does not generally give us Susan B. Anthony or Sacajawea dollars, or even shiny quarters, dimes, or nickels. Instead, He doles out the smallest denomination possible, "precept upon precept; line upon line, line upon line; here a little, and there a little." (Isaiah 28:10). As these coins accumulate in our piggy banks, we begin to increase "in wisdom and stature, and in favour with God and man." (Luke 2:52).

Pennies from heaven add up quickly, just like the coins thrown into Rome's Trevi Fountain. Over 3,000 Euros a day are removed from the fountain, and the proceeds are used to feed the poor. The difference is that pennies from heaven are used to feed the poor in spirit. Thus, "by small and simple things are great things brought to pass." (Alma 37:6).

It is said that if you throw three coins with your right hand over your left shoulder into the Trevi Fountain, it is guaranteed that you will return one day to Rome, and that you will have a new romance that will lead to marriage. Pennies from heaven have a similar purpose; they represent an investment by Heavenly Father in our future. They epitomize seed money that is designed to facilitate our return to heaven, solidify our commitment to the gospel, and secure our covenant relationship with Christ.

As pennies from heaven accumulate with compound interest, their value soars, and they are transformed into relationship capital. They take the form of guardian angels, priesthood leaders, home and visiting teachers, and friends. Positive cash flow with pennies from heaven frees us from the shackles of dependency and allows us to reach our potential.

Pennies from heaven bear the inscription "In God We Trust," and so we do. The pennies that are showered down upon us are date-sensitive, and have their greatest intrinsic value when they are uncirculated, are in mint condition, or are even of proof quality. They stand in sharp contrast to the spurious counterfeit coins that are circulated by those who lurk in the shadows hoping to negotiate a one-sided currency exchange favorable only to them.

It is said that every cloud has a silver lining, when, in fact, every cloud contains pennies from heaven, and a fortune in coins falls all over town, so we need to be sure that our umbrellas are upside down. Or, as Brigham Young similarly counseled: "Keep your dish right side up, so that when the shower of porridge does come, you can catch your dish full." (D.B.Y., p. 310). Surely, he too was thinking of pennies from heaven.

The world changes us from the outside, while Christ transforms us from the inside. The world alters our environment. Christ changes our nature.

Plan
Of Salvation

The focus of this essay is simply to explore the genius behind the construction of the Plan of Salvation, consider its compelling capacity to influence change, and quantify the inherently positive influence of the three words of its name, whether it is Plan of Salvation, Plan de Salut, Gottes Einfacher Heilsplan, Plan De Dios, or Guds Enfle Frelsesplan. (For an in-depth discussion of the Plan of Salvation itself, see my essay: "The Plan").

It is not my intention to oversimplify the elements of the Plan of Salvation. During my study, I have come to believe that many Christians, conscientious though they be, have only a shallow understanding of God's Plan. This influences them to conveniently shrink it down and neatly package it into a single finite point in time and space. To wit, evangelicals can often identify their precise moment of conversion, when they were "born again," and they can describe how an epiphany moved them to accept Christ and thus be "saved." Genuine though their feelings may be, their experience is only the first step of a conversion and refining process that should continue to their last breath. (See my essay: "Born Again"). In contrast, the Plan of Salvation is found only in the restored gospel of Jesus Christ and provides an educational experience that has been carefully designed to engage each of us in a rhapsody that lasts a lifetime. (See my essay: "The Purpose of Life").

"Born again" and "saved" evangelical Christians would be surprised to learn that "Plan of Salvation" (count the words: Plan-1, of-2, Salvation-3) may be the most etymologically connected three word phrase in the English language, inasmuch as it brings to mind "council in heaven," "agency and opposition," "justice and mercy," "apostasy and restoration," "modern day prophets," "latter day revelation," and "Jesus the Christ," all triads in their own right. When we invite the Spirit to guide us, we learn that God has a Plan that cannot be ignored, trivialized, or easily dismissed.

Joseph Smith's theophany in the Sacred Grove (another three-word blockbuster) is a powerful example that even a heavenly manifestation by Deity is not enough to save us. The intensity of Joseph's initial personal experience with the Godhead was necessarily followed by angelic instruction, personal revelation, diligent obedience, the bestowal of authority, the making of covenants, and repentance when required. Conversion follows testimony building, and is accompanied by an expanding awareness of principles, the digestion of doctrine, and a commitment to covenants that culminate in an endowment of power that makes sure our calling and election as children of promise.

The freely given Light of Christ (a three-word smash hit) is enough to kindle a spark of interest within each of us that motivates us to ponder the depths of eternity. But it would be wrong to leave it at that, underestimate the magnitude of the Plan, or define it in a way that demeans its overarching relevance to every aspect of our lives. At the end of the day, the Plan of Salvation provides us with tools that allow us to monitor with precision our relationship with God. It is founded upon the very points of doctrine that focus on Salvation, and it is upon these elements that its correct understanding hinges. The "Plan of Salvation," as it turns out, is a very good choice of words when describing the intimacy that our Heavenly Father desires to have with each of us.

In the world, we find three-word headliners that are a shadow of the Plan of Salvation. In physics, the Unified Field Theory explains almost everything. It falls short of the power inherent in the "Plan of Salvation," but in many ways these two concepts are reflections of each other. If the Unified Field Theory could be mathematically quantified, it would allow the fundamental forces and elementary particles of the physical world to be written in terms of a single field. In fact, this sounds a lot like the Plan of Salvation, which is really a working construct that allows us to reconcile our place in the cosmos with practical instruction relating to our divine potential. In science, the Unified Field Theory comes close to being a theory of everything; a single, coherent framework that explains all of the physical relationships within our universe. In a religious context, the Plan of Salvation does that and more. For the faithful, it doctrinally quantifies the links between the realities of our physical world and the promises of eternity, and seamlessly harmonizes the two in ways that provide us with a model within which we may hash out the details that relate to our progression. The Plan of Salvation provides more than physical laws that permit the tides to rise and fall, cause the seasons to change, and make the sun to rise. It articulates commandments and covenants of a spiritual nature that allow God's children to expand their capacities in ways that would be otherwise impossible and that cannot be rationally explained.

After Moses had been shown the visions of eternity, it was not for the space of many hours that he "did again receive his natural strength like unto man; and he said unto himself: Now, for this cause I know that man is nothing, which thing I never had supposed." (Moses 1:10). Until the Spirit touched him, he had no idea how magnificent the Plan of Salvation was, and he could not appreciate its capacity to fit one such as he into its grand design.

Later, God further revealed to Moses His Own binding association with the Plan of Salvation, when He declared: "This is my work and my glory - to bring to pass the immortality and eternal life of man." (Moses 1:39). This brings to mind Henri Bergson's expansive declaration: "The universe is a machine for the making of Gods."("Two Sources of Morality and Religion," p. 306).

There is also a powerful three-word theory of particle physics called "The Standard Model" that deals with the electromagnetic, weak, and strong nuclear interactions, all of which regulate the behavior of particles on a subatomic level. The Standard Model was developed during the latter half of the 20th century in a collaborative effort of scientists around the world. The discovery of quarks, tau neutrinos, and Higgs bosons has confirmed the validity of The Standard Model. It is called The Theory of Almost Everything because it doesn't adequately deal with gravity, which is the fourth force of nature, describe the expansion of the universe, or explain the existence of dark matter. While its experimental predictions have been validated, its equations leave some phenomena unexplained. Perhaps we could compare The Standard Model to the imperfect doctrines of those "among all sects, parties, and denominations, who are blinded by the subtle craftiness of men, whereby they lie in wait to deceive." The Standard Model version of gospel doctrine only keeps us from the truth because we "know not where to find it." (D&C 123:12).

In relation to the Unified Field Theory and The Standard Model with which we are becoming more familiar, the Plan of Salvation embraces questions that run the gamut from trivial to profound, and that may take a lifetime to comprehend. A shopping list may take only 5 minutes to compile and can be written on a scrap of paper; a daily task list can be completed in about 10 minutes, and assembling a Fisher Price toy (accompanied by pages of incomprehensible instructions written by a Chinese engineer with a rudimentary understanding of English grammar) might take 24 hours. Putting together a back-yard swing set using the enclosed plans may take 3 days, while building a house from blueprints may require the labor of a dozen subcontractors over a span of 6 months or more, even taking into account a dozen change-orders. The Empire State Building was erected in 1 year and 54 days. Planning and executing the construction of an entire city can require decades, while creating a new world order, beginning with the organization of the United Nations, on October 24, 1945, has taken generations, and is an on-going project.

While physicists have been toying with the Unified Field Theory, and now The

Standard Model, for a hundred years or so, family planning is a never-ending process that is fundamental to the successful implementation of the Plan. As the Lord Jehovah promised Abraham: "I give unto thee a promise that...all the families of the earth (shall) be blessed, even with the blessings of the gospel (Plan), which are the blessings of salvation, even of life eternal." (Abraham 2:11).

The Plan of Salvation is also described in The Book of Mormon in just three words as the Plan of Mercy, Plan of Redemption, Plan of Deliverance, Plan of Restoration, and Plan of Happiness. Its objectives are mercy, deliverance, redemption, restoration, and happiness, to name a few. Its three-word antonyms include Plan of Gadianton, and Plan of Wickedness. "There is," after all, "an opposition in all things." (2 Nephi 2:11).

The three words of the Plan of Salvation keep secular company with The New Deal, Social Security Act, War on Poverty, Voter Registration Act, The New Frontier, The Great Society, Language, Culture, Borders, and I Like Ike. (However, bureaucratic plans can get wound up in verbosity. Consider, for example, The Health Insurance Portability and Privacy Act, and The Patient Protection and Affordable Care Act. In the private sector, convoluted language is also sometimes employed with no demonstrable benefit. For example, when announcing layoffs to save costs (how hard was that to say), Citigroup issued this press release: "Today a series of repositioning actions was initiated that will further reduce expenses and improve efficiency across the company while maintaining Citi's unique capabilities to serve clients, especially in the emerging markets. These actions will result in increased business efficiency, streamlined operations and an optimized consumer footprint across geographies." The observation of Polonius comes to mind: "Since brevity is the soul of wit, and tediousness the limbs and outward flourishes, I will be brief." ("Hamlet," Act 2, Scene 2). (See my essay: "Brevity").

Many of the most significant concepts in mankind's struggle for freedom have been articulated in three simple words that convey meanings of earth-shaking import: Rights of Man, Power and Responsibility, Declaration of Independence, Articles of Confederation, The Federalist Papers, United States Constitution, Bill of Rights, The Executive Branch, The Legislative Branch, and The Judicial Branch, not to mention Faster, Higher, Stronger (Citius, Altius, Fortius).

It is entirely appropriate that the Plan of Salvation is articulated in three words, because the sacred number three pops up throughout religious history and all over the world, and not just because of its obvious association with the Christian Holy Trinity. The ancient Greeks wrote of a divine triad, Theos (God), Logos (the Word), and Psyche (the Soul). The father, mother, and son gods of the Egyptians were Osiris, Isis, and Horus. In Norse mythology, Yggdrasil supported the world with three roots: one extended into Asgard, the abode of the Gods, one into Jotenheim, the home of the Giants, and the third into Nifleheim, the region of the Unknown. Three precious gifts were given to the Jews; the Law of Moses, the Land of Israel, and Paradise.

The number three points us to what is real, essential, perfect, substantial, complete, and divine. It is almost universally understood as a key to the integrity and interdependence of all existence. The triangle is the most perfect geometrical figure, inasmuch as it is the first form complete in itself. There are three spatial dimensions: width, depth, and height. Time has three categories: past, present, and future, and their related divisions are birth, life, and death. Three persons in grammar represent all of our relationships: I, You, and They. The simplest forms of argument are completed with a major premise, a minor premise, and a conclusion. Thought, word, and deed represent the sum of our capabilities. The three sister virtues are faith, hope, and charity. There are three states of matter: gas, solid, and liquid, and three kingdoms represent our understanding of its composition: animal, vegetable, and mineral, not to mention land, sky and water, or sun, moon, and stars. God has three attributes: omnipresence, omniscience, and omnipotence. The number three represents the unity of body, mind, and spirit. Oak, ash, and thorn are called the triad of trees, and it is said that when they are found together, fairies thrive. Many world religions embrace triple deities or concepts of deity, including the Hindu Trimurti of Brahma, Vishnu, and Siva, (Creator, Preserver, and Changer), the Three Jewels of Buddhism, the Three Pure Ones of Taoism, and the Triple Goddess of Wicca. For these reasons and more, Pythagoras called the number 3 the noblest of all digits.

Classical mythology explores the trios of Graces, that are Fates, Furies, and Muses. The Graces were charm, beauty, and creativity. The Fates were Clotho, who spun the thread of life, Lachesis, who chose one's lot in life and measured how long it was to be, and Atropos, who at death cut the thread of life with her shears. The Furies were the three Greek goddesses of vengeance: Tisiphone (avenger of murder), Megaera (the jealous), and Alecto (constant anger). The Muses were the inspiration for literature, science, and the arts. Poseidon carried a trident, a three-pronged spear representing, among other things, birth, life, and death, mind, body, and spirit, and past, present, and future. The Greek Gorgons were Stheno, Euryale and Medusa, who had hair made of living, venomous snakes, as well as a horrifying face that turned to stone those who beheld it. The three judges of Hades were Minos, Æacus, and Rhadamanthus. Pluto's dog Cerberus had 3 heads. During the siege of Troy, the Greeks dragged Hector's body around the city three times.

In ancient Ireland, among the household officials of the High King of Erin were three royal jugglers, three jesters, three head charioteers, three equerries, three swineherds, three janitors, and three drink-bearers. The emblem of the Emerald Isle, the Shamrock, has a three-lobed leaf. Harder to explain are The Three Stooges: Moe, Larry, and Curly, and The Pep Boys: Manny, Moe, and Jack.

It is said that it is our nature to fall into sin, which is human, to lie in sin, which is diabolical, and to rise out of it again, which is angelical. Harmony contains 3 symphonies, the Diapason, the Diapente, and the Diatessaron. In civil life, the usher of a court repeats 3 times the warning Oyez, Oyez, Oyez, which means "hear" or "listen." In religious ceremonies, (Latter-day Saints think of the endowment), the expression of sacred covenants may be repeated three times. We eat three meals a day. Dinner often consists of an appetizer, an entrée, and dessert. Theatre often consists of a prelude, a main act, and a postlude. The three-act play is familiar to all. Writers often use the device of a prologue and epilogue to frame the main body of the work. The bounds of education are limited by the 3 Rs. The third time is the charm, and three is company, but four is a crowd. There is nothing particularly sacred about the number 4, however. Consider the dreadful Four Horsemen of the Apocalypse: War, Famine, Pestilence, and Death.

Many superstitions utilizing the number 3 have been a part of Jewish life through the ages. One is to spit three times for good luck in reaction to something that is either especially worthwhile or particularly evil. Solomon's Temple was divided into three important areas: the Holy of Holies, the Holy Place and the outer courtyard. In Jewish tradition, there will be three temples, Solomon's Temple (the first temple), the Temple of Zerubabel (the second temple), and a third temple, to be built on Mount Zion at some future date. When Catholics are greatly excited, they sometimes cry out: "Jesus, Mary, and Joseph!" Shakespeare's "Macbeth" prominently features three witches.

In our own Latter-day Saint religious tradition, we express some of our most cherished concepts with three words. For example, justice and mercy, articles of faith, Abraham, Isaac (and) Jacob, The Holy Bible, Garden of Gethsemane, The Old Testament, The New Testament, Doctrine and Covenants, Book of Mormon, The Holy Trinity, Our Heavenly Father, Jesus The Christ, The Holy Ghost, prophet, priest (and) king, baptism by water, baptism by fire, take the Sacrament, bear your testimony, choose the right, serve a mission, return with honor, Latter-day Saints, brothers and sisters, child of God, our ward family, share the gospel, perfect the Saints, redeem the dead, keep the commandments, follow thou Me, love your neighbors, families are forever, time and eternity, family home evening, stay the course, Word of Wisdom, Law of Tithing, Law of Sacrifice,

Law of Consecration, Law of Chastity, the temple endowment, The First Presidency, The Telestial Kingdom, The Terrestrial Kingdom, The Celestial Kingdom, The Three Witnesses, and The Eight Witnesses. In our religious educational programs we have Duty to God, Young Women Values, early morning Seminary, Institute of Religion, and Seminaries and Institutes. Our religious tradition also includes three degrees of glory, and three levels of glory within the Celestial Kingdom. The fulness of The Godhead is expressed in the number three. (Colossians 2:9). We are all familiar with the three-fold admonition to get ready, get set, and go, and with President Spencer W. Kimball's encouragement to "Do it. Do it right. Do it right now."

Three times is the blessing given in Numbers 6:23-24: "The Lord bless thee and keep thee; The Lord make His face shine upon thee and be gracious unto thee; The Lord lift up His countenance upon thee and give thee peace." King Solomon's Seal (the Star of David) is expressed by interlaced triangles. The Divine Feminine (popularized in the movie: "The Da Vinci Code") is represented by a downward facing triangle. There are three primary colors, (red, green, and blue) from which all other colors may be created.

The scriptures identify these three things as essential: water, spirit, and blood. "By the water ye keep the commandment; by the Spirit ye are justified, and by the blood ye are sanctified. (Moses 6:60). In baptismal fonts, twelve oxen support the font itself, with three looking to each of the cardinal points of the compass. In the mouths of three witnesses, and in the testimony of three witnesses, was The Book of Mormon prophesied to be established. (Ether 5:4). In the sacramental prayer, we promise to do three things: Take upon ourselves the name of Christ, always remember Him, and keep His commandments. (See D&C 20:77).

The waters of the River Jordan were thrice divided. (Exodus 24, Joshua 4, & 2 Kings 2:8). During His 40 day fast in the wilderness, the Savior was three times tempted by the adversary. (Luke 4:1-13). His subsequent ministry lasted three years. During that time, He raised three persons, that we know about, from the dead. (Luke 7:15, 8:55, & John 11:44). At His crucifixion, Pilate had the inscription "Jesus of Nazareth the King of the Jews" put on the cross in three languages: Hebrew, Latin, and Greek. (John 19:19-20). At the crucifixion, there was great destruction in the Land of Zarahemla for the space of three hours. (3 Nephi 8:19). Following the destruction, darkness covered the land for three days. (Helaman 14:27). The voice of the Risen Savior was heard three times by the Nephites in Bountiful before they understood His words. (See 3 Nephi 11:5-6). Suffering, sacrifice, and resurrection figure prominently in our liturgy.

The angels who usher the faithful through the veil into the presence of God announce their intention to do so with three distinct knocks, and heavenly messengers on God's errand often seek the attention of mortals with three inquiries or exhortations. (Genesis 18:21, Daniel 3:24, Isaiah 6:3). Likewise does the Savior. (See Matthew 26:44, & Mark 14:41). In the Garden of Gethsemane, thrice did Jesus come to Peter, James, and John only to find them asleep each time. He was crucified at the third hour, Peter denied him three times before the cock crowed, and He rose from the dead on the third day. The third time Jesus showed Himself to His disciples following his crucifixion, He asked Peter three times if he loved Him. Three times the same answer was given: "Feed my sheep." (John 21:17). Three years elapsed after the First Vision before the visit to Joseph Smith by the Angel Moroni. Then, three times in a single night did the Angel Moroni appear to the boy prophet in his bedchamber.

Perhaps the most significant questions we can ask ourselves are these three: "Where did I come from? Why am I here?" and "Where am I going?" These inquiries relate to the Plan of Salvation. The number three also pops up repeatedly when we consider church government. There were Three Witnesses, there are three members of The Quorum of the First Presidency, in Temple presidencies, and in the composition of Area Authorities, Stake Presidencies, Bishoprics, Aaronic Priesthood Quorum Presidencies, Auxiliary Presidencies, not to mention the Godhead itself. Even acronyms frequently employed by church members come in groups of three: These include L.D.S., C.E.S., C.T.R., E.F.Y., P.P.I., P.E.C., B.Y.C., F.H.E., M.T.C., C.C.H., and B.Y.U.

Pythagoras may have been right, that reality can be expressed mathematically, and that the number 3 is at the foundation of the Divine Proportion. However, there are no built-in scholastic prerequisites relating to our accessibility to the principles of the Plan of Salvation. Those without formal education are welcome to participate, as are those with advanced degrees from the most prestigious institutions of higher learning, like M.I.T., B.Y.U., L.S.U., and U.S.C.. (Hmmm. There is the number three again!) It is the poor in spirit, those with broken hearts and contrite spirits, who seem to have an advantage, though, when it comes to fully embracing and implementing the principles of the Plan.

Nor does the Plan impose any age restrictions. Three year olds, thirty year olds, and ninety year olds may all sing with equal fervency: "I Am a Child of God." The Plan is non-discriminatory, as well. It was designed for the world's heaviest person, who weighed in at 1,400 pounds, for the world's tallest person, at 8 feet 11 inches, for the world's shortest adult, at just 21.5 inches, the world's wealthiest person, who boasts $73 billion in assets, as well as the world's smartest person whose I.Q. is 210, as well as for the other 7 billion of us who fall somewhere within these extremes. As a matter of fact, God invites all of us to "partake of his (Plan); and he denieth none that come unto him," including these three groups, "black and white, bond and free, male and female; and he remembereth the heathen; and all are alike unto God, both Jew and Gentile." (2 Nephi 26:33).

There is no enrollment expiration date built into the Plan of Salvation. While an unrefrigerated creampuff will spoil in 2 hours, a banana will turn black in a few days, potatoes will grow "eyes" in a few months, and although wheat may stop germinating only after decades of storage, the Plan's vitality remains in effect forever. Its boundaries encompass the theories of evolution, relativity, quantum mechanics, the Big Bang, string theory, and every other theory that may have been or ever will be conceived by our finite minds to bring order out of chaos. The operating parameters of the Plan include the three laws of thermodynamics that define the fundamental physical quantities of temperature, energy, and entropy. The Plan trumps every postulate, supposition, or theoretical construct devised by man in an attempt to explain why the sun rises and sets, what keeps the planets in motion, and how the order of the cosmos was created and is maintained. While it circumscribes every physical law governing the temporal universe, its overarching influence also embraces every spiritual law governing the eternities.

God gave Abraham a glimpse of all "the works which his hands had made…which were many; and they multiplied before (his) eyes, and (he) could not see the end thereof," so comprehensive was the scope of the Plan. (Abraham 3:11-12). In 2015, NASA reported the discovery of a single quasar (WISE J224607.57-052635.0), sitting at the edge of the visible universe, that shines with the light of 300 trillion stars. This discovery reminds us of the line from the Anglican hymn: "All things bright and beautiful. The Lord God made them all." (Cecil Francis Alexander).

As it turns out, the benefits that spring from the "Plan of Salvation" will never cease to exist. New discoveries will continue to be made, at an accelerating rate, as the expanding boundaries of our knowledge interface with equivalent borders of darkness. When we turn our cheeks to be bathed in warm sunlight, we will feel the gentle caresses of the hand of our Father in Heaven. It was He Who organized the forces of nature, (the strong force, the weak force, electromagnetism, and gravity), that have held our universe together for 13.7 billion years. It was He Who anticipated the cosmic microwave background radiation that is left over from the Big Bang, and caused it to uniformly radiate at 2.73 degrees Kelvin, which happens to be just enough to warm our blood. His Plan of Salvation shines with the ethereal luster of a crown jewel standing alone in the cosmos.

The Plan has been humming along at a constant and unchanging level of energy since He implemented it following the Council in Heaven before the world was.

When its elements were first explained to us, we jumped to our feet and "shouted for joy." (Job 38:7). Like the rumble of thunder in the distant sky, we can almost hear the faint echo of the exclamations: "Hosanna, to God and the Lamb!" (D&C 109:79). When Jacob taught it to his brethren, he too was moved to exclaim: "How great the Plan of our God!" (2 Nephi 9:13).

The Plan of Salvation takes into account every conceivable exigency that could confront us. It has no finite depth or breadth, is temporally boundless, and has no restricting spatial conditions. To comprehend its universal applicability, we must make fundamental postulations about time that stretch our minds, expand our presumptions, and nudge us out of our complacency. As Steven Hawking has said: "One can think of ordinary, real, time as a horizontal line. On the left, one has the past, and on the right, the future. (This is the linear aspect of time with which we are all familiar. The arrow of time moves in one comfortable direction only, and that is forward). But there's another kind of time that moves in a vertical direction (in the sense that we are moved out of our three spatial dimensions, at right-angles to them, if you will). (See my essay: "Higher Dimensional Realities"). This is called imaginary time, because it is not the kind of time we normally experience. But in a sense, it is just as palpable as what we call real time." It even makes more sense than real time, when you stop to think about it, because it helps us to better understand the matrix within which the Plan finds expression; or, in pragmatic terms, the space-time continuum that for more than a hundred years has provided a new physical definition of existence that was needed to help to explain Einstein's theories of relativity.

The new reality of space and time existing in four interrelated dimensions (3 physical dimensions and one temporal dimension) is a continuum in the sense that there are no missing points in space or in moments in time, and both can be subdivided without limits in size or duration. Additionally, space-time does not evolve; it simply exists. Once again, the Plan of Salvation trumps the accumulated wisdom of science by embracing these concepts, and much more. When the veil is parted and you have been privileged to see God's realty much more. When the veil is parted and you have been privileged to see God's realty more clearly, (what we might now call "imaginary time"), if you could "hie to Kolob in the twinkling of an eye, and then continue onward with that same speed to fly, do you think that you could ever, through all eternity, find out the generation where Gods began to be, or see the grand beginning, where space did not extend, or view the last creation, where Gods and matter end? Methinks the Spirit whispers, 'No man has found pure space,' nor seen the outside curtains, where nothing has a place. The works of God continue, and worlds and lives abound; improvement and progression have one eternal round. There is no end to matter; there is no end to space; there is no end to spirit; there is no end to race. There is no end to virtue; there is no end to might. There is no end to wisdom; there is no end to light. There is no end to union; there is no end to youth. There is no end to priesthood; there is no end to truth. There is no end to glory; there is no end to love; there is no end to being; there is no death above. There is no end to love; there is no end to being; there is no death above." (William W. Phelps, "If You Could Hie to Kolob").

While there may be metaphorical interpretations relating to Kolob, no one can dispute that William W. Phelps was a keen observer and visionary who understood his place in the cosmos. He was one who related it to the elements of the Plan of Salvation. Hie to Kolob is yet another triad that grabs our attention.

In this vein, Steven Hawking continued: "One could say that the boundary condition of the universe (read: "of the Plan") is that it has no boundary. (Joseph Smith simply said that Kolob is the star that is nearest to the throne of God. See Abraham 3:2-3). Yet, the universe is completely self-contained and is not affected by anything outside itself. It has neither been created nor will it be destroyed. It just is. (Here, Hawking gets tantalizingly close to the mark). This might suggest that so-called imaginary time is the real time, and that what we call real time is just a figment of our imaginations. In real time, the universe has a beginning and an end at singularities that form a boundary to space-time and at which the laws of science break down. But in imaginary time, there are no singularities or boundaries. So maybe what we call imaginary time is really more basic, and what we call real is just an idea that we have invented to help us describe what we think the universe is like."

Perhaps God has fabricated real time to deal with the veil that has been drawn across our minds, preventing us from seeing the bigger picture that would compromise our opportunity to fully participate in the Plan during a brief period called mortality that is not our natural condition. Perhaps, when the veil is parted and we are more visionary, imaginary time will surge over us in a flood that envelops us in a new reality, as it carries us to new heights of awareness and new appreciation of the magnitude of The Plan. Were we to paraphrase both Hawking and Phelps, we might then realize that "there is no end to matter; there is no end to space; there is no end to spirit, and there is no end to race." The boundary condition of the Plan of Salvation would be that it has no boundary.

Even though we can only "imagine" what that "time" might be like, we can take comfort in the Lord' counsel: "My thoughts are not your thoughts, neither are your ways my ways. ...For as the heavens are higher than the earth, so are my ways higher than your ways, and my thoughts than your thoughts." (Isaiah 55:8-9).

Maybe our physical universe had a beginning in real time, at the Big Bang, the point of singularity when all things were circumscribed in one great whole. But maybe, in a stroke of creative genius, God caused the Plan to utilize "imaginary time" that exists at right angles to real time, in a vertical dimension, as it were. In this larger context, the universe would have no beginning and no end. This fits in neatly with the Latter-day Saint concept of the Plan of Salvation.

Daniel was told: "God hath numbered thy kingdom, and finished it." (Daniel 5:26). The grand design of our Father in Heaven is evidence that He plans His work and works His Plan. It validates our testimony that proper prior planning prevents poor priesthood performance. As we have seen, He has quietly woven a golden tapestry on a cosmic loom, and has ennobled His efforts with the frequent insertion of the number 3 into His master design to subtly remind us to make course corrections and re-focus our efforts in the right direction.

"Even the humblest human
beings, Pope John Paul I observed, are naturally
philosophic, asking themselves such questions as "Who
and I? Where do I come from and where am I going?"
Religious revelation provides answers to these
questions, the pope acknowledges."
("Time" magazine, 10/26/1998).

Premortal Life

I had never thought of the possibility that we lived before we were born, until I took the missionary lessons. I was unaware of William Wordsworth's poem that teaches: "Our birth is but a sleep and a forgetting. The Soul that rises with us, our life's Star, hath had elsewhere its setting, and cometh from afar. Not in entire forgetfulness, and not in utter nakedness, but trailing clouds of glory do we come from God, Who is our Home." ("Ode on Intimations from Early Childhood, from Recollections of Early Childhood"). Had I been familiar with these lines, I am sure they would have touched tender chords.

I had read the King James Version of the Bible, but had overlooked the verses that provide hints about our pre-earth life. Among them are the following: "Before I formed thee in the belly I knew thee; and before thou camest forth out of the womb I sanctified thee, and I ordained thee a prophet unto the nations." (Jeremiah 1:5). "Ye are the children of the Lord your God." (Deuteronomy 14:1). We "are the sons of the living God." (Hosea 1:10). "All of you are children of the most High." (Psalms 82:6). He is "the Father of all." (Ephesians 4:6). "In him we live, and move, and have our being (for) we are the offspring of God." (Acts 17:28-29). I did not yet know that, when I die, "shall the dust return to the earth as it was: and the spirit shall return unto God who gave it." (Ecclesiastes 12:7).

If I had deeply pondered these things, I might have received answers to the questions I had not yet thought to ask. Emerson wrote: "The man who has seen the rising moon break out of the clouds at midnight has been present like an archangel at the creation of light and of the world." On another occasion, he declared: "If the stars should appear but one night in a thousand years, how would men believe and adore, and preserve for many generations the remembrance of the city of God which had been shown." I had not yet discovered the key doctrinal information that had been given to Abraham and Moses, that would have astonished even Emerson, because they answer the fundamental questions of existence, such as pre-mortal life, agency, creation, and foreordination.

As he stood before the Burning Bush on Sinai, Moses became the first person in recorded history to ask: "Who am I?" (Exodus 3:11). In the Book of Moses, which was received as revelation by Joseph Smith when he was translating the Bible, and which is probably one of the plain and precious parts of the Bible that is missing from our K.J.V. of Exodus, we learn how Moses discovered the answer to that question.

It came from God as an explanation to Moses of his relationship with Deity. (See Moses 1:1-2). In fact, his identity was intertwined with that of God. "And God spake unto Moses, saying: Behold, I am the Lord God Almighty, and Endless is my name; for I am without beginning of days or end of years; and is not this endless? And behold, thou art my son." (Moses 1:3-4).

Today, we describe ourselves in the same way. The missionaries teach investigators and we teach our children who they are, using the same parameters. Think of the words of the Primary hymn: "I am a Child of God." (Lyrics by Naomi W. Randall). Because of the restoration of priesthood authority, our character is largely defined by our covenant relationship with God. This begins with the Baptismal Covenant and only ends, really, with our Calling and Election.

We know that God is moral, because he has put us under covenant to obey the law of chastity. We know that He has charity, because he commands us to love Him and each other. We better understand His discipline as we conform our lives to the Law of Obedience. We know that He must have been a righteous steward, because He has provided us with the Law of Consecration. We learn how much He must love His less fortunate children, because he has given us the opportunity to obey the Law of the Fast. Our observance of the Word of Wisdom reminds us of His perfected, resurrected body. Our desire to seek knowledge recalls His omniscience. We carry a prayer of thanksgiving in our hearts for the laws that are anchored to the principles of the Plan of Salvation, and realize that if it were not possible to become as God is, covenants would be unnecessary. Covenants ground our almost unspeakable heritage and our equally unimaginable destiny to reality. They are the cables that are strung in the rarified atmosphere of a celestial aether that anchor eternity to our temporal world.

We know that we are begotten spirit children of Heavenly parents, and that we lived in a pre-earth existence with them before we began our sojourn in this second estate known as mortality. In moments of deep reflection, we "think of stepping on shore, and finding it heaven! We visualize taking hold of a hand, and finding it God's hand. We envision breathing a new air, and finding it celestial air. We imagine feeling invigorated, and finding it immortality. We dream of passing from storm and tempest to an unbroken calm, and of waking up, and finding it home." (Anonymous).

We imagine what it will be like coming home from our mortal mission. "It will seem like the time passed too quickly. We will think of the people we met, the people we helped, and of how our experiences helped us to grow spiritually. We will recall that we were like children, so immature, when we left home such a short time ago. We will find mother waiting to embrace us, standing just a bit behind father, who is bursting with pride. We will see tears of happiness falling from mother's cheeks. Father will be the first to strike hands with us, and then warmly embrace us. Our feelings will resonate with familiarity, and we will feel the Spirit as we never have before. We will know this is where we belong, and it will be a real homecoming as we return with honor to Heavenly Father and Mother." (Anonymous).

God taught these fundamental truths to Abraham, who was pondering, as so many of us have, the majesty of God's resplendent handiwork. "Thus I, Abraham, talked with the Lord, face to face, as one man talketh with another; and he told me of the works which his hands had made; And he said unto me: My son, my son (and his hand was stretched out), behold I will show you all these. And he put his hand upon mine eyes, and I saw those things which his hands had made, which were many; and they multiplied before mine eyes, and I could not see the end thereof." (Abraham 3:11-12).

As He had earlier done with Moses, the Lord defined Abraham based on His relationship with him. Then God revealed to Abraham "the intelligences that were organized before the world was; and among all these there were many of the noble and great ones; And God saw these souls that they were good, and he stood in the midst of them, and he said: These I will make my rulers; for he stood among those that were spirits, and he saw that they were good; and he said unto me: Abraham, thou art one of them; thou wast chosen before thou wast born." (Abraham 3:22-23).

Joseph F. Smith saw in vision those who "were also among the noble and great ones who were chosen in the beginning to be rulers in the Church of God." (D&C 138:55). He taught that these were chosen during a Council that was held in Heaven. We know we were also present at this council, because Job rhetorically asked: "Where wast thou when I laid the foundations of the earth? ...When the morning stars sang together, and all the sons of God shouted for joy." (Job 38:4 & 7).

"It is extremely important to get straight what happened in that premortal council," taught Neal A. Maxwell. "It was not an unstructured meeting, nor was it a discussion between plans, nor a brain-storming session, as to how to formulate the plan for salvation and carry it out. Our Father's plan was known, and the actual question put was whom the Father should send to carry it out." ("Deposition of a Disciple," p. 11).

Satan did not offer a viable alternative plan. It was probably only after he had stormed from the meeting, that he gathered the media together to announce his unworkable, counterfeit proposal. That he was a liar from the beginning, and drew so many away from Heavenly Fathers Plan, underscores the effectiveness of his strategy to engage in "ideological warfare." (See D&C 93:25). But just who (and how many) were cast out of heaven as a result of rebellion remains unclear. "For behold, the devil was before Adam, for he rebelled against me, saying, Give me thine honor, which is my power; and also (not a third, but) a third part of the hosts of heaven turned he away from me because of their agency. And they were thrust down, and thus came the devil and his angels." (See D&C 93:25). "He had drawn away many after him." (Moses 4:6). "Many followed after him." (Abraham 3:28). The Father's Plan suggests that the mighty doctrine of foreordination underlies this pure knowledge offered unto Abraham.

On the other side of the coin, Lucifer became the purveyor of propaganda. With extreme prejudice, he promoted what was really a political cause, that he might further his agenda and form what was probably the first instance of a vocal minority among his brothers and sisters who were in opposition to His Father's Plan. His inflammatory alternative elicited an emotional reaction, rather than a measured, response, among those who listened to him. Once bitten by his infectious jaws, the saliva of Satan became a contagion that contaminated his followers with the rabies of rebellion. Photophobia inevitably followed. The scriptures characterize this extreme aversion to light as "war in heaven." (Revelation 12:7).

God, Who from the beginning saw the bigger picture, explained how the divine gift of agency would interact with foreordination to give the lives of His obedient children purpose and meaning. Immediately after describing Abraham's seeds of greatness, He declared: "We will go down, for there is space there, and we will take of these materials, and we will make an earth whereon these may dwell; And we will prove them herewith, to see if they will do all things whatsoever the Lord their God shall command them; And they who keep their first estate shall be added upon; and they who keep not their first estate shall not have glory in the same kingdom with those who keep their first estate; and they who keep their second estate shall have glory added upon their heads for ever and ever." (Abraham 3:24-26).

This revelation makes clear that our divine right to exercise our agency in an atmosphere of opposition was intertwined with our creation, that we might freely choose God and his commandments. We are foreordained, because of the Plan, to have glory added upon our heads forever, on the condition of our faithfulness to God as we humbly assist Him in His great work. We can better understand the blessings and foreordinations specific to our lives if we turn to the personal scriptures from the Lord that are known as our patriarchal blessings.

Foreordination is like any other blessing. It is a conditional bestowal of gifts that is subject to our faithfulness. "Prophecies foreshadow events without determining their outcomes, because of a divine foreseeing of that outcome. So, foreordination is a conditional bestowal of a role, responsibility, or a blessing that, likewise, foresees but does not fix the outcome." (Neal Maxwell, B.Y.U., 10/10/1978).

"Our Heavenly Father has a full knowledge of the nature and disposition of each of His children, a knowledge gained by long observation and experience in the past eternity of our primeval childhood. By reason of that surpassing knowledge, God reads the future of men individually and of men collectively as communities and nations. He knows what each will do under given conditions, and sees the end from the beginning. He foresees the future and as a state which naturally and surely will be; not as one which must be because He has arbitrarily willed that it should be." (James E. Talmage, "The Great Apostasy," p. 20).

Harold B. Lee taught: "Now a further word about this matter of foreordination. The Prophet Joseph Smith taught that "every man who has a calling to minister to the inhabitants of the world was ordained to that very purpose in the grand council of heaven before this world was." ("Teachings," p. 365). So, likewise, declared the Apostle Paul, "for whom he did foreknow...them he also called." (Romans 2:29-30). But do not misunderstand that such a calling and such foreordination pre-determine what you must do. A prophet on this western continent has spoken plainly on this subject: "Being called and prepared from the foundation of the world, according to the foreknowledge of God on account of their exceeding faith and good works; in the first place being left to choose good or evil." (Alma 13:3). This last passage makes the other preceding passages more understandable. God may have called and chosen men in the spirit world or in their first estate to do a certain work, but whether they will accept that calling here and magnify it by faithful service and good works while in mortality is a matter in which it is their right and privilege to exercise their agency to choose good or evil." ("Decisions for Successful Living," p. 168-169).

Moses asked, "Tell me, I pray thee, Why are these things so?" (Moses 1:30). In response, the Lord once again answered indirectly, in a way that would require Moses to make an expenditure of the currency of faith before spiritual understanding would come. He replied: "This is my work and my glory, to bring to pass the immortality and eternal life of man." (Moses 1:39). Our own expanding awareness teaches us that Creation was structured to give us expanding opportunities to be nurtured by God, that we might ultimately be glorified in light and truth and know all things. (See D&C 93:28).

The more we contribute to this work, the greater will be our happiness and joy, and the more fully will we fulfill our own foreordained destiny. When I finally learned that my birth had been a sleep and a forgetting, and that my life's star had come from afar, I determined anew to be faithful to the great cause of Zion. The knowledge of my pre-mortal existence sanctified my individual effort, dignified my timid achievements, and validated my faltering progress toward the achievement of my goals. One of my greatest personal challenges became my struggle to have the humility to recognize, and then to magnify, my foreordained calling.

"This writing seemeth to me, as far as a man can judge of his own work, not much better than that noise or sound which musicians make while they are tuning their instruments, which is nothing pleasant to hear, but yet is a cause why the music is sweeter afterwards. So have I been content to tune the instruments of the muses, that they may play that have better hands."
(Francis Bacon).

Preparation

We need "clean hands, a pure heart, and a willing mind, to touch heaven." (Thomas S. Monson, C.R., 10/1990). We need to "go and do the things which the Lord hath commanded, for (we) know that the Lord giveth no commandments unto the children of men, save he shall prepare a way for them that they may accomplish the thing which he commandeth them." (1 Nephi 3:7).

President Monson said to the brethren of the church: "May we be filled with gratitude for the right of choice, accept the responsibility of choice, and ever be conscious of the results of choice. As bearers of the priesthood, all of us qualify for the guiding influence of our Heavenly Father as we choose carefully and correctly. We are engaged in the work of the Lord Jesus Christ. We, like those of olden times, have answered His call. We are on His errand. We shall succeed in the solemn charge: "Be ye clean, that bear the vessels of the Lord." (C.R., 4/2010).

It is wonderful when The First Presidency and Quorum of the Twelve give apostolic blessings. I still remember the dedicatory prayer at the Pacific Palisades, California, chapel, delivered by Elder Robert D. Hales in the late 1970s. I specifically recall him blessing our new chapel, that it would be protected from the fires that periodically ravaged the Santa Monica Mountains in which it was nestled. That protection was required just a few years later, when a raging wildfire, fanned by the flames of a Santana Wind, burned the hillsides surrounding the chapel, but spared the building itself. I also remember Boyd K. Packer's April 2010 General Conference address, when he closed by saying: "I invoke the blessings of the Lord upon you who are struggling against this terrible plague (of immorality), to find the healing that is available to us in the priesthood of the Lord."

I once read how Elder Holland "left an apostolic blessing on those attending a stake conference, in Bahrain. He challenged the brethren to live up to their priesthood offices and become true disciples of Christ, counseled the sisters to be proud they are women in the kingdom of God, and the young people to be safe, happy and loved. He blessed the children, the sick, the ill and the grieving, saying his greatest desire was to bear the same witness and extend the same blessings that the Savior would, if He were present." (Reported in the "Church News," 3/7/2009)

In his April 2010 Conference Address, President Monson said: "One of my most vivid memories is attending priesthood meeting as a newly ordained deacon and singing the opening hymn "Come, All Ye Sons of God." Tonight I echo the spirit of that special hymn and say to you, 'Come, all ye sons of God who have received the priesthood.' The message of that hymn is to spread the gospel, listen to the Shepherd, repent, and be baptized, get the Spirit's zeal, and pray."

President Monson continued: "Twenty years ago I attended a sacrament meeting where the children responded to the theme "I Belong to The Church of Jesus Christ of Latter-day Saints." One of my grandsons, who was 11 years old at that time, had spoken of the First Vision as he presented his part on the program. Afterward, as he came to his parents and grandparents, I said to him, "Tommy, I think you are almost ready to be a missionary." He replied, "Not yet. I still have a lot to learn."

We all still have a lot to learn, and hopefully, we have the gift of time on our side. If we do, perhaps we should think about what we would like to learn in the next twelve months. How would we like to be different then, from what we are now? How could President Monson's counsel help us to make positive changes in our lives? How could we prepare to receive his apostolic blessing?

We can begin by making conscious efforts to avoid temptation. "God…will not suffer you to be tempted above that ye are able; but will with the temptation also make a way to escape, that ye may be able to bear it." (1 Corinthians 10:13). This puts the responsibility for yielding to temptation squarely where it belongs, on our own heads.

We can cultivate good friendships. Gordon B. Hinckley famously said that every convert needs three things: "a friend in the church, an assignment, and to be nourished by the good word of God." We all need these things.

We can treat everyone with kindness and dignity. We can do as Thumper counseled, in the Disney film "Bambi." "If you can't say nuttin' nice, don't say nuttin' at all." We can strive to be the kinds of people our dogs think we are.

We can be honest. George Washington famously wrote: "I hope I shall always possess firmness and virtue enough to maintain what I consider the most enviable of all titles, the character of an 'Honest Man." (Letter to Alexander Hamilton, Mount Vernon, 8/28/1788).

A young man who sought employment, in competition with a number of other equally qualified applicants, echoed Washington's wish. "If I hire you," asked the owner of the company, "can I count on you to be honest?" "You can count on me to be honest whether you hire me or not!" responded the young man. Do you think he got the job?

We can use uplifting language. Mark Twain said that we should so live that we would be willing to sell our parrot to the town gossip. We can avoid murmuring and idle conversation. In fact, "there is so much good in the worst of us, and so much bad in the best of us, that it hardly behooves any of us to talk about the rest of us." (Anonymous).

We can seek after "anything virtuous, lovely, or of good report or praiseworthy." (12th Article of Faith). This includes avoiding the use of illicit drugs, the abuse of prescription medication, and the use of coffee, tea, alcohol, and tobacco products that destroy our physical, mental, and spiritual well-being. Then we shall be as those who "wait upon the Lord (who) shall renew their strength, (and who) mount up with wings as eagles. (Then) they shall run, and not be weary, and they shall walk, and not faint." (Isaiah 40:31).

As we strive to abide by the principles of the Word of Wisdom, we think of Heraclitus, a philosopher of the Golden Age of Greece, who left this sage observation that is applicable in every epoch, but especially in our own: "When health is absent, then wisdom cannot reveal itself, culture cannot become manifest, strength cannot fight, wealth becomes useless, and intelligence cannot be applied."

We can listen to wholesome music that invites us to draw closer to our Heavenly Father. The purpose of music should be to inspire, to motivate, to comfort, to strengthen, and to calm our troubled souls. Music and worship are inseparably interrelated. Because music is part of a unified whole, the instruments utilized, the way they are played, the volume and tempo, the lyrics if a vocal, the accompaniment, the attire and attitude of the performers, and the atmosphere in which the music is presented significantly influence the message conveyed and its impact on the listener. When we have been privileged to touch the face of God, it has often been facilitated by the medium of music. Even before the foundations of the earth were laid, music filled the celestial air, when "the morning stars sang together, and all the sons of God shouted for joy." (Job 38:7).

We can be sure to maintain absolute fidelity in marriage, and to think clean thoughts. "This much I can tell you," declared Mosiah, "that if ye do not watch yourselves, and your thoughts, and your words, and your deeds, and observe the commandments of God, and continue in the faith…ye must perish." (Mosiah 4:30). As President Monson said: "May each of you be able to echo in truth the line from Tennyson spoken by Sir Galahad: "My strength is as the strength of ten, because my heart is pure." (C.R., 10/1990).

We can remember that prayer is our passport to spiritual power that will transport us into the presence of the Holy Ghost. We want to collect as many of His visa stamps as possible. These validate that we have been keeping the commandments of God and repenting when necessary. President Monson closed the October 2010 General Conference with these words: "May God bless you, my brothers and sisters. May heaven's blessings be with you. May your homes be filled with love and courtesy and with the Spirit of the Lord. May you constantly nourish your testimonies of the gospel, that they will be a protection to you against the buffetings of Satan. Conference is now over. As we return to our homes, may we do so safely. May the spirit we have felt here abide with us as we go about those things that occupy us each day. May we show increased kindness toward one another. May we ever be found doing the work of the Lord. I love you. I pray for you."

"Meet Joe Black" was a film that was loosely based on the 1934 motion picture "Death Takes a Holiday." At its conclusion, the protagonist, who is about to die, asks Death: "Should I be afraid?" When Death answers him and says: "Not a man like you," we know that, in the face of the inevitable, everything is going to be all right. May we so live that when we reach out and are embraced by heaven, we are similarly blessed.

"Pride is the universal sin, the great vice.
The antidote for pride is humility."
(Ezra Taft Benson).

Pride

Author's note: Next to my essay on Humility, I think this is the best one I've ever written. ☺

This essay is as much about humility as it is about pride, because for every character trait that is synonymous with pride, its counterpart defines humility. For example, pride looks over to man and argues who is right, while humility looks up to God and cares about what is right. Pride asks only: "What do I want out of life?" while humility quietly implores: 'What would God have me do?' Pride is motivated by self-will, while humility is inspired by God's will. Pride is driven by the fear of man, while humility is nurtured by the love of God. The applause of the world rings in the ears of pride, while the accolades of heaven warm the hearts of the humble.

The Book of Mormon repeatedly speaks of pride, which could have just as easily been called "Nephite Disease." Remembering that the past is prologue, we read Moroni's warning: "Behold, the pride of this nation, or the people of the Nephites, (that) hath proven their destruction." (Moroni 8:27). To the Latter-day Saints, the Lord cautioned: "Beware of pride, lest ye become as the Nephites of old." (D&C 38:39). In the beginning, before the world was made, it was pride that was at the root of the rebellion of Lucifer, who not only competed with his Father's Plan, but also desired to dethrone God by seeking honor for himself. The Savior, on the other hand, was moved by humility. As His Father declared: "Behold, my Beloved Son, which was my Beloved and Chosen from the beginning, (Who) said unto me - Father, thy will be done, and the glory be thine forever." (Moses 4:2).

The prideful are self-centered, conceited, boastful, arrogant, and haughty, as opposed to the modesty, self-effacement, and deference of the humble, but the central feature of pride is enmity toward God and our fellowmen. There is no room for charity in the hearts of the proud. Hatred, hostility, and blind opposition are the raw manifestations of pride by which Satan wishes to reign over us, and with which he feeds his lust for power, while the sociability, approachability, and accommodation of the humble starve his strategy for domination.

The proud feel more comfortable with their own perception of truth than they do with God's omniscience. They pit their own abilities against His priesthood power, their own paltry accomplishments against His mighty works, and their stubborn will against His gentle counsel, never recognizing that it is from Him that all blessings flow. Those who refuse to accept His influence and authority have hard-hearts, stiff-necks, and are unashamedly rebellious. They lack the pliability and malleability of the humble. The proud are unrepentant because they are enamored with themselves, while the humble are smitten by the Spirit with remorse as they realize they are less than the dust of the earth. The proud are easily offended, and are sign seekers, and because they are past feeling, they require greater and greater intensities of stimulation to receive the same level of temporal or theological gratification. The humble are long suffering and faithful, and when things seem that they could not be worse, they are at their best, because they are particularly sensitive to the influence of the Holy Ghost.

The proud secretly wish that God would agree with them more frequently. They are uninterested in changing their opinions or in aligning themselves with His direction. They believe that they don't get what they deserve. Instead, they consume themselves in a senseless scramble of self-serving negotiation. Their objective is to receive more than their fair share. But then, their lives become a series of compromises, with no end in sight. They blindly make every man their adversary by pitting their intellect, opinion, works, wealth, and talents against all others. The humble, on the other hand, foster an atmosphere of cooperation and conciliation, and they pool their resources with those with whom they work in order to achieve mutually satisfying solutions to their problems.

The proud believe that it's not about having enough of the world's goods for their needs, but rather it's about accumulating more than their neighbors have. It's not about keeping up with the Joneses. It's about stepping on and climbing over the Joneses as they scramble up what they mistakenly think is the ladder of success. It's not about cooperation, but competition. As C. S. Lewis observed: "Pride gets no pleasure out of having something, only out of having more of it than the next man. It is the comparison that makes you proud, the pleasure of being above the rest." ("Mere Christianity," p. 109–110). Pride feeds on competition, and once that is gone, it hasn't got a leg to stand on.

The fear of what others may think of them blinds the proud to their potential, and to what God sees in them. Pride was the engine that drove the Jews to demand the crucifixion of the Savior. It was pride that compelled Saul to see David as his enemy, and to seek his life. An appeal to the pride of King Noah sent Abinadi to the flames. Because of pride, Herod's hands were stained with the blood of John the Baptist.

The proud argue, fight, exercise unrighteous dominion, and abuse their position. The humble speak softly, seek peaceful solutions, invite the Spirit to guide them in their interpersonal relationships, and honor the priesthood of God as the engine that drives their righteous behavior. The proud set the stage for secret combinations that are built up with one purpose in mind: To get gain and the glory of the world. (See Helaman 7:5). The humble work openly. They know that "nothing is secret, that shall not be made manifest; neither any thing hid, that shall not be known and come abroad." (Luke 8:17). Their lives are open books, for all to read, and to profit thereby.

The proud correctly believe that life is about opposition, but they have chosen poorly, by entering the fray on the wrong side of the line between right and wrong. "They have sown the wind, and they shall reap the whirlwind." (Hosea 8:7). They are in a constant state of competition for the approval of others, and love "the praise of men more than the praise of God." (John 12:42-43). Their sins lie in their motivation, as well as in their execution. The proud are not concerned about whether their wages meet their needs, and do not believe in equal pay for equal labor. They only want to be sure that they receive more than their co-workers do. The humble, on the other hand, are only vaguely aware of the promise that "he that exalteth himself shall be abased, and he that abaseth himself shall be exalted," because it is inherent to their nature to be their brother's keeper. (D&C 101:42, see Genesis 4:9).

When we are caught up in the snare of pride, we can lose both our physical and spiritual independence because we deliver our freedom to the bondage of the judgment of those who do not really matter, do not really care about us or our welfare, and who, ironically, may not even wield significant influence over either our successes or our failures. When we succumb to pride, we lose our perspective and can no longer make sound judgments, because the Holy Ghost, Who has no desire to compete with the noise and commotion of the world, withdraws to a safe distance in order to wait out the storm. When the proud allow the wiles of the adversary to overwhelm the revelations of God, they are quick to let go of the Rod of Iron, and instead rail against the truth.

The haughty recognize pride as a poison in others, but they rarely treat, or even acknowledge, their own infection. Their feverish appetite for telestial fast-food becomes a self-defeating addiction, and they ignore the dietary counsel of the One Who could teach them how to adopt a healthier spiritual lifestyle. They may point to the pride of the rich and the learned, but they fail to recognize the beam in their own eye, and they never look in the mirror, other than to admire themselves. Upon closer examination, they might recognize the telltale signs of arrogance and egotism, such as murmuring, which is the subdued and continually repeated expression of indistinct or inarticulate complaints or grumbling. Like an earthquake, the murmuring of the smug can build into harmonic waves with the power to undermine the foundations of relationships and institutions. Because the conceited and the proud expect results without responsibility, their murmuring is a cowardly act. While it is often conducted anonymously or behind the cloak of secrecy, its effects are felt publicly. The pride of those who murmur compels them to expect tangible returns without having made legitimate initial individual investments.

The proud are prone to gossip, which is a kindred spirit of murmuring, but is more focused on mindless chatter and speaking without real purpose. It is just as damaging, however, because it feeds voraciously on rumor, hearsay, second-hand information, innuendo, and vanity. Left unchecked, it may build into a self-perpetuating frequency leading to a cascade of unfortunate consequences. In its many forms, gossip has one common characteristic. The words once so loosely spoken cannot be gathered up later on. Gossip is like a pile of feathers left on the doorstep of those with whom one engages in idle conversation. As it drifts to the four winds, it cannot be recalled. Words so carelessly scattered about in gossip suggest that the mouth has been brought on-line before the brain.

The proud are fault-finders, who throw dirt, but lose ground in the process. They are like flies, whom we have all witnessed with revulsion, as they pass over healthy parts of the body to feed at open sores. At the dedication of the Kirtland Temple, Joseph Smith referred to those predatory individuals who sought to tear down the Latter-day work through fault finding. "We ask thee," he prayed, "to confound, and astonish, and to bring to shame and confusion, all those who have spread lying reports abroad, over the world, against thy servants, if they will not repent." (D&C 109:29).

Too often, the proud forget that when they point their finger at someone, there are three other fingers pointing right back at them. On the other hand, when the humble seek to discover the best in others, they somehow bring out the finest in themselves. How refreshing, when their appraisals reflect a nobler estimate of others and celebrate their potential. Even if but little good is known, the humble still speak in glowing terms of that which they do know to be true. If the humble are the first to discover a fault in others, they are the last to make it known to the world. They practice restraint, and are always ready to give courage and hope, and to speak kind words that come from the heart to awaken the soul to cheerfulness, "'til heart meets with heart and rejoices in friendship that ever is true." (Joseph L. Townsend, "Let Us Oft Speak Kind Words").

In their twisted thinking, the proud believe that they are somehow demeaned by those who have earned their own authority and respect. They do not feel that they need guidance or direction from priesthood leaders, and do not easily receive counsel or take correction. Their disobedience is the manifestation of a power struggle against those who legitimately rule over them, who may be parents, priesthood leaders, teachers, or even God. The proud do not easily admit their mistakes, and are not easily taught. They fanatically cling to their beliefs, because they redouble their efforts even as they lose sight of their objectives. They feel uncomfortable with the thought of changing their minds, because to do so would imply that they had been wrong.

Their behavior contrasts with that of the humble, who in their assessments and judgments are prone to praise loudly and blame softly. The humble understand that when straightening a bent nail, a pat on the back is better than a bump on the head. Before being critical, the humble remember that others may have had fewer advantages. The humble have learned to seek out supportive and sustaining experiences in the peaceful and pastoral countryside of clarity of the spirit, and they encourage others to remove themselves from the madding crowd, to clear their heads, to listen more attentively and see more plainly, to breathe more deeply, to inhale the fresh air of truth, and to be caressed by its gentle breeze, if they have not beforehand been refreshed by such influences and invigorated by such whisperings.

The proud often have only a weak foundation of doctrinal understanding of the gospel, and risk falling into transgression in consequence of their shallow comprehension of its principles. As they pick apart the scriptures or the words of those who preach, they distort the doctrines into meaningless fragments without any coherent connection. As Alma declared to the inhabitants of Ammonihah: "Behold, the scriptures are before you; if ye will wrest them it shall be to your own destruction." (Alma 13:20).

The appearance of pride is multi-faceted, but the Spirit provides face-recognition software to help identify its shape-shifting manifestations. What may have begun as a selfish tendency can morph into self-absorbed and self-seeking character flaws such as self-conceit, self-pity, self-fulfillment, and self-gratification. The humble rely upon intrinsic and self-reinforcing countermeasures such as altruism, self-denial, self-discipline, self-restraint, and self-sacrifice. The proud are easily offended and hold grudges, believing that they have been wronged by others who do not deserve their forgiveness, which they perversely withhold to keep them in their debt and to justify their own injured feelings. In their defensiveness, they rationalize their weaknesses, frailties, and failures, rather than seeking the peace that comes with repentance and forgiveness by God. Their self-esteem hinges upon their approval by the world. They only feel validated if others suffer disapprobation. Pride is particularly ugly because it says: "If you succeed, I am a failure," and "If I have value, that makes you worthless."

The antidote to pride is humility, meekness, and submissiveness. As Rudyard Kipling put it: "The tumult and the shouting dies; the captains and the kings depart. Still stands, thine ancient sacrifice, an humble and a contrite heart. Lord God of Hosts, be with us yet, lest we forget, lest we forget." ("Recessional").

We can choose to humble ourselves by accepting counsel and chastisement, by forgiving those who have offended us, by rendering selfless service, and by our good example that teaches others. We can unconsciously choose to be humble by adopting a lifestyle that complements and honors God, and that acknowledges His "glory, honor, power, majesty, might, dominion, truth, justice, judgment, mercy, and an infinity of fulness, from everlasting to everlasting." (D&C 109:77).

The antidote to pride, the principle that has been woven into this essay, is frustratingly simple. The quiet example of the Savior is illustration enough. Humility will conquer our pride and cleanse our inner vessel as we yield to the enticings of the Holy Spirit, put off the natural man, and become Saints through the Atonement of Christ.

"The task ahead of us is never as great as the power behind us."
(J. Reuben Clark, Jr.).

Priesthood Keys

Our 5th Article of Faith states: "We believe that a man must be called of God, by prophecy, and by the laying on of hands by those who are in authority, to preach the gospel and administer in the ordinances thereof." We have respect for our priesthood leaders, and we honor their authority to exercise these keys. This Article of Faith resonates within us, because as Brigham Young taught: "Every gospel principle carries within itself its own witness of the truth." (D.B.Y., p. 65). The principle of authority requires no external corroborating witness. Because it is revelatory, it stands independently.

David O McKay alluded to authority when he said of the personal interview each of us will one day have with the Savior: "He will want a summary of your activity in your church assignments. He will not necessarily be interested in what assignments you have had, for in his eyes the home teacher and a mission president are probably equals, but he will request a summary of how you have been of service to your fellow man in your church assignments." (Reported by Cloyd Hofheins in an address to the Seventies Quorum of the Provo Utah Oak Hills Stake, 5/16/1982).

We are taught to obey those who preside over us in the exercise of their priesthood responsibilities. For example, just a year after N. Eldon Tanner took his place as the least senior member of the Quorum of The Twelve, he was called as a Counselor in the First Presidency, a position in which he presided over Joseph Fielding Smith, who was the President of the Quorum of the Twelve. President Tanner later expressed his gratitude for President Smith's support. "When I was called to the First Presidency, though he was the senior member of the Twelve and had been in office for over fifty years, he showed great respect for me in that position and gave me full support and confidence." ("Ensign," 8/1972).

One time during Joseph Fielding Smith's service as an Apostle, the First Presidency and Quorum of the Twelve Apostles were engaged in an ongoing discussion about a difficult question. "Elder Smith had expressed a strong opinion about the issue. One day, Heber J. Grant, who was then the President of the Church, came to Elder Smith's office. President Grant explained that after prayerfully considering the issue, he had felt impressed to recommend an action that differed from Elder Smith's views. Immediately Elder Smith voiced his support for President Grant's decision. He later declared, "So far as I am concerned, when the President of the Church says the Lord has manifested to him or inspired him to do anything, I support him fully in that action." ("Joseph Fielding Smith: Gospel Scholar, Prophet of God," p. 342).

Elder Smith respected the priesthood keys that gave President Grant the power and authority to direct the work of the Lord. As he explained: "There is a difference between receiving an office in the priesthood and in receiving the keys of the priesthood. While all men hold the priesthood who are ordained to any office, yet there are special, or directing, authorities, bestowed upon those who are called to preside. These authorities are called keys. Priesthood keys are the right of presidency; they are the power and authority to govern and direct the Lord's affairs. Those who hold them have power to govern and control the manner in which others may serve in the priesthood." (C.R., 4/1967).

Priesthood keys are our secret weapons in the ideological war in which we are engaged against the powers of darkness. They unlock the chains that would otherwise bind us to sin and drag us down to hell. In some cases, they may be our only defense against moral equivocation. When we stand against the world, and against a rule of law that has fallen far below gospel standards, priesthood keys can make us invincible.

On the stake level, the stake president holds priesthood keys. In the ward, the bishop, elder's quorum president, teacher's quorum president and deacon's quorum president hold priesthood keys. The high priest group leader and auxiliary presidents do not hold priesthood keys. The amazing thing about priesthood keys is that when those who hold them exercise their power, the service of others within auxiliary organizations is guided with spectacular results. In fact, when we "are commissioned by the one who holds these keys, then our acts are valid. That which we do is sealed and ratified in the church both on earth and in the heavens." (Joseph Fielding Smith, C.R., 4/1967).

The importance of priesthood keys cannot be overstated. Following the mortal ministry of the Lord, a long night of apostasy ensued because of the loss of priesthood authority. There needed to be a restoration of these priesthood keys in order to legitimately administer the gospel. When the Lord revealed to Joseph Smith the doctrines of salvation, members of the church began to characterize him as the "Prophet of The Restoration." We believe that "the Lord does not recognize any ordinance or ceremony, even though it be made or performed in His name, unless it is in accordance with His will and done by one who is recognized as His authorized servant. It was for that reason that He sent from His presence holy messengers to Joseph Smith and others, to restore that which had been taken from the earth, even the fullness of the gospel, and the fullness and the keys of priesthood." (Joseph Fielding Smith, "Ensign," 1/ 1972).

It was not enough that John The Baptist had come to restore the keys of the Aaronic Priesthood, or that Peter, James, and John restored the keys of the Melchizedek Priesthood. It is true that by virtue of this authority the church was organized. But the single-minded sacrifice of the Saints to build the Kirtland Temple attests to the fact that "all the keys of all dispensations had to be brought in order to fulfill the words of the prophets and the purposes of the Lord in bringing to pass a complete restoration of all things. Therefore, the father of the human family, the first man on the earth, Adam, had to come, and he came with his power. Moses came, and others. All who had keys came and bestowed their authorities. We have not the dates when some of these authorities were made manifest, but the Prophet Joseph Smith, in writing to the Saints in Nauvoo in regard to the salvation of the dead, declared, as we have it recorded in D&C 128:17-21, that all these prophets came with their keys in the dispensation in which we live." (Joseph Fielding Smith, "The Keys of the Priesthood Restored," p. 101).

There came "the voice of Michael, the archangel; the voice of Gabriel, and of Raphael, and of divers angels, from Michael or Adam down to the present time, all declaring their dispensation, their rights, their keys, their honors, their majesty and glory, and the power of their priesthood; giving line upon line, precept upon precept; here a little, and there a little; giving us consolation by holding forth that which is to come, confirming our hope!" (D&C 128:21).

Paul taught that "in the dispensation of the fulness of times" there would be gathered "together in one all things in Christ, both which are in heaven, and which are on earth." (Ephesians 1:10). Just so, Joseph Smith recorded that in the Kirtland Temple, "the heavens were again opened unto us; and Moses appeared before us, and committed unto us the keys of the gathering of Israel from the four parts of the earth, and the leading of the ten tribes from the land of the north. After this, Elias appeared, and committed the dispensation of the gospel of Abraham, saying that in us, and our seed, all generations after us should be blessed. After this vision had closed, another great and glorious vision burst upon us; for Elijah the prophet, who was taken to heaven without tasting death, stood before us, and said: Behold, the time has fully come, which was spoken of by the mouth of Malachi - testifying that he (Elijah) should be sent, before the great and dreadful day of the Lord come - To turn the hearts of the fathers to the children, and the children to the fathers, lest the whole earth be smitten with a curse - Therefore, the keys of this dispensation are committed into your hands; and by this ye may know that the great and dreadful day of the Lord is near, even at the doors." (D&C 110:11-16).

Today, the President of the Quorum of The First Presidency holds the keys over all the church. These keys came from Joseph Smith to the Twelve Apostles, with the right of Presidency vested in the senior apostle. When the President of the church dies, the senior apostle (the President of the Quorum of The Twelve) is set apart as President of the church by the Quorum (who hold the keys). Shortly before his martyrdom, Joseph Smith bestowed upon the Twelve Apostles, who constitute the second quorum in the church, the First Presidency being the first quorum in the church, all the keys and all the ordinances and priesthood necessary for them to hold in order to carry on the work. "This priesthood and these keys have been given to each man who has been set apart as a member of the Council of the Twelve. But since they are the right of presidency, they can only be exercised in full by the senior apostle of God on earth, who is the President of the church." (Joseph Fielding Smith, "Eternal Keys and the Right to Preside," p. 87).

"The President of the church holds the keys over all the church. In him is concentrated the power of the Priesthood. He holds all the keys of every nature, pertaining to the dispensation of the Fulness of Times. All the keys of former dispensations which have been revealed are vested in him." (Joseph Fielding Smith, "Doctrines of Salvation," 3:135). He may delegate and withdraw authority as he sees fit and receives inspiration so to do.

This authority includes the sealing power of the priesthood. "No man can officiate in and confer the blessings of the temple without the authority to do so being delegated to him by the President of the church. No man can officiate in any capacity in this church without the virtue accompanying him in that act, as it is obtained through the power and keys held by the President of the church." (Joseph Fielding Smith, C.R., 4/1967).

When the apostles or other brethren visit the stakes of Zion and are appointed to set in order anything therein requiring attention, they do so by virtue of the commission, or authority, delegated to them by the President of the church. Their authority is general, in nature.

In short, the united voice of those who hold the keys of the kingdom will always guide the church and its members. Joseph Fielding Smith reassured us: "I think there is one thing which we should have exceedingly clear in our minds. Neither the President of the church, nor the First Presidency, nor the united voice of the First Presidency and the Twelve will ever lead the Saints astray or send forth counsel to the world that is contrary to the mind and will of the Lord."

He continued: "An individual may fall by the wayside, or have views, or give counsel that falls short of what the Lord intends. But the voice of the First Presidency and the united voice of those others who hold with them the keys of the kingdom shall always guide the Saints and the world in those paths where the Lord wants them to be.

Finally, he testified "that if we shall look to the First Presidency and follow their counsel and direction, no power on earth can stay or change our course as a church, and as individuals we shall gain peace in this life and be inheritors of eternal glory in the world to come." ("Eternal Keys and the Right to Preside," p. 88).

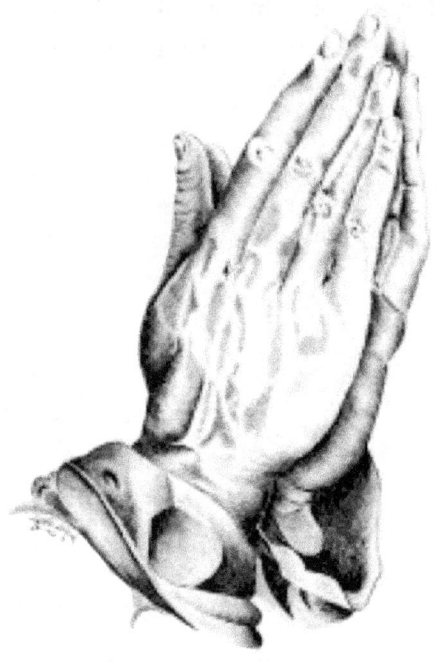

The Kirtland Temple Dedicatory Prayer,
given by the Prophet Joseph Smith.

A Primer
On Addressing Deity

The prayer that has been preserved for us as D&C Section 109 was "offered at the dedication of the temple at Kirtland, Ohio, March 27, 1836. According to the Prophet's written statement, this prayer was given to him by revelation." (Superscript to D&C 109). In the 80 verses of this prayer, Deity is addressed 42 times by at least 14 different name-titles, including once as the "Lord God of Israel, the "Most High," "God," the "Mighty God of Jacob," the "Lord God Almighty," "Jesus Christ the Son of thy bosom," the "Holy Father," "the Son of Man," and "God and the Lamb," three times as "Jehovah," six times as the Holy Father," and no fewer than nineteen times as "Lord."

"Latter-day Saints believe that Elohim is our God and Father, and Jehovah is Jesus Christ. (See D&C 110:1-4). Although these titles may not have always been used in this way anciently, Latter-day prophets have reinforced this belief, for example, in the following statement by President Joseph F. Smith: "Among the spirit children of Elohim the firstborn was and is Jehovah or Jesus Christ to whom all others are juniors." ("Improvement Era," 8/1916).

These titles may be thought of as a naming convention used in the modern church for clarity and precision. Since Christ may appropriately be spoken of as "the Father" in many situations, Latter-day Saints use these name-titles to avoid ambiguity, regardless of in which 'role' a divine Personage is being characterized.

Since this terminology was not standardized for convenience and clarity prior to the twentieth century, readers are cautioned not to expect the early writings of the church to always reflect a practice that arose only decades later. Likewise, attempting to read the Bible as if its writers followed the same modern protocols is anachronistic, and may lead to confusion and misinterpretation.

Terminology can also be confusing because in the scriptures and even in modern revelation, Jesus often speaks for the Father by right of divine investiture. "Since he (Jesus) is one with the Father in all of the attributes of perfection, and since he exercises the power and authority of the Father...the Father (sometimes) puts his own name on the Son and authorizes him to speak in the first person as though he were the Father." (Bruce R. McConkie, "Mormon Doctrine," p. 130-131).

There are numerous examples of divine investiture in scripture. The clearest biblical examples involve angels speaking in behalf of God or Christ (see Genesis 22:11-12, Exodus 3:2 & 6, 23:20-21, and Revelation 1:1, 19:9-13, and 22:8-16), although Christ also spoke as though he were the Father" on many occasions throughout the Old Testament. (See, for example, Genesis 17:1, 35:11, and Exodus 6:3). Christ is also referred to in scripture as "the Almighty." (See Revelation 1:8 & 18, 4:8, and 11:17). It is probably for this reason that many Christians mistakenly identify Elohim and Jehovah as the same person.

The concept of Christ as the Father is clearly set forth in a 1916 statement entitled, "The Father and the Son: A Doctrinal Exposition by the First Presidency and the Twelve." Additional support for the LDS differentiation in the use of divine titles is found in New and Old Testament scriptures, as cited above. Matthew and Mark reported that, while on the cross, Jesus cried out to his Father using the name Eli (See Matthew 27:46) or Eloi (see Mark 15:34). Both of these names are regarded by scholars as the Aramaic equivalents of El or Elohim.

Although allusions to Christ's sonship are somewhat rare in the Old Testament, they do exist. Daniel 3:25 describes a fourth individual in Nebuchadnezzar's furnace whose form was like a "Son of God (Elah)." Proverbs 30:4 speaks of the "son" of the creator, and Daniel 7:13 refers to the glorious coming of the "Son of man." (Compare John 3:13 and Moses 6:57). Hosea 11:1 was quoted by Matthew, in chapter 23 verse 15, as a prophecy that God's "son" would be called out of Egypt, and we should not forget that Isaiah's famous messianic prophecy foretold the birth of a son who would also be known by the titles "everlasting Father" and "mighty God." (Isaiah 7:14 & 9:16). All of these scriptures provide evidence that, as Nephi stated, many do now "stumble exceedingly" because of the "plain and precious thing which have been taken away" from the scriptures." (1 Nephi 13:26-30, 34, and 40).

The relevant verses in D&C Section 109 are:

Verse 1: "Thanks be to thy name, O **Lord God of Israel**."
Verses 3, 4, 31, 33, 43, 44, 46, 47, 48, 49, 50, 51, 54, 60, 68, 69, 71, 72, & 78: "**O Lord**"
Verse 4: Heavenly Father is addressed as "Holy Father in the name of **Jesus Christ, the Son of thy bosom.**"
Verse 5: Jesus Christ is referenced as "**the Son of Man.**"
Verse 6: The Prophet addresses **Heavenly Father** and makes reference to a revelation given by Him. (D&C 88:117-120). However, D&C Section 88 is clearly a revelation given to Joseph Smith by Jesus Christ.
Verses 10, 14, 22, 24, 29, & 47: "**Holy Father.**"
Verse 13: The temple is referred to as both "the **Lord's house,**" and as "**thy house.**"

Verse 16: The temple is referred to as "a house of glory and of **God**."

Verse 17-19: The Prophet prayed "that all the incomings of thy people, into this house, may be in the name of the **Lord**; That all their outgoings from this house may be in the name of the **Lord**; And that all their salutations may be in the name of the Lord, with holy hands, uplifted to the **Most High**."

Verse 22: "**Holy Father**" is again addressed, and then in the same verse the Prophet asks "that thy name may be upon them." (The name is commonly accepted as "Jesus Christ").

Verses 34, 42, and 56: "O **Jehovah**" (A name title of Jesus Christ).

Verse 47: In this verse, the Prophet address God as both "**Holy Father**" and as "**Lord**."

Verse 68: The Prophet refers to God as both "Lord" and as the "**Mighty God of Jacob**."

Verses 71 – 73: The Prophet refers to the church as "thy church."

Verse 75: The Prophet pleads for the day when "we shall be caught up in the cloud to meet thee, that we may ever be with the **Lord**."

Verse 77: "O **Lord God Almighty**."

Verse 79: The Prophet prays for acceptance of "this church, to put upon it thy name." Then he references "**God and the Lamb**."

"From the prophet of the
Restoration to the prophet of
our own year, the communication
line is unbroken, a light, brilliant and
penetrating. The sound of the voice of
the Lord is a continuous melody
and a thunderous appeal."
(Spencer W. Kimball).

A Primer
On Personal Revelation

We take for granted that prophets, seers, and revelators receive revelation. But, wouldn't it be wonderful if, for each of us, the sound of the voice of the Lord that is so familiar to them were for us "a continuous melody and a thunderous appeal?" (Spencer W. Kimball, C.R., 4/1977).

It is possible that one of the reasons the Lord provided us with the Doctrine & Covenants was that we might utilize it as a resource to fine-tune our revelatory sixth sense? "Most of the revelations of the Prophet Joseph Smith in this holy record," observed Spencer W. Kimball, "came as deep impressions." ("The Teachings of Spencer W. Kimball," p. 455–456). In fact, "most recorded revelations in the Doctrine and Covenants were a consciousness of direction from above. This is the sort of revelation individuals often have for their own needs." (Spencer W. Kimball, "Faith Precedes the Miracle," p. 30). When we have these impressions, we are experiencing revelation from above.

D&C 6:22-23 provides counsel to Oliver Cowdery that confirms the teachings of President Kimball: "Did I not speak peace to your mind concerning the matter?" the Lord asked. "What greater witness can you have than from God?" Have we not all experienced peace to our minds concerning matters of great personal importance?

Members of the church do not have a monopoly on revelation. Millions believe there are "angels among us." (Lyrics by "Alabama"). Countless newlyweds believe that their match was made in heaven. Others believe that they have been "touched by an angel" in one way or another. Promptings and impressions influence "black and white, bond and free, male and female (and) both Jew and Gentile" to move in positive directions. (2 Nephi 26:3). Persons of conscience among all creeds believe their actions are guided and directed by the Spirit. Christopher Columbus said after his epic voyage of discovery: "The Lord was well disposed to my desire and he bestowed upon me courage and understanding. Knowledge of seafaring he gave me in abundance, and of geometry and astronomy likewise. The Lord with provident hand unlocked my mind, sent me upon the sea, and gave me fire for the deed. Those who heard of my enterprise called it foolish, mocked me, and laughed. But who can doubt that the Holy Ghost inspired me?" ("Columbus, the Don Quixote of the Seas," p. 19-20).

Before they commit to baptism, those who have seriously investigated the church receive the confirming witness of the Spirit that what they are studying is true. They may have the same intensity of experience as that reported by Lorenzo Snow, who recalled: "Previous to accepting the ordinance of baptism, in my investigations of the principles taught by the Latter-day Saints...I was thoroughly convinced that obedience to those principles would impart miraculous powers, manifestations and revelations. With sanguine expectations of this result, I received the baptism and ordinance of laying on of hands by one who professed to have divine authority; and, having thus yielded obedience to these ordinances, I was in constant expectation of the fulfillment of the promise of the reception of the Holy Ghost.

(Shortly thereafter), I heard a sound, just above my head, like the rustling of silken robes, and immediately the Spirit of God descended upon me, completely enveloping my whole person, filling me, from the crown of my head to the soles of my feet, and O, the joy and happiness I felt! No language can describe the almost instantaneous transition from a dense cloud of mental and spiritual darkness into a refulgence of light and knowledge. As it was at that time imparted to my understanding, I then received a perfect knowledge that God lives, that Jesus Christ is the Son of God, and of the restoration of the holy Priesthood, and the fulness of the gospel. It was a complete baptism—a tangible immersion in the heavenly principle or element, the Holy Ghost; and even more real and physical in its effects upon every part of my system than the immersion by water; dispelling forever, so long as reason and memory last, all possibility of doubt or fear in relation to the fact handed down to us historically, that the 'Babe of Bethlehem' is truly the Son of God; also the fact that He is now being revealed to the children of men, and communicating knowledge, the same as in the Apostolic times. I was perfectly satisfied, as well I might be, for my expectations were more than realized, I think I may safely say, in an infinite degree." ("Biography and Family Record of Lorenzo Snow," p. 7-9).

But why don't more people have such powerful revelatory experiences? Why isn't it more common to have "a tangible immersion in the heavenly principle or element?" President Kimball said: "We do not expect the people of the world to understand such things, for they will always be quick to assign their own reasons or to discount the divine process of revelation." ("New Era," 4/1980, p. 36). While revelation can only be recognized on God's terms, curiously, He waits on the initiative of His children in a process that they cannot summarily influence or amend.

The feeble efforts of the worldly to disparage its delivery in order to bring revelation into harmony with their views ring hollow against the thunder and lightning of Sinai. Their determination to synchronize its circulation with their expectations cannot marginalize its importance. Their attempts to meddle with its manifestation in order to satisfy prurient interest cannot amend His inevitable decrees. Though they tamper with its expression to indulge their wicked and adulterous cravings, the signs and tokens remain untarnished. They may reinvent its flow and rework its stream according to Satan's counterfeit coin of spurious currency; they may tinker with its phrasing to homogenize its powerful message and to assuage their consciences; they may modify its distribution to greedily capture greater market share among the masses, and they may demean its delivery in a weak attempt to hustle the heavens. But they will fail in their efforts to hush the host of angels who are only waiting for a confirmation of our faith, that they might sound the clarion call of their trumpets in our ears. The wicked cannot erase the simple fact that it is God in whom we trust.

As Joseph Smith taught: "Does it remain for a people who never had faith enough to call down one scrap of revelation from heaven, and for all they have now are indebted to the faith of another people who lived hundreds and thousands of years before them, does it remain for them to say how much God has spoken and how much He has not spoken?" ("Teachings," p. 61).

"How presumptuous and arrogant," declared President Kimball, "for any man to say God is unapproachable, unknowable, unseeable, or unhearable because he has not prepared himself for the experience? ("Church News," 6/4/1966). Even members of a church that embraces revelation as a tenet of its faith run the risks associated with their neglect of preparation to receive streams of enlightenment from the heavens.

As the prophet Mormon warned: "Yea, wo unto him that shall deny the revelations of the Lord, and that shall say the Lord no longer worketh by revelation, or by prophecy, or by gifts, or by tongues, or by healings, or by the power of the Holy Ghost!" (3 Nephi 29:6). His warning extends to members of the church whose shallow understanding of the scriptures, or whose lack of commitment to follow the teachings the Lord's authorized servants, betrays their implicit denial of the revelations.

Even among the ranks of the righteous, perhaps the failure to recognize revelation constitutes a denial of sorts, as well. President Kimball observed: "Many people expect that if there be revelation it will come with awe-inspiring, earth-shaking display. For many it is hard to accept revelations as deep, unassailable impressions settling down on the mind and heart as dew from heaven or as the dawn dissipates the darkness of night. Expecting the spectacular, (they) may not be fully alerted to the constant flow of revealed communication." That may explain the process of revelatory experience in the church. When the Spirit settles upon the mind of the Saints and settles in their hearts as the dew from heaven, it is akin to having had a tangible immersion in the heavenly principle or element.

President Kimball went on to explain: "When, after prayer and fasting, important decisions are made (by General Authorities), new missions and new stakes are created, new patterns and policies initiated, the news is taken for granted and possibly thought of as mere human calculation. But to those who sit in the intimate circles and hear the prayers of the prophet and the testimony of the man of God; to those who see the astuteness of his deliberations, to them he is verily a prophet. To hear him conclude important new developments with such solemn expressions as 'the Lord is pleased,' 'that move is right,' or 'our Heavenly Father has spoken,' is to know positively." ("Instructor," 8/1960, p. 257).

Should we not also be able to say, after prayerful inquiry: "The Lord is pleased, the move is right, our Heavenly Father has spoken?" We do not have to be ecclesiastical leaders of the church to receive revelation from the Lord. "God hath not revealed anything to Joseph, but what He will make known unto the Twelve, and even the least Saint may know all things as fast as he is able to bear them." (Joseph Smith, "Teachings," p. 149).

We need personal revelation, perhaps as never before. In 1991, at the dawn of the creation of the Internet (1990), and before the introduction of I Pads, smart phones, snap-chat, Facebook, HBO, and Netflix, Boyd K. Packer said: "No one of us can survive in the world of today, much less in what it soon will become, without personal inspiration" (C.R., 10/1991). His statement underscores an observation made long ago, by Helen Keller: "The only thing worse than being blind is having sight but no vision."

When honing our revelatory capabilities, we can build upon the experiences we have already had, that includes confirmation of the Spirit relating to our testimonies of Jesus Christ and of His gospel, of the divine authenticity of The Book of Mormon and of the mission of the prophet Joseph Smith, of divine truths including tithing, the law of the Fast, and the Word of Wisdom, of the ordinances of the temple, and of our familiarity with personal revelation to receive guidance beyond our own limited understanding in answering life's questions, meeting challenges, and making decisions. How fitting when our testimony meetings consist of our discreet expressions relating to our familiarity with these revelatory experiences.

Each day, we spend roughly sixteen hours going about our daily business in confident expectation of an outpouring of the gifts of inspiration, or divine creativity, and discernment, or keenly selective judgment. Our anticipation is justified and will enjoy fruition if we have first qualified for such guidance "by setting our lives in order and by becoming acquainted with the Lord through frequent and regular conversations with him." (Spencer W. Kimball, "Ensign," 6/1975). He "will not force himself upon people; and if they do not believe, they will receive no visitation. If they are content to depend upon their own limited calculations and interpretations, then, of course, the Lord will leave them to their chosen fate." (Spencer W. Kimball, C.R., 10/1966). As He counseled Oliver Cowdery through Joseph Smith, so it is with each of us: "You must study it out in your mind; then you must ask me if it be right, and if it is right I will cause that your bosom shall burn within you; therefore, you shall feel that it is right." (D&C 9:8).

The Prophet Joseph can be our example. What he did in preparation for his great theophany in the Sacred Grove can be our pattern, as well. His "mind was called up to serious reflection and great uneasiness." His "feelings were deep and often poignant," and he "attended...meetings as often as occasion would permit." His "mind at times was greatly excited" to understand the will of God." He wondered to himself: "How shall I know" and recognize the truth? (J.S.H. 1:8-10). His experience underscores several basic principles. As we study matters out in our own minds preparatory to receiving answers to our prayers, we become actively, rather than passively, involved in the processes of inquiry and discovery. We dust off our agency, and actually use it as it was envisioned. We expand our capabilities as we exercise the gifts, resources, and reserves provided by the principles of the Plan of Salvation. President Kimball promised: "If there be eyes to see, there will be visions to inspire. If there be ears to hear, there will be revelations to experience. If there be hearts which can understand, know this: that the exalting truths of Christ's gospel will no longer be hidden and mysterious, and all earnest seekers may know God and his program." (C.R., 10/1966).

The Doctrine & Covenants illustrates how studying and contemplating the scriptures can help us to grow spiritually. Joseph F. Smith recalled therein how he had sat in his room "pondering over the scriptures, and reflecting upon the great atoning sacrifice" of the Savior. He wrote that as he did so, he "was greatly impressed" by the scriptures, so much so that "the eyes of (his) understanding were opened, and the Spirit of the Lord rested" upon him. (D&C 138:1-11).

Joseph Smith's similar experience when reading James 1:5-6 speaks for itself. He recalled: "Never did any passage...come with more power to the heart of man than this did at this time to mine. It seemed to enter with great force into every feeling of my heart. I reflected on it again and again." (J.S.H. 1:11-12). As Dallin Oaks explained: "We do not overstate the point when we say that the scriptures can be a Urim and Thummim to assist each of us to receive personal revelation. Because we believe that scripture reading can help us receive revelation, we are encouraged to read the scriptures again and again." ("Ensign," 1/1995). Boyd K. Packer pointed out: "No message appears in scripture more times, in more ways, than: 'Ask, and ye shall receive.'" (C.R., 10/1991). In fact, most of the revelations in the Doctrine and Covenants came as answers to questions that the Prophet Joseph Smith had posed to the Lord.

When we act in faith, we will be blessed, as was Oliver Cowdery, with "a knowledge of whatsoever things (we) shall ask in faith, with an honest heart, believing that (we) shall receive." (D&C 8:1). But we must ask in earnest, with sincerity, and with genuine humility and meekness. "Do you offer a few trite words and worn-out phrases, or do you talk intimately to the Lord?" asked Spencer W. Kimball. "Do you pray occasionally when you should be praying regularly, often constantly? When you pray, do you just speak, or do you also listen? Do you give thanks or merely ask for favors?" ("New Era," 3/1978).

The example of Joseph Smith in the Sacred Grove teaches us how to pray with equal intensity, and with a power of concentration that unlocks and then nudges open the door to heaven, allowing shafts of celestial light to flood our minds and our spirits. He prayed vocally, knelt in humility, and offered up the desires of his heart, and when necessity required it, he exerted all of his powers to call upon God. (J.S.H. 1:13–16).

Later, when the Lord spoke through him, the Savior said to those who followed his example: "Blessed art thou for what thou hast done; for thou hast inquired of me, and behold, as often as thou hast inquired thou hast received instruction of my Spirit." (D&C 6:14). As President Kimball promised: "The Lord is eager to see (our) first awakening desires and (our) beginning efforts to penetrate the darkness. Having granted freedom of decision, he must permit (us) to grope (our) way until (we) reach for the light. But when (we) begin to hunger, when (our) arms begin to reach, when (our) knees begin to bend and (our) voices becomes articulate, then and not till then does our Lord push back the horizons, draw back the veil, and make it possible for (us) to emerge from dim uncertain stumbling to sureness, in heavenly light." (Munich Germany Area Conference, 8/1973). He further counseled: "If (we) rise from (our) knees having merely said words, (we) should fall back on (our) knees and remain there until (we) have established communication with the Lord." ("The Teachings of Spencer W. Kimball," p. 124).

Dallin Oaks taught: "We cannot have the companionship of the Holy Ghost - the medium of individual revelation - if we are in transgression, or if we are angry, or if we are in rebellion against God's chosen authorities." ("Ensign," 3/1997). We must seek revelation from God in an attitude of deep humility, which is a character trait that does not come consciously or easily. David Whitmer recalled that one morning when Joseph Smith was getting ready to continue his translation of The Book of Mormon, "something went wrong about the house and he was put out about it. Something that Emma, his wife, had done. Oliver and I went upstairs and Joseph came up soon after to continue the translation but he could not do anything. He could not translate a single syllable. He went downstairs, out into the orchard, and made supplication to the Lord; was gone about an hour—came back to the house, and asked Emma's forgiveness and then came upstairs where we were, and then the translation went on all right. He could do nothing save he was humble and faithful."("Comprehensive History of the Church," 1:131).

Boyd K. Packer taught (back in 1991): "Inspiration comes more easily in peaceful settings. The world grows increasingly noisy. Clothing and grooming and conduct are looser and sloppier and more disheveled. Raucous music, with obscene lyrics blasted through amplifiers while lights flash psychedelic colors, characterizes the drug culture. Variations of these things are gaining wide acceptance and influence over our youth. This trend to more noise, more excitement, more contention, less restraint, less dignity, less formality is not coincidental nor innocent nor harmless. The first order issued by a commander mounting a military invasion is the jamming of the channels of communication of those he intends to conquer. Irreverence suits the purposes of the adversary by obstructing the delicate channels of revelation in both mind and spirit." (C.R., 10/1991).

Revelation is at the foundation of the living gospel of Jesus Christ, and is a cornerstone of God's perfect Plan of Salvation. "There are those who would assume that the printing and binding of these sacred records would be the "end of the prophets." But again, we testify to the world that revelation continues and that the vaults and files of the church contain these revelations, which come month to month and day to day. Of all things, that for which we should be most grateful today is that the heavens are indeed open and that the restored church of Jesus Christ is founded upon the rock of revelation. Continuous revelation is, indeed, the very lifeblood of the gospel of the living Lord and Savior, Jesus Christ." (Spencer W. Kimball, C.R., 4/1977).

The Plan provides the loom upon which we are free to weave the complex tapestry of our lives, to create our own coat of many colors. But central to the vitalization and execution of our efforts is direct contact with our Father in Heaven. Our introduction and our active participation in the Plan presupposes the establishment of ongoing two-way communication with its Author.

Chauncey Riddle seriously accepted that challenge, and his expressions echo the similar experiences of countless members of The Church of Jesus Christ of Latter-day Saints. He wrote: "I felt I had received some revelation before. However, I saw that random revelation was not sufficient. To be a rock, a bastion of surety, revelation must be something on which one can count and receive in every occasion of real need. I began to seek it actively. I prayed, I fasted, and I lived the gospel as best I knew. I was faithful in my church duties. I tried to live up to every scruple that my conscience enjoined upon me. And dependable revelation did come. Intermittently, haltingly at first, then steadily, over some years it finally came to be a mighty stream of experience. I came to know that at any time of day or night, in any circumstance, for any real need, I could get help.

That help came in the form of feelings of encouragement when things seemed hopeless. It came in ideas to unravel puzzles that blocked my accomplishment. It came in priesthood blessings that were fully realized. It came in whisperings of prophecy that were fulfilled. It came in support and even anticipation of what the General Authorities of the church would say and do in general conference. It came in the gifts of the Spirit, as the wonders of eternity were opened to the eyes of my understanding. That stream of spiritual experience is today for me a river of living water that nourishes my soul in every situation. It is the most important factor of my life. If it were taken away, all that I have and am would be dust and ashes. It is the basis of my love, life, understanding, hope, and progress. My only regret is that although this river is so wonderful, I have not been able to take full advantage of it, as yet. My life does not yet conform to all that I know. But now I do know; I do not just believe." ("Sunstone," 5/1988).

"Give me six hours to chop down a tree,
and I will spend the first four sharpening the axe."
(Abraham Lincoln).

Proper Prior Planning
Prevents Poor Priesthood Performance

Long before he saved the Union, Abraham Lincoln famously said: "I will prepare myself, and someday my chance will come." LaVelle Edwards, one of the most successful college football coaches of all time, often said that the key quality he looked for in his players was not the will to win, but the will to prepare.

Our preparation makes us fit to act honorably, to make our word our bond, to do our very best, and to be guided by the Spirit in everything we attempt to do. Our preparation is measured against our own high standards. When we too easily reach our goals, a frank reappraisal may be necessary. We may need to acknowledge that we have aimed too low, and we have achieved our objectives far too easily, with too little effort, and with too little expenditure of energy. We may need to recalibrate and refocus our vision so that it is trained on celestial objectives.

Trying times demand that we do our duty to God. That quality of courage requires availability. Brigham Young once declared: "I never count the cost of anything. I just find out what the Lord wants me to do, and I do it." That is this kind of total commitment and dedication that establishes the baseline of spirited action in the kingdom.

We owe our best efforts to execute our responsibility to do our duty to our country, as well; to recognize our sphere of influence as citizens and members of the church; to follow guidelines that will lead us to make wise choices; to help others at all times; to keep ourselves physically strong, and to take care of our bodies so that they will serve us well throughout our lifetimes.

We need to keep ourselves mentally awake; to develop our minds both in the classroom of academia as well as in the laboratory of life; to be curious about everything around us, and to work hard to make the most of our opportunities. We need to remember that the best education is to be perpetually thrilled with life.

We need to be morally straight, and prepare ourselves to be persons of strong character; to be as George Washington, who wrote to his friend Alexander Hamilton: "I hope I shall always possess firmness and virtue enough to maintain what I consider the most enviable of all titles, the character of an 'Honest Man.'" (Mount Vernon, 8/28/ 1788).

We prepare ourselves to lead well-rounded and productive lives through service and education, as we enlarge our perspective and gain experience, so that we will be better prepared to live in eternity in the mansions of our Father.

"Once we had wooden chalices and golden priests. Now we have golden chalices and wooden priests."
(Ralph Waldo Emerson).

Recognizing
The Church Of Jesus Christ

Today, in my community (in Spokane, Washington) there are a lot of churches. Among them are the following fifty: Jehovah's Witnesses, The Church of The Resurrection, The Cornerstone Pentecostal Church, Jesus is The Answer, The Living Truth Tabernacle, Amazing Grace Fellowship, The Assembly of God, The Crosswind Church, The Glad Tidings Church, The Trinity Lighthouse, The Baptist Church, The Living Water Community Church, The Shiloh Hills Fellowship, Christ Our Hope Bible Church, The Church of The Nazarene, The Catholic Church, The Christian Life Church, The Calvary Chapel, The Presbyterian Church, The Methodist Church, The Holy Temple Church of God in Christ, The Slavic Christian Church, The Refreshing Soaring Church of God in Christ, The Unity Church of Truth, The Life River Fellowship, The Cornerstone Pentecostal Church, The Northview Bible Church, The Lutheran Church, The New Beginnings Church, The Pentecostal Evangelical Church, The River of Life Open Bible Church, The Spokane Dream Center Women's Discipleship, The Unity Church of Truth, The New Hope Christian Reformed Church, The First Church of Christ Scientist, The Church of Christ, The Jesus Lord Church of the Living God International, The Church of Jesus Christ of Latter-day Saints, The Heritage Congregational Church, The First Covenant Church, The All Nations Christian Center, The Christ our Hope Bible Church, The Christ the Savior Orthodox Church, The First Church of The Open Bible, The Shalom Church, The Fellowship of The Messiah, A Fresh Start Ministries, and The Unitarian Universalist Church.

You would think that Christians of all faiths would ask the questions: "Does my church have, at the very least, these seven features?" (1). "Does my church believe that God speaks to its leaders who have the authority to act in His name?" (See Amos 3:7). (2). "Does the organization of my church bear a resemblance to the church during the ministry of Christ and His Apostles?" (Ephesians 2:19-20). (3). "Does my church believe, as Peter taught on the Day of Pentecost, that the first principles and ordinances of the gospel are faith in the Lord Jesus Christ, repentance for sins, baptism by immersion for the remission of sins, and receiving the gift of the Holy Ghost by the laying on of hands by those who hold the authority of the holy priesthood?" (See Acts 2:37-38). (4). "Does my church believe, as did Paul, that God is no respecter of persons, whether living or dead, and that the dead should have the same opportunities as the living to accept the ordinances of the gospel and to make covenants with Him?" (1 Peter 4:6). (5). "Does my church believe, as did Paul, in the gifts of the Spirit?" (1 Corinthians 112:4-10). (6). "Does my church believe in the biblical prophecies relating to an apostasy?" (Acts 20:28-30). (7). "Does my church believe not only in the Reformation and the Protestant movement, but also in the necessity of the Restoration foretold by Paul and others?" (2 Thessalonians 2:1-3).

Perhaps the reason that people don't ask these questions is because they are completely unaware of Act One, only vaguely aware of the purpose of Act Two, and relatively uninterested in the drama to come in Act Three, of the Three Act Play (The Plan of Salvation: Where did we come from? Why are we here? Where are we going?). Somehow, the religious educational system upon which they rely, that is supposed to teach these foundation truths, has been broken; it has failed them They behave as though they skipped kindergarten, barely made it out of high school with a G.E.D., and don't recognize the need for college-level courses. They are as the honorable men and women among the sects, parties and denominations, "who are blinded by the subtle craftiness of men (who) lie in wait to deceive, and (who are) are only kept from the truth because they know not where to find it." (D&C 76:75 & 123:12).

Satan is responsible for darkening the minds of many who dwell upon an earth that has been corrupted and is scarcely fit for sacred use. Isaiah suggested that it has been defiled and is polluted, "under the inhabitants thereof; because they have transgressed the laws, changed the ordinance, (and) broken the everlasting covenant." (Isaiah 24:5). It is hard to understand how a church could function today with even one or two of the seven features of revelation, authority, organization, first principles, work for the dead, spiritual gifts, and the illumination of restoration following a long night of apostasy.

Our 6th Article of Faith states: "We believe in the same organization that existed in the Primitive Church, namely, apostles, prophets, pastors, teachers, evangelists, and so forth." For some reason, this fundamental structure is not obvious to Christians of other faiths, who simply don't see things as we do. And yet, the Pope himself has stated the obvious: "Even the humblest human beings," he observed, "are naturally philosophic, asking themselves such questions as "Who am I? Where do I come from, and where am I going?" Religious revelation provides answers to these questions, the pope acknowledged." ("Time" magazine, 10/26/1998).

Paul believed in a "God, who at sundry times and in divers manners spake in time past unto the fathers by the prophets, (and who) hath in these last days spoken unto us by his Son." (Hebrews 1:1-2). "Whom say ye that I am?" the Savior asked. "And Simon Peter answered and said, Thou art the Christ, the Son of the living God. And Jesus answered and said unto him, Blessed art thou, Simon Bar-jona, for flesh and blood hath not revealed it unto thee, but my Father which is in heaven. And I say also unto thee, That thou art Peter, and upon this rock" of revelation "I will build my church." (Matthew 16:15-18). Joseph Smith explained that the rock upon which the church would be built was revelation. (See "Teachings," p. 274, and H.C., 5:258.) We believe in the Father, and in the Son, and in the Holy Ghost. The Savior taught: The Holy Ghost is a revelator, "whom the Father will send in my name. He shall teach you all things, and bring all things to your remembrance, whatsoever I have said unto you." (John 14:26).

The concept of authority builds on established revelation, and is given to ecclesiastical leaders by the grace of God. Martin Luther lamented the homogenization of the exercise of supposed authority: "A shoemaker, a smith, a farmer, each has his manual occupation and work; and yet, at the same time, all are eligible to act as priests." Walt Whitman said: "There will soon be no more priests. They may wait awhile, perhaps a generation or two, dropping off by degrees. A superior breed shall take their place. A new order shall arise and they shall be the priests of man, and every man shall be his own priest." Whitman, however, did not understand what had inspired Luther to resist the profane and apostate authority of Catholicism; it was that institutional revelation comes only to those whose lives merit the bestowal of divine authority, for as Paul correctly understood it, "no man taketh this honour unto himself, but he that is called of God, as was Aaron." (Hebrews 5:4).

"For the Son of man is as a man taking a far journey, who left his house, and gave authority to his servants, and to every man his work, and commanded the porter to watch." (Mark 13:34). "Ye have not chosen me," Jesus explained, "but I have chosen you, and ordained you." (John 15:16). Following His ministry, the Apostles "ordained them elders in every church." (Acts 14:23). Their authority was intertwined with a formal church organization that was quickened by the functional foundation of revelation and authority. Jesus Christ established a church that was a carefully crafted construct compared by Paul to a structure that was "built upon the foundation of the apostles and prophets, Jesus Christ himself being the chief corner stone." (Ephesians 2:20). Accordingly, "he gave some, apostles; and some, prophets, and some, evangelists; and some, pastors and teachers; for the perfecting of the saints, for the work of the ministry, for the edifying of the body of Christ: Till we all come in the unity of the faith, and of the knowledge of the Son of God, unto a perfect man, unto the measure of the stature of the fulness of Christ." (Ephesians 4:11-13).

Jesus foresaw the need for other priesthood leaders to assist the Apostles in the work of the ministry. He sent officers called Seventies in pairs to preach the gospel. (See Luke 10:1). Others who held callings in the church included evangelists (patriarchs), pastors (presiding leaders), high priests, elders, bishops, priests, teachers, and deacons. These positions were established to instruct and inspire church members, perform missionary work, and perform saving ordinances, or, in other words, to perfect the Saints, preach the gospel, and cement family relationships both in time and in eternity. Those who labored in these callings helped the members come to a "unity of the faith, and of the knowledge of the Son of God." (See Ephesians 4:13).

Authority empowered the leaders of the church to administer the first principles and ordinances of salvation. Those who held the priesthood in former times taught the two basic principles of faith and repentance, and then, the two basic ordinances of baptism and the receipt of the Holy Ghost. As the Savior taught: "Except a man be born of water and of the Spirit, he cannot enter into the kingdom of God." (John 3:5).

A dramatic application of this principle of authority that had been taught by the Savior occurred on the Day of Pentecost, when over three thousand people "were pricked in their heart, and said unto Peter and to the rest of the apostles, Men and brethren, what shall we do? Then Peter said unto them, Repent, and be baptized every one of you in the name of Jesus Christ for the remission of sins, and ye shall receive the gift of the Holy Ghost." (Acts 2:37-38). "And they continued steadfastly in the apostles' doctrine and fellowship, and in breaking of bread, and in prayers." (Acts 2:42). The ordinances of salvation propelled them along on the pathway of progression that would eventually lead to exaltation in the kingdom of God.

These ordinances were for the benefit of the dead as well as for the living. The scriptures plainly teach that Christ preached to the dead, between His own death and resurrection. "For Christ also hath once suffered for sins, the just for the unjust, that he might bring us to God, being put to death in the flesh, but quickened by the Spirit: By which also he went and preached unto the spirits in prison. Which sometime were disobedient, when once the longsuffering of God waited in the days of Noah, while the ark was a preparing, wherein few, that is, eight souls were saved by water." (1 Peter 3:18-20).

He performed these labors because the requirements to enter heaven are the same for all. They are equivalent for the living and for the dead, because God is no respecter of persons. (See Acts 10:34). As Peter further explained: "For this cause was the gospel preached also to them that are dead, that they might be judged according to men in the flesh, but live according to God in the spirit." (1 Peter 4:6). "Else what shall they do which are baptized for the dead," asked Paul, "if the dead rise not at all? Why are they then baptized for the dead?" (1 Corinthians 15:29).

While we tarry on earth, ordinances expose the Saints to a multitude of spiritual gifts that allow them to walk in the light of the gospel. Paul told the Corinthians: "Now there are diversities of gifts." (1 Corinthians 12:4). These gifts enabled the image of God to be engraven upon their countenances. "Who shall ascend into the hill of the Lord," asked the Psalmist, "or who shall stand in his holy place" to partake of the Divine Nature? "He that hath clean hands and a pure heart; who" is a partaker of spiritual gifts, and "hath not lifted up his soul unto vanity, nor sworn deceitfully." (Psalms 24:4-5).

Unfortunately, the seven features that distinguish the church of Christ have been neutralized by apostasy from the truth, resulting in a darkening of the minds of men. When the Saints in former times closed their hearts to spiritual promptings, darkness superseded the light. The loss of spiritual gifts resulted in apostasy. Paul prophesied to the Thessalonian Saints: "Be not soon shaken in mind, or be troubled, neither by spirit, nor by word, nor by letter as from us, as that the day of Christ is at hand. Let no man deceive you by any means: for that day shall not come, except there come a falling away first." (2 Thessalonians 2:2-3). "For behold," an angel taught Nephi, the apostasy has "taken away from the gospel of the Lamb many parts which are plain and most precious; and also many covenants of the Lord have they taken away." (1 Nephi 13:26).

Even if they are not Catholic, and their evangelical roots trace back to the Protestant Reformation, conscientious Christians may not realize that there has been a Great Apostasy. (See Amos 8:11-12). Perhaps Latter-day Saints need to learn how to explain that reality in different words that might be perceived as less harsh and therefore more easily understood. When Christians of all faiths acknowledge the reality of the Apostasy, it will be easier for them to accept the Restoration. When that is the case, it will be easier to establish a dialogue relating to the features of the primitive church (the church in Former Times), such as revelation, authority, church organization, first principles, work for the dead, spiritual gifts, apostasy, and restoration, that should be identifying markers of the Lord's restored church in the latter days, that was foretold by the Apostles so long ago. (See Acts 3:21 & D&C 27:6).

A restoration has been eagerly anticipated by visionaries seeking to redress the wrongs resulting from the corruption of the basic principles relating to the covenants we make with God. "I have sought nothing beyond reforming the church in conformity with the Holy Scriptures," declared Martin Luther. "I simply say that Christianity has ceased to exist among those who should have preserved it." ("Luther and His Times," p. 509). Roger Williams is reported to have declared: "There is no regularly constituted church on earth, nor any person authorized to administer any church ordinance; nor can there be until new apostles are sent by the Great Head of the church for Whose coming am seeking." (See "TimesandSeasons.org "For whose coming I am seeking," 6/15/2012).

After the Reformers paved the way, it was only natural that a Restoration would burst upon the scene. John saw in vision the angel Moroni, who would, in the Last Days, "fly in the midst of heaven, having the everlasting gospel to preach unto them that dwell on the earth, and to every nation, and kindred, and tongue, and people." (Revelation 14:6). How wonderful it would be to put to rest the long night of darkness with a visit by the Resurrected Lord Himself. As Luke had prophesied: "He shall send Jesus Christ, which before was preached unto you: whom the heavens must receive until the times of restitution of all things, which God hath spoken by the mouth of all his holy prophets since the world began." (Acts 3:20-21).

Revelation, authority, organization, first principles, work for the dead, and spiritual gifts are illustrations of principles in which "the power of godliness is manifest. And without" the driving force of these principles, "the power of godliness is not manifest unto men in the flesh," and there can be no Restoration, but only a continuation of the Great Apostasy. "For without this (restoration of light and truth) no man can see the face of God, even the Father, and live." (D&C 84:20-22). The manifestation of energy that animates the latter-day church speaks for itself, and is a seamless continuation of the vitality that quickened the church in former times.

Resource Material

1. Concerning the name of His church, the Lord told the Nephites: "If it be called in my name then it is my church." (3 Nephi 27:8). The essential qualifying prerequisite of the church was, as the Savior said, that it be "built upon my gospel." (3 Nephi 27:8).

Interestingly, of all the churches in the world when the Lord restored His church in this dispensation, there was not a single one that bore His name. It must have been very satisfying for Him to declare to Joseph Smith: "For thus shall my church be called in the last days, even The Church of Jesus Christ of Latter-day Saints." (D&C 115:4). Before this revelation, the Lord's Church was variously called The Church of Christ, The Church of Jesus Christ, The Church of God, and The Church of The Latter-day Saints. Even today, it is sometimes inaccurately called The Mormon Church, or The L.D.S. Church. But in 1830, this revelation from the Lord resolved the issue once and for all.

Today, "there is no valid reason why the Latter-day Saints should speak of themselves as 'Mormons,' or of the church as 'The Mormon Church.' We emphasize that we belong to The Church of Jesus Christ of Latter-day Saints, the name the Lord has given by which we are to be known and called." (Joseph Fielding Smith, Jr., "Answers to Gospel Questions," 4:174-175).

2. "The word 'saint' is a translation of a Greek word also rendered 'holy,' the

fundamental idea being that of consecration or separation for a sacred purpose; but the word came to mean 'free from blemish,' whether physical or moral. In the New Testament, the saints are all those who by baptism have entered into the Christian covenant." ("Bible Dictionary," p. 768).

Hence, Paul addressed "all that be in Rome, beloved of God, called to be saints." (Romans 1:7). He saluted "the church of God which is at Corinth, to them that are sanctified in Christ Jesus, called to be saints." (1 Corinthians 1:2). He introduced himself and his missionary companion Timothy as "the servants of Jesus Christ, to all the saints in Christ Jesus which are at Philippi." (Philippians 1:1).

Book of Mormon prophets also characterized the members of the church as 'saints.' "Behold, the righteous," Nephi declared, "the saints of the Holy One of Israel." Then he described them as those "who have believed in the Holy One of Israel, (and) who have endured the crosses of the world." (2 Nephi 9:18).

Benjamin taught: "The natural man is an enemy to God, and has been from the fall of Adam, and will be, forever and ever, unless he yields to the enticings of the Holy Spirit, and putteth off the natural man, and becometh a saint through the atonement of Christ the Lord." He characterized the Saints as children, "submissive, meek, humble, patient, full of love, willing to submit to all things which the Lord seeth fit to inflict upon him, even as a child doth submit to his father." (Mosiah 3:19).

Moroni explained that "the remission of sins bringeth meekness, and lowliness of heart; and because of meekness and lowliness of hearth cometh the visitation of the Holy Ghost, which Comforter filleth with hope and perfect love, which love endureth by diligence unto prayer, until the end shall come, when all the saints shall dwell with God." (Moroni 8:26).

Author's Note

As you peruse Appendix One on pages 419 - 431, you will notice that Volume One contains 59 essays, Volume Two contains 76 essays, Volume Three contains 71 essays, Volume Four contains 69 essays, and this volume (Volume Five) contains 56 essays. These, together with the 55 essays in the final volume (Volume Six) bring the grand total to 386. It was a push, but I wanted to provide at least a full year's worth of reading in the six-volume set. I leave for readers to do with these essays what they will. As for me, I can breathe a deep sigh of relief, and move on to other writing projects!

In all, the six volumes contain somewhere around 1,250,000 words. By comparison, there are just over 268,000 words in The Book of Mormon, which gives me pause, as I contemplate the ramifications of the observation of Polonius that "brevity is the soul of wit, and tediousness the limbs and outward flourishes. (Therefore,) I will be brief." ("Hamlet," Act 2, Scene 4).

My writing style stands in sharp contrast to the process of the translation of the plates from which The Book of Mormon was produced. I best express myself after I have pondered a topic for a while, taking the time to turn it over and over in my mind. Then, in a flurry of activity, I write a preliminary draft. Afterward, I let it simmer on my cerebral back burners for a few days or weeks. Finally, I consciously return to the task with renewed enthusiasm, and add final flourishes. If I leave it alone again, there is always the risk of coming back one more time with fresh eyes and a clear head, to make another revision or two. At last, I put it to rest, having created a product that contains a third again as much material as I initially had thought would be sufficient to adequately address the subject. So much for brevity!

Because this is a process that seems to work for me, and is one with which I am comfortable, I am often struck by how different was the experience of the Nephite prophets. Instead of putting pen to paper, or keystrokes to a word document, they made records on plates of ore that allowed no room for error or later revision. (For a look into that process, see my essay entitled "Writing on Metal Plates was a Pain," in Volume Four). If each essay has taken me a couple of weeks to complete, following the scenario outlined above, these six volumes represent around 15 years of mental gymnastics and soul sweat. Joseph, on the other hand, completed his translation of The Book of Mormon in an astonishing 65 days, offering it for all the world to see, without apology or alteration. (See "How long did it take Joseph Smith to translate the Book of Mormon?" "Ensign," 1/1988).

The admittedly unrealistic goal of my far more tedious efforts was to provide readers with enough material to tackle one essay each day, for a year. At 55 words per minute, that's only a little over an hour's worth of reading per day. A more practical suggestion, however, would be for you to instead spend quality time reading the scriptures. For example, accept the challenge to read The Book of Mormon in a year. (See: "Taking the Challenge," "Ensign," 12/2006). You'll be far better off for having done so. But, if after doing that, you're tired of late-night T.V. or movie re-runs, crack open one of these volumes, and give one of the 386 essay a shot. You should quickly be able to find a topic that will help you fall asleep more easily, dream more pointedly, and awaken more refreshed. Enjoy!

Appendix One

List of Essays
(Volumes One – Six)

Volume One: Spray from The Ocean of Thought

1. A Christmas Miracle
2. A Letter To A Non-member Friend
3. A Mailbox Marked With An "X"
4. A Personal Mission Statement
5. A Perspective On Civil Liberties (Alma 50-51)
6. A Perspective On The Apostasy
7. A Recipe For Success
8. A Standard Of Excellence
9. A Testimony Of Christ
10. A Thirty-Day Spiritual Fitness Program
11. A Whirlwind Into Heaven (The Doctrine of Translation)
12. Abstinence In A Permissive World
13. Agency And Opposition
14. Alma's Discourse On Faith (Alma 32)
15. An American Gospel
16. An Elect Lady (D&C 25)
17. Apostasy
18. Are Christians Mormon?
19. Are Life And Death Mutually Exclusive?
20. Are Mormons Christians?
21. Are We Alone In The Universe?
22. Baptism: A Foundation Ordinance
23. Baptism: The Gateway To The Celestial Kingdom
24. Batteries Are Not Included
25. Be Happy Attitudes
26. Because Of The Book Of Mormon
27. Become As Little Children
28. Before A Wound Can Heal
29. Being L.D.S. Is Like Being A Pumpkin
30. Being Well-Grounded
31. Benevolent Blindness
32. Book Of Mormon Hiking Song
33. Book Of Mormon Historicity
34. Born Again
35. Bosses And Leaders
36. Brevity

37. Buddy, Can You Spare A Dime?
38. Caesar (Mosiah 29)
39. Celestial Marriage And Eternal Families
40. Chastity Amid Permissiveness
41. Cherubim And A Flaming Sword Or Mercy And Justice
42. Christmas Is The Season Of The Year When
43. Christmas Thoughts
44. Church Organization And Government (D&C 20)
45. Combating Evil
46. Common Consent (D&C 26)
47. Conference (D&C 44)
48. Covenant Consciousness
49. Conversion: An Ongoing Process
50. Dentistry In The Scriptures
51. Detecting Satan's Fingerprints
52. Diversity
53. Do Justly And Love Mercy (Micah 6:8)
54. Do We Dye Our Skins?
55. Does God Obey The Speed Limit?
56. Edward Partridge: First Bishop Of The Church (D&C 36)
57. Embrace The Gospel (D&C 49)
58. Enduring To The End
59. Entropy In The Physical World

Volume Two: Ripples on a Pond

60	Eternal Progression In A Dynamic Universe
61	Everyone Wants To Go To Heaven
62	Evidences Of God
63	Faith, Hope And Charity
64	Faith Is A Principle Of Power
65	Faith, Knowledge And Education
66	Fasting: A Principle Of Perfection
67	Fayette, New York – The Last Revelation (D&C 38)
68	Focus
69	Focusing On The Important Things
70	Follow The Prophet
71	For Unto Us A Child Is Born
72	Gifts Of The Spirit
73	Goal Setting
74	God, Give Us Men!
75	God Goes Green
76	Godly Qualities (D&C 4)
77	Good, Better And Best
78	Gratitude Is An Attitude
79	Happiness And Sharing The Gospel
80	Having Been Commissioned Of Jesus Christ (D&C 22)
81	Higher Dimensional Realities
82	How Does God Get Things Done?
83	Huckleberries And Chokeberries
84	I Am The Light Of The World (John 8:12)
85	I Have Fought A Good Fight (2 Timothy 4:7)
86	I Have Overcome The World (John 16:33)
87	I Will Obey – James Covill (D&C 39)
88	If It Seems Too Good To Be True, It Probably Is
89	Is Heaven Hotter Than Hell?
90	It's Our Book! (Mormon 3)
91	Joseph Smith History
92	Just Get Back On The Bike
93	Justice And Mercy (Alma 42)
94	Lamanites By The Waters Of Sebus (Alma 17:37)
95	Let A History Be Kept (D&C 47)

96	Let Me Be Perfectly Honest
97	Life Is A Three Act Play
98	Life Is Like A Game Of Racquetball
99	Life's Greatest Questions
100	Life Support And Decisions (Life's Important Decisions)
101	Light
102	Light And Darkness
103	Look Who's Coming To Town (It Isn't Santa Claus)
104	Lucifer
105	Maintaining A Positive Mental Attitude
106	Management By The Spirit
107	Marriage Is Ordained Of God
108	Missing Scripture
109	Missionary Work: Our Greatest Call
110	Moral Discipline
111	Mothers In Zion
112	Multi-tasking
113	Navigating On The Snake
114	Ninety Nine Questions Answered By The Book Of Mormon
115	No Greater Call
116	Obedience Is The First Law Of Heaven
117	Obtaining The Spirit Of Revelation
118	One Hundred And One Things
119	One Lord, One Faith, One Baptism
120	Open Your Gates To The Gospel (D&C 32)
121	Orson Pratt: A Son Of God (D&C 34)
122	Our Educational Responsibilities
123	Our Eternal Nature
124	Our Family Constitution
125	Our Limiting Beliefs
126	Our Talents
127	Our Weaknesses
128	Overcoming Adversity
129	Parallelism In Hebrew Poetry
130	Pioneer Day Perspectives
131	Power: The Ultimate Test Of Character
132	Professors
133	Proper Prior Preparation
134	Putting Labels On Others
135	Quorum Sensing

Volume Three: Serendipitous Meanderings

136	Receiving Revelation (D&C 8)
137	Removing The Barnacles Of Life
138	Restoration Of The Aaronic Priesthood (D&C 13)
139	Revelation
140	Reverence
141	Sacramental Waters
142	Salvation By Grace
143	Satan
144	Seraphim
145	Set Apart
146	Sharper Than A Two-Edged Sword (D&C 33)
147	Signs
148	Sixty Five Ways To Express Gratitude
149	So You're Getting Married
150	Speak Kind Words To Each Other
151	Spiritual Calisthenics
152	Spiritual Identity Theft
153	Spiritual Manifestations
154	Steadying The Ark
155	Strangers In The Land Success
156	Studying The Scriptures
157	Success Strategies
158	Sydney Rigdon: Scribe To The Prophet (D&C 35)
159	Symbolism In The Scriptures
160	Symbols
161	Teaching In The Church
162	Teaching Key Doctrine
163	Technological Traps
164	Temple Work
165	Testimony
166	The 13th Article Of Faith
167	The 14th Article Of Faith
168	The Ablest Mariner
169	The Best Education Is To Be Perpetually Thrilled With Life
170	The Bible And Other Scripture
171	The Bible: Basic Information Before Leaving Earth

172	The Biggest Loser
173	The Character Of God
174	The Church In The Last Days
175	The Church Of Jesus Christ In Former Times
176	The Circle Of Knowledge
177	The Creation Of The World
178	The Desert Shall Rejoice (D&C 57)
179	The Door Swings Both Ways
180	The Dust Of The Earth
181	The Duty Of The Priest (D&C 20:46)
182	The First Revelation (D&C 2)
183	The First Revelation In Ohio (D&C 41)
184	The Heavens Were Opened
185	The Holy Ghost
186	The Hour Glass Of Opportunity
187	The Isaiah Chapters In The Book Of Mormon
188	The Last Judgment
189	The Law Of The Church
190	The Little Princess
191	The Lord's Prophet
192	The Lost Manuscript
193	The Lost Ten Tribes
194	The Manifestation Of Spirits (D&C 50)
195	The Meaning Of Doctrine
196	The Millennium
197	The Mind Of God
198	The Nature Of God And Our Covenants
199	The New And Everlasting Covenant (D&C 22)
200	The Order Of Revelation (D&C 28)
201	The Parable Of The Pencil
202	The Plan Of Salvation
203	The Prime Directive
204	The Prophet Joseph Smith
205	The Purpose Of Life
206	The Q Continuum

Volume Four: Presents of Mind

207	The Rapids Of Life
208	The Recipe For A Successful Church Address
209	The Sabbath
210	The Sacrament
211	The Spirit Of Gathering
212	The Second Coming
213	The Secret Garden
214	The Seeds Of Apostasy (D&C 31)
215	The Signs Of The Times
216	The Spirit
217	The Spirit World
218	The Springtime Of The Year
219	The Switch Points In Our Lives
220	The Temple
221	The Testimony Of Phil Hudson
222	The Third Part
223	The Three Witnesses
224	The Thrill Of Victory / The Agony Of DeFeet
225	The Voice Of Prophetic Warning
226	The Windows Of Heaven
227	The Word Of Wisdom
228	Then The Pig Got Up And Slowly Walked Away
229	This Is A New Day
230	Those "Gold" Plates
231	Thoughts On The Atonement (Alma 7:11-13)
232	Time
233	To Err Is Human; To Forgive Is Divine
234	Touching His Garment
235	Tough Questions (Alma 5)
236	Travel At The Speed Of Dark
237	True To Our Covenants
238	Twenty-Five Qualities Of High Achievers
239	Unity
240	Up / Down
241	Updates Are Ready
242	We Are Foreordained To Greatness

243	We Are His Hands
244	We Lived Before We Were Born
245	Well, That's Life
246	Were There Two Cumorahs?
247	We Talk Of Christ
248	What About Cherubim?
249	What About The Mormons? (D&C 45)
250	What Did He Just Say?
251	What Falls Down, Must Go Up
252	What Goes Around Comes Around
253	What I Have Lost (James Covill) (D&C 40)
254	What I Say Unto One, I Say Unto All (D&C 19)
255	What Is A Christian?
256	What Is Happiness?
257	What Qualifies Us For The Work? (D&C 4)
258	What Think Ye Of Christ? (Matthew 22:42)
259	What's In It For Me?
260	Who Is Packing Your Parachute?
261	Why Do We Laugh?
262	Why Is Happiness So Elusive?
263	Why Read The Doctrine & Covenants? (D&C 1)
264	Why Was The Book Of Mormon Preserved For Our Day?
265	Wickedness Never Was Happiness
266	Without The Book of Mormon
267	Work
268	Worlds Without Number Have I Created
269	Worship In Music
270	Wresting The Scriptures
271	Writing On Metal Plates Was A Pain
272	You Took No Thought Save To Ask
273	Zion
274	Zion And The New Jerusalem (D&C 57)
275	Zion Versus Babylon

Volume Five: Mental Floss

276	Agency And Youth
277	Attributes Of God
278	Bah! Humbug!
279	Baptism And Accountability
280	Blood, Covenant, And Land Israel
281	Born Again Christians
282	A Change Of Heart
283	Choose The Harder Right
284	Choose Ye This Day
285	Christ's Church Is Restored
286	Citizenship In The Church And Kingdom
287	A Coat Of Many Colors
288	Commitment
289	Connections
290	Construction Zone: Proceed With Caution
291	Covenants
292	Dancing With The Stars
293	Diversity
294	Doctrinal Switch Points
295	Enduring To The End
296	Establishing The Word
297	Faith Is Like A Screw
298	Fate
299	Father, Forgive Them
300	Finding Balance In Our Lives
301	Friendship
302	General Conference: The Super Bowl Of Spiritual Symposia
303	God Is NowHere
304	God's Tactical Flashlight
305	Heaven Can Wait
306	How Then Can I Do This Great Wickedness?
307	I Am A Child of God
308	In Defense Of The Family
309	In Defense Of The Prophet Joseph Smith
310	Joseph Smith's History
311	Joseph Smith's World

312	Jumping Out Of Our Skin
313	Keep Smiling
314	Lest We Forget
315	Light And Truth
316	Living Water
317	Lost Books Of The Bible
318	Marriage And Family Are Ordained Of God
319	May The 4th Be With You
320	Our Father In Heaven Knows Us
321	Our Neighbors
322	Pennies From Heaven
323	Plan Of Salvation
324	Premortal Life
325	Preparation
326	Pride
327	Priesthood Keys
328	A Primer On Addressing Deity
329	A Primer On Personal Revelation
330	Proper Prior Planning Prevents Poor Priesthood Performance
331	Recognizing The Church Of Jesus Christ

Volume Six: Fitness Training for the Mind and Spirit

332	Reflections On Her Mission
333	Sealed For Time And For All Eternity
334	Service: Mission Reflection
335	Serving In The Temple
336	Sharing The Gospel
337	Similitudes In Hosea
338	Snowbiking Through Life
339	Strengths And Weaknesses
340	Swiss Chocolate
341	Take My Yoke Upon You
342	Teachings Of The Minor Prophets
343	Temple Blessings For All Mankind
344	The Bestowal Of Spiritual Gifts
345	The Church Has Been Restored
346	The Creation
347	The Fall
348	The Germination Of Our Faith
349	The Highways And Byways Of Life
350	The Holy Ghost: Getting To Know Him
351	The Holy Grail Of Religious Doctrine
352	The Hourglass Of Life
353	The Light Of The World
354	The Lord's Patient Protection And Affordable Health Care Act
355	The Lord's Touchstone
356	The Mantle Of The Prophet
357	The Martyr's Mirror
358	The New American Bible: Uninspired Version
359	The Number Of The Disciples Was Multiplied
360	The Parable Of The Hiawatha Trail
361	The Plan Of Salvation: 15 Names
362	The Political Spotlight
363	The Power Of Proverbs
364	The Priests Of Baal In Our Lives
365	The Principle Of Agency
366	The Prophet Joseph Smith: The Third Of The Three Pillars Of Testimony
367	The Sacrament

368	The Second Mile
369	The Seven Deadly Sins
370	The Strait And Narrow Path To Discipleship
371	The Tools Of The Trade
372	The Twelve Tribes Of Israel
373	The Unknown Possibilities Of Existence
374	The Year Without Summer
375	Thoughts Of Kolob
376	Thou Hast Done Wonderful Things
377	Tithing
378	Travel At The Speed Of Thought
379	True Discipleship
380	Walk In The Light
381	We Ask Thee In Humility
382	What Think Ye Of Christ?
383	William Tyndale: An Appreciation
384	Wo Unto You Hypocrites
385	Words Of Mormon
386	Work And Personal Responsibility

Appendix Two

Topical Guide to the Essays
(Volumes One - Six)

One hundred
fifty five topics are herein
cross-referenced to the three
hundred eighty six essays within
the six volumes, in order
to facilitate matching
source material to
a particular area
of study.

Aaronic Priesthood
Abstinence
Achievement
Adversity
Agency
Apostasy
Articles Of Faith
Atonement
Attitude
Attributes Of God
Authority
Baptism
Belief
Book Of Mormon
Born Again
Brevity
Character
Cherubim
Children
Christ
Christians
Christmas
Church
Church Government
Civil Liberties
Commandments
Compensation
Conversion
Courage
Covenants
Creation
Cumorah
Death
Darkness
Dentistry
Decisions
Devil
Discipline
Diversity
Doctrine
Doctrine & Covenants
Education
Emma Smith
Endurance
Environment
Eternal Progression

Evil
Example
Excellence
Faith
Family
Fasting
Feet
Focus
Forgiveness
Friendship
Gathering
Goals
Good And Evil
Gospel
Grace
Gratitude
Happiness
Heaven
History
Holy Ghost
Honesty
Humility
Improvement
Isaiah
Israel
Joseph Smith
Journal
Justice
Kindness
Knowledge
Labels
Language
Last Days
Laughter
Leadership
Life
Light
Marriage
Mercy
Millennium
Mission Statement
Missionary Work
Morality
Mother
Multi-tasking
Music

Nature
Obedience
Opportunity
Opposition
Perseverance
Pioneers
Plan Of Salvation
Potential
Prayer
Pre-Earth Life
Preparation
Priesthood
Professors
Prophecy
Prophet
Public Speaking
Questions
Renewal
Repentance
Restoration
Resurrection
Revelation
Reverence
Sabbath
Sacrament
Satan
Scholarship
Scripture
Second Coming
Seraphim
Service
Set Apart
Signs
Spirit
Spirit World
Spiritual Fitness
Spiritual Gifts
Spirituality
Success
Symbolism
Talents
Teaching
Technology
Temple
Tenacity
Testimony

Third Part
Time
Tithing
Tolerance
Transgression
Translation
Unity
Universe
Walking In His Footsteps
Weakness
Wisdom
Wishful Thinking
Witnesses
Word Of Wisdom
Words
Work
Zion

Aaronic Priesthood

- Restoration of The Aaronic Priesthood (D&C 13)
- The Duty of The Priest (D&C 20:46)

Abstinence

- Abstinence in a Permissive World

Achievement

- Heaven Can Wait
- Twenty-five Qualities of High Achievers
- We are Foreordained to Greatness

Adversity

- Construction Zone: Proceed with Caution
- Finding Balance in our Lives
- Overcoming Adversity
- Spiritual Calisthenics
- Spiritual Identity Theft
- The Highways and Byways of Life
- The Martyr's Mirror
- The Rapids of Life
- The Seven Deadly Sins
- This is a New Day
- Travel at The Speed of Dark

Agency

- Agency and Opposition
- Agency and Youth
- Choose the Harder Right
- Fate
- The Prime Directive
- The Principle of Agency
- The Q Continuum

Apostasy

- A Perspective on The Apostasy
- Apostasy
- Christ's Church is Restored
- God is NowHere
- Recognizing the Church of Jesus Christ
- The Church Has Been Restored
- The New American Bible: Uninspired Version
- The Seeds of Apostasy (D&C 31)
- William Tyndale: An Appreciation

Articles of Faith

- The 13th Article of Faith
- The 14th Article of Faith

Atonement

- Thoughts on The Atonement

Attitude

- Be Happy Attitudes
- Finding Balance in Our Lives
- I am a Child of God
- Maintaining a Positive Mental Attitude
- The Martyr's Mirror
- This is a New Day
- Twenty-five Qualities of High Achievers
- We are Foreordained to Greatness

Attributes of God

- Does God Obey The Speed Limit?
- Evidence of God
- Godly Qualities (D&C 4)
- How Does God Get Things Done?
- Our Heavenly Father Knows Us
- The Character of God
- The Tools of The Trade
- The Mind of God
- The Nature of God and Our Covenants
- Touching His Garment
- Travel at The Speed of Thought

Authority

- Steadying the Ark

Baptism

- A Change of Heart
- Baptism: A Foundation Ordinance
- Baptism and Accountability
- Baptism: The Gateway to The Celestial Kingdom

Belief

- Commitment
- Our Limiting Beliefs
- We are Foreordained to Greatness
- What Think Ye of Christ?

Book of Mormon

- Because of The Book of Mormon
- Book of Mormon Historicity
- Book of Mormon Song
- It's Our Book! (Mormon 3)
- Ninety-nine Questions Answered by The Book of Mormon
- The Lost Manuscript
- Those "Gold" Plates
- Words of Mormon
- Why Was The Book of Mormon Preserved for Our Day?
- Without The Book of Mormon
- Writing on Metal Plates Was a Pain

Born Again

- A Change of Heart
- Born Again
- Born Again Christians
- Connections
- The Hourglass of Life
- Walk in The Light

Brevity

- Brevity

Character

- A Change of Heart
- A Coat of Many Colors
- Godly Qualities (D&C 4)
- I am a Child of God
- The Lord's Touchstone
- The Martyr's Mirror
- The Seven Deadly Sins

Cherubim

- Seraphim
- What About Cherubim?

Children

- Become as Little Children
- I am a Child of God

Christ

- A Testimony of Christ
- For Unto Us a Child is Born
- I am The Light of The World (John 3:12)
- I Have Overcome The World (John 16:33)
- Look Who's Coming to Town (It Isn't Santa Claus)
- The Ablest Mariner
- The Second Coming
- Touching His Garment
- We Talk of Christ
- What Think Ye of Christ? (Matthew 22:42)

Christians

- A Coat of Many Colors
- Are Christians Mormon?
- Are Mormons Christian?
- The Martyr's Mirror
- What is a Christian?

Christmas

- A Christmas Miracle
- Bah Humbug!
- Christmas is The Season When…..
- Christmas Thoughts
- For Unto Us a Child is Born

Church

- Being L.D.S. is Like Being a Pumpkin
- Christ's Church is Restored
- Church Historian (D&C 47)
- Church Organization & Government
- Citizenship in The Church and Kingdom
- Conference
- General Conference: The SuperBowl of Spiritual Symposia
- One Lord, One Faith, One Baptism
- Recognizing the Church of Jesus Christ
- The Church Has Been Restored
- The Church in The Last Days
- The Church of Jesus Christ in Former Times
- The Lord's Patient Protection and Affordable Healthcare Act
- What About The Mormons? (D&C 45)

Church Government

- Caesar
- Common Consent
- Conference
- Edward Partridge: First Bishop of The Church (D&C 36)
- Fayette, New York: The Last Revelation (D&C 38)
- General Conference: The SuperBowl of Spiritual Symposia
- Quorum Sensing
- Sydney Rigdon: Scribe to The Prophet (D&C 35)
- The First Revelation (D&C 2)
- The First Revelation in Ohio (D&C 41)
- The Law of The Church (D&C 42)
- The Lord's Patient Protection and Affordable Healthcare Act
- The Political Spotlight
- The Three Witnesses

Civil Liberties

- A Perspective on Civil Liberties
- The Martyr's Mirror

Commandments

- What I Say Unto One, I Say Unto All (D&C 19)

Compensation

- What Goes Around Comes Around

Conversion

- Bah Humbug!
- Connections
- Conversion
- We are Foreordained to Greatness

Courage

- Choose the Harder Right
- God, Give us Men!
- May the 4th Be With You
- The Martyr's Mirror
- This is a New Day

Covenants

- Covenant Consciousness
- Covenants
- The Nature of God and Our Covenants
- The New and Everlasting Covenant (D&C 22)
- True to Our Covenants

Creation

- Are We Alone in The Universe?
- Diversity
- Higher Dimensional Realities
- The Creation
- The Creation of The World
- The Dust of The Earth
- Worlds Without Number

Cumorah

- Were There Two Cumorahs?

Death

- Are Life and Death Mutually Exclusive?
- Everyone Wants to Go to Heaven

Darkness

- Travel at The Speed of Dark

Dentistry

- Dentistry in The Scriptures

Decisions

- Choose the Harder Right
- Construction Zone: Proceed with Caution
- Finding Balance in our Lives
- Heaven Can Wait
- The Highways and Byways of Life
- The Martyr's Mirror
- The Switch Points in Our Lives

Devil

- Combating Evil
- Detecting Satan's Fingerprints
- Lucifer
- Spiritual Identity Theft
- Wickedness Never Was Happiness

Discipline

- Choose the Harder Right
- Choose Ye This Day
- Commitment
- Construction Zone: Proceed with Caution
- Finding Balance in our Lives
- May the 4th Be With You
- Moral Discipline
- Spiritual Calisthenics
- Taking My Yoke Upon You
- The Lord's Touchstone
- The Number of Disciples was Multiplied
- The Second Mile
- The Seven Deadly Sins
- The Strait and Narrow Path to Discipleship
- This is a New Day
- True Discipleship
- We are Foreordained to Greatness
- What Think Ye of Christ?

Diversity

- Diversity

Doctrine

- Teaching Key Doctrine
- The Meaning of Doctrine
- The New American Bible: Uninspired Version

Doctrine & Covenants

- Why Read The Doctrine & Covenants? (D&C 1)

Education

- A Coat of Many Colors
- Our Educational Responsibilities
- The Best Education is To Be Perpetually Thrilled with Life

- The Highways and Byways of Life

Emma Smith

- An Elect Lady

Endurance

- Endure to The End
- Enduring to The End
- I Have Fought a Good Fight (2 Timothy 4:7)
- Spiritual Calisthenics
- The Highways and Byways of Life
- The Martyr's Mirror
- The Parable of The Hiawatha Trail
- The Seven Deadly Sins
- This is a New Day

Environment

- God Goes Green

Eternal Progression

- A Coat of Many Colors
- Connections
- Entropy in The Physical World
- Eternal Progression in a Dynamic Universe
- We are Foreordained to Greatness

Evil

- Combating Evil
- Detecting Satan's Fingerprints
- Lucifer
- May the 4th Be With You
- Satan
- Spiritual Identity Theft
- The Seven Deadly Sins
- Travel at The Speed of Dark
- Wickedness Never Was Happiness
- Zion Versus Babylon

Example

- Orson Pratt: A Son of God (D&C 34)
- The Ablest Mariner
- The Lord's Touchstone
- The Martyr's Mirror
- Then The Pig Got Up and Slowly Walked Away

Excellence

- A Standard of Excellence
- Good, Better, and Best
- Experiencing the Highways and Byways of Life
- Spiritual Calisthenics
- This is a New Day
- Twenty-five Qualities of High Achievers

Faith

- Alma's Discourse on Faith
- Faith is a Principle of Power
- Faith is Like a Screw
- Faith, Hope, and Charity
- Faith, Knowledge, and Education

Family

- I am a Child of God
- In Defense of The Family
- Marriage and Family are Ordained of God
- Our Family Constitution

Fasting

- Fasting: a Principle of Perfection

Feet

- The Thrill of Victory / The Agony of DeFeet

Focus

- Being Well-Grounded
- Choose ye This Day
- Construction Zone: Proceed with Caution
- Focus
- Focusing on The Important Things
- May the 4th Be With You
- The Martyr's Mirror
- This is a New Day
- Twenty-five Qualities of High Achievers

Forgiveness

- Father, Forgive Them
- The Door Swings Both Ways
- The Martyr's Mirror
- The Secret Garden
- The Third Part
- To Err is Human, To Forgive is Divine

Friendship

- Connections
- A Letter to a Nonmember Friend
- Friendship
- Our Neighbors

Gathering

- Blood, Covenant, and Land Israel
- Covenant Consciousness
- Strangers in The Land
- The Gathering
- The Lost Ten Tribes
- The Twelve Tribes of Israel

Goals

- Goal Setting
- Spiritual Calisthenics
- This is a New Day
- Twenty-five Qualities of High Achievers

Good and Evil

- May the 4th Be With You
- Finding Balance in our Lives
- The Seven Deadly Sins
- Up/Down
- Wickedness Never Was Happiness

Gospel

- An American Gospel
- Embrace The Gospel
- Establishing the Word
- Living Water
- The Lord's Patient Protection and Affordable Healthcare Act
- The New American Bible: Uninspired Version
- The New and Everlasting Covenant (D&C 22)

Grace

- Salvation by Grace
- The Martyr's Mirror
- Thou Hast Done Wonderful Things

Gratitude

- Gratitude is an Attitude
- I am a Child of God
- Pennies from Heaven
- Sixty Five Ways to Express Gratitude

Happiness

- Happiness and Sharing The Gospel
- Keep Smiling
- What is Happiness?
- Why is Happiness so Elusive?
- Wickedness Never Was Happiness

Heaven

- Heaven Can Wait
- Is Heaven Hotter Than Hell?

- Up/Down

History

- Let a History be Kept (D&C 47)
- The Parable of The Pencil

Holy Ghost

- Batteries are Not Included
- Management by The Spirit
- The Holy Ghost
- The Holy Ghost: Getting to Know Him

Honesty

- Let Me Be Perfectly Honest

Humility

- Pride
- The Dust of The Earth
- The Seven Deadly Sins
- We Ask Thee in Humility
- Wo Unto You Hypocrites

Improvement

- A Coat of Many Colors
- Choose the Harder Right
- Construction Zone: Proceed with Caution
- Our Limiting Beliefs
- Spiritual Calisthenics
- The Highways and Byways of Life
- The Lord's Patient Protection and Affordable Healthcare Act
- The Seven Deadly Sins
- This is a New Day
- Twenty-five Qualities of High Achievers
- Updates are Ready
- We are Foreordained to Greatness

Isaiah

- The Isaiah Chapters in The Book of Mormon

Israel

- Blood, Covenant, and Land Israel
- Covenant Consciousness
- Strangers in The Land
- The Gathering
- The Lost Ten Tribes
- The Twelve Tribes of Israel

Joseph Smith

- In Defense of The Prophet Joseph Smith
- Joseph Smith History
- Joseph Smith's History
- Joseph Smith's World
- The Lord's Prophet
- The Mantle of The Prophet
- The Prophet Joseph Smith
- The Prophet Joseph Smith: The Third of the Three Pillars of Testimony
- The Year Without Summer

Journal

- The Parable of The Pencil

Justice

- Cherubim and a Flaming Sword
- Do Justice and Love Mercy
- Justice and Mercy (Alma 42)
- The Last Judgment
- The Third Part

Kindness

- Benevolent Blindness
- Speak Kind Words to Each Other
- The Lord's Touchstone
- The Martyr's Mirror

Knowledge

- I am a Child of God
- The Circle of Knowledge

Labels

- A Coat of Many Colors
- Blood, Covenant, and Land Israel
- Putting Labels on Others

Language

- What Did He Just Say?

Last Days

- Blood, Covenant, and Land Israel
- The Church in The Last Days
- The Twelve Tribes of Israel

Laughter

- Keep Smiling
- Why Do We Laugh?

Leadership

- Bosses and Leaders

Life

- Are Life and Death Mutually Exclusive?
- Life is Like a Game of Racquetball
- Life's Greatest Questions
- Life Support and Decisions (Life's Important Decisions)
- The Highways and Byways of Life
- The Purpose of Life
- The Seven Deadly Sins
- Well, That's Life

Light

- God's Tactical Flashlight
- Light
- Light and Darkness
- Light and Truth
- May the 4th Be With You
- The Light of the World
- Walk in the Light

Marriage

- Celestial Marriage and Eternal Families
- Marriage and Family are Ordained of God
- Marriage is Ordained of God
- Sealed for Time and All Eternity
- So You're Getting Married

Mercy

- Cherubim and a Flaming Sword
- Do Justice and Love Mercy
- Justice and Mercy (Alma 42)
- The Martyr's Mirror
- The Third Part

Millennium

- Blood, Covenant, and Land Israel
- The Millennium
- The Twelve Tribes of Israel

Mission Statement

- A Personal Mission Statement

Missionary Work

- Conversion
- Establishing the Word
- Happiness and Sharing The Gospel
- Missionary Work: Our Greatest Call
- No Greater Call
- Open Your Gates To The Gospel (D&C 32)
- Sharing the Gospel
- Swiss Chocolate
- We Talk of Christ

- What About The Mormons? (D&C 45)
- What Qualifies Us For The Work? (D&C 4)

Morality

- Abstinence in a Permissive World
- Chastity Amid Permissiveness
- The Seven Deadly Sins

Mother

- Mothers in Zion

Multi-tasking

- Finding Balance in Our Lives
- Multi-tasking
- This is a New Day

Music

- Worship in Music

Nature

- Our Eternal Nature
- We are Foreordained to Greatness

Obedience

- Construction Zone: Proceed with Caution
- Do We Dye Our Skins?
- How Then Can I Do This Great Wickedness?
- I Have Fought a Good Fight (2 Timothy 4:7)
- I Will Obey – James Covill (D&C 39)
- Navigating on The Snake
- Obedience is The First Law of Heaven
- The Hourglass of Life
- The Seven Deadly Sins
- What's In It For Me?

Opportunity

- Heaven Can Wait
- The Hourglass of Opportunity

Opposition

- A Coat of Many Colors
- Agency and Opposition
- Huckleberries and Chokeberries
- I Have Fought a Good Fight (2 Timothy 4:7)
- Lamanites by The Waters of Sebus (Alma 17:37)
- May the 4th Be With You
- The Priests of Baal in our Lives
- Spiritual Identity Theft
- The Seven Deadly Sins
- This is a New Day
- Zion Versus Babylon

Perseverance

- Just Get Back on The Bible
- Spiritual Calisthenics
- The Highways and Byways of Life
- The Parable of The Hiawatha Trail
- This is a New Day
- Twenty-five Qualities of High Achievers
- We are Foreordained to Greatness

Pioneers

- Pioneer Day Perspectives
- The Martyr's Mirror

Plan of Salvation

- Connections
- Life is a Three-Act Play
- Life is Like a Game of Racquetball
- Life's Greatest Questions
- The Fall
- The Germination of our Faith
- The Holy Grail of Religious Doctrine

- The Lord's Patient Protection and Affordable Health Care Act
- The Plan of Salvation
- The Plan of Salvation (V. 6)
- The Plan of Salvation: 15 Names
- The Purpose of Life
- The Third Part
- The Isaiah Chapters in The Book of Mormon
- The Little Princess

Potential

- Connections
- May the 4th Be With You
- The Little Princess
- The Unknown Possibilities of Existence

Prayer

- A Primer on Deity

Pre-Earth Life

- I am a Child of God
- Life is a Three-Act Play
- Life's Greatest Questions
- Pre-mortal Life
- We Lived Before We Were Born

Preparation

- Preparation
- Proper Prior Preparation Prevents Poor Priesthood Performance
- Snowbiking Through Life
- Who is Packing Your Parachute?

Priesthood

- General Conference: The SuperBowl of Spiritual Symposia
- Having Been Commissioned of Jesus Christ (D&C 22)
- Priesthood Keys
- The Mantle of the Prophet

Professors

- Commitment
- Professors
- The Martyr's Mirror

Prophecy

- Blood, Covenant, and Land Israel
- The Voice of Prophetic Warning

Prophet

- Follow The Prophet

Public Speaking

- The Recipe for a Successful Church Address

Questions

- Tough Questions (Alma 5)

Renewal

- The Springtime of The Year

Repentance

- Before a Wound Can Heal
- Removing The Barnacles of Life
- The Biggest Loser
- The Door Swing Both Ways
- The Secret Garden
- To Err is Human, To Forgive is Divine

Restoration

- Blood, Covenant, and Land Israel
- Christ's Church is Restored
- God is NowHere
- The Church Has Been Restored
- The Desert Shall Rejoice

- The New American Bible: Uninspired Version
- The Twelve Tribes of Israel
- William Tyndale: An Appreciation

Resurrection

- What Does Down Must Go Up

Revelation

- A Primer on Personal Revelation
- Fayette, New York: The Last Revelation (D&C 38)
- Obtaining the Spirit of Revelation
- Receiving Revelation (D&C 8)
- Revelation
- The First Revelation (D&C 2)
- The Heavens Were Opened
- The Manifestation of Spirits (D&C 50)
- The New American Bible: Uninspired Version
- The Order of Revelation (D&C 28)
- Thoughts of Kolob
- You Took No Thought Save to Ask

Reverence

- Reverence

Sabbath

- The Sabbath

Sacrament

- Sacramental Waters
- The Sacrament
- The Sacrament (V. 6)

Satan

- Combating Evil
- Detecting Satan's Fingerprints
- Satan
- The Seven Deadly Sins
- Travel at The Speed of Dark

- Wickedness Never Was Happiness

Scholarship

- You Took No Thought Save to Ask

Scripture

- Blood, Covenant, and Land Israel
- Lest We Forget
- Lost Books of the Bible
- Missing Scripture
- Parallelism in Hebrew Poetry
- Sharper Than a Two-edged Sword (D&C 33)
- Similitudes in Hosea
- Studying The Scriptures
- Symbolism in The Scriptures
- Teachings of The Minor Prophets
- The Bible and Other Scripture
- The Bible: Basic Information Before Leaving Earth
- The Isaiah Chapters in The Book of Mormon
- The New American Bible: Uninspired Version
- Wresting The Scriptures
- Writing on Metal Plates Was a Pain

Second Coming

- The Second Coming

Seraphim

- Seraphim
- What About Cherubim?

Service

- The Lord's Touchstone
- We are His Hands

Set apart

- Set apart

Signs

- Blood, Covenant, and Land Israel
- Signs
- The Signs of The Times

Spirit

- Batteries are Not Included
- Jumping Out of Our Skin
- Management by The Spirit
- Spiritual Identity Theft
- Spiritual Manifestations
- The Spirit

Spirit World

- The Spirit World

Spiritual Fitness

- A Coat of Many Colors
- A Thirty-Day Spiritual Fitness Program
- Construction Zone: Proceed with Caution
- Jumping Out of Our Skin
- May the 4th Be With You
- Spiritual Calisthenics
- The Highways and Byways of Life
- The Seven Deadly Sins

Spiritual Gifts

- Gifts of The Spirit
- Pennies from Heaven
- The Bestowal of Spiritual Gifts

Spirituality

- Connections
- Spiritual Calisthenics

Success

- A Recipe for Success
- Finding Balance in Our Lives
- Success Strategies
- This is a New Day
- Twenty-five Qualities of High Achievers
- We are Foreordained to Greatness

Symbolism

- A Coat of Many Colors
- Similitudes in Hosea
- Symbols
- Symbolism in The Scriptures

Talents

- I am a Child of God
- Our Limiting Beliefs
- Our Talents

Teaching

- Teaching in The Church
- Teaching Key Doctrine

Technology

- Technological Traps

Temple

- Connections
- Sealed for Time and All Eternity
- Service in The Temple
- Temple Blessings for All Mankind
- Temple Work
- The Temple
- Tithing

Tenacity

- A Coat of Many Colors
- Choose Ye This Day
- Finding Balance in Our Lives
- I Have Fought a Good Fight (2 Timothy 4:7)
- The Highways and Byways of Life

- The Seven Deadly Sins
- Twenty-five Qualities of High Achievers
- We are Foreordained to Greatness

Testimony

- A Change of Heart
- Testimony
- The Testimony of Phil Hudson
- We Talk of Christ

Third Part

- The Third Part

Time

- Time

Tithing

- The Windows of Heaven
- Tithing

Tolerance

- Do We Dye Our Skins?

Transgression

- What I Have Lost (James Covill) (D&C 40)

Translation

- A Whirlwind into Heaven

Unity

- May the 4th Be With You
- Unity

Universe

- Are We Alone in The Universe?
- Dancing With The Stars
- Higher Dimensional Realities
- May the 4th Be With You

Walking in His Footsteps

- A Change of Heart
- The Highways and Byways of Life
- The Lord's Touchstone
- The Martyr's Mirror
- The Seven Deadly Sins
- The Thrill of Victory / The Agony of DeFeet

Weakness

- Our Weaknesses
- Spiritual Calisthenics
- Strengths and Weaknesses
- The Seven Deadly Sins
- We are Foreordained to Greatness

Wisdom

- One Hundred and One Things I've Learned
- The Word of Wisdom

Wishful Thinking

- If It Seems To Good To Be True, It Probably Is

Witnesses

- The Three Witnesses

Word of Wisdom

- The Word of Wisdom

Words

- What Did He Just Say?

Work

- Work
- Work and Personal Responsibility

Zion

- Zion
- Zion and The New Jerusalem (D&C 57)
- Zion Versus Babylon

About the Author

Phil Hudson and his wife Jan have 7 children and over 20 grandchildren. They enjoy spending time with their family at their cabin nestled in the Selkirk Mountains, on the shores of Priest Lake, the crown jewel of North Idaho. Phil had a successful family dental practice in Spokane, Washington for 43 years, before retiring in 2015. He has an eclectic mix of hobbies, and enjoys riding motorcycles and ATVs. In his free time, he can be found hiking, boating, cycling, snow biking, and traveling with Jan. He always finds time, however, to record his thoughts on his laptop. He understands Isaac Asimov's response when he was asked: "If you knew that you only had 10 minutes left to live, what would you do with your time?" He answered: "I'd type faster."

As this volume was about to be published, Phil and Jan accepted a call to serve as full time missionaries for The Church of Jesus Christ of Latter-day Saints, in the Kingdom of Tonga. While there, they will celebrate their 50th wedding anniversary.

Also By The Author

Essays

- Volume One: Spray From The Ocean Of Thought
- Volume Two: Ripples On A Pond
- Volume Three: Serendipitous Meanderings
- Volume Four: Presents Of Mind
- Volume Six: Fitness Training For The Mind And Spirit

Book of Mormon Commentary

- Born In The Wilderness
- Voices From The Dust
- Journey To Cumorah

Doctrine & Covenants Commentary

- Volume One
- Volume Two

Minute Musings: Spontaneous Combustions of Thought

- Volume One
- Volume Two
- Volume Three

Calendars:

- In His Own Words: Discovering William Tyndale
- As I Think About The Savior
- Scriptural Symbols

Children's Books

- Muddy, Muddy
- The Thirteen Articles of Faith

Diode Laser Soft Tissue Surgery

- Volume One
- Volume Two
- Volume Three

These, and other titles, are available from online retailers.

www.ingramcontent.com/pod-product-compliance
Lightning Source LLC
Chambersburg PA
CBHW082107280426
43661CB00090B/920